Richards on Rhetoric

Richards on Rhetoric

I. A. Richards: Selected Essays (1929–1974)

Edited by Ann E. Berthoff

New York   Oxford
Oxford University Press
1991

Oxford University Press

Oxford   New York   Toronto
Delhi   Bombay   Calcutta   Madras   Karachi
Petaling Jaya   Singapore   Hong Kong   Tokyo
Nairobi   Dar es Salaam   Cape Town
Melbourne   Auckland
and associated companies in
Berlin   Ibadan

Library of Congress Cataloging-in-Publication Data
Richards, I. A. (Ivor Armstrong), 1893–1979
Richards on rhetoric :
I. A. Richards, selected essays, 1929–1974
edited by Ann E. Berthoff.
p. cm.   Includes bibliographical references.
ISBN 0-19-506426-7
1. Rhetoric—Philosophy.   2. Semiotics.   3. Criticism.
4. Meaning (Philosophy)   I. Berthoff, Ann E.   II. Title.
P301.R49   1991   808'.001—dc20   89-77995

1 3 5 7 9 8 6 4 2

Printed in the United States of America
on acid free paper

Acknowledgments

This book would not have been possible without the support of Richard Luckett, Pepys Librarian at Magdalene College (Cambridge), and Ivor Richards' literary executor and keeper of the Richards archive. I have benefited from our discussions of Richards' ambitions and achievements, and I gratefully acknowledge Dr. Luckett's permission to reprint material in copyright now held by Magdalene College. I am also happy to have had the support of the late Mrs. Dorothea Pilley Richards in this enterprise. And, in a sense, I have been encouraged by Dr. Richards himself. John Constable, who edited a selection of Richards' letters, has shown me a letter Richards wrote to his wife in which he stated that he wished to prepare an anthology of his writings, thus making accessible to teachers the ideas he believed would be most helpful. Actually, he was temperamentally incapable of doing so: he preferred to write a new piece rather than cut, amalgamate, or rearrange what had already been written; he preferred preparing notes and glosses to revising. But I like to think that, on the whole, he would have approved of what I have attempted here.

I enjoyed a brief correspondence with I. A. Richards in his later years and am happy that he endorsed my interpretations of his theory and practice, as well as encouraging my own. I never studied with Dr. Richards, but like all those who enrolled in Andrews Wanning's course in seventeenth-century prose at Harvard in the postwar years, I benefited from an imaginative interpretation of Richards' methods. Professor Wanning, who had studied with Richards at Cambridge, brought to bear on prose style the principles of practical criticism in ways that profoundly changed how his students read literature and thought to teach it. I have been grateful for that experience throughout my teaching career. And I appreciate the encouragement I have had in my study of I. A. Richards from W. Jackson Bate, in whose courses I first read him.

Over the years, I have enjoyed conversations with friends and colleagues about I. A. Richards and what we might do with what he had to say about language and learning. T. Y. Booth, who has seen more clearly than anyone else the importance Richards has for what was once called "general education," has encouraged me with his interest in this project. James Broderick, who was one of Dr. Richards' teaching assistants in "Gen. Ed." at Harvard in the postwar years, has followed out in his teaching some of the most original and provocative principles of Richards' philosophy of rhetoric, especially the role of perception as a model for analysis. He was also one of the first to consider the philosophical presuppositions of composition pedagogy. As colleagues for some thirty years, we have often discussed what would happen if Richards could influence the teaching of writing as he once did the teaching of critical reading.

I arrived at the choice of selections presented here chiefly on the basis of my own experience with what has helped me in my teaching, but I have also learned from the response to selected passages from Richards' oeuvre by participants in the NEH Summer Seminar ("Philosophy and the Composing Process") I directed in 1980 at the University of Massachusetts at Boston. I am especially grateful to Lil Brannon, William Geiger, the late Eugene Green, Warren Herendeen, Paul Kameen, and John Ramage. I have also been guided by the suggestions of fellow and sister Ricardians Stuart C. Brown, Thomas Derrick, Janet Kotler, and Ann Raimes. I appreciate their help.

A grant from the American Philosophical Society enabled me to spend some time in the Richards Room at Magdalene, reviewing some thirty notebooks, with special reference to Richards' methods of composition and his interest in C. S. Peirce.

Concord, Mass.   A.E.B.
March 1989

Contents

Introduction

This selection of essays and passages from among I. A. Richards' twenty or so books is offered to teachers of English in the belief that he is a critic we urgently need. He can help protect us from certain "gangster theories" (his term) which have proliferated in current criticism; he can explain the triadic semiotics of C. S. Peirce, which he thought should supplant a dyadic linguistics; he can guide a reassessment of the mission of English departments; and, most important, he can show us how best to confront the challenge of illiteracy.

Richards was one of the great teachers of the twentieth century; he was also, of course, an influential literary critic. Both his theory and practice were important to the New Criticism, but he is virtually unread today, even by critics who pretend to be assessing his status and evaluating his critical ideas. Most graduate students have probably read the chapters on metaphor in *The Philosophy of Rhetoric* or at least heard of tenor/vehicle, but they (and their instructors) seldom have any notion of I. A. Richards' contributions to pedagogy, to a critique of modern linguistics, and to an understanding of semiotics. The seven books in which Richards set forth his principal ideas of learning and language are out of print or are available only in special editions. The present selection of essays has been edited with the aim of making Richards' ideas about language and learning more accessible.

The title I have selected for this volume—*Richards on Rhetoric*—is meant to echo two of Richards' own titles: *Mencius on the Mind* and *Coleridge on Imagination* For I. A. Richards, rhetoric was both the study of "how words work" and the study of "misunderstanding and its remedies": to analyze this nexus of what would today be called semiotics and hermeneutics he held to be the principal aim of a philosophy of rhetoric. The dialectic of meaning and interpretation, of "what is said" and "what is meant," of imagination and form, of encoding (or "Morsing," as he called it) and purposing, of the mind and the contexts of its activity (what he called "interdetermination") was Richards' principal concern throughout his long life.

Despite the accuracy of his sense of what it is we should account for and take account of, Richards has long been neglected. The reasons are not hard to find. There is, first of all, the matter of his style. He deliberately used ambiguous terms because he wanted to foreground the difficulties; Richards is never unaware of the possible misunderstandings of language used about language. His often fascinating excursuses on words which should or should not be terms of a discourse can at times become distracting; it is very easy to lose the thread of his argument. Digression is his favorite rhetorical strategy, and now and then he seems to be mumbling to himself for the good reason that nobody seemed to be listening. In this book I have sought to address these problems in several ways.

But even if he had always written with the lucidity and straightforwardness that characterize his best essays, Richards would have suffered neglect because of the unpopularity of his purposes. He was committed to improving the public schools when few people in higher education deigned to concern themselves with "elementary" education. (He enjoyed the pun.) He was hopelessly optimistic (he would have enjoyed the oxymoron) about the capacity of education to change society, to say nothing of saving the planet, energetically demanding of himself practical demonstrations of just what was required in language teaching in order to make a crucial difference in the way we conceive of the human future.

The most significant reason for the neglect of I. A. Richards is his brand of semiotics. He followed C. S. Peirce in holding that the sign is triadic (i.e., three-valued), not dyadic, as in Saussurian linguistics. In Peirce's triadic semiotics, interpretation is a logical constituent of the sign, not a psychological additive. (This distinction accounts for the difference between "reader-response" theory as set forth by Louise Rosenblatt—another Peircean—and other varieties, which focus on "identity themes" and "subjective" reactions.) Since modern linguistics, in all its varieties, is based on the concept of the dyadic sign, and since current rhetorical theory, from problem-solving to "expressive" discourse, is founded on this positivist linguistics, there has been little chance for I. A. Richards, who tirelessly questioned what was going on, to get a fair hearing.

Nor are recent developments any more welcoming to rigorous conceptions of triadicity. Postmodern critical theory has discovered "interpretation," but in the perspective of the dyadic sign this critical concept has no heuristic value. It is not unusual, for instance, to find a professor of English proclaiming the high truth of deconstruction in one book and simultaneously publishing a "rhetoric" based on the tenets of positivist linguistics, in which thought is *clothed* in language, *aligned* with words, or *poured* into linguistic slots like batter into muffin tins or molten iron into pigs. The faddishness commonplace in the curious field of rhetoric and composition is symptomatic of a decidedly unphilosophical understanding of the hermeneutic enterprise. This selection of essays is intended to make accessible a triadic conception of the meaning relationship which legitimates *interpretation in teaching* as revolutionary pedagogy and not another fad.

Richards, more than any other literary critic, educational theorist, linguist, or philosopher, can help us reclaim teaching as an intellectually challenging enterprise—teaching as dialogic action in classrooms conceived as "philosophic laboratories" for the study of the making of meaning. Sixty years ago Richards startled the academic world with his findings that the best and brightest often could not construe, could not always read for sense, could not dependably differentiate variant readings from misreading. The practical criticism he offered as analysis and remedy became one of the principal points of departure for the New Criticism, but his further analyses and his more radical remedies were disregarded. The time has come when we can usefully return to the rest of what I. A. Richards had to say to teachers of English. He wrote very little about composition per se, but in *everything* he wrote, there are important implications with respect to how we think about teaching writing and the ways we go about it. It might well be that in considering Richards' writings on rhetoric—defined as the study of "how words work" and of "misunderstanding and its remedies"—new attitudes and a revived sense of what can be done will emerge.

We will, in any case, discover that wherever we look, I. A. Richards has been there before us. What is now being called "writing across the curriculum" was for him "general education in a free society." His experimental designs in second language learning can show us why certain approaches in ESL pedagogy are valid for native speakers. Richards can help us rethink "errors and expectations." Some English teachers who once dutifully abjured a concern for "errors" now rush in either of two directions: toward basic skills and language labs, where drill is given a human face, or toward doctrines of interpretation and community that make any attempts to teach critical reading and writing absurd. I. A. Richards offers trustworthy guidance in rejecting the conceptions of language which underlie both tough-minded positivism and its mystical variants, as put forth by theoreticians who do not know what or how to teach. Our pedagogical "expectations" need the inspiriting that can come from a fresh appreciation of the resources of language itself.

Richards' philosophy of rhetoric can help to develop such understanding because he realized that the limits provided by the formal system of language are "virtuous and necessary": it is thoroughly grounded in a triadic semiotics which makes interpretation the motive power of a process of determination. Or, as he preferred to put it, his theory of practical criticism *depends from* certain principles of the nature of meaning as emergent in contexts of situation. That is to say, Richards profoundly understood that Peirce's semiotics entails his pragmaticism. The chief consequence of triadicity is the recognition of mediation and thus the need for what Richards called a continuing *audit* of meaning, the process of interpreting our interpretations, of "arranging our techniques for arranging," of thinking about our thinking, an infinite regression that is arrested when we ask: "What difference would it make to our practice if we stop here and put it this way, if we hold that this is probably the situation?" Richards' pedagogy, like that of Paulo Freire, is supported by (or depends from) a philosophy of language that can account for meaning as a process of determination and can thus guide the accounts we give of the meanings we make by means of emergent meanings.

The selections included in this volume have been organized in four parts, titles for which I have borrowed from Richards' own books: *Practical Criticism, The Philosophy of Rhetoric, The Meaning(s) of Meaning* (written with C. K. Ogden), and *Design for Escape,* his meditation on world education as the means of avoiding global catastrophe. When an essay has been printed more or less in its original form, I have retained Richards' title. To a series of short chapters I have amalgamated and to those he simply calls "Introductory" or "Retrospect" I have given new titles, usually drawing on the text for the wording. Scarcely a single selection could not easily appear in another section. The basic principles of early experiments in practical criticism are discernible in designs Richards was working on forty years later; his conception of "reader-response" theory is consonant with his triadic understanding of symbol systems; an interest in situation and context apparent in early books also finds expression in the language learning experiments of the 1960s; his theory of comprehending, developed in the 1950s, grew from his theory of translation, first sketched in 1932.

By juxtaposing early and late disquisitions, as well as pedagogical and critical exercises, I have tried to highlight some of the chief principles of Richards' critical thought and practice. But my primary aim has not been to trace the development of his ideas: omissions and repetitions alike are intended to bring into focus the Richards we most need in thinking about the philosophy of rhetoric and the challenge of inventing new pedagogies. Thus, I have included nothing from *Principles of Literary Criticism,* a mechanistic, behaviorist account he refused to disown but rather quickly set aside, letting Coleridge lead him to a better understanding of language and its purposes. And only a few pages from *Practical Criticism* and *The Philosophy of Rhetoric* are included because both are in print and should be read in their entirety.

A few essays have been printed in their original form, but for the most part I have cut and trimmed. Richards is not, in my opinion, a great essayist, but he is a master of the paragraph and the paragraph sequence; my emendations have been made in the interest of allowing that strength to emerge. Richards felt compelled to offer readers (or audiences) pointers and maxims which allow him to recapitulate arguments developed at length elsewhere.

(Some are very tiresome indeed, for they reappear again and again.) I have generally omitted these since the reader will have the arguments themselves at hand in this selection. I have omitted references to prior explanations and subsequent arguments not reprinted in this volume, as well as allusions to contemporary matters now obscure. I have occasionally omitted reservations and qualifications which seemed distracting or simply unnecessary; indeed, I've been guided by I. A. Richards' vigorous warning to all who design educational projects: "Cut out the distracting!" There is now and then a coyness in Richards' style, a kind of sweet sarcasm which does not suit his argument. I have cut wherever I found this habit off-putting. Passages of substance have been omitted when they are not germane to the essay as I am presenting it. I have, however, frequently retained digressions in order to ensure that Richards' favored mode of exposition—oblique and indirect—may be fairly represented; or, rather, that his ideas may be presented in the mode he preferred. All omissions are indicated by ellipses except in the previously mentioned instance; roadsigns (e.g., "as we have seen in last week's lecture," "further examples may be found") have been silently emended. Richards published books in both Britain and the United States. I have not attempted to make spelling consistent, but generally punctuation has been standardized in conformity with American usage.

Following each chapter, I have added a short excerpt from another Richards essay to serve as a kind of sounding board. (In several instances the passages chosen are cited in his own footnotes.) Richards was a master of the aphorism, and in some cases a single sentence can clarify pages of difficult exposition. And I have supplied an "Index of Richards' Speculative Instruments," the chief ideas he thought *with,* the meanings he found it necessary to deploy in the process of making further meanings. This annotated list includes working definitions, explanations, and examples of a word being used speculatively.

My purpose has not been to represent the history of Richards' philosophy of rhetoric but to present it in such a way that practical implications can be drawn out and consequences hypothesized and brought to the test in our own practice. As Richards said of his discussions of Coleridge, the aim is not to establish *what he thought,* but to provide occasions to explore *what we might do with what he said.* I do not claim that we should make Richards' opinions our own, but I believe that in following out what he does with his ideas, we can learn to sharpen and redirect our own.

Richards on Rhetoric

Beginnings and Transitions:
I. A. Richards Interviewed
by Reuben Brower

I.A.R.   Good morning, Ben. Shall we sit as we did when you first came to Magdalene to see me? How many years ago is it?

R.B.   It will be forty years in late September or early October when I had the nerve—I don't know whether you can remember that—to stop you on the street and ask you if you would like to supervise me, and then I went to your rooms.

I.A.R.   There was that big window, looking out into the Master's garden. Suppose you sit on that side as I remember you did, and I'll sit this side. Here we are again. Isn't it extraordinary what a part accident plays in our life? There was another time we sat on opposite sides of a window. It was in a railway train going up by Amherst somewhere. There you are, and the contact was resumed. Pure accident.

R.B.   Do you know at all how you first developed an interest in poetry? Was that accident too?

I.A.R.   It seems so. You know, I think, I was laid up all my early teens with TB. A very near squeak. And as I had unlimited leisure, I read and read . . . Suddenly I got engulfed by Kipling. I was reading a story (in *Many Inventions*) where Muller, the Inspector General of Woods and Forests, meets Mowgli, the grown-up Mowgli, in the woods. He recites to himself in a kind of German English. I was so overwhelmed by this that I really set to work to find out what it was.

From *I. A. Richards: Essays in His Honor*, ed. Reuben Brower, Helen Vendler, and John Hollander (1973).

And sooner or later someone said "'Dolores.' Swinburne." I'd never heard of "Dolores." And I doubt if I had heard of Swinburne. But, hearing, I ran down immediately to the drawing room where there was a funny old collection called The International Library of Famous Literature. About twenty volumes with little bits and pieces of everybody in it.

R.B.   I've heard of it.

I.A.R. I turned up Swinburne in the index and of all things on earth, found *The Battle Chorus* from *Erechtheus*. About ten lines later I couldn't see the book. I just blubbered my way through the rest of the excerpt. I had to lie down on my back on the hearthrug with the book propped up on my chest to keep the tears out of the line of vision.

> From east to west of the south sea-line
> Glitters the lightning of spears that shine. . . .

I didn't know that was going to send me, after many days, to the *Iliad*. But that opening

> Ill thoughts breed fear, and fear ill words; but these
> The Gods turn from us that have kept their law.
>   Let us lift up the strength of our hearts in song
>   And our souls to the height of the darkling day.
>   If the wind in our eyes blow blood for spray,
>   Be the spirit that breathes in us life more strong.
>   Though the prow reel round and the helm point wrong
>   And sharp reefs whiten the shoreward way
> For the steersman time sits hidden astern
>   With dark hand plying the rudder of doom. . . .

And so on and so on. This stayed with me, after a very few readings.

For me, it was the divine vision. I've never, therefore, been able to think critically about it—though I do recall that when I found "Dolores," soon after, I decided that Muller had much improved what he quoted. But the *Erechtheus* stood by me. At fearsome moments it was a talisman to restore courage. And it took me to Cambridge. One day in class at Clifton a marvelous old schoolmaster—we called him Cabby Spence because he was the picture of an old-fashioned cabby—asked, "Does anyone here know which were the flowers, the sacred flowers of Athens?" I couldn't help myself.

> Violet and olive leaf purple and hoary,
> Song wreath and story the fairest of fame,
> Flowers that the winter can blast not or bend;
> A Light upon earth as the sun's own flame,
>   A name as his name,
>   Athens, a praise without end.

That suddenly made me a classroom figure. And by pure accident again someone said I ought to try for an exhibition. I did and won a twenty-pound exhibition—twenty pounds a year at Magdalene. Quite enough to dazzle me: an opportunity to get away to Cambridge a year earlier than usual.

R.B.   What was this master in? Was he a master in English?

I.A.R.   Fifth form. And he was a master of English . . . really. And of enormous influence on me. He read to his class what he himself wanted to read and let them come along. He'd suddenly come in one morning and read us the whole of William Morris' "Defence of Guinevere." I'll never forget that, you know. One year he suddenly thought, "I'll reread the *Purgatorio* . . ." and gave it us—skipping little right through. That's unusual.

R.B.   Very. Did you worry much about language that early? As such?

I.A.R.   No. Not till I got to Cambridge.

R.B.   Now how does the transition take place between this kind of young interest: it's still very present with you—I've just heard you recite Swinburne—to, somehow or other, the Moral Sciences? Did you do the Moral Sciences Tripos first? Of course there was no English Tripos.

I.A.R.   There was no English Tripos. I went up in 1911 and stayed there till '15. Taking a year out through TB trouble again. I was laid up on Dartmoor. A break of a year and a very good thing too . . . another fine accidental intervention that let me do some miscellaneous reading. But this is what happened about the Moral Sciences. I was supposed to be a History Exhibitioner, you see. I had a most understanding Supervisor, very young, a newcomer at Magdalene, Frank Salter, who remained a close friend until his death in 1970. I went to him one morning in a grim mood and said I didn't think History ought to have happened. I didn't see why we should study it. I was getting no benefit. I had nothing against him. Frank Salter simply said, "You know, what you'd better do is come to lunch on Tuesday." So I came to lunch and there was Frank Salter in tennis clothes. He apologized. Said he'd had a snack and he was going out to play tennis and left me alone with a little white-faced, large-glittering-spectacled undergraduate, four years older than me. A Senior, when I was a very raw Freshman. And we sat and had lunch together there in Frank Salter's rooms. And Ogden, it was C.K. Ogden, proceeded to tell me what I would have to read in every possible subject being taught at the University, who my chief instructors would be and why they would teach me the sort of doctrines they taught. He thoroughly believed in the economic and social determination of doctrine. I was given a view of Cambridge University teaching such as no other could have given me. And at the end, characteristically, he took me off to his rooms and sold me two books. I decided at that lunch table to read Moral Sciences. I didn't know before that there was any such thing.

R.B.   What stage was he at then?

I.A.R.   He was a Classic, waiting. He was supposed to be in that anomalous situation, hanging about, hoping that some College would pick him up. Some teaching job or perhaps a by-fellowship: the beginnings of a career. Everybody had put him down as a future Professor in Classics . . . without any doubt whatever. He just was unbelievable as an intelligence. Perfect recall and all those sorts of things. And very lively spirit. Well, that settled me. I went into Moral Sciences and then I got enthralled by G.E. Moore.

R.B.   I was going to ask you if Moore wasn't a key point.

I.A.R.   He was. I don't think I ever understood anything. But it was complete subjugation. I got really interested in language because I felt something must be done to stop the leakage of information that was going on there all the time. I knew I didn't understand Moore or what he was at. I always thought if I went back to him for a whole course of lectures once again an inkling would come. But . . . no.

R.B.   Was he already asking, "What do we mean?"

I.A.R.   Incessantly.

R.B.   Lovely irony in that, isn't there?

I.A.R.   Yes. Moore was vocally convinced that few indeed could possibly *mean* what they *said*. I was silently persuaded that they could not possibly *say* what they *meant*. These two balanced one another perfectly. Anyhow, I didn't do too badly in the Moral Sciences. Then I went away from Cambridge and cultivated other pursuits . . . which come into the picture again by accident. I got another attack of my lung trouble and went up to North Wales to cure it. It seems rather unlikely, but I became—for those days: nothing like the standards of today—a rather skilful cragsman. I was fairly good at floating up difficult rocks.

R.B.   How did this interest in mountaineering come about? Who started you?

I.A.R.   Whymper, I think, and Ruskin. I was a devotee of the fourth volume of *Modern Painters* while at Clifton. Whymper's *Matterhorn* sent me to Ruskin's. I was re-reading the other day Ruskin's "mica flake" paragraph and realizing again what a prodigious influence it must have had on me. May I read it to you?

R.B.   Please do.

I.A.R.   "Modern Painters," Volume 4, Chapter XVI, paragraph 17.

Is not this a strange type, in the very heart and height of these mysterious Alps—these wrinkled hills in their snowy, cold, grey-haired old age, at first so silent, then, as we keep quiet at their feet, muttering and whispering to us garrulously, in broken and dreaming fits, as it were, about their child-hood—is it not a strange type of the things which "out of weakness are made strong"? If one of those little flakes of mica-sand, hurried in tremulous spangling along the bottom of the ancient river, too light to sink, too faint to float, almost too small for sight, could have had a mind given to it as it was at last borne down with its kindred dust into the abysses of the stream, and laid, (would it not have thought?) for a hopeless eternity, in the dark ooze, the most despised, forgotten, and feeble of all earth's atoms; incapable of any use or change; not fit, down there in the diluvial darkness, so much as to help an earth-wasp to build its nest, or feed the first fibre of a lichen;—what would it have thought, had it been told that one day, knit-ted into a strength as of imperishable iron, rustless by the air, infusible by the flame, out of the substance of it, with its fellows, the axe of God should hew that Alpine tower; that against *it*—poor, helpless, mica flake!—the wild north winds should rage in vain; beneath *it*—low-fallen mica flake!—the snowy hills should lie bowed like flocks of sheep, and the kingdoms of the earth fade away in unregarded blue; and around it—weak, wave-drifted mica flake!—the great war of the firmament should burst in thunder, and yet stir it not; and the fiery arrows and angry meteors of the night fall blunted back from it into the air; and all the stars in the clear heaven should light, one by one as they rose, new cressets upon the points of snow that fringed its abiding place on the imperishable spire?

R.B.   So mountains weren't just a gymnasium to you.

I.A.R.   I had Ruskin's rebuke to the Alpine Club by heart while I was still a schoolboy, before I had any dream of ever owning an iceaxe. "The mountains themselves, which your own poets used to love so rev-erently, you look upon as soaped poles in a bear-garden, which you set yourselves to climb and then slide down again with shrieks of delight . . . red with cutaneous eruption of conceit and voluble with convulsive hiccup of self-congratulation."

R.B.   But still you took to climbing.

I.A.R.   Yes, and, for a while, was good enough at it to take those pleasures seriously.

When I got over my TB, I decided to go back to Cambridge and get a medical qualification in order to become a psychoanalyst.

R.B.   This is where physiology comes in.

I.A.R.   Physiology and much more; psychological reading and reflexion be-yond any I'd tried to do as an undergraduate. And what was in those days theory of linguistics and communication. Since that lunch with Ogden, I'd not met him again. We had everything in common, but we didn't meet. And then, here's another accident.

Armistice Day: 11 o'clock on the 11th day of the 11th month, 1918. Pandemonium broke out in Cambridge. I spent some time climbing up the pinnacle in the middle of the market place . . . which has since been removed. I was sitting on top of that and enjoying the scene when I heard a name. I came down to King's Parade to see a crash of glass breaking. Ogden, by that time, was the owner of three shops in Cambridge; one was a picture gallery, the others were book stores. There he was, standing by the door of one of them, busy at a peculiar trick. He used to take his glasses up to the top of his head and press the corners of his eyes with his fingers. He could distort the lens slightly and get better vision . . . so he believed. Partly because his hands were over his eyes and mouth, nobody recognized him. I took my stand beside Ogden. Twenty or thirty drunken medical students were sacking the shop. Pictures were coming out through the plate glass in very dangerous fashion . . . Duncan Grant, Vanessa Bell, Roger Fry . . . right out into the street; it was very lucky no one spotted Ogden. He'd have been in the river. That night he came to call on me, to see if I could help him in recognizing any of the rioters. And later, in the small hours, we stood together on the little winding stair in 1, Free-School Lane and for the first time we talked together—for three hours, outlining the whole *Meaning of Meaning*.

R.B.   Already?!

I.A.R.   We agreed so easily on every point then. Twenty years later there came a time when we couldn't write a line to one another without grossly misunderstanding. It happens. But that was the moment when *The Meaning of Meaning* came into being.

R.B.   Had he already been pursuing things like that?

I.A.R.   Yes, for twenty years perhaps.

Now here's the next thing. Where my mountaineering comes in. I was suffering continuously from Hand to Mouth Disease, as Ogden called it. Very poor. I had to be careful. And I got tired of this life in Cambridge. It looked as though it would be twenty years before I got anywhere. So I went round to that Enchanter, Manny Forbes, of Clare College.

R.B.   Oh yes, I was hoping Manny would come in.

I.A.R.   Manny comes in very very much. He was the most saintly spirit I have ever had to do with . . . very bizarre.

R.B.   I heard him lecture.

I.A.R.   Well, you can see how he wouldn't strike everybody in the same way. But when you got to know him—spellbinding. I remember meeting him at the corner of King's Parade and Benet Street. He had a pile of books higher than his head in his arms. And a Newn-hamite passing by took pity on him and said, "May I help you?" Manny, holding some of his books with his chin and so forth said, "Pray do not disturb me; I have the stability of a pregnant Kanga-roo."

R.B.   Marvelous!

I.A.R. Always like that. I went to Manny because he knew all the Lairds of the Mountain Hebrides. I got him to write me a set of letters which would smooth my way to becoming a professional guide for mountaineering in Skye. We wrote the letters together, and he fell in love with the scheme. After we'd done it, we sat down by the fire and started talking about Wordsworth. Two hours later Manny tore up the letters and found another bit of paper. He could get two signatures, he told me, from people in the English school, just form-ing then, which would enable me to lecture next year . . . and collect fifteen shillings a head from anyone who came six times to the course. And that worked out. I only had to see Chadwick and Q and Aubrey Attwater and one or two others. And next year I came back and lectured: one course for distinction on Principles of Lit-erary Criticism and the other course for lucre—on the Contempo-rary Novel.

R.B.   Would this be about 1921? Or something like that?

I.A.R. More like 1919, when the English Tripos was just beginning.

R.B.   You've got to get in one more strand at this point. There is *The Foundations of Aesthetics*. Did that grow partly, I suppose, from Og-den, too?

I.A.R. That was a pure fluke, again, another fluke. It's the only time, I think, between the wars, that I didn't spend the entire summer in the Alps. I went out, I think it must have been in '20, to the Alps. I was rather unlucky . . . on an early expedition; and knocked myself out. And I gave up the season, a thing I never had to do any other year, and went back to Cambridge. In low spirits. And there I ran into a man I'd met once before, James Wood, who was staying in Cambridge. A good painter and a very close friend of Ogden's. He started talking art talk to me, and I said, "Why don't we spend some of our time as a triumvirate? Sorting out this art talk." I was doing bits and pieces of the *Meaning of Meaning* already.

R.B.   You must have been, to get that done by '23.

I.A.R. We did it all in a very queer way. Here is the picture of the three of us doing it. James Wood in the corner bicycling slowly upside down, doing his Muller's exercises, and supplying the ideas. It would be very late at night. Ogden lying on an immense high day-bed he had. We always called it Sardanapalus's Death Bed. Ogden would be on the Death Bed, pen in hand, writing it all down. And I would be walking up and down, doing a good deal of phrasing and rephrasing. The triumvirate would have sessions far into the night, being kept going by an ozone machine Ogden had picked up which produced sparks about a foot long and a tremendous smell of the Underground. But Ogden thought it was Brighton, and transported Brighton into Cambridge. He went to live in Brighton the later part of his life.

R.B.   Well, now, that interest . . . had you been reading Clive Bell and Vernon Lee and those people on your own?

I.A.R.   Yes. And so had James Wood.

R.B.   And Roger Fry, did he come in quite soon?

I.A.R.   Quite soon. But Roger Fry was a bit different from the others, I felt. I saw a lot of him later. In his whimsical way he touched realities.

R.B.   What about other minds that played some part in your experience then. You have mentioned Moore, and of course Ogden. How soon did Wittgenstein come to Cambridge and mean anything to you? Or didn't he mean much to you?

I.A.R.   He didn't, you know—ever. But he was very daunting and impressive. He turned up, the first time I saw him, at Moore's classes. Moore would lecture twice a week and at a third meeting we were expected to ask him questions. And almost nobody ever dared . . . to do it twice. So it tended to be a bit like a Quakers' meeting. Silence all round. Moore was quite unwittingly very savage. He would have to put his hands over his head and scream if you didn't use exactly the language that he would have used. If you used your own, he was baffled. Ogden—it was partly the impishness of the man—found a very distinguished physicist, A. A. Robb, who thought he had antedated and altogether outclassed Einstein. Robb was a huge Irishman with a head like a melon. And he completed it by always wearing a bowler hat, a *chapeau melon:* really a very odd figure for a great philosopher–mathematician. Ogden persuaded him to come to Moore's lectures, and he asked Moore a very simple question. He said, "When you say you see the sun, what do you think you see?" "The sun." "But, you know, about sunset, you can't see the sun. The sun is below the horizon. It's the refraction of the earth's atmosphere which enables you to see an image of the sun. Quite in a different location from where the sun is." Moore went nearly helpless with rage. "I can't see the sun," he cried. "I can't see the sun!" Everything broke down; that was what we were used to. And then suddenly there was this incredibly beautiful young Austrian, Wittgenstein, Lucifer before his Fall, oh, the most noble thing you ever saw. Rumour then had it he was an aeronautical engineer who had come to consult Russell as to whether any of Russell's and Whitehead's performances would assist him in some problems in aerodynamics. If so, he got involved deeper than he knew. Russell sent him to Moore. Wittgenstein started asking Moore questions.

For the first time in our many years' experience of Moore, Moore was submissive, gentle, doing his best to understand. It was a complete reversal. Mohammed was gone to the mountain. It was most extraordinary. And from that moment came Wittgenstein's dominance over Moore and over Cambridge. It went up preternaturally.

R.B.   I was wondering whether your meeting with Wittgenstein had much to do with how you thought about language.

I.A.R.   I shouldn't think it had. I was very negative. Wittgenstein was a personality who required utter devotion. And I've never been able to be even amused in any way with anyone who makes such enormous claims. People who saw much of Wittgenstein acquired what I irreverently christened "Saint Wittgenstein's Dance." They twitched and they pulled faces and they stopped to stare upwards . . . in the manner of the Master. And I shrank away from it all. I had one long session with Wittgenstein when I came back from one of our visits to China. First week. He came to breakfast and in the end we gave him supper. It was an all-day business, walking round Magdalene Garden and then coming in to talk. Various people joined us from time to time to relieve the strain. It was heavy. He pointed out to me early that there were two mistakes in *Tractatus*. I said, "Oh, that's no trouble, is it? It will be reprinted next year, I believe, and you can put an errata slip in." I realized as I said it that I had lost caste. He was staring at me like a Pillar of Society looking at a self-confessed rapist. "How could I," he said, "how could I touch it? It is my child." I just couldn't deal with that. And later he spent about an hour trying to convince a small group that if anyone were to drink one drop of perfectly pure water, he would die instantly. He had beliefs of that order . . . amongst the other things. He was a very odd character in many ways. I wrote a poem much later . . . about his lectures in Trinity. I used to go to them occasionally. They weren't lectures. You've heard descriptions, haven't you?

R.B.   Yes, I have. When you say lectures: wasn't this still a very small group?

I.A.R.   About twenty people, lying down in deck chairs. He thought that that was more propitious—they were supposed to be relaxed. And Moore was in an armchair, at his elbow, taking down every syllable. When Wittgenstein would start a sentence ten times, Moore would write it on his pad ten times up to the point where he broke it off. Absolute devotion. Most peculiar. It gave me the creeps.

R.B.   Well, now, we'll round another corner. How did you turn from that intense interest in meaning to the *Principles*?

I.A.R.   It grew out of my current lecturing, and I am a little tired of its being taken as my final word. I've certainly had enough of the first sentence: "A book is a machine to think with." That was just borrowed from Le Corbusier. "A house is a machine to live in. A chair is a machine to sit on. A book is a machine to think with." But it was a very early use of Le Corbusier, before he was much of a figure. It was James Wood who brought Le Corbusier to my attention. He read in the arts very very widely. But I like *Principles* still: parts of it; and I like what Hugh Gaitskell said of it. He came to Harvard to give the Godkin Lectures. Somebody introduced us. And I said, "*Principles of Literary Criticism*," and he said, "No, Principles of Intellectual Rectitude. That's what I learned through that book."

What mattered was that I was interested in psychology, a rather old-fashioned psychology: prebehavioristic, although I did know a good deal about behaviorism and did something towards joining them up. But my psychology came out of G.F. Stout, out of the big James Ward article in the Encyclopedia Britannica, and William James's two volumes, *The Principles of Psychology*. Those were the real formative things. Those and Sherrington's *Integrative Action of the Nervous System* to put the physiology in it. I was someone really saturated in psychology and neurology making up a book about the literary approaches. That was a bit of luck really. Two quite different concerns crossing at a crucial point.

R.B.   Then *Practical Criticism* . . . which was perhaps even more upsetting.

I.A.R.   It was to me. It went home. That and *Interpretation in Teaching*, which in my own private judgment is a much better, bigger book.

R.B.   I agree also that it's a very much neglected book, most unjustly neglected.

I.A.R.   It was written too fast. Did I tell you what happened with that book? It is worth putting on record. The Rockefeller Foundation had just begun to take me up. They took me up for about ten years. John Marshall said, for them, "Will you write an equivalent to *Practical Criticism* about prose? Do the lectures. Write the book, and we'll have a big conference in New York. And get everyone to come and we'll try and make this a subject: *Interpretation*." So I did. I gave a course. I collected the protocols. Enormous quantities of them. I saw Marshall again, when I'd got my materials piled up. And he said, "Now you've got to put down a figure that represents the worth of what you're going to do for the Foundation. I gave it a lot of thought and with great daring came up with the sum of $600. Then I had six weeks given me to write the book. It so happened that Dorothea caught scarlet fever. And was wafted off to an isolation hospital in Tooting Graveney. I wasn't allowed to do anything but stay away, and I wrote night and day. I found the extracts from the protocols (which took some finding), and arranged them and wrote the whole book in six weeks. It doesn't, I know, seem possible.

R.B.   The last part of the book saw you going in at least two directions toward a new kind of analysis of uses of language. I suppose it was the beginnings of *The Philosophy of Rhetoric*?

I.A.R.   I wrote that in those same six weeks. It's a derivative built from bits and pieces that I didn't use in *Interpretation in Teaching*. There is a sort of proportion sum: *Philosophy of Rhetoric* is to *Interpretation in Teaching* as *Science and Poetry* is to *Principles of Literary Criticism*. Each was a replaying on a more popular level, as I thought.

    Interpretation in Teaching has been out of print. But now, after all these decades, I am glad to say Routledge are reissuing it.

R.B.   In writing it, were you still thinking of how you could directly help teachers of literature?

I.A.R.   Yes. I was . . . and more than just teachers of literature.

R.B.   This is where you made the big transition.

I.A.R.   This is where it is. Actually, those two books sickened me for life of trying to read examination papers fairly. It's too hard to judge how foolish a comment really is and there are too many, too big a proportion of foolish comments. Do you know when I decided to back out of literature, as a subject, completely, and go into elementary education, I learnt something. I learnt where the academic railway tracks are. I was crossing the railway tracks in a most sinister fashion. I was told so again and again. Russell had tried to do it, you know. He'd founded a school and written a book on education. And people had said, "No wonder. He hadn't anything more to say." There's a very severe penalty attaching to going the wrong way across the railway tracks.

R.B.   The guilt feeling, yes.

I.A.R.   And in a way you are betraying a cause, showing things up. All that sort of thing. I remember one extraordinary moment when I was talking with T. S. Eliot. He was staying with Pickthorn, then the Junior Burgess (Member of Parliament) for Cambridge. I went round, Pickthorn had to go out and Eliot seemed hungry for serious conversation. I knew Eliot pretty well. He'd come and stay with us. But I always had a difficulty in making him talk about truly serious matters. He preferred not to on the whole.

R.B.   This was characteristic always, wasn't it?

I.A.R.   I thought so. He may have had special cronies with whom he could be intimate, but with me he usually dodged it. But at this point I took courage and asked him very, very straight, to advise me. Would I be making a mess of things . . . if I did what I in fact did. And he was about the only man I asked that question of who was cordially ready to approve. He had authority and dignity, Eliot had, that made you weigh his opinion. I was much comforted that he thought it would be a good thing to do.

R.B.   One wouldn't have expected him to have seen why you were doing it.

I.A.R.   I expect I took a good deal of trouble trying to spell it out.

R.B.   That transition must have been really something. *Interpretation in Teaching* is sort of the grand hinge from one way to another.

I.A.R.   From things which had been strangely successful to things very much otherwise.

R.B.   There is another transition I'm curious about. Your transition to Plato.

I.A.R.   I suppose that was partly due to Coleridge, to finding out that he was even more a Platonist than he himself sometimes knew. But, more still, making a Basic English version of *The Republic*. I'd neglected Plato. Everybody I knew in Cambridge had. They were strangely unaware of Plato. He didn't seem to be alive in any of them. They didn't seem to think he was anything but a Spartan anticipator of Mussolini or something as silly. That kind of thing was the View. It's very significant to me that for some reason or other even that noble figure, G.E. Moore, after being a distinguished Classic, when he turned to philosophy, never—so far as I know—made any reference to anything he'd learnt from Plato.

R.B.   And yet the kind of debate Moore said, at least, he wanted—it sounds as though he didn't want it when he got it—would be the essence of dialectic. After all, he was always asking Socratic questions.

I.A.R.   He was. And answering them himself. Wouldn't allow other people to answer them. He shows extraordinarily little concern with any other thinker than Moore. A dangerous sign, maybe, in him. A great mind, but—so it seems to me now—strangely immature: in some ways intellectually childlike.

R.B.   What's interesting is that you should have come out of the very heart of what one thinks of as the scientific, positive Cambridge, and made this transition where there was almost nobody around doing it. I suppose there was a little "Platonizing" in some corners of Cambridge . . . did Lowes Dickinson mean anything to you?

I.A.R.   Yes.

R.B.   He would have been one of the great exceptions.

I.A.R.   He was. Of course, old Goldie was glorious really in lots of ways. But I don't think he had at the time any influence on me on that front. He *had* a tremendous influence on me politically. *A Modern Symposium* was a book I would be able then to recite. It was a sort of Bible. And we joined up through his passion for things Chinese. But it was James (Jas) Wood who first awakened my interest in the multiple potentialities of Chinese phrases. We compared different translations of them together in a kind of rapture. It was he who brought the Chung Yung into our *Foundations*. Typically, he made "The Lodge of Leisures" a catchword among us. H.A. Giles had translated the Chinese collection of yarns as *Stories from a Chinese Studio*. Jas Wood pointed out that in the English translation of Soulié de Morant's version it was *Tales from the Lodge of Leisures*. We delighted in having such a name for wherever we might be doing our hardest work. It must have been an inverse impulse that made us give a really clamant title to the little book we had so enjoyed writing.

R.B.   This reminds me of another deviation or transition: *Mencius on the Mind.* Is that picking up your early *Meaning of Meaning* interest? Or is it also looking into the very next step, which seems to me to be broadly connected with translation?

I.A.R.   Both perfectly true. It was a sort of natural growth for me in Peking. Here was I doing my best to take part in academic activities which illustrated incomprehension—unknown, unrecognized failure of understanding and on such a scale, always hitting you. I felt I must do something. So I got together a very able team of four and I sat in more or less as secretary. I didn't pretend to any Chinese. I could just distinguish one character from another, but I didn't know anything. I couldn't be sensitive to the terrific, universewide, reverberations. And these four people were so sensitive in their various ways, and they did their best to explain to me some of the key things. I took . . . curiously enough . . . the passages in Mencius which might be parallel to passages in Coleridge.

R.B.   That's just the question I was about to ask. *Coleridge on Imagination, Mencius on the Mind.* Isn't there some deliberate coming together here?

I.A.R.   Yes, but with a difference. What got into *Coleridge on Imagination* was a sort of free reconstruction. I wasn't so much concerned to say what Coleridge had thought as to suggest what might be done with what he had said.

R.B.   This too was a transition.

I.A.R.   It was. In my then view it was being scientific.

R.B.   Which many people didn't understand. It baffled many "pure scholars." Because they didn't see that what you were trying to do—as I understood it—was to show us what could be rescued and continued.

I.A.R.   Yes, that is exactly right. And I tried to do something for Mencius of the same sort. Only I had to lay out the problems much more thoroughly in Mencius. My informants (and I had to rely on them), although they were devout Mengtzists, or whatever you call it, were very diverse in their understanding of the Master. I came to feel that this diversity was what mattered.

R.B.   Well, I gathered from that book that it was just this very variety of interpretation that you were talking about. The book gave you an enormous opportunity for it. This was where I came in, incidentally. You were getting the proofs of Mencius just at that time. And occasionally I used to sit by your side on the sofa in Magdelene when you were tearing your hair out over these choices of Mencius and saying to yourself sometimes: "Whatever did I mean?"

I.A.R. One way and another Mencius taught me so much that I got the Rockefeller to stake me to go back and try to found a movement in China for teaching English in a way that would make it more useful to the Chinese, for understanding what they (and we) most need. And there I learnt a lot of politics again.

R.B. You and Ogden had already worked out the vocabulary of Basic English.

I.A.R. He did it. It's Ogden's, all the detail; the general plotting is a good deal me, but all the hard work was Ogden's . . . tremendous, too. The way he did it was as individual as it was original.

R.B. Can you reconstruct how the two of you thought of doing this at all? If I may say so, this was a really new idea.

I.A.R. Ogden had been playing with artificial languages for perhaps ten years.

R.B. Had he gone back to . . .

I.A.R. He'd read Wilkins and Leibnitz; he knew Newton's proposals backwards. He was deep in it, and in all the artificial languages too. He had a gift for that kind of thing. And when he wrote a chapter, in *The Meaning of Meaning,* "On Definition," at the end of it we suddenly stared at one another and said, "Do you know this means that with under a thousand words you can say everything." If a word can be defined in a descriptive phrase of not more than ten words, you can substitute the descriptive ten words for the word and get rid of it. Oversimple, extremely—but, for most purposes, good enough. We found we'd worked out the principles of such rephrasings in writing that Chapter. And at the end of it, we very nearly switched to a new task. I remember I went home to Clifton and spent my time drafting what was to be Basic. And Ogden had been doing exactly the same thing in my absence. When we came together again we said, "Look here, shall we drop the *Meaning of Meaning* because this is a much bigger thing." It was only half written, the book, you see, and this was a much bigger thing. But Ogden had got himself deeply involved. He'd already set up the publication of *The Meaning of Meaning.* Did you ever hear how that was done? He created a project which finally grew to two hundred volumes called The International Library of Psychology, Philosophy and Scientific Method—just in order to print the *Meaning of Meaning* among suitable supporting works.

He had been publishing then, very successfully, a penny weekly magazine, which he turned into a digest of the world news as an aid to the war. When all *that* was put an end to by drunken medicos rioting on Armistice Day, he wrote a letter to the subscribers, some 15,000, including Charlie Chaplin, I remember, saying that the unexpired part of their subscription would be met by their receiving instead of the penny Weekly a Quarterly—very handsomely produced. He designed the Quarterly so that each page of it was four pages of *The Meaning of Meaning*. That cut down expense and trouble. So we wrote the *Meaning of Meaning* in a tremendous hurry for publication, in bits and pieces quarter by quarter. We cut up the *Cambridge Magazine* proofs as they came in and I pasted them on the walls of my room. In time we had the whole book pasted up there. So we could put a *not* in any sentence we thought would benefit from having a *not* put into it. Oh, it was fun! That's how we did it.

R.B.   I suppose this interest—going over into Basic—is very much a part of your move to this Cambridge, isn't it.

I.A.R.   Couldn't be more so. Though, actually, I came in '39 because of the war. When it broke, I went to the man I knew best in the field: Stephen Gaselee, Senior Ambassador, Librarian of the Foreign Office and a Fellow of Magdalene. I asked what I should do. I didn't care to get out of the war, and I had in my pocket an invitation to come to Harvard. The answer was: If you've got an invitation to Harvard, you've got to go. So I came. The invitation was mainly the work, I think, of David Stevens of the Rockefeller. They fixed up my appointment here because they wanted some Basic English texts turned out and some people trained and so on. They gave me an endowment for three years.

R.B.   You would think now with all the new interest in the teaching of English as a second language all over the world, that there would be lessons to be learned from Basic.

I.A.R.   Anyway, my gifted collaborator, Christine Gibson, and I turned out, through the years, a great amount of rather fundamental redesign of instruction—for Beginning Reading and Languages—in all the Media. I hope more people will be using it along with our other derivatives from Basic. Otherwise, I fear a big experimental resource for education will be missed. But I have put all that in my paperback: *Design for Escape*.

R.B.   It seems natural to go on now to translation because these two interests are one, aren't they?

I.A.R.   I never thanked you rightly for that dedication to me of your *On Translation*. That was enheartening.

R.B.   That book really started from looking in Magdalene at those proofs of *Mencius on the Mind*. (I very nearly did Classics in college, but soon shifted to a combination of Greek and English.) It suddenly dawned on me then that here was a whole interest that I had been on top of, though unconscious of. But what I would like to ask about is the step from that kind of analytical interest to your actually trying your hand at translation?

I.A.R.   Making Basic or Everyman's versions? Well, I needed to do that for China. But I also felt that there was a population here in the schools that would benefit from something really lucid. So, there we are. And I'm quite happy about the way *The Wrath of Achilles, Why So,*

Socrates? and the *Republic* hold to their purpose . . . and are serving it. It's not every purpose. There must be a variety of interpretations aimed at different companies of addressees.

R.B.   Right. The attempt to get *everything* into the scholarly translation finally defeats the reader.

I.A.R.   It produces the Loeb versions—thank everyone for them.

R.B.   Right in the middle of all this comes *How to Read a Page*. At least it was published in 1942. This seemed like a very good shot at Chicago and its Great Books Program and the way it was conducted.

I.A.R.   You hit the nail on the head. I had admired Mortimer Adler immensely but I somehow got irritated by *How to Read a Book*. So I wrote a counterblast: *How to Read a Page*. Instead of a hundred *books*, chosen regardless of what translation, version or anything, I wanted to take just a hundred *words* and then I revolted again and made it a hundred and three. And it so happens that the Great Books are now a hundred and three. It was partly a bit of fun. But it was a very serious book, unusable, I know now, for the populations I hoped I was addressing. I did have one surprise. It was made into a paperback. And about six months after that, I suddenly got a telegram from the editor of the paperback series, who simply said, "Hold on to your hat. They've ordered 15,000 of it." And I looked forward, as you imagine, to next year's returns. I think they sold forty-two copies the next year. It didn't go down where it was hoped it would go down. One has to be used to that.

R.B.   It went down . . . perhaps where the ground was prepared . . . when the teachers who at that time were feeling, as I was—many of us were—feeling really swamped by the Chicago sort of thing. And all of our effort had been, you know, in the opposite direction. There were so many badly conceived courses that just grabbed Great Authors right and left, and threw them in. No consideration of what translation, or of how the teacher could intelligently teach a translation.

I.A.R.   Or how much a mind can take in by the week.

R.B.   Let's not end on this because I'm interested in the experiments you are now active in. I suppose it was Basic that led you to thinking about visual media?

I.A.R.   Yes, because I had to draw, I had to turn *English through Pictures I* into comic strip technique. That's an awfully good little book that Dr. Wiese produced about the man who invented the comic strip, Rodolphe Töpffer: *Enter the Comics* (University of Nebraska Press, 1965).

R.B.   She was in my translation seminar when she was working on that.

I.A.R.   I learnt a lot from it. What happened was very simple. I'd long wanted to have a comic strip version for teaching Basic. I did the sequencing, the overall design; I drew the pictures for the book myself and then, very mistakenly, got a draughtsman to redo them. And he gave them a kind of woodenness that I'm against. There's a great deal of thinking involved in drawing *really clear* diagrammatic representations of meanings. It's a way of studying meanings that's unexpectedly revealing. It started me on what may be a key idea: that the multiplicity of our channels is our best hope. The eye can check what the ear hears and vice versa. Our habits of writing may teach us a great deal about what we're saying. I found myself recently having twice written on a single page *competition*—very clearly, in my clearest handwriting—in place of *composition*. It hadn't occurred to me in oral or visual words so sharply ever before that any composition is a competition between the choices that are open to it. Here was my hand—unknown to me—speaking for a deeper awareness: writing *competition*. It was reminding me, drawing my attention to a primal fact.

R.B. I hoped we might end on your poetry. Were you always writing verse?

I.A.R. Almost never, until recently. It was a very queer set of impulsions, not accidental, that led me to write verse. I was finishing a play called *A Leak in the Universe;* it seemed definitely to require a lyrical component. So I just had to write the lyrical component. And that got me into it.

R.B. And this would be about when?

I.A.R. I must have been sixty, or over. The *Leak* is quite late (Playbook, New Directions, 1956). It is listed in my *Internal Colloquies:* my poems, up till 1970.

R.B. And you've gone on.

I.A.R. As Robert Lowell said to me recently: "Why not, if writing verse is the most fascinating thing there is to do?" Perhaps I might close this self-indulgent talk with my latest poem? It's not, I hope, my last. The title is *Acquiescence.*

> His young Mont Blanc could say,
>   For Shelley, what he would.
>   O serene Throne
>   Unseen, Unknown!
> Mine, threescore years away,
>   For other searchings stood:
>
> Spoke to me of Beyonds
>   But too well gainable,
>   Of means and aims
>   Dwindling to games.

Now what in me responds
  To the Unattainable?

Lo! Ruskin's Matterhorn!
  Not Whymper's mortal prize.
    That craze dispelled,
    The Unbeheld
Returns, as if reborn,
  To disillusioned eyes.

Hence, to the Lodge of Leisures
  With easy steps and few,
    Being intent
    Less to repent
Than re-appraise those pleasures,
  Assess these aches anew.

Study the antic flight
  From shiver to sun to shade;
    The fervours past,
    The rigours last
Into the chills of night
  That shake strong hearts afraid.

Now the proud rage for doing,
  That passion for What's On,
    That feckless
    Restlessness,
That frenetic pursuing . . .
  Had best be seen as gone.

Hopes that would hint of treasures
  Repaying such to-do
    Have stept ahead
    As leaves are sped.
So redesign your measures,
  Align your ends anew.

Sorrows that might not tell
  Of Loss beyond your thought:
    Yearnings forbid,
    By chagrin hid.
Old strains and dreads as well:
  Old aches gone where they ought.

From what may this forefend?
  Such transformations steal
    So past recall

Through all;
Foreshadowings so impend,
　How sense now how we feel?

Who less than ever guess
　What we may yet conceive
　　So insecure
　　Each "To be sure . . ."
In which we acquiesce;
　Nor know for what to grieve.

Failure comes first: first
　Forepang, gathering strength;
　　To have so failed,
　　Left unfulfilled
What most we tried: the worst
　Now realized, at length.

Each muscle that won't pull,
　Each sense and joint to stall,
　　Enacting old
　　Assaults gone cold,
Speaks to us, to the full,
　Of what might now appall.

The body wearing out
　Backs still each changed regime:
　　What to refuse,
　　What not accuse,
Learning to live with gout . . .
　Mind has its graver theme.

Parallel though: to keep
　Viable itself,
　　Being not,
　　Now, longer what
It was, but half-asleep,
　The old codes on the Shelf.

What we might do has sought
　To shape and set our scope.
　　Which shutting in,
　　We may begin
Refurbishing our thought,
　Untarnishing our Hope.

Of what? Ah, none can tell.
　But see what's risen there:

That Towerer, sheer
Transcending fear,
Whereby, composed, to dwell,
Dare, share, forbear.
And murmurings spare.
The Alps, July–October 1972

I

Practical Criticism

Richards reclaimed *practical criticism*—both idea and phrase—from Coleridge, using it as the title for his best-known book, which was at once a study of literary form and an enormously influential account of how people read: *Practical Criticism* became a founding charter of the New Criticism. Richards' aim was to provide documentation of how people actually read, hoping thereby to avoid debate in order to move toward an authentic criticism. To the habit of disputation Richards opposed research—systematic procedures and experimental techniques. All were devised to put theory to the test: "How we use a theorem best tells us what the theorem is." He wanted to develop what he called a "natural history of opinions" (later, of "meanings"), tracing the sources of misunderstanding so that remedies could be arrived at more rationally; for Richards, authentic criticism is always pedagogic at its core.

From the first, Richards thought of reading—indeed, of learning and teaching—as a matter of interpretation, but with interpretation conceived of not as a psychological additive but as the logical condition of signification. The meaning relationship for Richards is not two-valued, as in Saussure's conception of the sign, but three-valued: interpretation empowers signification and is itself a process of determination. Nothing is more important in Richards' theory and practice than this semiotic principle of triadicity, which he learned early on from C. S. Peirce.*

*The triangle with the dotted base line is the emblem of Peirce's theory of the meaning relationship; this curious triangle, which Richards uses in his discussion of how *Truth* means (see pp. 141–42), made its first appearance in *The Meaning of Meaning*, written with C. K. Ogden and published in 1923. C. S. Peirce also made his first appearance there outside the philosophical journals: Ogden and Richards included as an appendix Peirce's disquisition on the sign.—ED

Richards seems to have understood from the first a principle which has escaped the New Pragmatists, namely, that pragmatism (which Peirce renamed *pragmaticism,* after deciding that William James had misrepresented the theory) is entailed in the triadic conception of the sign. All that we know is mediated; all that is represented must be interpreted; all interpretations must themselves be interpreted, since there can be no direct access to the reality of our experience. Pragmatism recognizes the consequences of triadicity: it does not mean being hard-nosed or tough-minded or cost-conscious or limiting oneself to "empirical findings." To be pragmatic is to understand that the logically infinite regress of interpreting our interpretations requires that we ask "What difference does it make to our practice if we put it this way? If we hypothesize thus and so, how would it change the way we proceed?" In developing multiple definitions, Richards is showing us how to cultivate an attitude of "fallibilism," as Peirce recommends. For Richards, keeping things tentative is the chief principle of all learning and teaching.

What is now called "reader response theory" was given an early formulation in *Practical Criticism.* It is noteworthy that the theory in this case determined the course design. The number of "texts" was severely limited; rereading was invited; writing was free and open-ended; no topics were assigned. Student "texts" provided the point of departure for the lectures; their misunderstandings were the occasion for considering remedies. Richards' classes at Cambridge must have been more like Grand Rounds at a teaching hospital than like academic lectures.

In *Practical Criticism,* poetry was Richards' "instrument of research"; the first opportunity to set down what he had worked out came in connection with his interest in the theory and practice of translation. He insists on the necessity of a "logical machinery" by which we can alert ourselves to the contexts, to the meanings through which we discover and represent our interpretations in the form of new meanings. I have included a later essay in which Richards returns to the image of translation as going through the looking glass.

When Mortimer J. Adler of the University of Chicago offered to the public a treatise called *How to Read a Book,* Richards countered with *How to Read a Page.* He is at his energetic best here, and what energizes him is the impatience he feels with those who do not know how complex the challenges of reading are; how virtually inevitable misreading is; and how challenging it is to theory and practice to correct it. His chief remedy is to emphasize the systematic character of ambiguity, offering as a technique for understanding its role his list of "one hundred *great* words," a variant of the eight hundred *basic* words of Basic English.

After *How to Read a Page,* Richards did not again write a book conceived as a whole until his last-published volume, *Techniques in Language Control.* But in all the intervening books—collections of articles, papers, talks—he continued his explorations of how we read and how we might improve.

I

An Experiment in Criticism

I have set three aims before me in constructing this book. First, to introduce a new kind of documentation to those who are interested in the contemporary state of culture whether as critics, as philosophers, as teachers, as psychologists, or merely as curious persons. Secondly, to provide a new technique for those who wish to discover for themselves what they think and feel about poetry (and cognate matters) and why they should like or dislike it. Thirdly, to prepare the way for educational methods more efficient than those we use now in developing discrimination and the power to understand what we hear and read.

For the first purpose I have used copious quotations from material supplied to me as a Lecturer at Cambridge and elsewhere. For some years I have made the experiment of issuing printed sheets of poems—ranging in character from a poem by Shakespeare to a poem by Ella Wheeler Wilcox—to audiences who were requested to comment freely in writing upon them. The authorship of the poems was not revealed, and with rare exceptions it was not recognised.

After a week's interval I would collect these comments, taking certain obvious precautions to preserve the anonymity of the commentators, since only through anonymity could complete liberty to express their genuine opinions be secured for the writers. Care was taken to refrain from influencing them either for or against any poem. Four poems were issued at a time. I would,

From *Practical Criticism* (1929), parts I and IV.

as a rule, hint that the poems were perhaps a mixed lot, but that was the full extent of my interference. I lectured the following week partly upon the poems, but rather more upon the comments, or protocols*, as I call them.

Much astonishment both for the protocol-writers and for the Lecturer ensued from this procedure. The opinions expressed were not arrived at lightly or from one reading of the poems only. As a measure of indirect suggestion, I asked each writer to record on his protocol the number of "readings" made of each poem. A number of perusals made at one session were to be counted together as one "reading" provided that they aroused and sustained one single growing response to the poem, or alternatively led to no response at all and left the reader with nothing but the bare words before him on the paper. This description of a "reading" was, I believe, well understood. It follows that readers who recorded as many as ten or a dozen readings had devoted no little time and energy to their critical endeavour. Few writers gave less than four attacks to any of the poems. On the whole it is fairly safe to assert that the poems received much more thorough study than, shall we say, most anthology pieces get in the ordinary course. It is from this thoroughness, prompted by the desire to arrive at some definite expressible opinion, and from the week's leisure allowed that these protocols derive their significance.

The standing of the writers must be made clear. The majority were undergraduates reading English with a view to an Honours Degree. A considerable number were reading other subjects but there is no ground to suppose that these differed for this reason in any essential respect. There was a sprinkling of graduates, and a few members of the audience were non-academic. Men and women were probably included in about equal numbers, so, in what follows "he" must constantly be read as equivalent to "he or she." There was no compulsion to return protocols. Those who took the trouble to write—about 60 percent—may be presumed to have been actuated by a more than ordinarily keen interest in poetry. From such comparisons as I have been able to make with protocols supplied by audiences of other types, I see no reason whatever to think that a higher standard of critical discernment can easily be found under our present cultural conditions. Doubtless, could the Royal Society of Literature or the Academic Committee of the English Association be impounded for purposes of experiment we might expect greater uniformity in the comments or at least in their style, and a more wary approach as regards some of the dangers of the test. But with regard to equally essential matters occasions for surprise might still occur. The precise conditions of this test are not duplicated in our everyday commerce with literature. Even the reviewers of new verse have as a rule a considerable body of the author's work to judge by. And editorial complaints are frequent as to the difficulty of obtaining good reviewing. Editors themselves will not be the slowest to agree

---

*Richards' experiments in *Practical Criticism* (and in *Mencius*) feature *protocols* and multiple definitions which depend on *grammatico–logical* analysis. This terminology parodies Wittgenstein's procedure and title—the propositions numbered 1.1, 1.2, 1.3, and so on and his title *Tractatus Logico-Philosophicus.*—ED

with me upon the difficulty of judging verse without a hint as to its prove-
nance.

Enough, for the moment, about the documentation of this book. My second aim is more ambitious and requires more explanation. It forms part of a
general attempt to modify our procedure in certain forms of discussion.
There are subjects—mathematics, physics and the descriptive sciences supply
some of them—which can be discussed in terms of verifiable facts and precise
hypotheses. There are other subjects—the concrete affairs of commerce, law,
organisation and police work—which can be handled by rules of thumb and
generally accepted conventions. But in between is the vast *corpus* of problems,
assumptions, adumbrations, fictions, prejudices, tenets; the sphere of random beliefs and hopeful guesses; the whole world, in brief, of abstract opinion and disputation about matters of feeling. To this world belongs everything about which civilised man cares most. I need only instance ethics,
metaphysics, morals, religion, aesthetics, and the discussions surrounding liberty, nationality, justice, love, truth, faith and knowledge to make this plain.
As a subject-matter for discussion, poetry is a central and typical denizen of
this world. It is so both by its own nature and by the type of discussion with
which it is traditionally associated. It serves, therefore, as an eminently suitable *bait* for anyone who wishes to trap the current opinions and responses
in this middle field for the purpose of examining and comparing them, and
with a view to advancing our knowledge of what may be called the natural
history of human opinions and feelings.

In part then this book is the record of a piece of fieldwork in comparative
ideology. But I hope, not only to present an instructive collection of contemporary opinions, presuppositions, theories, beliefs, responses and the rest,
but also to make some suggestions towards a better control of these tricksy
components of our lives. The way in which it is hoped to do this can only
be briefly indicated at this point.

There are two ways of interpreting all but a very few utterances.

Whenever we hear or read any not too nonsensical opinion, a tendency so
strong and so automatic that it must have been formed along with our earliest
speech-habits, leads us to consider *what seems to be said* rather than the *mental
operations* of the person who said it. If the speaker is a recognised and obvious
liar this tendency is, of course, arrested. We do then neglect what he has said
and turn our attention instead to the motives or mechanisms that have caused
him to say it. But ordinarily we at once try to consider the objects his words
seem to stand for and not the mental goings-on that led him to use the words.
We say that we "follow his thought" and mean, not that we have traced what
happened in his mind, but merely that we have gone through a train of thinking that seems to end where he ended. We are in fact so anxious to discover
whether we agree or not with what is being said that we overlook the mind
that says it, unless some very special circumstance calls us back.

Compare now the attitude to speech of the alienist attempting to "follow"
the ravings of mania or the dream maunderings of a neurotic. I do not suggest that we should treat one another altogether as "mental cases" . . . but

merely that for some subject-matters and some types of discussion the alien-ist's attitude, his direction of attention, his order or plan of interpretation, is far more fruitful, and would lead to better understanding on both sides of the discussion than the usual method that our language habits force upon us. For normal minds are easier to "follow" than diseased minds, and even more can be learned by adopting the psychologist's attitude to ordinary speech-situations than by studying aberrations.

It is very strange that we have no simple verbal means by which to describe these two different kinds of "meaning." Some device as unmistakable as the "up" or "down" of a railway signal ought to be available. But there is none. Clumsy and pedantic-looking psychological periphrases have to be employed instead. I shall, however, try to use one piece of shorthand consistently. In handling the piles of material supplied by the protocols I shall keep the term "statement" for those utterances whose "meaning" in the sense of what they *say,* or purport to say, is the prime object of interest. I shall reserve the term "expression" for those utterances where it is the mental operations of the writers which are to be considered.

When the full range of this distinction is realised the study of criticism takes on a new significance. But the distinction is not easy to observe. Even the firmest resolution will be constantly broken down, so strong are our na-tive language habits. When views that seem to conflict with our own pre-possessions are set before us, the impulse to refute, to combat or to recon-struct them, rather than to investigate them, is all but overwhelming. So the history of criticism, like the history of all the middle subjects alluded to above, is a history of dogmatism and argumentation rather than a history of research. (We shall meet in the protocols plenty of living instances of famous critical doctrines that are often thought to be now merely curiosities of opin-ion long since extinct.) And like all such histories the chief lesson to be learnt from it is the futility of all argumentation that precedes understanding. We cannot profitably attack any opinion until we have discovered what it ex-presses as well as what it states; and our present technique for investigating opinions must be admitted, for all these middle subjects, to be woefully in-adequate.

Therefore, the second aim of this book is to improve this technique. We shall have before us several hundreds of opinions upon particular aspects of poetry, and the poems themselves to help us to examine them. We shall have the great advantage of being able to compare numbers of extremely different opinions upon the same point. We shall be able to study what may be called the same opinion in different stages of development as it comes from different minds. And further, we shall be able in many instances to see what happens to a given opinion, when it is applied to a different detail or a different poem.

The effect of all this is remarkable. When the first dizzy bewilderment has worn off, as it very soon does, it is as though we were strolling through and about a building that hitherto we were only able to see from one or two distant standpoints. We gain a much more intimate understanding both of the poem and of the opinions it provokes. Something like a plan of the most usual approaches can be sketched and we learn what to expect when a new object, a new poem, comes up for discussion.

It is as a step towards another training and technique in discussion that I would best like this book to be regarded. If we are to begin to understand half the opinions which appear in the protocols we shall need no little mental plasticity. And in the course of our comparisons, interpretations and extrapolations something like a plan of the ways in which the likely ambiguities of any given term or opinion-formula may radiate will make itself apparent. For the hope of a new technique in discussion lies in this: that the study of the ambiguities of one term assists in the elucidation of another. To trace the meanings of "sentimentality," "truth," "sincerity," or "meaning" itself, as these terms are used in criticism, can help us with other words used in other topics. Ambiguity in fact is systematic; the separate senses that a word may have are related to one another, if not as strictly as the various aspects of a building, at least to a remarkable extent. Something comparable to a "perspective" which will include and enable us to control and "place" the rival meanings that bewilder us in discussion and hide our minds from one another can be worked out. Perhaps every intelligence that has ever reflected upon this matter will agree that this may be so. Everyone agrees but no one does any research into the matter, although this is an affair in which even the slightest step forward affects the whole frontier line of human thought and discussion.

The indispensable instrument for this inquiry is psychology. I am anxious to meet as far as may be the objection that may be brought by some psychologists, and these the best, that the protocols do not supply enough evidence for us really to be able to make out the motives of the writers and that therefore the whole investigation is superficial. But the *beginning* of every research ought to be superficial, and to find something to investigate that is accessible and detachable is one of the chief difficulties of psychology. I believe the chief merit of the experiment here made is that it gives us this. Had I wished to plumb the depths of these writers' Unconscious, where I am quite willing to agree the real motives of their likings and dislikings would be found, I should have devised something like a branch of psychoanalytic technique for the purpose. But it was clear that little progress would be made if we attempted to drag too deep a plough. However, even as it is, enough strange material is turned up.

After these explanations the reader will be prepared to find little argumentation in these pages, but much analysis, much rather strenuous exercise in changing our ground and a good deal of rather intricate navigation. Navigation, in fact—the art of knowing where we are wherever, as mental travellers, we may go—is the main subject of the book. To discuss poetry and the ways in which it may be approached, appreciated and judged is, of course, its prime purpose. But poetry itself is a mode of communication. What it communicates and how it does so and the worth of what is communicated form the subject-matter of criticism. It follows that criticism itself is very largely, though not wholly, an exercise in navigation. It is all the more surprising then that no treatise on the art and science of intellectual and emotional navigation has yet been written; for logic, which might appear to cover part of this field, in actuality hardly touches it.

That the one and only goal of all critical endeavours, of all interpretation, appreciation, exhortation, praise or abuse, is improvement in communication may seem an exaggeration. But in practice it is so. The whole apparatus of critical rules and principles is a means to the attainment of finer, more precise, more discriminating communication. There is, it is true, a valuation side to criticism. When we have solved, completely, the communication problem, when we have got, perfectly, the experience, *the mental condition* relevant to the poem, we have still to judge it, still to decide upon its worth. But the later question nearly always settles itself; or rather, our own inmost nature and the nature of the world in which we live decide it for us. Our prime endeavour must be to get the relevant mental condition and then see what happens. If we cannot then decide whether it is good or bad, it is doubtful whether any principles, however refined and subtle, can help us much. Without the capacity to get the experience they cannot help us at all. This is still clearer if we consider the use of critical maxims in teaching. Value cannot be demonstrated except through the communication of what is valuable.

Critical principles, in fact, need wary handling. They can never be a substitute for discernment though they may assist us to avoid unnecessary blunders. There has hardly ever been a critical rule, principle or maxim which has not been for wise men a helpful guide but for fools, a will-o'-the-wisp. All the great watchwords of criticism from Aristotle's "Poetry is an imitation" down to the doctrine that "Poetry is expression," are ambiguous pointers that different people follow to very different destinations. Even the most sagacious critical principles may, as we shall see, become merely a cover for critical ineptitude; and the most trivial or baseless generalisation may really mask good and discerning judgment. Everything turns upon how the principles are applied. It is to be feared that critical formulas, even the best, are responsible for more bad judgment than good, because it is far easier to forget their subtle sense and apply them crudely than to remember it and apply them finely. . . .

[Richards continues with a list of the "chief difficulties of criticism," as follows: making out the plain sense, difficulties of sensuous apprehension and of imagery, the influence of mnemonic irrelevance, stock responses, sentimentality, inhibition, doctrinal adhesions, technical presuppositions, general critical preconceptions. The protocols themselves constitute Part II, Documentation. In Part III, IAR returns to the ten difficulties of criticism, considering them in the light of the distinctions to be made among four kinds of meaning. *Practical Criticism* then concludes with Summary and Recommendations, excerpts from which follow.]

It is *not* inevitable, or in the nature of things, that poetry should seem such a remote, mysterious, unmanageable thing to so large a majority of readers. The deficiencies so noticeable in the protocol writers (and, if we could be franker with ourselves, in our own reading) are not native inalterable defects in the average human mind. They are due in a large degree to mistakes that can be avoided, and to bad training. In fact, does anyone ever receive any useful training in this matter? Yet, without asking more from average humanity than even a misanthrope will grant, something can be done to make men's spiritual heritage more available and more operative. Though I may seem to be traversing, in what follows, ground with which every teacher (and every person thrust into close contact with humanity) is familiar to the point of desperation, I am confident that the last word in this matter has not been spoken. A better technique, as we learn daily in other fields, may yield results that the most whole-hearted efforts fall short of if misapplied. And the technique of the approach to poetry has not yet received half so much serious systematic study as the technique of pole-jumping. If it is easy to push up the general level of performance in such "natural" activities as running or jumping (not to insist upon the more parallel examples of mountaineering, fly-fishing and golf) merely by making a little careful inquiry into the best methods, surely there is reason to expect that investigation into the technique of reading may have even happier results. With this not extravagant hope to encourage us, let us try to see what exactly is needed, and what is within our power to do.

The men and women who supplied the protocols are products of the most expensive kind of education. I would like to repeat, with emphasis, that there is no reason whatever to suppose that a higher capacity for reading poetry will be manifested by any similar group anywhere in the world. Sons and daughters of other Universities who are tempted to think otherwise may be invited to bring experimental evidence collected under the same conditions. But no experienced teacher will be surprised by any of the protocols; no teacher, at least, who has refrained from turning his pupils into sounding-boards that reflect his own opinions. And, candidly, how many of us are convinced, with reason, that we would have made a better showing ourselves under these conditions?

Thus the gaps in these readers' equipment are very significant. First may be placed the general immaturity of the readers. Their average age would be between nineteen and twenty. Yet with several of the poems one important reason for erratic opinions seems undeniably to be lack of general experience. I wish very much that I could include as a frontispiece a good group photograph of the protocol-writers. It would help us to realise, better than pages of discussion, the concrete significance of some of these revelations. Statistics as to the proportion of the writers who are going later to be teachers would also assist this realisation. Yet it may be doubted whether any large proportion of those who showed themselves to be under age—not in intelligence alone but in emotional development also—are destined to become much more mature with the passage of time. In some respects the years will do their work, for good and ill, but in others there is little reason to expect any essential change. Much though there is to be said, on general anthropological grounds, in favour of a delayed maturity, an educational and social system which encourages a large proportion of its most endowed and favoured products to remain children *permanently* is exposing itself to danger. The point is a familiar one; I merely bring my mite of evidence.

A strong suspicion that I developed in looking over the protocols, that the women-writers were of higher average discernment than the men, is perhaps relevant in this connection. For the young woman of nineteen is generally supposed to be nearer to her final settled character, in most respects, than the equivalent young man. A better explanation would be the greater familiarity with poetry that is certainly possessed by the average girl. A lack of experience with poetry must be placed next to general inexperience of life in this list of deficiencies. A large number of writers showed clearly (a fact which one knew well enough already) that they had hardly any reading at all to serve them as a background and means of orientation. And those readers who did try to use their background often proved the naïvety of their outlook and the poverty of their literary experience by the comparisons and identifications they made. Apart from this wide experience it is hard to see how any but the most gifted readers can help being impressed, for example, by work which is merely a feeble echo of something else. We may sometimes say, then, that it is the original work which is at second-hand the source of the impression. . . .

Also, but more rarely, the condition of poetic starvation appears. The reader, having discovered some value in poetry, swallows all he can of it for a while, hoping that it will do him good, and improve his taste, even when he does not really like it. But there is not a great deal of this in our examples. We could have safely inferred from the protocols that the relatively cultivated youth of our age spends extremely little of its time over poetry.

Partly to this well-recognised fact, but partly to more interesting causes, we may trace the wide-spread inability to construe meaning, which is perhaps the deficiency made most apparent in my selections. But it is not only those with little experience of poetry who fail in this. Some who appear to have read widely seem to make little or no endeavour to understand, or, at least, to remain strangely unsuccessful. Indeed, the more we study this matter the more we shall find "a love for poetry" accompanied by an incapacity to understand or construe it. This construing, we must suppose, is not nearly so easy and "natural" a performance as we tend to assume. It is a craft, in the sense that mathematics, cooking, and shoemaking are crafts. It can be taught. And though some gifted individuals can go far in the strength of their own sagacity alone, instruction and practice are very necessary for others. The best methods of instruction remain to be worked out. At present, apart from not very satisfactory exercises in translation from other languages and some still less satisfactory experiments with *précis* writing and paraphrasing, this instruction ceases at too early a stage. No attempt at imparting a reasoned general technique for construing has yet been made. Perhaps because the need for it has not been sufficiently realised. Two problems for reflection, suggested by this low capacity in construing, may be noted. (1) What is the worth of poetry for readers who cannot make out what it means? (2) How far can we expect such readers to show themselves intelligent, imaginative and discriminating in their intimate relations with other human beings? Neither question can be answered summarily, but it is not doubtful that certain "sentimental" addictions to poetry are of little value, or that this poor capacity to interpret complex and unfamiliar meanings is a source of endless loss, for those whose lives need not be narrowly standardised at a low level. If anything *can* be done, educationally, that is not already being done to improve it, the attempt would be worth much trouble. . . .

It is natural to inquire how far insensitiveness, poor discrimination, and a feeble capacity to understand poetry imply a corresponding inability to apprehend and make use of the values of ordinary life. This is a large and awkward question which we shall answer in different ways as our experience varies. Two answers, however, would certainly be wrong: the view that a man who is stupid with poetry *must* be as stupid with life, and the view that obtuseness in literary matters implies no general disabilities. Doubtless to some degree poetry, like the other arts, is a secret discipline to which some initiation is needed. Some readers are excluded from it simply because they have never discovered, and have never been taught, how to enter. Poetry translates into its special sensory language a great deal that is given in the ordinarily daily intercourse between minds by gesture, tones of voice, and expression, and a reader who is very quick and discerning in these matters may fail for purely technical reasons to apprehend the very same things when they are given in verse. He will be in the same sad case as those Bubis of Fernando Po, who need to see one another before they understand what is said. On the other hand, it is sometimes not difficult in reading through the protocols to distinguish those who are incapacitated by this ignorance and *lack of skill in reading* from those whose failure has deeper causes. And, moreover, those who have naturally a fine imagination and discrimination, who have a developed sensibility to the values of life, do seem to find the password to poetry with great ease. For there is no such gulf between poetry and life as overliterary persons sometimes suppose. There is no gap between our everyday emotional life and the material of poetry. The verbal expression of this life, at its finest, is forced to use the technique of poetry; that is the only essential difference. We cannot avoid the material of poetry. If we do not live in consonance with good poetry, we must live in consonance with bad poetry. And, in fact, the idle hours of most lives are filled with reveries that are simply bad private poetry. On the whole evidence, I do not see how we can avoid the conclusion that a general insensitivity to poetry does witness a low level of general imaginative life. There are other reasons for thinking that this century is in a cultural trough rather than upon a crest. I need not expatiate here upon them. But the situation appears sufficiently serious to force us to consider very carefully what influences are available as remedies. When nature and tradition, or rather our contemporary social and economic conditions, betray us, it is reasonable to reflect whether we cannot deliberately contrive artificial means of correction.

It is arguable that mechanical inventions, with their social effects, and a too sudden diffusion of indigestible ideas, are disturbing throughout the world the whole order of human mentality, that our minds are, as it were, becoming of an inferior shape—thin, brittle and patchy, rather than controllable and coherent. It is possible that the burden of information and consciousness that a growing mind has now to carry may be too much for its natural strength. If it is not too much already, it may soon become so, for the situation is likely to grow worse before it is better. Therefore, if there be any means by which we may artificially strengthen our minds' capacity to order themselves, we must avail ourselves of them. And of all possible means, Poetry, the unique linguistic instrument by which our minds have ordered their thoughts, emotions, desires in the past, seems to be the most serviceable. It may well be a matter of some urgency for us, in the interests of our standard of civilisation, to make this highest form of language more accessible. From the beginning civilisation has been dependent upon speech, for words are our chief link with the past and with one another and the channel of our spiritual inheritance. As the other vehicles of tradition, the family and the community, for example, are dissolved, we are forced more and more to rely upon language.

Yet, as the protocols show, such reliance as we place in it at present is quite unjustified. Not a tenth of the power of poetry is released for the general benefit, indeed, not a thousandth part. It fails, not through its own fault, but through our ineptitude as readers. Is there no means to give the "educated" individual a better receptive command of these resources of language? . . .

There is little room for doubt that some progress in this direction can be made through such experiments as the one upon which this book is based. We are quicker to detect our own errors when they are duplicated by our fellows, and readier to challenge a pretension when it is worn by another. But the logic of the situation can be made in time too strong even for the vainest. And when a systematic publicity is given to these ordinary phenomena of misinterpretation that usually remain so cunningly hidden, the stoutest self-confidence is shaken. Language is primarily a social product, and it is not surprising that the best way to display its action is through the agency of a group. The only way perhaps to change our attitude to language is to accumulate enough evidence as to the degree to which it can be misunderstood. But the evidence must not only be accumulated; it must be pressed home. The wild interpretations of others must not be regarded as the antics of incompetents, but as dangers that we ourselves only narrowly escape, if, indeed, we do. We must see in the misreadings of others the actualisation of possibilities threatened in the early stages of our own readings. The only proper attitude is to look upon a successful interpretation, a correct understanding, as a triumph against odds. We must cease to regard a misinterpretation as a mere unlucky accident. We must treat it as the normal and probable event.

But this distrustful attitude takes us but a little way towards a cure. We must, if possible, gain some power of diagnosis, some understanding of the risks that interpretations run, and some capacity to detect what has occurred. This may be considered too abstruse and baffling a matter, bad enough for the determined adult, and self-condemning as an educational suggestion. The reply is that those who think so have probably forgotten how abstruse and baffling every subject is—until it has been studied and the best methods of learning it and of teaching it have been worked out. It would have seemed fairly absurd if somebody in the seventeenth century had suggested that the Method of Fluxions (though with an improved notation) could be profitably studied by schoolboys, and not very long ago Elementary Biology would have seemed a very odd subject to teach to children. With innumerable such instances behind us, we ought to hesitate before deciding that a Theory of Interpretation in some slightly more advanced and simplified form (with perhaps a new notation and nomenclature to help it) may not quite soon take the foremost place in the literary subjects of all ordinary schools. No one would pretend that the theory as it is propounded in this book is ready, as it stands, for immediate and wide application. But a very strong case can, I think, be made out, both for the need and the possibility of practical steps towards applying it. No one who considers the protocols closely, or considers with candour his own capacity to interpret complex language, will, I think, deny the need. As to the possibility, the only improvements in training that can be suggested must be based upon a closer study of meaning and of the causes of unnecessary misunderstanding.

This, then, may be made a positive recommendation, that an inquiry into language—no longer confused with the grammarian's inquiry into syntax and into comparative linguistic morphology, or with the logician's or the philologist's studies—be recognised as a vital branch of research, and treated no longer as the peculiar province of the whimsical amateur.

But it is possible without too much rashness to go further. However incomplete, tentative, or, indeed, speculative we may consider our present views on this subject, they are far enough advanced to justify some experimental applications, if not in the school period then certainly at the Universities. If it be replied that there is no time for an additional subject, we can answer by challenging the value of the time at present spent in extensive reading. A very slight improvement in the capacity to understand would so immensely increase the value of this time that part of it would be exchanged with advantage for direct training in reading. This applies quite as much to

such studies as economics, psychology, political theory, theology, law or philosophy, as to literature. For though the material handled in this book has
not allowed me to demonstrate it (except perhaps in ways which I should
deplore), quite as many readers blunder unnecessarily over intricate argumentation and exposition as over poetry. And a direct study of interpretation
here can be made quite as useful. The incidental training that every one is
supposed to receive in the course of studying other subjects is too fragmen-
tary, accidental and unsystematic to serve this purpose. Sooner or later interpretation will have to be recognised as a key-subject. *But only the actual effort
to teach such a subject can reveal how it may best be taught.*

There is this to be added in favour of the subject. It enlists at once a natural
interest, a cousin belonging to that family of interests which govern the cross-
word puzzle, acrostics and detective fiction. And a type of curiosity about
words and their meanings that infants and primitive savages share with sophisticated philologists (very different from a psychological interest in the
problem of meaning, and sometimes in conflict with it), can also be engaged—with discretion. Thus, although it would probably be wisest to begin
with advanced classes in the Universities, it would be rash to say how far
from the Elementary School we need in the end stop. . . .

[In concluding, Richards returns to Coleridge.]
"Poetry gives most pleasure when only generally not perfectly understood."
"Perfect" understanding might here be a product, something which a sufficiently delicate and elaborate account might represent, an end-state of
thought and feeling to which understanding had led. It would obviously be
possible to make up a rough scale with specimens of poetry arranged according to the degree to which their meanings settled down finally and remained
fixed. We might then find that this scale agreed often with our usual rank-
ings. Some would find this so, others not.

Whether this were so or not, one moral of immense critical importance
emerges undeniably from any close study of the process of interpretation, of
understanding, of reading. Like most critical morals it is hardly a novelty,
though its observance would have novel results. It is this, that a judgment
seemingly about a poem is primarily evidence about a reading of it. There
are ways of reading almost any poem so as to make it magnificent or ludi-
crous. Opinions about it to either effect really tell us how it has been read.
Every critical opinion is an ellipsis; a conditional assertion with the conditional part omitted. Fully expanded it would state that if a mind of a certain
sort, under certain conditions (stage of its development, width of its recover-
able experience, height of its temporary vigilance, direction of its temporary
interest, etc.), has, at scores, or hundreds, or thousands of points in the
growth of its response to certain words, taken certain courses; then such and
such. But, as a rule, it seems to be immediately about a certain fictional public

object, a projected experience, the poem. It pretends to be, and is usually taken to be, a categoric assertion, discussible as though it were in simple logical relations, of agreement or contradiction and so on, with other assertions of the same type. But these also are collapsed conditional statements. Marvellously alike though we are, it would be fantastic to suggest that our interpretations are often sufficiently similar for critical discussions to yield *the kind of profit we profess to expect*. But they may yield a different profit in increased knowledge of, and skill with, ourselves and others.

It may seem that on this view the difference between good and bad reading has gone; that there is no sense left for "correct" as applied to interpretations. This would be a mistake. We can always give a sense to a word if we want one, and here we more than want, we *need* a sense for "correct," or rather, we need several. One for occasions when we are asking about communication, another for semantics, another for orthology, another for general critical purposes, and yet another for the comparison of readings. To take this last only, the *tests,* we should ordinarily say, for the correctness of any interpretation of a set of complex signs are its internal coherence and its coherence with all else that is relevant. But this is an unnecessarily fictitious way of talking. We can say instead that this inner and outer coherence is the correctness. When an interpretation hangs together (without conflicting with anything else: history, literary tradition, etc.) we call it correct—when it takes into account all the items given for interpretation and orders the other items, by which it interprets them, in the most acceptable manner. There are problems behind such a formulation. Correct interpretations of bad and good writing will not hang together in the same specific ways, for example, but though these problems are large ones there seems nothing to prevent an inquiry which would be repaying. We may not have "the correct interpretation" of a passage and we probably won't have it and we might not recognize it for such if we had it; in this our definition agrees nicely with the ordinary use of "correct"—which perhaps follows some such definition as "corresponding" to what was in "the poet's mind." But ours has this advantage, that we need not, in judging correctness, attempt, even by fiction, to trespass across Acheron.

"Fifteen Lines from Landor," from *Speculative Instruments* (1955).

2

Towards a Technique
for Comparative Studies

. . . The problem, put briefly, is this. Can we in attempting to understand and translate a work which belongs to a very different tradition from our own do more than read our own conceptions into it? Can we make it more than a mirror of our minds, or are we inevitably in this undertaking trying to be on both sides of the looking-glass at once? To understand Mencius, for example, must we efface our whole tradition of thinking and learn another; and when we have done this, if it be possible, will we be any nearer being able to translate the one set of mental operations into the other? Is such translation, at best, only an ingenious deformation, in the style of the clever trick by which the children's entertainer makes with his fingers and thumbs a shadow really very like a rabbit?

It is not to be supposed that most Orientalists, Egyptologists, classicists, mediaevalists, field-anthropologists have not had their wakeful nights over the problem. To put it more precisely, can we maintain two systems of thinking in our minds without reciprocal infection and yet in some way mediate between them? And does not such mediation require yet a third system of thought general enough and comprehensive enough to include them both? And how are we to prevent this third system from being only our own familiar, established, tradition of thinking rigged out in some fresh terminology or other disguise? There is nothing new about the problem, that is obvious. What would run some risk of novelty would be an attempt to discuss it explicitly, to bring it out of the realm of midnight dubiosities and initial misgivings into the field of arguable methodology or technique.

From *Mencius on the Mind* (1932), chap. 4.

The problem seems to grow still more formidable as we realize that it concerns not only incommensurable concepts but also comparisons between concepts and items which may not be concepts at all. If we agree that most literary meanings are likely to combine at least four components ((1) Intention or purpose; (2) Feeling, or attitude towards what is being spoken about; (3) Tone, or attitude to those spoken to; and (4) Sense, or reference to what is being spoken about), and if we confine the term "concept" to the fourth of these component functions, we shall frequently suspect that our business with a passage concerns the first three functions much more than the fourth. It is possible even to grow a doubt as to whether this fourth component is necessary, though at first sight we may suppose that an utterance about nothing (not symbolizing a thought of something, however vague) must be nonsense or, at the best, merely music. But certainly cases seem to occur where the meaning of the passage is *almost* exhausted by a consideration of the first three functions, and the concept (reference) that is present hides itself and almost fades out behind the speaker's intention and his attitudes as guided by his intention.

To recognize the multiplicity of the meaning-components may sometimes make matters easier for us. In place of a baffling and obscure *concept*, translation has in such extreme cases to deal with a relatively describable blend of intention, feeling, and tone. (Or, if we distrust the blending metaphor, with an integral meaning from which abstractive analysis can derive these functions.) But we do not often get off so lightly. As a rule the meaning does contain a concept—so wrapped up with other functions as to be unintelligible and untranslatable apart from them. Even with our own most familiar meanings, it is not often easy to distinguish what we are thinking of from what we are feeling about it or what we want to do with it. . . . The explicit description of the meaning is not at all a substitute for the meaning. The implicit concept is capable of connections (notably those of confusion) with other concepts which the explicated concept (after analysis) escapes or resists.

Movements of thought involving vague concepts can have a power and coherence which analysis would destroy. And once analysis is introduced, the especially troublesome problems of the logical machinery (fictions, mythology) we use in analysis are on our hands. Our Western tradition provides us with an elaborate apparatus of universals, particulars, substances, attributes, abstracts, concretes, generality, specificities, properties, qualities, relations, complexes, accidents, essences, organic wholes, sums, classes, individuals, concrete universals, objects, events, forms, contents, etc. Mencius gets along without any of this and with nothing at all definite to take its place. Apart entirely from the metaphysics that we are only too likely to bring in with this machinery, the practical difficulty arises that by applying it we deform his thinking.

There are many people, of course, who are satisfied that this machinery (or some brand of it) is necessary not only convenient for our traditional type of thinking, but inevitable for all thought and correspondent to (or valid for) the structure of any possible universe. One may envy them their confidence but demur to it in the present stage of comparative studies. With such an author as Mencius, for whom logic is so little developed, dogmatic assumptions of this kind are little interfered with, and perhaps not very dangerous. But with such a thinker as Chu Hsi, to try to fit his distinctions into a framework taken from Aristotle, or Mill, Kant, or Bradley, appears exceedingly risky; and the assimilation of Buddhist or Vedanta philosophic apparatus to our Western machinery is probably not much wiser.

But we need not go round the world to appreciate these dangers. The long-drawn-out and still drawn struggle between Aristotelianism and Platonism, or the beautiful specimens of mutual misunderstanding that any controversy between Oxford and Cambridge logicians of the last generation will provide, should convince us of the folly of using any logical machinery dogmatically in *comparative* studies. One of the first conditions for genuine comparisons would seem to be ability to use logical apparatus *tentatively*.

In practice this ability is only gained through the cultivation of a certain habit—the habit of multiple definition, of accompanying any definition or distinction we make use of with a set of rival definitions in the background of the mind. Only so can we protect ourselves from the coercive suggestion of any one interpretation which seems for the moment to fit. It is not enough simply to resolve that we will regard our logical *schema* as hypothetical. By itself this is only a rechristening of tradition. New hypothesis is but old dogma writ large. Unless we do actually and constantly sketch out alternative definitions using different logical machinery we shall not gain the ability to *experiment* in interpretation which comparative studies require.

That our current procedure is inadequate is shown by the ease with which any Cambridge-trained realist can demonstrate the confusions in a product of Oxford idealism and vice versa—a situation which would be comical if it were not so wasteful. To show that an improvement in interpretative technique is possible may be not so easy. The habit of mind required is that of regarding all thinking—even the most seemingly autonomous—as purposive, and of expecting the form of the thinking to be not independent of the purpose. With this habit we may be readier, when we analyse our thought, to treat any structure we find in it (or give to it in the course of analysis) as no more than an instrument convenient or not for the purpose in hand. The subject–predicate, universal–particular, relational, syncretic, discrete, or organic structures we use in the analysis we shall regard as not necessarily structures that the thought intrinsically has (still less as necessarily the structure of the aspect of the world the thought is "of"), but merely as forms which it is useful, for certain purposes, to regard the thought as having. And as the purposes governing the thought and governing our examination of it change, we shall expect the logical machinery used by the thought and by our analysis of it to change also. It may not do so, but methodologically the assumption that it is likely to is prudent.

For we do not yet know enough about how we think (if, indeed, we know anything about this in any strict sense of "knowing") to say: "All thinking must use *this* or *that* kind of machinery (or have this or that kind of structure) and no other." The danger to be guarded against is our tendency to force a structure, which our special kind of Western training (idealist, realist, positivist, Marxist, etc.) makes easiest for us to work with, upon modes of thinking which may very well not have any such structure at all—and which may not be capable of being analysed by means of this kind of logical machinery. As we do so all chance of genuine comparative studies is wiped out.

What is needed, in brief, is greater imaginative resource in a double venture—in imagining other purposes than our own and other structures for the thought that serves them. . . . What steps can be suggested to encourage this imaginative freedom? The answer, I suggest—since no capacity can be expected to develop without exercise—is the exercise of Multiple Definition.

Multiple Definition, though it cannot yet call itself a technique, is at least a plan for a technique, and it is as such that I push it forward here, hoping that it may be considered on its merits *as a plan*; a proposal for a systematic survey of the language we are forced to use in translation, of the ranges of possible meanings which may be carried by our chief pivotal terms—such as Knowledge, Truth, Order, Nature, Principle, Thought, Feeling, Mind, Datum, Law, Reason, Cause, Good, Beauty, Love, Sincerity—and of our chief syntactic instruments, "is," "has," "can," "of," and the like. Everyone will flaccidly agree that such words are ambiguous. And most philosophers have remarked that if they are to be used they must first be defined, and that their main endeavour is to define them. But the definitions they have given have been for their own use in their own thinking, not for other people's use in different thinking. The chief reason why such words are still viciously ambiguous as instruments for *general* communication is, in fact, to be traced to the survival in philosophic practice of the combative habit of mind. As every disputant knows, definitions are key positions; a philosopher who is ready to abandon his own definitions and adopt his opponent's on any considerable scale is quickly out of action. The first effect of a general practice of multiple definition would be a strange peace in philosophy. . . . With the increasing pressure of world contacts, we do pitiably need to understand on a scale we have never envisaged before. Warfare in the intellectual world as in the physical is a wasteful survival. But there are signs that it is declining in prestige. We are becoming methodologically more self-critical.

The task of Multiple Definition includes a survey both of the senses and the gestures of a word. It will often be found that the apparently "indefinable" peculiarities of a sense can be resolved into features of its range of gestures; and the definer's job is much simplified by the seeming complication. . . .

Concepts (senses) which seem extremely abstruse and recondite may get this appearance mainly from their accompanying gestures. One complication especially deserves notice. When a word has been much used with a sense that is naturally associated with a strong and rich emotive reverberation, it frequently carries this gesture over to senses that give no natural support for any such stirrings. Normally we tend, I think, unless we are on our guard, to expect the rest of a word's meaning to be consonant with and dependent on the sense. It sounds a reasonable expectation; but the analysis of poetry would go very little distance on this principle. The chief danger, however, is that we may insist upon giving a word a far more elaborate sense than it really has, in order to justify its gesture, because we have not noticed what other senses it may have on other occasions from which its stirring qualities derive.

As examples which may make the plan for a technique I am calling Multiple Definition seem more capable of development and application, I will take *Knowledge, Truth,* and *Order* [omitted here], choosing them as terms fundamental enough to be worth some trouble, likely to raise at least as many difficulties as most others, and directly relevant to any interpretation of Mencius. Once again, may the confusions and inadequacies of my treatment *not* be allowed to discredit the general proposal. As should be overwhelmingly apparent there is no faintest pretence of completeness or finality at any point with any of these lists. The essence of the method is in its tentativeness and freedom.

SENSES OF *KNOWLEDGE*

A grammatico–logical ambiguity runs through most of these; "knowledge" may stand for "what is known" and for the "knowing of it." Some senses, however, resist, abrogate, or surpass this distinction; for them "what is known" and "the knowing of it" are one.

1. *Knowledge as Response*

    A knows B = A varies with B.

    a) Response in Action.

    > A magnetic needle knows the North.
    > Thermometers know the temperature.
    > Pigeons know their way home.
    > A dog knows his master.

    A scale from simple to complex can plainly be drawn up for this sense and it will be arguable that at a certain point, where we pass from the physical to the psychological, the sense changes.

    > He knew the Koran by heart at the age of two.
    > I know how to ride a bicycle.
    > I know French.

    B (the known) with which A (the knower) varies is a situation which increases in complexity in these examples, and the knowing in all of them can be regarded as a form of action, or observable behaviour.

But the same sense can be applied to cases of feeling and thought, where no observable behaviour need result.

b) Response in Feeling.

He had never really known happiness or misery until she came.
The babe in arms knows how to love its parents.
Beauty is Truth, Truth Beauty; that is all ye know.

c) Response in Thought.

He knows his subject well.
He knows what you mean.
We know that the other side of the moon is convex.

The last example (indirect knowledge) can be interpreted in several ways, of which this is only one. So can some cases of knowledge of "imaginary objects," e.g. "We know Hamlet better than we do most of our friends"—where Hamlet might be taken as a complex internal stimulus–situation, and this imaginative construction would be what is known. But equally it might be Shakespeare's imaginings which were said to be known. In all cases of interpretation which goes by many stages or steps a series of possible "knowns" is generated and a corresponding series of "knowings."

All the above *can,* I think, be taken as cases of "knowledge how." The knowers here all "know" in the sense of being able to vary appropriately. And for "knowledge how" what is "known how" is the possible scale of exercise of "knowing how." To "know how to multiply" is to be able to perform appropriate operations of a certain type; we may still "know how" even though—having a secretary—we never do any multiplications.

A sense for "knowledge of" can be derived from knowledge how—the situations to which we appropriately respond being what we have "knowledge of." But usually "knowledge of" has other senses, for, evidently we respond appropriately to innumerable situations (digestive, for example) of which we should ordinarily be said to have no knowledge. We "know how" to digest without necessarily knowing anything relevant about it.

2. *Knowledge as Participation*

a) To be known is to be part of the life-history of the individual who knows, part of his stream of consciousness.

The mind knows its own states or experiences.

By metaphor an inanimate thing—e.g., a mountain—may be said to know winter and summer; and a nation to know good and evil days. Other interpretations of *these* "knows"—in terms, for example, of (1)—are obviously possible.

b) By extension, states or experiences which *have been* part of a knower's life history can be said to be known by him; (1) though he is not conscious of them—he knows all sorts of things which he may never have occasion to be conscious of again; (2) though he has never been conscious of them and never will be—so-called unconscious perceptions would be an example. "To know something is to have it in consciousness or in the unconscious as determining consciousness."

c) "The act of knowledge requires within the knowing subject the presence of the object known."
This is a part of the thomistic view of knowledge: "To know something is a manner of becoming it."

d) Senses in which "to be known" is to be "in" the mind—with various interpretations of "in"—are numerous both in Idealist doctrines and in others.

3. *Knowledge as Involving a Unique Relation or Act.*
   a) "Knowledge is a relation of a unique kind between a conscious subject and a presented object."
   b) "Knowledge is a modification of the conscious subject arising with the *presentation* of an object."
   c) "Knowledge is a state or act of the mind accompanying, but not caused by, certain states or acts of the body" (Psychophysiological Parallelism).

4. *Knowledge as Reflection.*
   "Knowledge is a copy or image in the mind of what is known."

5. *Special Senses*
   a) "Knowledge is of the necessary only. Opinion is of the contingent."
   b) "Knowledge is of data only, with which the mind is in *immediate contact*. The rest is hypothesis."

It would be idle to carry this list further here—unless it were carried so very much further as to overbalance the book. The danger is that it turns so easily into a classification and dissection of theories of knowledge—half a library of philosophy—whereas it aims to be merely a list of senses of knowledge. No doubt a thorough analysis of the theories would be useful for studies of authors who may be suspected to have theories . . . , but most people who employ the word, or words we have to translate by "knowledge," have not been epistemologists, and the list we need is one which will help us with these people—with Mencius for example. The list I have sketched may be enough to suggest, at least, that we are usually content with a very vague understanding of what an author may be saying with the word.

"I always remember meeting the eyes of a gypsy woman, for one moment, in a crowd in England. She knew, and I knew. What did we know? I was not able to make out. But we knew." What kind of knowledge is this that D. H.

Lawrence wrote so much about? I have not put it in my list—nor his antith-
esis between "mind-knowledge" and "knowledge by the blood" (though 1*b*
and 2*b* might provide places for them)—because no indication of a possible
sense for the words which neglected their gesture would help us much.
"Knowledge," just because its sense is sometimes so important, is most often
used, without any precise sense at all, to awaken the feeling that whatever is
happening matters immensely. Such sense as it carries is the vague one that
can only be indicated by extension:—

X is known = X is somehow along with A.B.C. . . . which are also said to
be known.

This, of course, is the way in which most words, for all but a very small
minority of users, get such sense as they have. Even the small minority uses
its words thus most of its time, for this is the way by which we learn our
language—not by systematic investigation into senses. So the fact that we
seem so often to have a very definite sense for a word without our being able
in the least to say what it is—even whether it is *this* rather than *that*—ought
not to surprise us. Our definiteness comes from our tact in deciding when
we may and when we may not use the word and our tact comes from the
prolonged social drill we have been through. But tact is not enough if thinking is our aim—the most accomplished writers may not have even dim ideas
of what they are writing so pleasantly about—and the very conditions which
make tact successful are absent when we study a strange language or a remote
author. Nonetheless, we have to realize that, though *we* need a conscious
control of possible senses and gestures, he, e.g., Mencius, most likely used
his words mainly under the guidance of tact—and how to bridge this difference is just our problem.

A good instance arises with *Truth,* which, for Mencius, seems to have had
only a small part of our Western ranges.

SENSES OF *TRUTH*

I. Senses Deriving from the Symbol-situation

It is convenient in indicating these to place the three sets of items
concerned—Symbol, Thought, and Referent (or State of Affairs thought
of)—at the angles of a triangle,* and to give the three relations—between
Symbol and Thought; between Thought and Referent; between Symbol and
Referent—the names "symbolize," "of," and "stands for," respectively. For

---

*See chapter 12 for a discussion of this triangle, a diagrammatic representation of the role
of meaning as a means of making meaning. We can get from the symbol to what it represents
only by way of a mediating idea, which Peirce called the Interpretant.—ED

"True" in different senses is defined in terms of each of these relations. Thus we have:—

X is true =
1. a) The symbol X corresponds to the state of affairs it claims to correspond to;
   b) The thought X corresponds to the state of affairs it claims to correspond to;
2. The symbol X corresponds to the thought it claims to correspond to.

It will be noticed that the kind of correspondence is different in the three cases. In (*a*), where the relation "stands for" is reducible to "*symbolizes* a thought which is *of*," the correspondence is also reducible and becomes a double correspondence. In (*b*) the correspondence, which makes the thought true in this sense, between a thought and what it is *of*, is a fundamental matter. But in (2) the correspondence is more easily discussed. It may be:—

   a) Correct or prudent usage.
      If we do not use language perfectly (and no one does), we may say something which does not misrepresent our thought to ourselves but does misrepresent it to other people. We shall not then have *truly* reported our thought. But, as often happens, we may also be misrepresenting it to ourselves (largely through the equivocations of language) and a second kind of falseness comes in. The above ambiguities can be displayed as rival interpretations of the seemingly simple remark "What he said was untrue."
      If we extend (2) to cover not thought only, but feelings, attitudes, intentions, etc.—the emotive functions of words—we get:—
   b) Truth as sincerity, in various senses. These range from that which can be given to "truly" in "Yours truly"—when the document thus attested is to be read only for its sense—to that in which a true-lover might display no feelings but those he has. All sorts of questions as to degrees of self-understanding, accord between the conscious and the unconscious, and so forth, plainly come in.
3. a) The statement X is consistent with all other statements relevant to it (Coherence Truth).
   b) The thought X is consistent with all other thoughts relevant to it. (The difficulties of relevance here parallel those of correspondence in 1*b*.)
4. X (a thought, state of mind, or statement) works—
   a) explains what we needed to explain (Methodological Pragmatism)
   b) suits our purposes when these suit our needs (Politico–ethical and voluntaristic–metaphysical pragmatisms).
5. X (a thought, state of mind or statement) reveals or apprehends Reality— what is *really so* "behind" appearances. Appearances here may be what are imposed on us by our bodily constitution or our mental constitution, or what science (being abstract nonvaluative, etc.) deals with and so on.

Derivatively, Truth = Reality = what is. This logico–grammatical shift—from truth as a property of thought to truth as what a true thought is *of*—may be made, I think, for all senses which allow a thought and what it is "of" to be distinguished. Some of the severer forms of Methodological Pragmatism (4*a*) and Coherence Idealism (3*b*) should not permit it. But a sense in which "The Truth" = "the totality of all truths" = the Universe = The Absolute is well known. By this shift, truths = facts, and "fact" (as we have noticed above) comes to have many of the ambiguities of "truth."

6. *Metaphoric Truth*.

Here X (symbol or statement) while not *literally* true (in any sense above) may (if the proper transference of its sense to a new context is performed, and the metaphor is thus *reduced*) be made to yield a statement that is true in one of the above senses (or some other sense).

The problem here concerns *reduction*. Sometimes the metaphorical expression is a convenience only; it is not difficult to substitute another nonmetaphorical expression in its place. But sometimes the metaphor is *irreducible*—no literal expression seems to be a satisfactory substitute. It then becomes doubtful whether the metaphorical expression has a sense at all, and, in any case, discussion and examination of it grow exceedingly difficult. For example, much of the language (and thought) used in psychology is metaphoric ("apprehension," "conception," "attention," "understanding"); how to reduce it satisfactorily is half the problem of psychology. It is possible that statements about the soul, the spirit, mental energy, vital forces, etc. are metaphoric and irreducible, or, if reducible, hitherto unreduced. It may be that their *gestures* not their senses are what we should concern ourselves with. The extent of this linguistic problem is only less remarkable than its undeveloped and undiscussed state.

II. *Senses Not Deriving from the Symbol-situation*

X is true =
1. X is straight (of a line). Cf. True north; out of the true, i.e., crooked; true virtue.
2. X acts in accordance with a given set of conditions, e.g., the wheel is true. Be true to yourself, your true self, your ideal.
3. X is faithful, loyal. Cf. Troth, allegiance. This sense of being true is of some importance in early Chinese writings and is easily mistaken for the symbolic senses of truth-speaking or truth-seeking.

GESTURES OF *TRUTH*

X is true —
1. You ought to believe X! Accept X! "Belief" and "acceptance" or "assent" are obviously very ambiguous in these connections. Cf. "I never feel certain of any Truth but from a clear perception of its Beauty" (Keats).

2. X is needed! The need may be anything from a local requirement to the largest general need—the fullest development of a form of life.
3. X is as it should be! Good for X! Since True in its various senses carries with it more vigorous gestures than perhaps any other English word, we should not be surprised to find it possessed of these gestures even in cases where none of its senses would be relevant. E.g., "We need no critical precepts to judge of a true rhythmus, and melody of composition." (I (4*b*), or II (2), or merely a gesture?)

[Richards next provides the same sort of analysis for *Order* and then suggests that "nothing could better conduce to understanding between the Chinese and the West than well-prepared tables of ranges of our principal moral themes and theirs." He then makes the case for preparing multiple definitions for the fundamental terms in Chinese.]

The objections likely to be brought against the proposal are, I think, of two main kinds: sociological and epistemological. It is doubtful whether argument in such matters is of avail; but it will be well to mention them to show that supporters of the scheme are not quite blind to them. The first, relying on the doctrine that ideas and attitudes are socially determined, will object that without intimate participation in the life of a people its most important meanings are incomprehensible, that they cannot be represented except by literature (bulky and mainly untranslatable), and that the proposed lists of meanings will merely consist of abstract deformations. We may reply that these considerations would perhaps show that an ideal performance is inexecutable; but still something useful can and should be done.

The second objection claims greater depth and urges that the task proposed is merely the age-long task of philosophy. That all critical thought is simply the analysis and comparison of meanings. That this supremely difficult study is here hastily dressed up with philological trimmings and treated as though it were capable of summary settlement. It will be added perhaps that fundamental ideas must naturally be insusceptible of analysis or comparison, and that nothing is intelligible if you ask too insistently if it is, or on what it rests. Do not all complex meanings allow of pyramidlike analyses by which the noticed top-stone is shown to rest upon scores of incomprehensible others hidden from sight in the sand? We may reply that this objection would be damaging perhaps, if we were concerned with "ultimate" analyses (or considered that "ultimate" had reference to anything but our present, very undeveloped, skills in analysis), but that what we seek are descriptions of the natural history of meanings (not answers to such questions as, What is Life?). We might even retort against most epistemology that it refuses itself the use of microscopes or even of the eye until it has solved the problem of the nature of light.

Such disputes, however, may themselves wait until techniques for manipulating meanings have been advanced. Meanwhile, the urgency of the matter, as regards the passage of Western meanings into Chinese currency needs more emphasis than I have given to it in these pages. Few who have not been in close contact with Chinese students in China—the pick of whom are certainly among the finest intellects in the world—can realize the gravity of the problem. We have been discovering during the last century how much we lost through Greek ideas coming into post-Renaissance currency in confused or misconceived translations. Similar avoidable accidents on a vastly greater scale threaten the new language of modern China. The superb work of many Chinese scholars—quite comparable in difficulty and success to the greatest feats of our Renaissance men—is still insufficient to protect China from these dangers. An enormous crop of maladjusted hybrid meanings—from the crossing of our ambiguities with Chinese ambiguities—seems certain to be perpetuated in language to the unnecessary distress and confusion of many generations. Unless, that is, a deliberately devised technique for recording and comparing the ranges of our words and their words can be brought into action *in time*. . . .

With an increased awareness of the danger, ways of meeting it are likely to be found. This, at least, seems the conclusion to be drawn from human development in the large biological sense and in the smaller historic sense. Clear consciousness of what we are doing is our best means of control. The limited development of a conscious criticism of methods was probably a chief reason for the long stagnation of Chinese culture. There are dangers, of course, that we may incur by too sudden an extension of consciousness. The well-known rhyme about the centipede* illustrates them. But there could hardly be any advantages if there were no accompanying dangers. We may well feel, after a fuller development of multiple definition, that thinking is harder than we found it formerly. And it may well be that some kinds of thinking proceed more successfully if we are not too conscious therein. Certainly there seem to be *feelings* to which inspection is unpropitious. But by becoming conscious of which these are we may perhaps better avoid such prying interference.

With Multiple Definition, however, there is reason to suppose that it is only the unfamiliarity of the exercise on any large scale that makes it, at first sight, seem to increase the difficulties and confusions of discussion. It asks us to distribute our attention in an unwonted fashion, to watch our thoughts as well as think; and to notice their forms as much as their contents. At first the effort is distracting, the sense of an almost unlimited spider's web of radiating allied meanings may be daunting, we easily lose our way—I have illustrated this abundantly—among trivialities of mere possibility. And as we persist the fascination of the formal schematic aspect of possible types of

---

*I append it for the benefit of those who cannot remember:—

> The centipede was happy—quite !
> Until the toad in fun
> Said, "Pray, which leg moves after which?"
> This raised her doubts to such a pitch
> She fell exhausted in the ditch
> Not knowing how to run!

connection between meanings may distract us again. It is as though a doctor should neglect his patient through too curious an interest in cytology. I have illustrated this also. But there is at least a chance that a persistent study of the general forms of ambiguity, the types of ranges of meaning, might give us a greatly increased control over our thinking, and provide—in an expanded "logic"—the general technique that we need. We have been using our words for some 20,000 years at least (and perhaps a million) *incuriously,* as primitive man used his sticks and stones, his animals and plants. It is time perhaps to study words and their meanings in the ways in which metallurgists and biologists have recently been studying our material instruments and resources. The results might be equally surprising, particularly in the technique of education. The nonspecialist—the ordinary reader and speaker—meanwhile need not be too much disturbed in his habits. And, after all, a generation which is cheerfully becoming more and more self-, sex-, race-, and world-conscious should not complain if it is required to become word-conscious also. And in such word-consciousness may be found the solvent for these other problems.

For though a few students of primitive mentality or of the language and thought of the child have begun to give serious attention to the evolution of thinking, on the whole our historians of philosophy have been too much preoccupied with results. Their eye has been on the thoughts as products rather than on the thought-processes. They have written too often as though *we,* in this haphazard, transitional century (or Plato and Aristotle, or Galileo and Bacon) had finally learnt how to think. An assumption which in a thousand years' time is likely to seem rather childish. They have not enough remembered that the fruit of comparative studies should be in an increase in our own powers—a systematized general technique by which to avoid confusion. Mere natural sagacity—the light of reason—works marvels, but we should not put more strain upon it than we must; and, as the history of the natural sciences has shown us, method is not its enemy. In matters of interpretation and those comparative studies which must precede any attempt to trace the development of thinking and its aberrations, we have as yet hardly any method. We are forced to put too great a strain upon sagacity. These pages make no claim to supply a method. Their purpose is fulfilled if, through their defects, they help to make the need for one more evident. To contribute positively to such a method would be to make one of the great steps in human progress. Few can hope to do that; but, meanwhile, those of us who are not born for such achievements can at least be grateful that we live in an age which offers unparalleled opportunities for intellectual adventure.

Imagine yourself teaching Hardy's *Tess of the D'Urbervilles* to a class of some forty highly motivated, superbly efficient Chinese students. In spite of their poor command of English, their assiduity at the dictionary enabled them to construct views on almost every sentence in the book. I wore through to the end, not without heavy misgivings. I had read aloud as clearly and slowly and eloquently as I could all the key passages. I had worked very hard, and at last I came to the last paragraph which I read aloud too. I came to the raising of the black flag to show that Tess has been hanged: "Upon the cornice of the tower a tall staff was fixed. Their eyes were riveted on it. A few minutes after the hour had struck, something moved slowly up the staff and extended itself upon the breeze. It was a black flag." At that moment my class burst into spontaneous applause, the only applause that marked the whole passage of the course. I couldn't get out the next sentence. I couldn't break through the applause. I thought, here is a chance, so I issued sheets of paper instantly and got them to say what they liked about what they had just been applauding. There it was, the great majority all agreeing together, in step. You see in their protocols what it was. Tess had been an unfilial daughter in the very beginning of the book. She hadn't treated her father with proper respect, and they had been waiting all through a very long book to see her get her due, and at the very end, that great artist, that wonderful man, Thomas Hardy, had seen that she got it: to be hanged to death—just what she deserved.

That sort of thing was decisive for me, and when I came back from China to Cambridge, I felt I had realized too deeply ever to forget it what extreme dangers lay for the future of mankind in the miscomprehensions that were active between the Western world, our tradition, and the Chinese tradition, miscomprehensions of such depth and scale between China and the West.

"The Future Reading," from *The Written Word* (1971).

3

Mencius Through the Looking-Glass

Classroom mistakes are often enough due to cultural divergences to make them directly relevant to international miscomprehensions. There may be something to be gained by considering them together. In both, what may at first sight seem perversity, mere stupidity or malice, may, when more adequately examined, be found to have its explorable etiology and to be open to treatment. The gravest wrenchings of meaning frequently come from intelligence operating on insufficient or distorted evidence, or from self-protective efforts prompted by an alien situation.

This essay is intended to serve as a reminder that immense and threatening divisions in mankind can spring from differences between virtues as well as from envies and greeds. When the virtues on each part are largely inapprehensible by the other, the danger is heightened by Man's natural fear of what he does not understand, and his inclination to suppose it not worth understanding. To attack it easier than to study. There are also, in this case of China and the West, intense and complex cultural vanities on both sides to be taken into account: vanities largely inexplicable the one to the other. . . .

. . . Making up for ourselves as good an account as we can of the society and tradition Mencius lived in, soaking ourselves in his reading and writing—the way of scholarship—may be our best resource; but it cannot be expected to turn us into Mencius. It is much more likely to turn Mencius into us! Mencius was not a modern scholar, trained in the fabulous discipline of con-

So Much Nearer (1966), chap. 8.

temporary research, balanced and sobered by an awareness of the hopes and despairs of how many ages.

Knowing even *all about* the thought of Mencius would not be the same thing as *having* it. It wouldn't even be a good preparation for that. And, to have it in some measure and if possible make a reader *have it* is my aim here. I will delay only a few pages before beginning this essentially magical, dramatic or poetic attempt.

Mencius was a teacher, not an expositor. He was *not* giving a lecture on Mencius. At important points, he did talk about his teaching, but that was to make it stronger. His audience was to be helped and improved. He was not presenting a view to be discussed and criticized. When from time to time he gives out one of his great secrets of the conduct of life in an anecdote or a formula, the thing to do is to remember it, treasure it up and live with it for a time, and see what it does to you thereafter.

Mencius gets these secrets himself by a process he hints to us. It is up to us to guess what it was. It certainly was not in the least like anything the main Western philosophic tradition would recognize as philosophic method. It is a question indeed if the ˢʷthoughtˢʷ ˣ of Mencius is ˢʷthoughtˢʷ at all in any accepted Western interpretations of that word.

That might sound derogatory. We are apt to give ˢʷthoughtˢʷ a higher rank and dignity than ˢʷfeelingˢʷ. The point is that for Mencius no such division has been made. For Mencius, the intellectual and the moral are not separate. The suggestion that there was some important distinction to be made between intellectual knowledge in general and right living would probably have made no recognizable sense at all to him.

For Mencius—and this seems to be true, with some doubtful exceptions, of all early Chinese philosophers possibly until Sung times—the mind was not so split. There was no *separate* problem of truth or problem of knowledge. There was no epistemology, no theory of ideas, no logic—in the modes of these things which belong to the intellectual mainstream of Western thinking. There was no such thinking in Mencius or for Mencius. In a sense, the intellect was never invented by the Chinese, and it may be doubted whether, outside the sciences, it has been imported and transplanted by them. One of the interests of Chinese ˢʷthoughtˢʷ is that it lets us ask ourselves sharply whether the intellect has been on the whole a useful invention to man. It is well for those who believe in it to say so, in an age in which it has been openly and variously attacked (think of Bergson, D. H. Lawrence and Hitler). Chinese studies help us to realize that the intellect (as something separate from the whole man, as an instrument of pure theoretic inquiry, the rational organ) is a cultural invention. Man is not born with it; he is not, by nature, a rational animal. He becomes one through education into a tradition which gives him a ˢʷreasonˢʷ (in this sense), which installs in him this feature of

*See pp 270–73 for an explanation of these superscripts.—ED

possible human design, as a given feature may be put into one airplane and not into another.

It is well to remind ourselves too that even such a fundamental feature as ᵍʷthe intellectˢʷ may seem to be has upkeep charges. As William Angus Sinclair put it, such a selecting and grouping "is a continuing process which must be sustained if our experience is to continue as it is. . . . If for any reason a man follows a different way of grouping in his attention then the experience he has will be different also. . . . Knowing is not a passive contemplation, but a continuously effort-consuming activity." Take this far enough and the probabilities of our comprehending Mencius will look low. It asks us to conceive that our concepts are less stored in containers than kept up as a breed may be. . . .

All this is preparatory. What we have to prepare for is the probability that, as Mencius begins to speak for himself, the words will mainly carry ideas of the Western tradition which Mencius would know nothing of. I have listened to very learned scholars, Chinese and Western, lecturing to me on Mencius. What I mostly learned was which *Western* philosophers had most captured their imaginations. Probably that, in my own case, is all that I will be able to show you.

I ought to give one other example for those not familiar with the condensed and cryptic style in which Mencius spoke—to let them see how easy it is to read different things into his words. One of his key remarks (IV, II, 26) has been translated as follows:

LEGGE   All who speak about the natures of things have in fact only their phenomena to reason from, and the value of a phenomenon is in its being natural.

UGALL   That which everyone below heaven calls nature is nothing but habit; and habit has its roots in gain.

COUVREUR   Everywhere under heaven, when we speak of nature, we have in mind natural effects. The special characteristic of natural effects is that they are self-acting.

Three utterances on three different topics. Word for word it goes like this:
Heaven below their talk Nature about causes only
Causes use profit as root.

And now I do my best to disappear, and we will pretend it is Mencius who comes through the mirror and addresses you.

(IV, II, 26) "What I dislike in your wise men is the way they niggle and chip. If those wise ones would do like Yü when he moved the waters, no dislike for wisdom. Yü moving the waters did what was without toil. If the wise ones did what is without toil, their wisdom *would* be great."

(VI, I, 6) A disciple, Kung Tu-tse, said to Mencius: "Kao Tzu says 'Man's nature: without good, without not-good.'"

"Others say, 'Some natures good, some not good.'"

"But *you* say, 'Nature good.'"

"All these wrong? Are they?"

Mencius said, "In the impulses which make it up, our nature may be seen to be good. Thus I call it good. When men do evil, that is not the fault of their *natural* powers."

> Sympathetic pity; all men have that.
> Shame and avoidance; all men have that.
> Respect and reverence; all men have that.
> Sense of right and wrong; all men have that.

> Sympathetic pity is human-heartedness.   JEN
> Shame and avoidance is righteousness.   YI
> Respect and reverence is good behavior.   LI
> Sense of right and wrong is wisdom.   CHIH

Human-heartedness, righteousness, good behavior and wisdom are not influences infused and molded into us from without. We already have them; only we do not realize this. Therefore I say, "Seek then get it, let go then lose it." Men are incalculably different here because unable to make the most of their powers. In a fruitful year, the children are most of them reliable, in a bad year they are most of them violent. This is not because Heaven gives them different powers but because their minds were trapped and drowned. Only that!

Things of the same kind are alike. Why doubt it only of man? Mouths have the same tastes, ears hear sounds the same, eyes see the same beauty in colours: Are minds alone without their sameness? What is the mind's sameness? Its name is Order and Right. It is the Sage who first grasped the sameness of the mind. Order and Right are agree-able to our minds as grass-fed animals are agree-able to our mouths.

All men have a mind which pities others. The ancient kings had it, so they had a government which pitied others. With a pitying mind acting through a pitying government, ruling the whole world is like turning something round in the palm.

Why do I say, "All men have minds which pity others?" Even today a man suddenly perceived a child about to fall into a well has a shuddering qualm of sympathy and pity—*not* in order to strike up a useful acquaintance with the child's parents, *not* to get a great name for sensitivity with the neighbors, and *not* because he just dislikes the sound of the child thudding down into the well.

From such things we see that

Without pity and sympathy, man is not,
Without shame and avoidance, man is not,
Without respect and reverence, man is not,
Without sense of right and wrong, man is not.

Pity and sympathy is the active principle of (Jen) Human-heartedness.
Shame and avoidance is the active principle of (Yi) Righteousness.
Respect and reverence is the active principle of (Li) Good Behavior.
Sense of right and wrong is the active principle of (Chih) Wisdom.

To man these four principles are as his four limbs. Having them, to say "I cannot" is to rob himself; to say of the Ruler "he cannot" is to injure *him*. Since we all have these four principles, if we know how to develop and fulfill them, it is as a fire that begins to burn, as a fountain that begins to flow. If fulfilled, they are enough to guard the four seas; if not fulfilled, they are not even enough to let us serve our parents.

(IV, II, 18) A disciple said to Mencius, "Confucius praised water saying, 'Water! Water!' What did he so approve of in water?" Mencius said, "Here is a spring; it gushes out, unlessening day and night, fills its courses and flows to the four seas. Such is a source. This, in water, he praised. But, if there is no source, in the rainy months the fields are filled, but while you wait they are dried up. Therefore, when his reputation exceeds the facts, the superior man is ashamed."

(IV, II, 19) "That wherein man differs from the birds and beasts is small and slight; common folk let it go, the superior man keeps it."

These then are for Mencius the four virtues: Human-heartedness, Righteousness, Good Behavior and Wisdom, which together form man's essential nature and from the fulfillment of which his perfection comes. We easily misconceive them and obviously they are untranslatable by simple names in our tradition. The overtones of *Jen*, for example, are quite different from those of the word "Love" to us. *Jen* lacks the erotic, the affectionate and the theological uses which make the word "Love" for us one of the pivotal points of the Western mind. It spans no such hierarchy of meanings, from the most transcendent—for example, Aristotle's "All things are moved by Love" or Dante's inscription over Hell Gate, "What made me was . . . the eternal love," down to Alexander Bain's view that love is the response to soft surfaces at the right temperature or the schoolgirl's "I love candy." On the other hand *Jen* has plenty of widely spreading links and ample reverberations in Chinese. It sounds the same as the word for man. Its character looks as if it meant "What two men have in common" or "What is mutual between men." It is charged with some of the feelings we put into "human," "humane," "humanity"—though we must beware of just putting in *our* ideal of man. That was an invention of our tradition—a Greek invention. As Werner Jaeger strikingly put it, "The greatest work of art they had to create was Man." In this invention, and the invention of the Western type of education outlined in Plato's *Republic*, the education which could produce this type of man, the Greeks approached through the philosophical and the universal, the logos, as that which is common to all minds. And, as these words, universal, logos, idea, form and type suggest, this which is common to all minds—'the mind's sameness'—was for the Greeks something before them for contemplative realization. To quote Jaeger again, "The Greeks relied wholly on this clear realization of the natural principles governing human life, and the immanent laws by which man exercises his physical and intellectual powers."

That might be a description (an excellent one) of what Mencius is doing. And yet what great differences there are! The Greek interest in "the principles governing human life," which was to culminate in Plato, was theoretical in ways which never developed in Chinese thought. And when Mencius says, "We already have them; only not *realize* this," it is fair to note that the sort of "clear realization of the natural principles" Jaeger is talking about is not at all what Mencius' work led to in China. Greek cultivation became more and more intellectual and led toward *knowledge what;* Chinese cultivation remained primarily moral or social and led toward *knowledge how.*

It is not that the followers of Mencius failed to study "the immanent laws by which man exercises his physical and intellectual powers." The point is, rather, that they worked on them another way and in so doing, by their sort of philosophical or educative art, created (or developed) another type of man. So, the part of the meaning of *Jen* which we might translate by *human* or *manlike* must not be understood simply in terms of what *we* traditionally assume a man should be.

Similar considerations apply to the names of the other virtues. Thus *Yi*, Righteousness, may easily be given a too Hebraic meaning. Its seed or active principle is somewhat negative—shame and distaste. *Li,* Good Behavior, Good Form, decorum, propriety, is concerned with doing the socially right thing in view of one's position, in one's family and in society. And *Chih*, or Wisdom, combines sound judgment not only of what *is so* or *not,* but of what *should be* or *shouldn't be* so.

There is one parallel with Greek morals (as we find them in the *Republic,* say) which may be accidental or unimportant. Mencius and Plato alike list four main Virtues. Plato's four as commonly labeled are: Wisdom, Courage, Temperance and Justice, misleading though these names may be. There is more than a little in common between Mencius' *Li* and Plato's Justice. Both have to do with keeping in one's proper place and knowing what is due to it and especially what is due from it. Wisdom seems a more intellectual thing for Plato, though we must not exaggerate and must remember how Plato made the virtues the indispensable basis, without which the philosophic or dialectic activity could come to no good.

And we must not draw any inferences from the absence of Courage among Mencius' list of virtues here. Elsewhere he has much to say about Courage. He is concerned with military conduct. Plato, you remember, defined Courage as "the knowledge of what is truly to be feared." Mencius had this (VI, I, 10) which comes quite near to Plato:

"I like fish and I like bears' paws. If I cannot have both, I let the fish go, and take the bears' paws. I like life and I like right too. If I cannot have both, I let life go and take the right. I like life indeed, but I like some things more than life, and will not do wrong to keep it. I dislike death indeed, but I dislike other things more, so I do not always avoid danger. All men have what they like more than life, and what they dislike more than death; not only great men but all men. The great men are those who do not lose these things.

"Here is rice and the want of it means death. A beggar will not take it when it is offered with an insult. Yet a rich man will take 10,000 chung, regardless of what is decent or right. What can 10,000 chung add to him? Mansions and concubines? Was it not possible for him to refuse it? This is called losing one's first mind. The great end of learning is the recovery of the lost mind."

Here again we may feel not too far away from Plato:

"We have been talking of how it seems to us at present. We have been looking on the soul as men did on the sea-god Glaucus. What he was might hardly be made out because his arms and legs were broken off and cut and crushed by the waves, and he was coated over with shells and seaplants and stones so that, to look as he might have been any sort of beast in place of what he truly was. So do we see the soul, lowered to this condition by unnumbered evils" (*Republic*, 611D). But around this passage there are plenty of things to warn us that we are in another world from that of Mencius. Nonetheless, it is tempting to go on looking at their resemblances.

The first half of Mencius' life (c.390–c.305) coincided with the last half of Plato's (429–347). Each was as widely informed as any then living in his culture. Yet Mencius knew nothing of Greece and Plato seems hardly to have heard of China. Both were teachers, in terms of their influence on later men among the very greatest. But in what different ways! A remark that should be repeated, and with emphasis, each time any of their interesting correspondencies in life and work is mentioned. Both looked for a king who could put their doctrines into action, and failed to find him. Both were sure that "licentious words, and perverse theories, ought never to have been allowed to begin. Beginning in the mind, they cause harm to the practice of things" (Dobson, 3.3). "But one law our guardians must keep in force, never letting it be overlooked and guarding it with more care than all the rest. This law keeps new ways out of the state which already has its fixed and reasoned order . . . because forms and rhythms are never changed without producing changes in the most important political forms and ways" (*Republic*, 424).

Both had hoped to restore a former perfection and held that this could be achieved by a turning round, a conversion, of the mind. "It is when a man sets his face primarily towards the greater parts that the lesser parts are unable to obtrude. It is this, nothing more, that makes him a great man" (Dobson, 3.4). "The instrument of knowledge has to be turned round, and with it the whole soul, from the things of becoming to the things of being" (*Republic*, 518). Both put something for which "good" seems a good word at the heart of nature. "It is of the essence of man's nature that he do good. That is what I mean by good. If a man does what is evil he is guilty of the sin of denying his natural endowment" (Dobson, 4.11). "This good, then, every soul looks for, and for this every soul does all that it does, feeling in some way what it is, but troubled and uncertain and unable to see clearly enough" (*Republic*, 505).

In Mencius' four virtues there is a certain unifying bond. Together they are Man's nature. Man is essentially these virtues striving for operation; but he does not know it. Coming to know it is becoming *sincere*.

"All things already complete in us. Reflect and find ourselves sincere; no greater happiness. With effort become mutual and so act; in seeking *jen*, nothing is nearer." (Legge) "All things are complete within ourselves. There is no joy that exceeds that of the discovery, upon self-examination, that we have acted with integrity. And we are never closer to achieving Humanity than when we seek to act, constrained by the principle of reciprocity" (Dobson, 7.24).

Or again: "Do not be what you are not; do not desire what you do not desire; just this only!" (Legge.) Less arrestingly, "Do not do what you should not do; do not wish for what you should not wish—there is nothing more to it than that" (Dobson, 7.24). More literally: "Do not do (be) its-what-not-do, do not desire its-what-not-desire, just this only." (See *Mencius on the Mind*, Appendix 28.) There is another tempting parallel with early Greek thought here: the great utterance of Pindar's Second Pythian Ode: "Become what you are!" in which Werner Jaeger saw the seed of so much of the doctrine of ideas.

What was by Mencius' own account his own greatest merit? One day a disciple spoke to him as follows:

"Dare I ask, master, what you are best at?"

Mencius replied, "I know Words, I excell in cultivating my vast *chi.*"

(*hao jan chih ch'i:* vast flowing passion nature: animal spirits, vitality.)

"Dare I ask, master, what is this vast *chi*?"

Mencius replied: "Hard to say. Most great and adamant is *chi*. When straightforwardly cultivated without being injured, it fills everywhere between heaven and earth. It matches *Yi* (Right) and *Tao* (the Way) without being daunted by them. It comes from the accumulation of *Yi*. It is not something which single right acts may make use of. If our conduct dissatisfies us, then the *chi* is daunted."

The disciple asked again: "What is knowing Words?"

Mencius replied:

"When Words are one-sided, I know where the speaker is blind. When Words are extravagant, I know what pit he has fallen into. When Words are evil, I know where he is lost. When Words are evasive, I know where he is at his wit's end. Such Words growing in the mind are injurious in the government; carried out in government, they are injurious in affairs. A Sage, when another comes, must be in agreement with my Words."

The chief of Mencius' Words was that *Hsing,* human nature, is good.

Necessarily there is much in Mencius still pointing to our future. The designs being uncovered by modern biology and explored through the new models for the working of the brain may make his prime doctrine—*Man by nature is good*—especially relevant. To believe this may seem to some a mere feat of willful optimism. To a culture like ours, built in part upon the conception of original sin, such a belief may seem dangerous, either blind or pitfallen or lost or at an end of its poor wits. But Mencius was not blind to or unafraid of evil or at his wit's end. The world he lived in had plenty of evil to show. The seasons went astray; princes were cruel and incompetent; war raged throughout his time; floods broke loose; despair was widespread. "The black-haired people," he said, "do not know where to place their hands or feet." All this he deliberately set out to remedy. These evils were for him a gigantic reflection of a frustration in man's mind. Only if the mind could return to its true nature and find itself again could all this be set right. With the mind turned round, setting things right would be no more toil than turning a pebble round in the palm of the hand. For him the cardinal virtues were what can be trusted, and human nature was that in us through which they could be trusted—that which made them trustworthy, namely our true selves.

What is there here for us? Nothing directly perhaps. But such an opportunity as few other Sages offer of considering anew for ourselves what we may put *our* trust in. We have our resources too, on which we too little reflect. And we may learn to know ourselves the better for studying a teacher who has been second only to Confucius in his influence on the mores of the Chinese people, helping in a large measure to sustain the most stable, the longest lasting and one of the most satisfying modes of human living that have been tried.

"What to do! What to do?" said Confucius. "Indeed I do not know what to do with a man who does not ask himself this." We may ask ourselves this— and its companion question, What are we doing?—the better for traveling into an archaic world and imagining another order of morality no less lofty and exacting than any we may be trying to achieve.

Consider the role of monolingual restatement, which I have been calling vertical translation. As part of the training of teachers or preachers, and for speakers and writers addressing themselves to certain publics, it stands up well. With a class coming to grips with any passage of difficult reading, the greatest value will prove to be the disciplined operation of restating and the close thinking that discussion of alternative rephrasings can foster. For unlike traditional paraphrase which might be called horizontal restatement since it so often consists of synonym trading, of second-choice word substitutes set into a framework that does not hold them well, vertical translating probes and searches and has to recast most of its sentences.

"The Future of Reading," from *The Written Word* (1971).

4

How to Read a Page

A slip of the log I am sitting on by my campfire under Mount Sir Donald has given me as an alternative title, "How to *reap* a page," which perhaps better suggests the aim. We assume we know how to read: spell it r e a *p*, and we begin to wonder how we do it.

Twenty years ago a very inexperienced writer commenced authorship with the remark, "A book is a machine to think with" (*Principles of Literary Criticism*). Here he is trying to devise another sort of verbal machine: something which may be a help in using books as machines to *think* with. He seems to have been uneasy about the word "think" then, for he added in a later edition, "but it need not usurp the functions either of the bellows or the locomotive." Some books endeavor to transport their readers or to drag them passively hither and thither; others aim to stuff them, with facts or other supposedly fattening matter; others are microscopes, as it were, which can take the most familiar things and lay scraps and details of them before us, so transmuted by the new conditions under which we see them that we lose all power of recognizing or putting them together again; others behave rather as pulverizers or consolidators. My readers here will have to choose for themselves what sort of machine they will compare this book to. I do not believe that either a washing machine or a combination harvester is the right comparison.

How a page was read has often been a matter of life and death. Misread orders on the battlefield have sent thousands to unnecessary destruction.

How to Read a Page (1942), Introduction; chaps. 1–3.

Their readings of a page of Scripture have led as many to the stake. Written words are very dangerous things:

> Who hath given man speech
> Or who hath set therein
> A thorn for peril and a snare for sin

wrote Swinburne (*Atalanta in Calydon*). He was thinking of quarrels, but we are perhaps in most danger when we agree too readily, or think we agree when in fact we do not. One thing here, at least, I am clear about and I hope I can make myself clear on. Neither this book nor any other can say how a page *should* be *read*—if by that we mean that it can give a recipe for discovering what the page *really says*. All it could do—and that would be much— would be to help us to understand some of the difficulties in the way of such discoveries. "How the page should be read" is a typically ambiguous phrase. Everyone can see that it may mean: (a) the right reading, the authentic interpretation; or (b) the right general procedure, or way of tackling the page. I need hardly say that this book keeps its eye on the second of these, and will be content if it can display some of the things which make it easy for us to twist pages to mean what we please—whether in order to damn or to praise them.

It is concerned with pages of all sorts—from plain exposition or instruction, the battle order for example, to poetry or philosophy, or the pages of Scripture referred to above. With the *first* there should be no doubt that there is one right reading which can be discovered or the writer is horribly at fault. But with the pages which on a long view have mattered most to the world, the utterances of the great poets and sages, we may reasonably doubt whether there is one right and only right reading. These greatest sayings of man have an inexhaustible fertility. Different minds have found such different things in them that we would be very rash if we assumed that some one way of reading them which commends itself to us is the right one. And yet . . . to assume so, to suppose that some one reading is the only right one, is our natural and our traditional approach. We feel very strongly that unless there is a right reading, and unless our business is to find it, we are wasting our time with such writings. This would certainly be so if they were like the specifications of an airplane, say, or like a map. A map on which hills and valleys could reasonably change places according to the consulting eye would be condemned as worthless by all. But with the highest poetry and philosophy and moral teaching, something like this happens and rightly. And the great pages lose nothing of their perpetual value because it happens. Indeed, their value is perpetual because through them, as through nothing else, we gain such opportunities of surveying the possibilities of ourselves and our worlds. There are limitations here clearly. Not every vague saying becomes precious. You will not succeed in making up a sentence which, because it might mean anything, will be permanently interesting. The immortal pages are no such puzzles, though they are the great exercisers of the spirit. But if we read them as though they could say one thing only, or condemn them because they can say many different things, we will be cutting ourselves off from the best which has been known and thought in the world—to use Matthew Arnold's phrase.

A list of the vices of reading should put first, as worst and most disabling, the expectation that everything should be easily understood. Things worth thought and reflection cannot be taken in at a glance. The writer should, of course, have done his utmost to make things easy for us. He could have had nothing (could he?) more important than *that* to do. But where there is still some difficulty remaining, let us beware of blaming it on the author rather than on our own imperfect command of the language. To blame the writer will teach us nothing. To wonder if we are reading right may.

Next to this vice should come that shallow indifference which says, "Well, if the page can mean almost anything, what does it matter how I take it? One reading is as good as another." It isn't. All the value comes from the depth and honesty, the sincerity and stress of the reflection through which we choose which meanings among its possibilities we will take seriously into our considerations. These things have many meanings because they touch us at points at which each one of us is himself many-minded. Understanding them is very much more than picking a possible reasonable interpretation, clarifying that, and sticking to it. Understanding them is seeing how the varied possible meanings hang together, which of them depend upon what else, how and why the meanings which matter most to us form a part of our world—seeing thereby more clearly what our world is and what we are who are building it to live in.

A chief modern difficulty in such understanding comes from the recent development of the historical sense. Compared with our great-grandfathers, we know incredibly much about the past. Scholarship has made the authors, their times and social conditions, etc., etc., known to us as to no other generation ever. This, at first sight, should make good reading easier. In many ways it does. We can turn to a dictionary such as Dr. Johnson never dreamed of and see how a troublesome word has been used century after century in varying ways. Concordances show us all the other uses the author made of the word. On wider points we can consult histories and biographies. Vast collections of disparate interpretations and comments are available. Around almost every important author an enormous critical apparatus has come into being. Its prime aim is just to help us to read better. But somehow all this wealth of scholarly aid does not lift up our hearts as it should. It spreads attention out too thinly and daunts us with the thought that we would have to know everything before we could know anything. Doubtless this is true, philosophically, but to readers in search of a method it is unhelpful.

Modern historical scholarship especially terrorizes us with the suggestion that somewhere in the jungle of evidence there is something we happen not to know which would make the point clear, which would show us just what the author did in fact mean. That suspicion of a missing clue is paralyzing—unless we remember firmly that from the very nature of the case essential clues are always missing. However much evidence we amass, we still have to jump to our conclusions. Reading is not detection as the perfect detective practices it. We are never concerned with facts pointing conclusively to a central fact—what happened in an author's mind at a given moment. No facts could ever establish that. If psychoanalysis has done nothing else for the world it has at least helped us to realize that minds—including authors' minds—are private. All we can ever prove by factual evidence is *an act*—that the author wrote such and such words. But what he meant by them is another matter. Our conclusions there must rest, as best they may, upon another sort of consideration. Fundamentally they rest upon analogies—certain very broad similarities in structure between minds: "The all-in-each of every mind," as Coleridge called it.

To go deeper, the reader, as opposed to the biographer, is not concerned with what as historical fact was going on in the author's mind when he penned the sentence, but with what the words—given the rest of the language—may mean. We do not read Shakespeare, or Plato, or Lao Tzu, or Homer, or the Bible, to discover what their authors—about whom otherwise we know so little—were thinking. We read them for the sake of the things their words—if we understand them—can do for us. But understanding them, of course, is not making them mean something we know and approve of already, nor is it detecting their ignorance and limitations. It is using them to stretch our minds as they have stretched the minds of so many different readers through the centuries. The interest they have so long had for man is the proof of their importance for us.

Emerson estimated that a man might have, if he were fortunate, some hundreds of reasonable moments in a long life. He was thinking probably of moments of inspiration from sources less traceable than the book in one's hand. The great pages are the most constant and dependable sources of "reasonable moments," if we mean by them moments when we know more completely what we are, and why we are so, and thus "see into the life of things" more deeply than in our everyday routine of existence. Such reasonable moments are the highest aim of reading. In them we do more than communicate with our authors—in the humble sense of communicate. We partake with them of wisdom. This aim is not attained unless we also gain such skills in reading as serves us in all our communications with our fellow human beings. The arts of reading are a pyramid whose pinnacle rests on the stages below. No one can understand poetry well whose mind cannot take in the prose of discussion and necessary business.

We all enjoy the illusion that we read better than we do; not least, no doubt, those who set out to write about *How to read*. But most of us—or those at least, who are likely to open a book with this title—are satisfied that other people read badly, that they can miss any point and will put their own wild interpretations on even the most obvious remark. In recent years books, papers, and articles which labor this point and accuse the general reader of incompetence with language have been coming out in plenty. Some of them hint despondingly that things are getting worse and threaten us even with universal intellectual collapse unless something is done about it. Authorities tell vast conferences of English teachers every few weeks that they are failing to teach reading. Texts simplified and written down to tenth-grade level are adopted in university courses because the undergraduates cannot, it is alleged, read anything harder. Publicists lament, in popular volumes, the plain man's helpless acceptance of verbal nonsense. Specialists complain that their contributions are wasted because the other specialists do nothing but misread them. And prophets foretell the downfall of democracy through a decline in the citizen's ability to follow any discussion worth a hearing.

Behind all this there is enough solid evidence to make anyone who studies it very uncomfortable. If most people's reading is really as inefficient as it seems when carefully enough examined, the main staff of education is hardly worth leaning on. What is the advantage of toiling on through thousands of pages, if a chief outcome is an accumulation of misunderstandings? Surely it should be possible to go directly to the root of the trouble, to study verbal misunderstanding, its nature and causes, deeply enough to find and apply a cure?

Accordingly, a considerable literature is coming into being which discusses the theory of language: classification, abstraction, naming, metaphor, and the rest. Unfortunately, it cannot be said to offer us much hope of immediate remedies. And this is not surprising. The questions which our theory of language has to discuss are hardest of all to write clearly about. They are the meeting points of tremendous pressures coming from rival philosophic systems used consciously or unconsciously by those who discuss them. We should expect not only great divergences of view but persistent drastic misinterpretations among their students. Everyone who writes on such matters sighs to think how often he seems to be misread. The layman who looks into this literature extensively enough will be shocked to discover how much seemingly fundamental disagreement it contains. If he does not go into it far enough to see this, he should be warned not to suppose there is anything at present there corresponding to the agreed doctrines the sciences can offer him. There is no agreed theory of language—as elementary mechanics, for example, is an agreed theory. Later on in this book we will see why there cannot be. Moreover, to get any adequate view of what the rival professors are maintaining, the inquiring layman would have to become an adept at a peculiarly difficult sort of reading in which one is specially apt to suppose he has understood when in fact he has not. It is not likely, therefore, that perusal of those confusing pages will make many people better readers. There is evidence, on the contrary, that misunderstandings acquired from them have made intelligent people more foolish and imperceptive as readers than they would otherwise have been.

The belief that knowledge of linguistic theory will make a man a better reader comes itself from such a misunderstanding. Theory and practice are not so simply connected. It is true that bad theory does lead to bad reading. But good theory will not necessarily produce good reading. Between the principles in the theory and the actual words to be read comes the task of seeing which principles apply to which cases, the problem of recognizing what the actual situation is. Theory can give us no *direct* help in this, more's the pity! We have to rely on whatever sagacity we have developed. Nothing, alas, is easier than to fit our distinctions to the wrong instances. And in most reading there are strong motives at work which tempt us to do this.

We are all of us learning to read all the time. All our thinking is a part of the process as affecting the way we will on some occasion take some sentence. Whenever we use words in forming some judgment or decision, we are, in what may be a painfully sharp sense, "learning to read." The lover scanning his mistress's scribble or her scowling brows is learning to read. So is the theologian comparing the ideas of *eros* and *agape*.

There is an ambiguity here which is brought out by asking, learning to read what?—the written word? or by means of that word the face, or the heart, of Nature?

The answer, of course, is, "Both." We cannot separate them. We always read for some purpose—unless some sad, bad, mad schoolteacher has got hold of us. There is no such thing as merely reading words; always through the words we are trafficking or trying to traffic with things—things gone by, present, to come or eternal. So a person who sets up to teach reading should recognize that he may be more ambitious than he seems. He may pretend he is only concerned to help people not to mistake one word for another, or one construction for another. *That,* so far, doesn't look like an attempt to finger the steering wheel of the universe. But "Which word is it?" turns into "Which use?"; and the question "Which construction?" into "What implications?" Before long the would-be authority on interpretation has become indistinguishable from an authority on "What's what?"—a question which belongs to a more divine science than he may wittingly aspire to.

Nonetheless, by being more aware of this he will be better able to pursue his main task—the cultivation of general verbal sagacity.

Whence comes, then, the development of this sagacity so much needed if we are to see what is happening? The answer is "Experience," of course; experience of a certain sort. But "experience" is one of the words we are all always most likely to misunderstand, because we all use it in so many ways. As a rule, we are not more than dimly aware of the great differences between its possible meanings. In most sentences it can say very different, sometimes even contradictory, things to different readers. And these different meanings will, as a rule, all make fairly good sense. There is an interesting and not too obvious reason for this. With most uses of "experience," the other words round about in the neighboring sentences are ready to shift their meanings to conform with its meanings. Most explanations of "experience" will be found to contain words like "mind," "observation," "attention," "knowledge," "feeling," "consciousness," which systematically vary in meaning in corresponding ways. So to say what we may mean or what anyone else may mean by "experience" or by any of these words is no easy undertaking— though it is what these pages attempt.

It is no one's fault that these words behave so. It is a sign of their importance. All ᵠunderstandingᵠ* of anything of general importance turns on our mastery of the ranges of ideas which such words cover. I put ᵠunderstandingᵠ here in these specialized quotation marks (*q* for *query*) to note the fact that it is another of them and to suggest that in reading it we have to make out, if we can, which of its possible meanings it probably has. To assume that we know this too soon with any such word is the most frequent cause of bad reading.

This *systematic* ambiguity of all our most important words is a first cardinal point to note. But "ambiguity" is a sinister-looking word and it is better to say "resourcefulness." They are *the most important words* for two reasons:

1. They cover the ideas we can least avoid using, those which are concerned in all that we do as thinking begins.

2. They are words we are forced to use in explaining other words because it is in terms of the ideas they cover that the meanings of other words must be given.

A short list of a hundred such words will help to make these reasons for their importance clearer.

Amount, Argument, Art, Be, Beautiful, Belief, Cause, Certain, Chance, Change, Clear, Common, Comparison, Condition, Connection, Copy, Decision, Degree, Desire, Development, Different, Do, Education, End, Event, Example, Existence, Experience, Fact, Fear, Feeling, Fiction, Force, Form, Free, General, Get, Give, Good, Government, Happy, Have, History, Idea, Important, Interest, Knowledge, Law, Let, Level, Living, Love, Make, Material, Measure, Mind, Motion, Name, Nation, Natural, Necessary, Normal, Number, Observation, Opposite, Order, Organization, Part, Place, Pleasure, Possible, Power, Probable, Property, Purpose, Quality, Question, Reason, Relation, Representative, Respect, Responsible, Right, Same, Say, Science, See, Seem, Sense, Sign, Simple, Society, Sort, Special, Substance, Thing, Thought, True, Use, Way, Wise, Word, Work.

I have, in fact, left 103 words in this list—to incite the reader to the task of cutting out those he sees no point in and adding any he pleases, and to discourage the notion that there is anything sacrosanct about a hundred, or any other number. The very usefulness which gives them their importance explains their ambiguity. They are the servants of too many interests to keep to single, clearly defined jobs. Technical words in the sciences are like adzes, planes, gimlets, or razors. A word like "experience," or "feeling," or "true" is

---

*See pp. 270–73 for an explanation of these superscripts.—ED

like a pocketknife. In good hands it will do most things—not very well. In general we will find that the more important a word is, and the more central and necessary its meanings are in our pictures of ourselves and the world, the more ambiguous and possibly deceiving the word will be. Naturally these words are also those which have been most used in philosophy. But it is not the philosophers who have made them ambiguous; it is the position of their ideas, as the very hinges of all thought.

To say, then, that a reader's sagacity comes from *experience* in reading is not to say much unless we can do something to clear up what is meant here by ᵠexperience.ᵠ In a rough way everyone will agree. A good doctor gets his ability to diagnose from experience. A good judge gets his discernment from experience. But what is this experience which gives some men so much and others so little? It is not having many things happen to one merely. Some who have read little read well; others who have read much read badly. What happened and how it happened matter more than the quantity or variety of happenings. If we are to get any light on the reading process, on why it goes wrong and on how it might be improved, we must look as closely as we can into our own minds as we read and form as live a conception as we may of the sort of experience with words in sentences which makes better readers. . . .

The main source of any view, sound or silly, which we have of how we read must be our own observations of our own doings while we are reading. We should supplement this by observations of others' behavior and their reports, but inevitably in interpreting such other evidence we start from and return to that picture of a mind at work which only introspection can supply.

We do not realize what an opportunity our reading affords us for these self-observations. There, in the most convenient form, is an admirable experimental setup. We need no colleague to set us tasks; the author takes that duty over. All that we have to do is to cultivate the trick of changing our easily observed reactions from a communion or dispute with him into notes on our own deliberations. There must, however, be some difficulty in the page we face to stir us to noteworthy maneuvers. Otherwise this page prefaced by "I saw that . . ." would serve as a record of our doings. Any page which stretches our power of comprehending can teach us much about how we grope, and comparison of a number of pages—if we did not let our interest in the search too soon overcome our interest in the searching—could show us useful differences between guessing and grasping. On the other hand, there must be something on the page we really care about understanding. Otherwise we will go through the motions of reading only and the result will be uninstructive.

It is an advantage if the passages we use for these experiments form a series presenting in different settings and with different verbal expression somewhat similar problems to thought. The operations with which we work at them—generalization, abstraction, deduction, induction, division, exemplification, assumption, definition—have flavors of their own, which we learn to recognize as we become clearer as to what we are doing in them. As topics to *discuss* they are all but stupefying. Logicians long ago proved that to us. Only adepts long inured to them can keep awake. Only a minimum of such discussion will appear in these pages. We propose to practice these operations rather than to discuss them. And through practice we can become better aware of what they do than through even the clearest discussion.

In reading we are performing these operations all the time. Each has its own characteristic mishaps, and these stumblings have their own distinctive feelings. We can sometimes know that we are going wrong without being able yet to see what has happened. It is such observations that we will be on the lookout for.

I will add after each passage a commentary designed to help a reader:

1. to notice what he does with them in a first perusal.

2. to compare this with what happens in later, more questioning attention.

3. to compare both with various suggested possibilities.

4. to notice upon what points any decision about the meaning of the passage turns for him.

Inevitably I will have my own views about the interpretations of the passages. To hide them would be artificial and the attempt would probably fail. My aim will not be to get the reader to agree with me in my readings. I have no very robust confidence that they are right. So I will not be expounding them as I would if persuasion were the aim. Just what our passages say is, for our purpose here, less important than *how* they say it and how they may say different things to different readers. It is the reading process rather than the products we are to study.

On the other hand, it would be idle to invite so much attention to passages which could not say rather important things, or in which the ambiguities were not of a sort which recur everywhere in writing. My extracts will therefore be, most of them, from great writers, and will treat questions of the first order of importance. And these questions will be those we will inevitably have in mind in considering our experience while reading. Thus we may with them sometimes be catching more than one bird with the same throw of the net. Most of the passages will be difficult, some very. It is the difficulties of reading we are studying. In each case please read through once carefully. Then sit back and try to collect and survey what you have gathered before reading my remarks and returning to study the passage.

My first passage, which is among the hardest, gives us Aristotle's account of "learning by experience." It comes from the last pages (99^b 33–100^a 9) of the *Posterior Analytics*.

It will be followed by a version in Basic English. I shall be making much use of the techniques of Basic English throughout. Being pinched within the limits of 850 words forces one to look at the original one in translating with an intentness hard to keep up otherwise. By cutting out the easy synonym it makes one go into the possibilities of the forbidden words more deeply. Here "perception" (which Aristotle is describing for us) will be the only non-Basic word used.

Aristotle has asked how we get to know the basic, primary or immediate, premises from which demonstration leading to scientific knowledge sets out. Demonstration has to start from things undemonstrated. How have we come to know such things? Are we born with the knowledge and does the infant just fail to notice he has it? That would be too strange. On the other hand, it can't just pop into our minds complete without there being anything from which it is developed.

> Therefore we must possess a capacity of some sort, but not such as to rank
> higher in accuracy than these developed states. And this at least is an obvious
> characteristic of all animals, for they possess a congenital discriminative capacity
> which is called sense-perception. But though sense-perception is innate in all
> 5 animals, in some the sense-impression comes to persist, in others it does not. So
> animals in which this persistence does not come to be have either no knowledge
> at all outside the act of perceiving, or no knowledge of objects of which no
> impression persists; animals in which it does come into being have perception
> and can continue to retain the sense-impression in the soul: and when such per-
> 10 sistence is frequently repeated a further distinction at once arises between those
> which out of the persistence of such sense-impressions develop a power of sys-
> tematizing them and those which do not. So out of sense-perception comes to
> be what we call memory, and out of frequently repeated memories of the same
> thing develops experience; for a number of memories constitute a single experi-
> 15 ence. From experience again—i.e., from the universal now stabilized in its en-
> tirety within the soul, the one beside the many which is a single identity within
> them all—originate the skill of the craftsman and the knowledge of the man of
> science, skill in the sphere of coming to be and science in the sphere of being.

The first time we read through this we are likely at places to feel a little like those animals in whom no impression persists. What is said seems too cloudy or too folded over upon itself to be taken in. One such place will be perhaps at lines 6–7, where the *either . . . or* comes. This feels like a crumple in the discourse. It is as though Aristotle were saying the thing twice, or we were seeing double. And we may notice the same effect at other places, as in the following sentence: "animals in which it [What's *it*? The persistence of course] does come into being have perception and can continue to retain the sense-impression in the soul." Here if "the persistence does come into being" it seems unnecessary to add that the animals "can continue to retain the sense-impression in the soul." That is said already. This redundancy of expression is very characteristic of Aristotle and may have something to do with his lecturing technique. These are lecture notes, and the repetitions can be so inflected by the voice that they amount to emphasis, or a sort of soothing confirmation to the listener that he *has* got the point. In reading with the eye we miss these pointers as to when it is a new nail being driven or just another tap on one already home. It will be found in general that reading a passage aloud with this sort of thing in mind is an enormous help in giving perspective to an argument, making its structure more evident, and focusing one's attention on the right places.

Developing the structure of the argument in this way goes, of course, along with questioning the meaning of its words and phrases and with tentative decisions as to what is said. As a means of getting that ready for discussion, let me offer here a simplified translation. (Of the English passage as it stands, I have no pretensions to be able to comment on the fidelity of the Oxford version to the Greek.) This version may both bring out the structure, as I see it, and give you something to compare with what you have found.

> So we have to be able to get this knowledge in some way but not in a way which makes it righter than the knowledge which comes out of it. And this is clearly true of all animals, for they have from birth a power to see different things as different, which is named "sense-perception." But though all animals have
> 5 sense-perception by birth, some of them keep what it takes in, and some of them don't. Those which don't ever become able to keep these things have no knowledge at all when the act of sensing isn't going on. Those that are able to keep the effects of sensing and keep them again and again are of two sorts. There are those which become able through keeping them to put them into some order and those
> 10 which don't. So out of sense-perception comes to be what is named "memory." And out of frequent memories of the same thing comes experience; for a number of memories make up one experience. From experience again—that is, from the general form now fixed as a complete thing in the mind, the one thing which is the same in any number of examples—come the art of the workman and the
> 15 knowledge of the man of science, art as having to do with changing things and science as having to do with what is ever the same.

Now let us compare this rendering with the original and note some of the problems which came up in making it:

1. line *2, higher in accuracy: righter,* as one answer to a question is nearer to the right answer than another. *Accuracy, precision, exactness* are difficult words to be clear about. They share some of the troubles of *true* and some of those of *definite.* A definite answer need not be true, nor a true one definite. If we try hard enough to see what *true* and *definite* may mean we will not be surprised that true and definite interpretations are so hard to arrive at.

2. line *3, congenital discriminative capacity: power to see different things as different. See* is (by metaphor) short for "perceive through any of the senses." That would not mislead. But *see* might suggest that all animals do more than respond differently to some sorts of different things, that they *see* (i.e., understand as a philosopher might) what the differences are. Aristotle is thinking of no such intellectual feat. This discriminative capacity is just the ability to be affected differently when their surroundings are different in certain ways, that is, to vary with their surroundings in certain ways. Lifeless bodies have this ability too—in very limited ways, however. A billiard ball is affected differently by different pushes, but it is little influenced by smells if at all.

3. line *4, innate: by birth*. I hesitated between *by, from,* and *at birth* here. *By* might suggest that the process of birth gave them the power, but that is not a likely interpretation. *From* and *at* suggest that they have it the moment they are born. But an innate power may come into operation only later. Kittens have to open their eyes before they see different things as different. The notion of innate powers, like that of inheritance, collapses if we look at it too closely, as Aristotle knew. "Innate" and "congenital" say no more than that an animal has the power under the right conditions. What we are born with has to have certain conditions if it is to come out. So the contrast between heredity and environment is a false one if we make them independent. Under different conditions we would be found to have inherited different powers.

4. line *7–8, and when such persistence is frequently repeated: those that are able to keep the effects of sensing and keep them again and again*. The problem here is whether the impressions which have to be kept if the power of systematizing them is to develop are of the same sort or not. I was tempted to write "able to keep the *different* effects of sensing." That would make a more satisfactory theory. But Aristotle might only have in view the return again and again of the same impression $a_1 a_2 a_3 \ldots a_n$ leading to A, the universal or form which they share. On the other theory the thing would be more complex. By "the persistence is frequently repeated" he would mean that $a_1 \, a_2 \, a_3 \ldots$

$$\text{and } b_1 \, b_2 \, b_3 \ldots$$
$$\text{and } c_1 \, c_2 \, c_3 \ldots \text{ came}$$

back. Not only that but there would be such repetitions as

$$a_1 \, b_1 \, a_2 \, b_2 \, a_3 \, b_3 \ldots$$
$$a_1 \, c_1 \, a_2 \, c_2 \, a_3 \, c_3 \ldots$$
$$a_1 \, b_1 \, c_1 \, a_2 \, b_2 \, c_2 \, a_3 \, b_3 \, c_3 \ldots$$

The same sense impressions come back *in varying frames of other impressions,* and it would be through *that,* not through mere unvarying repetition, that "the power of systematizing them" would be developed. It is hard to see why any number of repetitions of the same impression, however well they are retained, should become anything other than an embarrassing crowd of them. But "the universal . . . the one beside the many which is a single identity within them all" is certainly not a swarm of impressions. The impressions are the many; the one is their form, that which makes them the same. The evidence *here* that Aristotle held the more complex theory is the next phase I now discuss.

5. line *9, systematizing them: putting them into some order*. I might have written (still in Basic), "sorting and ordering them and separating their different connections with one another," for that is what has to be done if this kind of knowledge is to arise. The systematizing which constitutes experience and supplies our basic premises is very much more than merely noting "thingumbob again!" A typical basic premise, guaranteed by experience, is: *tapping with one's fingernail on a table makes a sharp little sound.* This is woven in with such other premises as *tapping so on a can, on a stove . . . makes a different sound,* and *tapping so with the soft tip of the finger makes hardly any sound.* The

fabric these belong to is so vast that I could easily fill this book with nothing but such commonplaces of experience all connected with one another through universals. The universal which my wording makes prominent here is *tapping*. These are all instances of tapping. A much more embracing universal is *make,* which is indeed one of the topmost powers in the hierarchy (makes a sound, makes sense, etc.). *Tapping* is a fairly specific universal. It divides up into light-impacts-between-surfaces-of-solids, say, all of which are more general universals. *Make* is a very general universal and is perhaps indivisible. We meet a baffling simplicity if we try to say what making is. *Systematizing* here is the coming into the soul of universals and the growth of their connections with one another there. It is these connections which stabilize them. "The soul is the place of forms," says Aristotle elsewhere. Here he says, "within the soul." Maybe we confuse ourselves with this spatial metaphor *in* the soul. We would if we took it seriously. But the metaphor is too convenient to be abandoned. It might be more accurate to say that the soul just is the universals which knit together all it knows, as we might say that its knowledge (compare the metaphor in *cognition*) was that knitting together. But these are hardly lucid ways of talking. (Or overlucid? We have with them the same difficulty that we have in seeing empty space.)

6. line *12, soul: mind.* Basic does not include the word "soul," but adds it for its version of the Bible. "Soul" identifies for us Aristotle's word here (ψυκή), but we should not lightly identify Aristotle's conception of the soul with a Christian one or with any other. He is writing psychology here, and modern psychology in spite of its name has for such uses replaced "soul" by "mind." My change would therefore not mislead unless the reader were thinking of other Greek words which would have to be translated by "mind."

7. line *10, memory.* Psychology distinguishes memory from retention, the persistence Aristotle is talking of here, and limits "memory" to remembering and what is remembered. When we remember some event we look back to it. But the effects of the event may persist without our remembering it. We do not have to remember former acts of tapping tables in order to know what sound will be made. It is retention—the persistence of past events—which forms experience here. It is not memory in the sense in which you will use your memory when you write your memoirs.

8. line *11,* a number of memories *constitute a single experience: making up one experience.* "Experience" here plainly means something very different from the most frequent current use—"That raid was a terrific experience"—or the sense in which teachers, for example, talk so much about "worth-while experiences." In Aristotle's sense we do not get experience by just going through events but by learning something *general* or universal therein. "I regard as genuine knowledge only that which returns again as power," said Coleridge. The power is the ability to recognize, to know again that universal (or *with* that universal, if we make it the power of knowing rather than what is known).

Constitute is a troublesome word. Does it mean "set up" or "actually are"?

A number of words have this same trick: *compose, consist* ("By Him all things consist"—*Colossians* I:17), *form,* and *make* are examples. They are very convenient when we do not know which we mean, or when it does not matter, but they are a nuisance at places like this. The only thing to do is to explore both possibilities as far as we can. We get two theories:

A. That Aristotle is stating as a matter of fact that a number of persisting impressions develop into or cause to come into being *something else,* a universal.

B. That he is pointing out that, after all, an experience (as a universal) really is what is common to a number of persisting impressions. As soon as the impressions are taken together by the mind as being *of the same thing,* the universal is at work. They couldn't be of the *same* thing, without it.

Why a *single* experience? To raise the contrast driven home in the next sentence between the plural impressions and the one universal. We keep this use in sentences like "My experience is that such men don't go far." On the other hand, most pedagogic talk about "worth-while experiences" is about multifarious impressions.

9. line *12, in its entirety: as a complete thing.* Universals seem hard to think of, or even self-contradictory, chiefly because we try to imagine them, to see them in the mind's eye as if they existed in space. So when we say a universal is *in* many things and *in* many minds, if we do not take these *in*'s literally, at least we give them a ghost's body. We think of universals as having parts: the phrase "in its entirety" is there to defend us from this habit.

10. line *15, the sphere of being: what is ever the same.* Science is knowledge of the unchanging. This may seem odd since the scientific worker is studying changes all the time. But what he is trying to know is the law of some change; and laws are unchanging. *Art,* since for Aristotle here it is concerned with making things, or with practical activity as in medical treatment, is a knowledge of how to make changes. Both originate in experience. The scientist would have no changes to study and the artist-workman no *things* to change, if the universals had not been stabilized in their soul as experience. They would merely be indescribable chaoses.

We may now pause to consider what, so far, in the process of reading as we have been observing it here in our minds, offers any suggestion toward a technique for improving reading. A number of points seem worth noting. I believe most readers will confirm them.

1. When eye reading alone does not give us a clear sense of the grammar and of the logical structure, we tend to switch speaking and hearing on. We can do this in two ways which are, as it were, degrees of realization or actualization of the sentences.

A. We read it in imagination—producing *images* of the speech movements and of the sound of the words.

B. We really utter the words faintly or out loud.

Vocal reading can aid in giving structure to the argument. It is an experimental manipulation, a testing procedure on trial-and-error lines. While noting that reading a thing out loud may be a great help, we should not forget that it can be a great hindrance. As the name "trial and error" (rather than "trial and triumph") suggests, there are likely to be more errors than successes. The eye is a more neutral agent than the voice. Or, to put it more fairly, the voice, if there has been failure, can easily add a very persuasive garb or garble of rhythm and intonation to support the misinterpretation. This commonly happens when the cause of the misinterpretation has been prejudice—the interference of some sentiment. Nothing is easier than to make words ring out or fall flat as we please, to our own ears—especially if we don't know we are doing it. So the chances of our detecting the twist we are giving in our reading are much reduced. When other people read things to us, we often think, "So long as you read it *that way* you can't possibly understand what it says!" We should more often be saying the same thing to ourselves. In particular, a certain querulous questioning tone—"What *can* it mean?"—is an enemy of comprehension. Read it as though it made sense and perhaps it will.

2. In addition to reading the words on the page to ourselves in various ways and with various tones, we can add to them—anything from ejaculations, delighted or derisive, to an analytic commentary. Some people do no little talking to themselves while reading. For them, it is very much a part of the reading process. With argumentative matter the reader should talk back as much as possible unless he is merely fighting, talking for a victory there will be no one but himself to award. Though debate is silly, reasoning is still dialogue, as Plato said.

This touches a large theme—the different modes of reading suited to different types of writing. It is absurd to read everything—poetry, prose, pulp—alike, especially to read it all as *fast* as possible. Whom are they fleeing from, these running readers? I fear the only answer is, "Themselves." Anything that is worth *studying* should be read *as slowly* as it will let you, and read again and again till you have it by heart. Only so will the persistencies be repeated frequently enough for a power of systematizing them to develop. Most of us read too fast rather than too slowly. This opinion goes bang in the teeth, I know, of the massed professional teachers of the reading art, those who are telling one another so often that they are failing to teach it. They will brandish their figures to show that the fastest readers get most. One may still ask: How do you know they would not have got something of another order if they had not sped so fast? Have their speeding teachers themselves got quite enough out of their reading to be able to judge? And these are things which no "comprehension test" yet devised can measure. But all this belongs to our conclusions, when we have studied the process of reading in much greater detail.

3. From internal dialogue to rephrasing is a small step. Most people find that having two versions of a passage before them opens up the task of ex-

ploration immensely. This is true even when one version is clearly very inferior; its presence still throws the implications of the other into relief. So a black-and-white reproduction of a picture can make us see what the color in the original is doing. A better parallel, perhaps, is with photographic surveying. Two versions are like two views from slightly different angles. If we can fit them together, each tells us much about the things seen in the other.

These effects are striking enough to promise (if we can study them successfully) some real improvement in reading. And tradition in teaching backs up this hope. Translation work has been the main technique of literary education in the past. Now no one who knows how translation—whether from Latin into English or back again or with French or German either way—is ordinarily done and has ordinarily been done in the past will see in that dreary and largely mechanical routine any saving virtue. It is only in the best translation work, which comes after the mechanics of the strange tongue have been mastered, and only in the hands of teachers who are themselves exacting readers, that the incessant comparisons required between different ways of saying more or less the same thing become any royal road to good reading. *Thorough* mastery of a foreign language, no doubt, always improves our understanding of the mother tongue in some degree. Getting a smattering does not. Even the first steps in a foreign tongue *can* be made a profitable study of our own language, but current practice fails to do this; and the grim toil which follows consists mainly in replacing, one by one, words we hardly understand at all with words we have not time to consider—or vice versa. So my reference here to translation as a method of improving reading will not cheer up anyone to whom translation means primarily that. But there is an altogether different sort of translation in which both languages, as to the routine handling of their mechanics and the pocket-dictionary senses of their words, are fully grasped. The task then can become a deep exploration of meaning, a perfect exercise for developing resource and justice in interpretation.

The same merits can be possessed by English–English translation, if we put certain controls on it which bar out synonym trading and glosses which dodge or veil the difficulties (Basic English offers us many possibilities of such controls.)

Comparison seems to be the key to all learning of this type. Learning to read is not fundamentally different from learning to be a good judge of wine, or of horses, or of men. Persistence of effects must be repeated frequently enough to become systematized. And, for progress to be rapid, effects whose similarities and differences—their sameness amid difference rather—are instructive should persist together. Some people can compare things across wide intervals of time. They go ahead faster than the rest of us. Others cannot make subtle comparisons between things which do not overlap in their effects. Everything depends, of course, on what things are being compared by whom. What I have just been saying applies chiefly to first comparisons between somewhat novel things in somewhat novel respects—the earliest stages of the systematization about which Aristotle was talking. The more any body of perceptions becomes systematized, the easier it becomes to span vast stretches of time in comparing examples within it. A real expert can identify a wine and its condition even though he has not tasted any similar wine for years. But that is only because his experience became well systematized in the bygone days when he was tasting such wines. And then, no doubt, his comparisons were not very widely spaced apart.

Now, if reading is a matter of organized comparisons between meanings, as it certainly is, it should not be difficult to arrange things so that the best opportunities for the growth of this organization or systematization are secured. What we have to do is put the materials for distinctions and connections about which we are not clear enough *together,* so that the universals can develop through comparison. And we will do this best by using different ways of saying "the same thing" in close collocation.

But four very important qualifications must be made or this program will lead us into nothing but folly:

A. We must know which are the important distinctions and connections.

B. We must be very much on our guard with the phrase "the same thing."

C. We must respect the fundamental conditions of interest.

D. We must recognize that failure to see an important distinction or connection is most often due to our not *wanting* to see it.

I will take these up in turn, and then pass on to some experiments with another passage in the light of these reflections.

a. I have mentioned already—when listing my hundred great words—the chief reasons which make some distinctions and connections more important than others. Let me restate them here in another form. The most important ideas (and an idea here is a form of distinction and connection) are the *necessary* ones in the sense that we cannot do without them. They enter inevitably into all our thinking, for thinking is just another name for the operation of these ideas. Typical among them are the ideas covered by *same, different, change, cause, thing, idea, part, whole, abstract, concrete, general, special, form, implies, matter, quality,* and *relation.* Language has an inexhaustible variety of ways of expressing these ideas, and we may easily fail to notice that they are serving still as the structure of our thought. Sometimes, too, we may handle them better through language which does not make them prominent by using these bald and somewhat formidable words. More often, though, we miss a point or confuse an argument by failing to see that under the attractively novel phrasing, and behind its special graces, we have to do with the same familiar joints and muscles and bones.

To say we cannot do without these ideas may seem to get us into a difficulty. If we have them and use them all the time already, what is the point of working up great programs for teaching ourselves about them? The point is that no one is as skillful with them as he might be, and that much of the inefficiency of thought and language comes from needless blundering with these ideas. But here again we must note that skill with them is not in the least the same thing as being able to propound even the best theories about them. A first-rate authority on the foundations of mathematics might well be a poor mathematician. And so it is throughout. Our aim will not be improved theory of language but improved conduct with it.

If we can improve our conduct of these ideas, our reward is everywhere. That is why time given to the words which can handle them least confusingly is better spent than time given to distinctions and connections which are only locally useful.

If we open a dictionary of synonyms we are faced with thousands of subtle problems. The early nineteenth-century compilers used to attempt to *state* distinctions between usages—with all but uniformly absurd results. The only thing that will show us what these different implications are is watching them at work. And only then, when we see with the help of all around it what a word is doing, can we fruitfully attempt to state this, or by experiment explore differentiations. When we do so we discover that there is a certain limited set of words which we use most in such attempted elucidations. They form a language within a language—the words needed in explaining the rest of the language. The ideas these words cover are fewer than we suppose, though there is something very artificial about pretending that we can *count* such things as ideas. All we can say is that the meanings of words are relatively compound or simple, and that careful analysis *in contexts* can as a rule break down a complex meaning into simpler ideas acting together in a certain form. It is the simpler ideas (and the words which handle them best) that are the most important for us to study if we are to improve our reading. No one will pretend, of course, that an improved understanding of these ideas will by itself teach us what different things different complexes of them will do. For that we need experience of the complexes themselves at work. But better knowledge of the simples will certainly help to form that experience of complexes at work.

b. We have now to take a look at some of the problems behind the innocent-seeming words "say the same thing." Both "say" and "same" need our best attention. Their meanings are closely intertwined.

When something is *said*, words are uttered (whether through waves in the air or patterns of rays from the surface of paper does not matter here) which have certain effects. How widely and generally, or how narrowly and specifically, are we to take these effects? Looked at closely enough, they are never the same for two readers or for the same reader twice. Looked at undiscriminately enough, they are much the same always. (What other words come with them, what the situation is, and so on, must, of course, be kept in mind throughout.) Whether for practical purposes we account them *the same* depends upon two things: upon our purpose and upon the respects in which they are the same and different.

All this we all know in a sense very well. Yet we endlessly talk and frequently think as if in forgetfulness of it. We assert that two phrases say the same or that they do not, as if that were something which turned on the phrases alone—in utter independence of who reads them and when and why and within what setting. Probably when we do this we are assuming a host of things: including a standard reader with some sort of normal purpose and a standard setting and range of situations. We would be very hard put to it, indeed, if we had to be specific about these assumptions. But we are rather suspiciously careful not to explore them. We take them for granted and people are only too ready, in fact, to grant them. We seem even to suffer from a fear that questioning these assumptions will lead to no good, will shake the foundations of communication perhaps and let anyone with any word mean anything he pleases.

This background fear is empty, though its roots are perhaps deep in man's first speculations about language when he first began to experience its magical powers. Nobody perhaps, after reflection, now believes that words have their meanings in their own right, as our bodies have their minds. We have replaced that old belief with another which looks much more plausible but is as groundless. It is the belief in a sort of compact or agreement between all good users of the language to use words only in certain limited ways. It is true enough that we do behave with words *as if* some such compact ruled their uses. But the explanation in terms of usage agreement is wrong. The stability of the language has other causes. It comes from our experience of the ways in which words are tied up with one another. A language is a fabric which holds itself together. It is a fabric which, for the most part brokenly and confusedly but sometimes with startling and heartbreaking clarity, reflects the fabric of universals which is our world.

There is no risk whatever, then, in questioning the assumptions which make us say two phrases must or can't mean the same. And to be able to question them—not as a piece of linguistic theory but in practice as they come up—is a large part of the art of reading. We ought to be incessantly ready to ask of two phrases which seem "more or less to mean the same" just wherein (and for whom) are their effects alike and wherein different. And to decide whether—for the purpose in hand, which is what the whole passage is swayed by—the differences are relevant. If they are not, we can be indifferent to them. But with a slight change in the purpose they might become very important. Any ruling on such points which does not take the purpose into account *is* an attack on language. We ought to fear pedants who cry, "But that *isn't* the meaning of the word," much more than any rash or wanton innovator.

One other quirk in our behavior with phrases said to mean the same is also perhaps connected with remnants of magical beliefs. My Basic English version of the Aristotle passage, for example, says, *more or less,* what the Oxford translation says. In comparing two versions our minds sometimes perform this antic: instead of regarding them as two sets of words which in some ways have similar outcomes, in other ways different, we may suddenly find ourselves thinking, of one, "So *that* is what he was trying to say!" We are then likely to follow it up with, "It's a pity he didn't say it!" In extreme cases (and none such will probably occur in this instance) what happens is that the reader then identifies the thought with the *words* of the version he prefers. They become for him what the other passage is (inefficiently) saying, and he makes no comparison between meanings. He is helped in this by the chief regular systematic ambiguity of *say:* We say certain words and then *they* may say more than we are saying with them. These three *say's* say very different things—as we see if we replace them with more explicit phrases: We give voice to certain words and then they may be taken to mean more than we have in mind.

c. There are few important words which are not in varying patterns systematically ambiguous; *say* is typical. These *regular* shifts of sense as a rule give us little trouble in reading, but all untechnical words also *change* their meanings from place to place in discourse under the pressures of the purpose and the setting. And these Sense Content Changes, because they are so closely related to the purpose, are specially important to follow. We need not *notice* them and usually do not; but we must submit to them if we are not to misread. But because they are made against the resistance of the word's normal relations with other words, the likelihood of misreading is considerable. If we accept the change we will probably never be aware that it occurred. If we don't, then we will either boggle at the passage and find discontinuity or nonsense in it, or more probably we will go on happily assured of a meaning which a better reader would see was not intended. If an author's purposes leads him to change the meanings of too many words, people do not go on reading them. He becomes too hard to follow—unless he is so great a writer and so adroit in relating his changes to one another that he reshapes language for us. Shakespeare is the great example. The interest of what he is doing has made us accept an experimental handling of language which otherwise would have been unreadable. He wrote, though, for an audience which was very skillful in interpretation. Thus language protects itself

It is possible to collect examples of important words pushed out of their normal uses by various pressures. The great dictionaries contain such collections in an early, as yet little organized, stage of development. By drawing on these collections and appending paraphrases to show how words which in one place say one thing in another say another, tables and exercises affording unlimited opportunities for comparisons can be prepared. It might well be thought that these would provide the best means of improving reading. The traditional grammar books, however, by failing to teach the lessons they intended, have taught us another, of more value perhaps. We do not learn linguistic points from tables and examples; we learn through using the language—not in exercises but in the pursuit of a meaning we are seeking for a specific not a general purpose. In other words, the desire to improve our reading, worthy though it is, won't help us unless it operates through the work of puzzling out a passage because we care what it says. The persistencies of effects—no matter how well we make them overlap—will not systematize themselves into experience (knowledge that returns as power) unless they are heated by an immediate sustaining interest.

d. But interest, the great weldor (as the weldors spell it now, a *welder* being a machine: compare *actor* and *sailor*) of universals, is also the great logic-breaker. If we want to, or if something in us wants to establish something, we grow blind to any thwarting idea, however familiar it is or however obvious it might otherwise be; we deform our distinctions and connections to meet our aim, commit every sort of injustice and make the very word "argument" a term of derision. Mercury, the interpreter and messenger of Heaven, was also the patron god of rogues.

Most mistakes in reading look willful—not only to the man in the other camp but to the impartial eye. Few of them are, but it is harder to be fair-minded in reading than we know, and a passion for the truth is misinterpretation's favorite guise. . . .

———

A well-designed inquiry into the resourcefulness of the words which most occasion misunderstandings would amount to a study of metaphysic. (I don't know a subject in which study of the resourcefulness of its key terms doesn't amount to the subject, properly studied, itself.) It is perfectly compatible with close attention to selected passages from great books. I would say it required that. But it would be metaphysic approached from a different angle. We would not be attempting to show our students (much less tell them) what Plato or Aristotle really meant. That is a job for a superhuman historian of human thought a million years hence perhaps. We would be trying to help them to see for themselves some of the more important things the great texts may mean. And, since misunderstandings and corruptions of their thought may have played a great part in our tradition, we would be including these also. We would, I suggest, be giving little time to refutation or to the formal logical technique of philosophical proof or contention. Training in that is best given within a technically rigidified vocabulary; and we would above all try to defend our pupils from supposing that one philosophical view must necessarily be irreconcilable with another. This last amounts to throwing aside what has traditionally been held to be the chief business of philosophers. If you think it too drastic I can only confess that my own commerce with the disputatious has left me with a sad conviction that when you are refuting a view you become too busy to see what it is.

What we would aim at is a knowledge of *how* and *why* these central intellectual terms—*being, have, cause, connection, same,* and the like—can shift their meanings and thus give rise to varied misunderstandings. To develop the spatial metaphor here, which being all but unavoidable should be made as explicit as possible, all these words wander in many directions in this figurative space of meaning. But they wander *systematically,* as do those other wanderers, the Plane's. By fixing a limited number of positions, meanings, for them, we may help ourselves to plot their courses. But we should not persuade ourselves that they must be at one or other of these marked points. The laws of their motions are what we need to know: their dependence upon the positions of the other words that should be taken into account with them.

To early astronomers and travellers the wanderings of the planets may have seemed troublesome. Or, more probably, portentous. Full of significance indeed they were! When understood they became the key to all the other motions in the heavens that we have yet ascertained or conjectured. A similar human preference for "fixities" and "definites" and "absolutes" is perhaps the source of some of the opposition which these suggestions may encounter.

I have said that the wandering—the resourcefulness—of these central terms of discourse is systematic. I ought to say a word or two more on that; to be brief, the same misunderstandings endlessly recur. Few people ever commit a new and original misunderstanding. Misinterpretations run to type, to a small number of types. An adequate study of one intellectual mistake can be made to illumine countless other fields where invitations to similar mistakes are offered. It is this which makes insight into *the patterns of resource* able to knit different studies together. The same problems in interpretation arise in them all. We do not at present benefit as we should from the limited variety of our stupidities. This may be, in part, because we have not developed appropriate exercises. Are we perhaps like mathematicians who had never thought of using the working of examples as a technique of instruction?

"The Resourcefulness of Words," from *Speculative Instruments* (1955).

II

The Philosophy of Rhetoric

Theory and practice defined one another for Richards: one grows from the other; each feeds the other. His pragmatism demanded that a theory be brought to the test. It is no surprise, then, to learn that *The Philosophy of Rhetoric,* though it was published first, was written after *Interpretation in Teaching,* a book Richards hoped would do for prose what *Practical Criticism* had done for poetry.

All those who consider that they are turning away from Aristotle and the rhetoric of classical antiquity do so in the name of a "new" rhetoric. Most New Rhetorics fade quickly because they are focused too narrowly or they are co-opted, serving only to revivify what they aimed to supplant. Richards' "New Rhetoric"—he used the phrase—was to be micro, not macro; heuristic, not taxonomic. He made it part of his program that rhetoric would have to "take charge of the criticism of its own assumptions," not borrow them "ready-made." This self-critical stance, the reflection on principles, is what he meant by "philosophy." These assumptions concerned language, of course, and the most notable contribution Richards made here was his theory of metaphor. (I have not included the well-known disquisition, but readers who are unfamiliar with the tenor/vehicle model should read chapters 5 and 6 of *The Philosophy of Rhetoric.* Richards discusses tenor/vehicle in a semiotic context in "Powers and Limits of Signs"; see p. 212 in this volume.)

Of equal importance is his "contextual theorem of meaning." The claim that the New Critics believed poems should be considered as "words on the page" is meaningless unless one takes into account what they understood by that phrase; insofar as they followed I. A. Richards, they did not mean that words have no referents or that texts have no contexts! Richards saw that

Freud's importance for criticism lay in the theory of interpretation. And he cites the idea of "overdetermination" in his attack on the "Proper Meaning Superstition."

A rhetoric that provided for the critique of its principles could then guide the study of *how words work*. (Those who prefer now to speak of "production" instead of "creation" might find that characterization of rhetoric provocative.) Richards also held that rhetoric should be "a study of misunderstanding and its remedies." He never disdained medical metaphors in his philosophy or his pedagogy, a practice which could remind us that medical diagnosis is one of the chief paradigms for hermeneutics. The interpretation of *misreading* was an important prologomenon to the teaching of reading. This is precisely Schleiermacher's point of departure in his hermeneutics; indeed, Richards' theory of reading is through and through a hermeneutic. Richards never refers to Schleiermacher and seldom mentions the philosophers of German Romanticism; but of course the main channel for those ideas is Coleridge who, with Plato and Peirce had the greatest influence on Richards' theories of language and learning, of reading, translation, and interpretation.

Richards suggests a third working definition of rhetoric as "the art by which discourse is adapted to its end." He sets about specifying kinds of ends, exploring the fact that in the triadic perspective ends are means. The "third" required in order to study the relationship of ends and means is *purpose*. Some contemporary critics have declared that Richards is out of date because of an allegedly elitist focus on the self. The corrective to this misconception is to be found in his insistence that the self and its purposes are necessarily apprehended in social contexts. From the earliest books in which he explicitly stated his view that "language is a social product" to the very late meditation on the powers and limits of the sign, Richards held that the self is never merely private: "Like the words in a sentence we are meaningless unless we take our senses from one another."

In some of the selections here, it is notable that "instrument" has begun to supplant "machinery," because it represents more clearly the ideas of mediation and interpretation. Instrumentality is central to Coleridge's theory of Imagination and his philosophy of language. Richards has begun to concentrate on how the idea of the coalescence of subject and object can help us form the concept of forming, the concept of meaning as emerging in a process of interpretation. These different points of emphasis—on mediation, instrumentality, process—are dramatically represented in the notes and glosses Richards prepared for the second edition of *Science and Poetry* (1926), when it was reissued as *Poetries and Sciences* (1970).

5

The First Three Liberal Arts

The teaching they gave to their pupils was ready but rough. For they used to suppose that they trained people by imparting to them not the art but its products, as though anyone professing that he would impart a form of knowledge to obviate pain in the feet, were then not to teach a man the art of shoemaking, or the sources whence he can acquire anything of the kind, but were to present him with several pairs of shoes of all sorts: for he has helped him to meet his need, but has not imparted to him any art.

Aristotle, *De Sophisticis Elenchis*

Less by design than from the nature, history and life of its subject, this treatise has grown into three parts which correspond roughly to ancient provinces of thought. Rhetoric, Grammar and Logic—the first three liberal Arts, the three ways to intelligence and a command of the mind that met in the Trivium, meet here again. And though each is for us today cumbered with much deadfall and much obsolete technical tackle which we must shift from the path, neither the general problem nor the plan of attack can be new. To orientate, to equip, to prepare, to encourage, to provoke, a mental traveller to advance by his own energies in whatever region may be his to explore; to make him think for himself *and* make him able to do so sanely and successfully, has always been the aim of a civilizing education. How to hand back the gains of the more experienced to the less experienced in the least hampering and most available form is the general problem. And, since language must be the medium, the three traditional modes of the study of language keep or renew their importance. They meet and mingle incessantly; they cannot, as we shall see in detail, be separated without frustration, and separation has historically been the most frequent cause of failure. But still, Rhetoric, Grammar and Logic, if we set aside their repulsive terminologies and associations, are the headings under which to arrange what the student we hope to help needs most to study.

The prime obstacle in general education is a feeling of helplessness before the unintelligible. Every problem is new to the mind which first meets it and

Interpretation in Teaching (1938), Introduction.

it is baffling until he can recognize in it something which he has met and dealt with already. The all important difference between the mind which can clear itself by thought and the mind which remains bewildered and can proceed only by burying the difficulty in a formula—retained, at best, by mere rote memory—is in this power to recognize the new problem as, in part, an old conquest. Language, with its inexhaustible duplications (which here are duplicities), ceaselessly presents to us the old as though it were new, familiar ideas in novel disguises, understood distinctions as fresh opportunities for confusion, already assimilated combinations as unforeseeable conjunctions. The teacher meets with all this whenever he reads anything which stretches his intelligence; the pupil meets with it all the time, and if he is being well taught he should be expecting it and enjoying the sense of increasing power that his progressive mastery of it can afford. For this growth in power is, fundamentally, the vitalizing incentive with which education builds.

The beginner, in studying the most elementary matters, is doing nothing which is (or should be) *for him* any simpler than what we are doing when we try to follow a new and difficult author. And we can only help him in a fashion parallel to that in which we ourselves would wish to be helped or to help ourselves: that is, not by supplying the "right answer" to the difficulty (with some unexamined criterion of "right answers") but by making clearer what the difficulty itself was, so that when we meet it again we shall not have to "remember the answer" but shall see what it must be from our understanding of the question. A learner at all stages learns—for serious purposes—only in so far as he is a thinker, and the difficulties of thinking are never new. We overcome them—in elementary mechanics, and in the Theory of Relativity, in learning to read words of one syllable and in reading *Ulysses,* alike—by taking account of them, by seeing what we are doing and setting aside other things which we should not be trying to do there. We solve them finally by discovering how much more simple the task was than we had hitherto supposed.

As language, in its multiplicity of modes, and our always incomplete mastery of them, is the source of most of our preventable stultifications, so the study of how language works and fails is our great opportunity.

With reason did Coleridge dilate upon "the advantages which language alone, at least which language with incomparably greater ease and certainty than any other means, presents to the instructor of impressing modes of intellectual energy so constantly, so imperceptibly . . . as to secure in due time the formation of a second nature." Well did he urge his generation "to value earnestly and with a practical seriousness a means, already prepared for us by nature and society, of teaching the young mind to think well and wisely by the same unremembered process and with the same never forgotten results, as those by which it is taught to speak and converse" (*Biographia Litcraria,* II, p. 117). We cannot think, as Coleridge thought, about language, without recognizing that he is not overstating its powers. How to use them, how to develop the instructive possibilities of this universal switchboard, how, by investigating them, to improve, at the same time, our command of all the interconnections of thought, nonverbal as well as verbal, is our problem. We are better placed for this than Coleridge's contemporaries were, because we have come to see still more clearly how central the fact of language is.

The unintelligibility of a problem may sometimes be due to lack of special experience, but most often it is due to the language in which the problem comes to us—or to our lack of experience with such language, or with the ways of language as such. As Sayce said, in his *Introduction to the Science of Language*, "If we are suddenly brought into contact with experts in a subject we have not studied, or dip into a book on an unfamiliar branch of knowledge, we seem to be listening to the meaningless sounds of a foreign tongue. The words used may not be technical words; but familiar words and expressions will bear senses and suggest ideas to those who use them which they will not bear to us." From this situation there are two escapes. Acquaintance with the special topic, and, which is more widely useful, a general readiness to expect words to change their senses with their contexts, together with an aptitude for divining their probable meanings even in unfamiliar fields. And this last, which involves intelligence in its highest form, comes only from reflection upon our experience with language in fields with which we are already familiar.

To suppose that this necessary experience can be gained by mere practice with language, without reflective study of it, is an error which recurrently dominates education. Every great persistent error is perhaps a mode of escape from worse errors; in this case, recognition of the futility of those studies in grammar and logic which used to be inflicted upon the helpless pupil, is behind the widespread current opinion that it is better just to make the pupil read and write as much as possible rather than to waste his time so. . . . I am not sure, though, that the results obtained by even the dreariest early 19th Century drillings in parsing and the syllogism did not compare favourably with current output. But the comparison is not fair. There were, for one thing, fewer pupils. Setting this aside, however, we can see that these now obsolete forms of language study, if they sometimes did some incidental good, flagrantly violated the first principle of education—the principle of intelligibility which I have begun by stressing. We may recall how even a Milton complained that the Universities presented to "unlearned novices, at their first coming, the most intellective abstracts of Logic and Metaphysics."

In place of insight into language, they put subservience to rules—to rules which could not appear to the learner as anything but inexplicable arbitrary impositions from without. The Rules of Grammar and of Logic and of Good Usage were nothing but Orders, Commands laid down to be obeyed, utterly mysterious and incomprehensible both as to their origin and their justification. As such they were an outrage to every mind which realized—as every mind, however young, realizes when it is awake—that it must be its own keeper. "It is not only possible, but necessary," wrote Charles Hoole, in his *New Discovery of the Old Art of Teaching School,* with a flash of insight he never managed to put into effect, "to make children understand their tasks, from their very first entrance into learning; seeing that they must everyone bear his own burden, and not rely upon their fellows altogether."

It is no part of these proposals that anything at all resembling the traditional Grammar or Logic should be reintroduced into education. Nothing in the theory of the uses of language should be admitted which cannot, as it is admitted, be made satisfyingly intelligible. I hope to show however that it is possible, even under this restriction, to include much more of the supposedly recondite parts of the subject than most modern educationists have imagined.

These problems: as to why we may say one thing but not another, why one word or phrase is "right" and another "wrong," why one "reason" is fitter than another, have an absorbing interest, even for very young minds, an interest which none of the usual methods for damping it quite succeed in extinguishing. Granted that the Logic, Grammar and Rhetoric of the Manuals can go near to putting it out and can frighten all but the most obstinate intelligences from free speculation on these matters (and most others) for the rest of their lives, this is not the fault of the problems but of the fashion in which inquiry into them is discouraged. The speculative interest—which is thought at work on its own most urgent needs—is often far stronger in the pupil than in the teacher, who cannot afford to be too patently out of his depth. . . .

There can be no pretence, of course, that how language works can be fully explained. And there is much to be said for insisting early that in this as in everything else we have to start from as well as work towards the unintelligible. Evidently we cannot understand our foundations in anything; nor can we fly outside the Universe. We must accept our fundamental facts as unexplained, and we never reach a view which does not generate new questions. Thought about language keeps these limits constantly present to us; and there is nothing paralyzing about that kind of unintelligibility. An aeroplane must have a base as well as a ceiling. What is paralyzing is the frequent occurrence in our minds of unsuspected pockets of another kind of unintelligibility. Our thought is riddled with unnecessary vacancies where problems, which we could and should have thought through, have been encased, unexplored, in a phrase. Thereafter, since argument is very largely, and rightly, an exchanging and substitution of phrases, all kinds of confusion and distortion are made possible.

These blank and treacherous pockets of incomprehension must occur in proportion as we leave important and life-bringing questions unconsidered, or seal them with a fraudulently conclusive "answer." And the most important and most generally vitalizing of all questions are those which concern language. They are needed, not only for this particular problem or that, but for the reasonable conduct and discipline of all thinking. All instruction through words is, of course, a process of answering such questions more or less indirectly. Whether we are talking *about* words and their meanings or merely *with* them, we are finding our way through an endless series of alternatives between meanings. We may choose so quickly that the other possibilities never come into clear consciousness, but it is a disastrous error of oversimplification to suppose that we are not choosing, or that there are no alternatives balancing against one another in our interpretation. Fast or slow, thought, in this sense, is questioning. We may, and usually do, restrict the term "question" to the slower cases where the choice would be undecided without a supporting rally of further considerations. But whether the process is swift or leisurely, implicit and summary or explicit and discursive, our interpretation is never a mere taking up of an isolated self-complete and single meaning. For the meaning is itself a process of growth and the outcome of a balance between possibilities of being.

The ordinary answering of such merely local questions about language as all use of language entails, is not enough. By answering, say, sixty specific problems in the use of language that happen to be parallel, we shall not have made it easier to answer a sixty-first parallel problem *unless* the respects in which the problems are parallel have been reflected upon. Unless, that is, we have replaced the specific problems by a general problem. But the general problem must not merely replace them in space and time; it must genuinely represent, embody, offer them again, it must be a natural outgrowth and development from them. In understanding it we must know that we are understanding them also and see how we are doing this. Here, as we all recognize with sorrow, is the difficulty; and near it opens the gate to that Paradise of Teachers which notoriously so much resembles the Paradise of Fools. So easy is it to put general views in the place of particular perceptions—without the one having, necessarily, any effective connection whatever with the other. How *to generalize,* as opposed to how to learn general formulas, how to pass from a momentary triumph over a particular language-problem back to a perception of the problem *in itself* rather than of its answer, and so to achieve the power to recognize and meet (though *not* necessarily to classify) the problem again when it rises in a new instance, that is our problem here—and, I insist, not a whit more difficult essentially than the schoolboy's task in seeing what sort of a sum he has been set and how he is to tackle it.

The way to the generalizing power, or better, to the general insight that we seek, does not lie through classification or a listing of uniformities. This is another grand traditional error. Catalogues of predicaments and arguments, of typical fallacies with representative examples, tables of grammatical constructions with their appropriate breaches, classifications of tropes and modes and genres—these may have done some good; but time and effort have shown often enough that they will not give us what we want. They look like the fumbling first steps of young sciences: what we want is the further development of what is already an advanced art, the art of intellectual discernment. For this reason—and here I am probably turning my blows from dead donkeys to a live enough lion—educational psychology is not what we want. That, too, is still a toddling infant science and our ordinary tact and skill and common sense are far in advance of the utmost reach of its present purview. I would not (and could not if I would) discourage the labors of those who are enquiring methodically, in the psychological laboratories, into the learning process, into memorization, the conditions of retention and undistorted recall, into I.Q.s and other factors, and transferences of ability; into typology, needs, motivation and the rest. May they succeed beyond all expectations—but would they even *then* have found out anything which for practical purposes (as apart from theoretical interest) would add to our present powers? I wish I could hope so. What I have seen of this work makes me think that it will yield increasingly exact but *increasingly abstract* statements of laws with whose general form we are already sufficiently acquainted to be able to use them in practice, though we need not necessarily be able to state them. That these refinements will have much direct bearing upon teaching I doubt. Refinements in the Theory of Gravitation make no difference whatever to the way we throw stones. The sort of psychological laws we use in teaching are like the physical laws we use in playing baseball; if we knew them more precisely we still would not use the refinements. The complexity of the conditions would make the attempt unprofitable. *Theoretically,* on the other hand, it may happen—I believe it is happening—that exact experiment and abstract reflection, in that branch of biology which we call psychology and in its other branches, may make immense changes in our whole *conception* of education. The changed conception may well change our aim but we should still try to attain that aim by ways that we know about already—that we know about, at least, when we wake up to ask ourselves what we are doing.

Our errors in teaching technique can be corrected more easily, and more safely, I believe, from our own awareness of how we ourselves learn and think, than from the recommendations of educational psychology, which at present only confirm some parts of common knowledge. And where, as with some work on intelligence-testing, psychology offers to correct this vaguer common knowledge, difficult and unsettled matters of interpretation enter. The psychology and the common knowledge may not be judging the same things. There is therefore danger in attempting to make practical immediate use of psychological findings,—a danger that was illustrated in the days when the mental testers laid simple uncritical stress upon the speed with which tasks could be performed, as though problems could be identified merely through their formulation in a supposed standard context.

I have touched here upon educational psychology for three reasons. To explain why in what follows I shall be attempting no direct applications from it. Secondly, because it has recently had an increasing place in the training and studies of teachers, and I believe that they could learn whatever they learn from it that will be useful to them *as teachers* much more easily without it, and their time is badly needed for other studies and *for reflection.* Thirdly, because the replacement of insight into the learning process by a rote acquaintance with the jargon of the subject and its typical formulations is such an excellent example of the disease of abstractionism with which the whole undertaking is perennially afflicted. I know no sadder or more disheartening reading than some of the educational theory which leans upon psychology— unless perhaps the dreary pages of those masters of Rhetoric who thought themselves perfectly acquainted with the subject when they had learnt only to name some of its tools.

The direction then in which an enhancement of general intelligence and understanding must be sought is not in any introduction of "intellective abstracts," whether of Educational Psychology or of Rhetoric or of Logic or of Grammar, or of any other section of Pedagogy, into teaching. The history of the subject shows how great the danger of such blundering is. We may compare the odd fashion in which Prosody, Philology, and Phonetics, for example, followed Grammar in climbing from the humble handmaid station they originally held. They came to rival, and sometimes to dominate, the literature in the enjoyment of which they were to assist. Back to their combs* (or, if they are haughty, out among the sciences) with them all! And so too with the study of interpretation if it pretends to set itself up as a rival to the general practice of understanding and distracts the student from his work—which is to interpret, not to discourse on interpretation.

So, in what follows, I beg that the theoretical expatiations on interpretation, its assumptions, its conditions and its risks, be not confused with the practical exercises designed to improve students in their performance. I shall be analyzing and attempting to diagnose hundreds of representative misinterpretations; but I do not propose that such anatomizings should be imposed in teaching,—though they should be induced in our pupils' minds. If they were imposed in instruction, that fact would confess that the right plan had not been found. Our aim, to take the obvious examples, is not to produce Logicians, or Grammarians, but sound thinkers and clear writers, a different thing altogether.

But subject to this caution—which is appallingly easy to forget—a training in Rhetoric, Grammar and Logic, *as Arts* not as sciences, a training which is at present almost entirely lacking in the curriculum, is what is most needed. It may especially take the place of much of the unchecked perusal and undirected scribbling in which time is now spent. To expect those to write who have developed no power either to read or to think is both foolish and cruel. It is, at best, only encouraging a malady to which we are all too prone. To quote an unpublished note that Coleridge wrote in the margin of an essay by Southey, "The Pen is the tongue of a systematic dream—a Somniloquist. The sunshine comparative power, the distinct contra-distinguishing judgment of Realities as other than Thoughts is suspended!—During this state of continuous, not singlemindedness, but *one-side*-mindedness, writing is a manual somnambulism—the somnial magic superinduced on, without suspending, the active powers of the mind." But the business of a teacher is to

---

*Richards enjoyed deploying the language of mountaineering. *Combs* picks up the metaphor in *climbing*: it derives from the Welsh *cwm* and means a narrow, ravinelike valley.—ED

awaken, to bring "the sunshine comparative power" out of its clouds of dream, to stir his pupil into distinguishing between thought and fancy, into caring seriously whether he understands what he reads and says or not. We have to help him to know when he has understood and when he has not, and to prepare him, when he has not, to face and defeat the unintelligible with his own awakened intelligence.

Rhetoric I take to be "the art by which discourse is adapted to its end." This makes it very inclusive. . . . The most *general* task of the Art would be to distinguish the different sorts of ends, or aims, for which we use language, to teach how to pursue them separately and how to reconcile their diverse claims when, as is usual, the use of language is mixed. That our uses of language can be divided under several different main heads, no one will doubt; though just which divisions are the most illuminating and convenient in teaching may be a puzzling matter. This is that question of "the classification of the Language Functions" which makes a brief and unsatisfactory appearance among the preliminaries of many works on general linguistic.

How many things does language do? It is possible to make a very baffling tangle (Stern, for example, in his valuable *Meaning and Change of Meaning,* does so) out of the different answers: that it records or *communicates* thought, *expresses* mental processes, *symbolizes* states of affairs, *promotes* human cooperation, and so on. "The interrelations of the functions are not known in detail," observes Stern. They *cannot,* of course, be known, until the functions themselves have been more clearly determined and distinguished. Which we take to be fundamental and how we arrange the others, are not matters to be settled until we have decided *why* we are distinguishing them, for what purposes. This first language problem, like a hundred later ones, is apt to be stated in a way which from the start prevents any progress. Language has infinite uses, and which main categories we introduce to facilitate study of these infinite uses, depends upon the proposed scope and aim of our study. The psychologist, the jurist, the social historian, the logician, the lexicographer, the semanticist tracing the history of sense changes, the critic, and the pedagogue will use different principles of classification. The apple grower establishes *grades* among his fruit for marketing purposes which are of no significance whatever to the plant physiologist.

For our purposes the last thing we wish to do (literally the last thing) is to introduce a classification to be taught and relied on. To introduce one too early would interfere with one of the most healthy exercises that the student can indulge in. It is easy to offer him passages in a way which will force him to work out for himself some of the implications of the perception that a plain neutral statement of fact is in some way different from an appeal to passion. To start out, *in teaching,* from a division between, say, pure scientific impersonal or neutral statement, and emotive utterance which expresses and evokes states of feeling, is a good way of helping him to encyst, and so to dodge or hide from himself, just the very things whose differences and connections he should be puzzling over. I mention this here as another example of the danger, throughout the subject, of supposing that instruction in linguistic theory (whether Rhetorical, Logical or Grammatical) can replace insight into, self-discovery of and thus understanding of, the matters with which it is concerned. (If I insist too often upon this, the fault will be readily forgiven me by those who realize what a new world that would be in which there was no need especially to remind ourselves of this failing!)

The general task of Rhetoric is to give, not by dogmatic formula but *by exercise in comparisons,* an insight into the different modes of speech and their exchanges and disguises. The chief divisions of these general fields for comparison may be: statement, full and explicit, or condensed (by abstraction, ambiguity or implication, the hint, the aposiopesis); statement literal or direct, and indirect (by metaphor, simile, comparison, parallel etc.); suasion, open (from appeal to cajolery) or concealed (either as mere statement or as mere ornament) and so on.

But we should do little good by explaining this, even with examples. All our pupils know it already. What they do not know is how to distinguish and meet the varying modes of language *in practice.* The theory of the divisions is only useful when it comes in later to aid them in noticing explicitly what they are already doing—for good or ill.

The more special problems of Rhetoric have to do with the Figures of Speech—about which current theory is oddly out of date, and our practice most deceiving. Experiments with figures easily awaken a raging curiosity which, if it is suitably fed and not choked with formulas, can cut deep and spread wide. Well led, it should be able to fertilize almost any topic, redeeming it from the status of desert to be crossed to that of region to be cultivated.

Some figures of speech can be translated into relatively nonfigurative language with ease, others only with difficulty and some perhaps not at all. Such translation exercises (if used with discretion; they can be paralyzing) are an invaluable device for redirecting attention to what is being said and how it is being understood. They lead naturally and insensibly into Logic. I might equally say that Logic, for our purposes, is just a more thorough inquiry into these translations. For example, if we try to say what is said in one metaphor by means of another metaphor (e.g., try replacing the water-figure at the end of the last paragraph by a fire or light-figure) we find ourselves really studying in the most practical and immediate way the process of *abstraction* itself. And to ask whether or not a parallel, e.g.

Meaning is an arrow which reaches its mark when least encumbered with feathers

really supports the view it is introduced to state, or whether it weakens it unnecessarily, is a better exercise in argument than any that formal instruction in the syllogism provides. Generalization is systematic *abbreviated* parallelling, and choice among similes or metaphors is chiefly a matter of rapid recognition of likes and discrimination between unlikes. Mathematics and the sciences, so often praised, and rightly, for the training in Logic they provide, are the leisurely, analyzed, explicitly recorded, developments of the very same processes that, well or ill, operate in the main mode of metaphor.

For all thought is sorting, and we can think of nothing without taking it as of a sort. Logic is the Art or discipline of managing our sortings and it is of little use to study it only in an abstract science, if we have no command over the play of metaphor where logic should most intimately steer our thought. The logic required is of course subtler than that needed in a prepared abstract science, but if this is our peril it is at the same time our hope of remedy. Sentimental folk who "like to think" that the figures of speech (being "imaginative," sometimes) are beyond the reach of logic, may consider again what they are saying. They have probably some view of logic which makes it less than "the ethics of thinking," a principle of order upon which all good life, including all imaginative life, depends.

Rhetoric, then, leads naturally into Logic. But where does Grammar come in? Being, for *our* purposes, nothing but *the study of the cooperation of words with one another in their contexts,* it comes in everywhere. But Grammar is notoriously the subject in which it is hardest to remember what we are studying, in which a focus upon detail most blurs the background and the formation of opinion most occults the very assumptions which set the local problem. Nowhere more than in Grammar are utterly diverse inquiries likely to be mistaken for one another, and the right task be abandoned for others which are irrelevant though identical in their verbal formulation. These are reasons for despair of Grammar, as an educational discipline, if we do not recognize and deal with them in teaching. Recognized frankly and entered into carefully, they are, for this very reason, an irreplaceable opportunity for promoting insight, by natural development, into the key secrets of the use of language. The resentment, too, which all good minds feel against the futilities, unintelligible dogmas, and arbitrary rulings of so much traditional grammatical teaching is a useful handle.

A good way to arouse a lively interest in Grammar is to begin with specimens of the outrages of past grammarians, inviting and guiding some attempts to explain how such absurdities could ever have come about. What were they trying to do and what did they think they were doing? From this we may pass to a separation of the different kinds of inquiries which may masquerade as Grammar by using a common apparatus of questions; and thence to an understanding of the control of the setting upon interpretation. These are not difficult steps, though in an abstract exposition they would seem an intolerably confusing and recondite affair. So an anatomical description apart from suitable sections and preparations to consult will seem beyond the wit of man to follow.

With suitable examples by which to display these divergent interests and their contexts in operation, we can exploit a natural skill in interpretation that is as common as the developed capacity for sustained meditation in abstract terms is rare. More perhaps with Grammar than even with any other branch of teaching, we have to distinguish between ability to see the point in the actual (which is all that we wish to develop) and ability to describe it in the abstract—a gift hitherto of no great service even to professional grammarians.

These, of course, are sentiments that all, including the worst culprits in the history of Grammar, would applaud. "Don't bother the boys with the reasons! Give them *the rules,* with examples, and make them learn them and apply them!"—that is the recipe they would derive from them and *that* is the plausible program against which I most wish to protest. For it exploits a perilous equivocation in the sense of *Rules* (with *Law, Order and its other partial synonyms*) which goes right through every branch of language study; and will be found, in fact, dominating the most fundamental issues in biology. It may seem a far cry from the elementary teaching of Grammar to the problem of the constitutive laws of development of an organism (and the free-will, determinism, vitalism, mechanism, cross-purposed controversy); but when we learn anything we are quite obviously exemplifying biologic laws. How we suppose we learn, then (and thus how we propose to teach), is not independent of our theories, or assumptions, as to the process of growth and the laws of development. And though there is learning which may be regarded as a mere yielding to repetitive pressure from without, a mere moulding by an external law, which comes to us as a dark rule, still the learning that is fruitful—in such a matter as the development of the most highly organized of man's activities, the control of his thought through language—is better treated as growth from within; and *that* feels, as we make it, like insight. It feels not like an alien dark compulsion but like an enlightening discovery of our own making. The only *rules* in intellectual discipline that a teacher may willingly make use of are records of the pupil's own helpful self-determinations.

These, which are today the commonplaces of pedagogy in other subjects, are, for reasons upon which it is very profitable to speculate, still usually ignored in language study. We still here attempt to impose the forms upon the matter instead of encouraging the matter to develop for itself its appropriate forms. And the "matter" is here just the activity of self-discovering thought, which of all activities least deserves to be so distrustfully and disdainfully treated.

For, as a prime guiding principle, we have to remember that here, as in all teaching but more so, all that we can do is to provide opportunities for an extension and refinement of skills which are inexplicably, unimaginably and all-but-triumphantly, successful already. In the Confucian *Chung Yung* the clue to the self-completing growth of the mind is given in the aphorism:

In hewing an axe handle, in hewing an axe handle, the model for it is in our hand.

So here in this instance of language-study, the pupil, however stupid and inert he may seem, has already somehow learnt to talk, which is much more than we could teach him to do if he did not do it for himself! He comes to us with these uncanny powers already highly developed, and we have only, if we can, to help him to develop them a little further.

That, at present, we so often do no more than put unnecessary obstacles in his way is explained largely by our own unhappy histories. They are mostly the obstacles we encountered ourselves and did not really overcome as often as we may later suppose. But it would be painful to dwell upon this. A contributory cause is the influence, on the study of the native language, of procedures that should belong only to the quite different business of learning a foreign language. We do not enough realize what an artificial operation the grafting of a foreign language on a mind by systematic teaching is. Historically, Grammar has very largely developed as an aid in this violent grafting process. As such its schematizations are of no *direct* service in increasing our command over our own language.

What a book does, if it is good enough, can hardly be done otherwise and talking about it is seldom helpful. In contrast, how it manages itself is an eminently discussable and interesting matter. Questions of *how* are, as it were, anatomy, physiology, and warily speaking, psychology. But what is done is a moral issue, or better, one of those recognitions out of which moralities arise.

From a letter to the *New York Review of Books,* Dec. 3, 1970.

6

The Essential and the Accidental, and the Freedom in Definition

> Man, proud man,
> Drest in a little brief authority,
> Most ignorant of what he's most assur'd,
> His glassy essence, like an angry ape,
> Plays such fantastic tricks before high heaven
> As make the angels weep; who, with our spleens,
> Would all themselves laugh mortal.
>
> *Measure for Measure**

The reason for cultivating reflection upon the process of abstracting is that only so can we improve discrimination between what is essential and what is accidental in a matter.

The flounderings of the protocols† show how frequently people do not know what they are talking about: in this sense, that they cannot separate *the properties which determine the thing they are talking about* from other properties which may or may not belong to it *without* its being thereby any less itself. They wobble in a fatal indecision as to which exactly of the things they happen to know *about* a thing they will include *in* it, and constantly use accidents, or inessential properties, as defining "its very nature." The process, then, of clearing up their views must be that of giving them increased power to form new and better arranged *things* to think about. Or, rather, of making them recognize that what they mean by a word is within their own control—not given them inexorably by the language. And that in their choices here they create the things they are talking about. For example, every sentence

---

*This passage—especially the phrase "glassy essence"—was a great favorite with Peirce, for whom it was an emblem of the logic of necessity. (We cannot see ourselves seeing.) Richards offers an extended gloss of "glassy essence"—which he takes as a lens—in *Design for Escape* (1968), p. 46.—ED

†See note, p. 26. The protocols in *Interpretation in Teaching* come mostly from students at the Harvard Graduate School of Education in response to prose passages. They are not so complexly organized as those in *Practical Criticism,* but they provide points of departure for Richards' discussions of grammar, logic, and rhetoric.—ED

From *Interpretation in Teaching* (1938), chap. 23.

here may be confidently misread by those who wish to. "Create"? We do not create anything ever! "Its very nature"? As though things possessed natures of their own! "Not know what they are talking about"? Who does ever? And so on. . . .

What matters most in all such exercises is that the learner should be made to watch the consequences of his decisions, and see that what a word means (that is, here, what the *thing* is that he is talking about) depends upon the purpose in hand. It is no use expounding to him the difference between accidental, or contingent, and necessary, or essential, properties unless he sees that what is essential for one purpose is inessential for another and why. Thus many favorite ways of illustrating the difference do little good. If, as logicians have lately been fond of doing, we take our examples out of the exact sciences, or from those parts of them for which the problems of definition have been finally settled, we are likely to create an unhelpful impression that the task turns on *knowing* the answer, not on *finding* it. Thus, if we explain that "being a plane curve," "having its radii equal," and "having the angle in the segment subtending a diameter a right angle," are *essential* properties of a circle; but "having a diameter 3 inches long" is an *accident*, we will be illustrating the difference but may hide the reason. It suggests that circles *are* so; not that for the purposes of the geometer circles have been made so. And this often imports a notion of "correct meanings"—valid enough and for good reasons in the sciences—which is not valid and merely obstructive outside them. It is better to take some word like *man* or *beautiful* or *poetry* in place of *circle*, and try what happens with say,

> Human nature never changes
> Man is a creature of infinite variety

There is no "correct meaning" for man or human in such sentences. The task of interpreting them is that of finding out which meanings work best for which purposes. In other words, of trying various choices among properties which may be taken as essential to the meaning of *man* and seeing what happens with them.

Man is, in one way, better for such purposes than *beauty* or *poetry*. For it is not quite so likely as with other words that we will suppose that there is something which man *really is*, and that we could know what this is and thereby settle the question of his changeableness. But people do very frequently behave as though there were something which beauty *really is*, and another thing which poetry *really is*, and that doubts about questions using the words *beauty* and *poetry* are due to our ignorance about these things and not about our use of the words. . . . The peculiar paralysis which the mention of definitions and, still more, the discussion of them induces can be prevented, I believe, by stressing the purposive aspect of definitions. We want to do something and a definition is a means to doing it. If we want certain results, then we must use certain meanings (or definitions). But no definition has any authority apart from a purpose, or to bar us from other purposes. And yet they endlessly do so. Who can doubt that we are often deprived of very useful thoughts merely because the words which might express them are being temporarily preempted by other meanings? Or that a development is often frustrated merely because we are sticking to a former definition of no service to the new purpose?

The limitation of thought to successive moments, its discursive character, we can bear, . . . but that our thought, which is clear and in order one moment, should, in the next, be twisted, clouded, closed, merely because we are insufficiently supple in changing the meanings of our words, is harder to bear; for it is, in a large measure, unnecessary and remediable. Logic usually stresses the other aspect—the excessive ambiguity of words—but their excessive rigidity and obstinate attachments to inappropriate meanings should be at least equally noticed. It makes a happier starting point for a discussion.

Subject only to our purpose—which, I need hardly say, *includes communication*—we are free to define our words as we please. This, of course, applies also to the word "definition"; and I am availing myself of this freedom here. A first consequence is that there will be many different things which, for different purposes, will equally properly be called definitions. Logicians, who tend to neglect explicit discussion of purposes, usually attempt to restrict the word severely, and economize in their explanations. But a fairly full explanation is the only way to disperse the atmosphere of mystery, if not of hanky panky, which hangs over the topic. A statement of the connotation of a word is what is usually meant in Logic by a definition. I pass by the familiar troubles that afflict the question; "Does such a definition define a *word,* its *sense* or a *sort of things?*" noting only what an opportunity for exercises in the use of inverted commas it affords. Let us consider definitions by denotation, or exemplificatory definition.

As we all know, such a method is very often by far the most convenient and the clearest way of showing how a word is to be used. The most effective definition of a finger (or of "finger") is "This and this and anything like them!" Similarly an epic may often most conveniently be *"Paradise Lost, The Odyssey* and such." "And such" is, of course, the difficulty: "anything like them" in what respects? It may be excessively hard to say. In the limiting case there may be no relevant similarities whatever between our examples. Then we shall be deceiving ourselves, persuading ourselves that we are talking about a kind of things when there is no such kind. This happens probably more often than we would care to believe. Fairly often the only similarity is just that we call them alike. But, nonetheless, we do succeed frequently in using these exemplificatory, extensive, denotative definitions with great advantage, in spite of being unable at the moment, or perhaps ever, to *say* what are the common properties which make what we are talking about into a kind. Of course, they are a kind in so far as we call them by the same name; but they need to be a kind in another way, and this other way is, we hope, the ground for our calling them by a common name.

It is a fundamental truth that we can sort things rightly without knowing how we sort them. If we could not do this, we could never know anything. From our earliest, our behaviour is all sorting. William James' polyp with its "thingemabob again!" was sorting. We may pick out things as alike in relevant respects without necessarily being able to say (or even think) anything about the respects in which they are alike. Between merely *recognizing* things and being able, in reflection, to discern the respect of likeness there is an immense gap in development. Most human beings grow across it at some points. Chimpanzees may perhaps cross it here and there; the lower animals probably never do. But even the most reflective humans cross it, hitherto, at relatively few points. Those who pretend that there is little further scope for human development are being unimaginative. We might indeed describe general education as the process of advancing this development at the nodal points. And one of the nodal points is certainly this question of our use of the word "definition." . . .

We should recognize that definition is always *partial*. If we disregard all but a restricted purpose (or limited mode of communication, as Logic commonly does) we can overlook this and set ourselves very rigorous standards of precision. But a general theory of interpretation, which takes strict logical statement as only one mode of discourse, will remember our inevitable partiality, and point out that no expression whatever is entirely and in all respects equivalent to any other.

There is nothing lost but everything to be gained by using different sorts of definitions for different purposes, or giving the word "definition" various senses, provided we know and can make clear if need be to others what we are doing. That making clear will be itself a process of defining, of showing how we are proceeding. To put the matter in these terms is, I believe, a good way of dissipating the obstructive mystery about definition that is so daunting. Another is to invite the view that a definition is itself an invitation, a request, or, on occasion, an imperative; but *not* a statement. It is difficult in practice, so strong are normal writing habits, not to *urge* that this *IS so*. There is a temptation here to *insist* that definitions, properly regarded, are not statements, not true or false therefore, but only wise or foolish, prudent or imprudent, more like a resolve to eat six dozen oysters than a record of fact. But if we adopt this plan, then clearly we have no business to insist or make statements about it: we are offering a definition (of "definition") and if a definition is a request it should be expressed accordingly in the appropriate mood, which is not the indicative but the optative. So I should not say "A definition is a request" but "Come! let us understand by 'a definition' an invitation to regard a certain word as meaning so and so. Will you be so good as to accept?"

This is the principle of Freedom in Definition and, evidently, like other freedoms it increases our responsibilities. I would add a subprinciple, or special assistant, namely, the Equivalence in Grammatical Formulation—which may lighten them. To propose a defining choice *in one grammatical form only* is always dangerous. The classical examples have been "What is Truth?" and "What is Beauty?" These suggest that our job is to catch an already determined universal.* Let us agree instead that:

What sorts of things are beautiful?

When are what beautiful?

Beautiful things are which things?

How is "beautiful" used here?

With which logical form would it be
  convenient here to take "x is beautiful"?

and so on . . . are all proper alternative formulations for the definition question we are asking. If we do so, we are much better placed to avoid mistaking logical machinery for what it handles.

A choice of a grammatical form very often seems to impose the use of a logical form; this misleads us. A given sentence may, and often must, be read with varying logical forms. This principle, that we are free to use different grammatical forms in definitions as logically equivalent, states the complementary case and is a further defence against the tyranny (which feels like support) of logical machineries—against the restrictions we suffer if we forget that they are devices with no authority which does not derive from their services to us in analysis and comparison. They are modes of apprehension (mental forceps), not things we grasp; but, forgetting this, we take them to be the very things themselves we aspire to talk about. "Things themselves"! It is a notorious phrase and may make me seem here to be overlooking the limitations of thought. My point is only that what we think of is not to be regarded as necessarily having the logical form we find convenient in handling it. But still we can handle it only with some form of thought, with some logical instrument, though we can vary these—very much as we vary a word without changing our meaning. Logical machines are not themselves words; but they behave like language; so our handling of them reproduces the alternatives of the verbal situation.

In all this I am using my freedom of definition, offering an invitation to try how a view serves. . . .

If we recognized more frankly that *how* any word whatsoever is used is a matter of choice, of invitation and consent, not of regimentation, conformity and compulsion, should we not *then* better understand how artificial are the imagined discrete senses of our words, how dependent they are on the meaning we give to the sentence. The more optative our view of definition, the more humane Logic becomes. On this view we can do as we please and the more we take any sentence as an invitation or request, to be considered on its merits—rather than as a mere statement, like a blow, to be suffered or

*We may recognize universals to be logical machines and thus harmless and yet note the distortions that metaphysical beliefs in them induce. In this they are like ghosts—to be feared though not believed in.

repelled—the more we civilize communications. The thresholds of the moods are within our control, though as we change them, we are changed with them. And they shift perceptibly from generation to generation. What the mid-19th century parent thought was a mild appeal, we are apt to look upon as a bit of emotional bullying. So, all through the scale, the modes of utterance vary. Our meanings, not only in content but in modality, are in flux. Until recently, however, it would have been supposed that at least the indicative mood stood put! We are beginning to know better. . . . Nowadays, very evidently in Science, the indicative rests on an optative basis and is indicative (over widening fields) only within optative constancies. "Let us think so, and go on still further thinking so, while we see what happens," that is what we have to compare today, have we not? with "It is so." Admitting this, though *overt* syntax denies it in every sentence, we see that an optative, or invitational, Logic requires a more subtle and versatile, a better sustained and a more sensitively ordered art of interpretation. Otherwise our choice is only between crudity and chaos. An exploring writer not only uses more varied words than the ordinary man but he uses most of them in *many more ways*. He has to offer a far wider range of invitations to interpret, though never so many as Shakespeare was prepared to extend to *his* audience. Shakespeare's extreme freedom of definition has triumphed because he combined with it an unparalleled virtuosity in Grammar and, when he needed it, a supreme rhetorical tact. But let us remember how far we have come from the cradle, and then even Shakespeare will not seem too far above the generality of mankind to serve as an ideal of the command of life in language.

From this vantage point we may look back to observe the incessant interaction and interdependence of Rhetoric, Grammar and Logic, and the strategic importance of keeping their problems in mind together. The Optative view of Definition (which is the central problem of Logic) makes the creation of the-things-to-be thought of, that is, the demarcation of Sense from the other language functions (which is the central problem of Rhetoric), a matter of our choice—subject, however, always to the exigencies of communication, that is, the provision of sufficiently stable interverbal action (which is the central problem of Grammar). By Definition things arise. If Berkeley had said of the objects of thought that TO BE was, for *them*, TO BE THOUGHT OF, few would have hesitated to agree; and yet this is not far from what he was most concerned to say. If we choose, wittingly or unwittingly, to think as the passions rather than the reason—the most inclusive integrating action— would have it (thus forcing on Rhetoric its degraded sense), or to speak without regard to the extant articulations of the senses of the words in the language (the dehumanizing disintegration of Grammar), we thereby become incapable of human companionship, that is, insane. The two departures often go together; but not always, alas! There are several spell-binding maniacs among the great personages of the world today. But, in general, the loss of reason entails the loss of efficient speech. Perhaps, if we can take a long enough view, that may be true too of the ruling madmen, their speech may destroy them; but meanwhile it is only too effective upon the correlative madmen who are subservient to it. However that may be, it is still certain—

> That this pragmatical, preposterous pig of a world,
>   its farrow that so solid seem,
> Must vanish on the instant did the mind but change
>   its theme

We can, moreover, almost daily notice that it changes. "The eye altering, alters all," and the eye—the intellectual organ that, in defining, determines the limits of things—is always altering, for worse there, for better here, we hope. But no one eye, no one creative outlook, settles anything. Like the words in a sentence, we are meaningless unless we take our senses from one another. The individual, alone, is nothing; though the whole takes its value from the individuals within it. Society thus has a Grammar—the cooperation of its members. This breaks down easily unless the instruments of cooperation, the languages of its members, serve and grow with it. And the sciences, the operative Logic through which alone modern societies live, have equally to be preserved—from the distortions and the taints of disloyal desires. The physical sciences are comparatively free from this danger. The social sciences are much exposed to it, and among them the linguistic studies, the practice and theory of the teaching of literature, for example. Rhetoric guards from these contaminations both Logic, and the deeper integrations of myth which speak for reason. It contains religion, as Logic contains science, and Grammar contains communication, and has the largest scope of the three. For in Rhetoric's care is that unity or, as Coleridge would have written, coadunation of the mind which is, whatever the deviations, the aim behind and before our strivings—an increasing organic interinanimation of meanings, the biologic growth of the mind in the individual and in a social inheritance maintaining the human advance.

A modern student of the *Topica* ("Dialectic is a process of criticism wherein lies the path to the principles of all inquiries," 101*b*; "Moreover, it is well to expand the argument and insert things that it does not require at all . . . for in the multitude of the details the whereabouts of the fallacy is obscured," 157*a*) ought, I think, to be deeply troubled, though to be tolerant toward Aristotle's treatment of dialectic has been the tradition. The fundamental and double-edged old question which that treatment clouds and slights is as curative today as ever: What sorts of persuasion are there? and to what ends may we reasonably employ them? This is a question we all hope to dodge. To be local and specific in this matter: which sorts of points in literary history are capable of being established with what sorts of security? When a highly conjectural "Maybe so!" is the best we can hope for in a given case, how much collective toil and elaboration of detail is justified in its pursuit? Academic tradition (which may doom itself so) is apt to regard such queries as no more than graduate growing pains. The purity of the scholar's quest for knowledge is often supposed to sanction no matter what waste of time and talents, and in many quarters there is genuine ignorance as to what else a student of literature could be doing. It is well to remember that more than a little unemployment for academics is one of the more persistent of the economists' prophecies. In a time of high competition for needed endowment not many modern literary inquiries are going to be easy to justify.

"The Places and the Figures." from *Speculative Instruments* (1955).

7

A Study of Misunderstanding and Its Remedies

These lectures are an attempt to revive an old subject. I need spend no time, I think, in describing the present state of Rhetoric. Today it is the dreariest and least profitable part of the waste that the unfortunate travel through in Freshman English! So low has Rhetoric sunk that we would do better just to dismiss it to Limbo than to trouble ourselves with it—unless we can find reason for believing that it can become a study that will minister successfully to important needs. . . .

Rhetoric should be a study of misunderstanding and its remedies. . . . [Rhetoricians sometimes] claim that Rhetoric must go deep, must take a broad philosophical· view of the principles of the art, but nothing of the sort is attempted. What we are given instead is a very ably argued and arranged and discussed collection of prudential Rules about the best sorts of things to say in various argumentative situations, the order in which to bring out your propositions and proofs and examples, at what point it will be most effective to disparage your opponent, how to recommend oneself to the audience, and like matters. As to all of which, it is fair to remark, no one ever learned about them from a treatise who did not know about them already; at the best, the treatise may be an occasion for realizing that there is skill to be developed in discourse, but it does not and cannot teach the skill. . . .

[Richrads delares that the old macroscopic rhetoric must be supplanted by a microscopic inquiry.] To account for understanding and misunderstanding, to study the efficiency of language and its conditions, we have to renounce, for a while, the view that words just have their meanings and that what a

The Philosophy of Rhetoric (1936), Lecture I.

discourse does is to be explained as a composition of these meanings—as a wall can be represented as a composition of its bricks. We have to shift the focus of our analysis and attempt a deeper and more minute grasp and try to take account of the structures of the smallest discussable units of meaning and the ways in which these vary as they are put with other units. Bricks, for all practical purposes, hardly mind what other things they are put with. Meanings mind intensely—more indeed than any other sorts of things. It is the peculiarity of meanings that they do so mind their company; that is in part what we mean by calling them meanings! In themselves they are nothing—figments, abstractions, unreal things that we invent, if you like— but we invent them for a purpose. They help us to avoid taking account of the peculiar way in which any part of a discourse, in the last resort, does what it does only because the other parts of the surrounding, uttered or unuttered discourse and its conditions are what they are. "In the last resort"—the last resort here is mercifully a long way off and very deep down. Short of it we are aware of certain stabilities which hide from us this universal relativity or, better, interdependence of meanings. Some words and sentences still more, do seem to mean what they mean absolutely and unconditionally. This is because the conditions governing their meanings are so constant that we can disregard them. So the weight of a cubic centimeter of water seems a fixed and absolute thing because of the constancy of its governing conditions. In weighing out a pound of tea we can forget about the mass of the earth. And with words which have constant conditions the common sense view that they have fixed proper meanings, which should be learned and observed, is justi- fied. But these words are fewer than we suppose. Most words, as they pass from context to context, change their meanings; and in many different ways. It is their duty and their service to us to do so. Ordinary discourse would suffer anchylosis if they did not, and so far we have no ground for complaint. We are extraordinarily skilful in some fields with these shifts of sense— especially when they are of the kind we recognize officially as metaphor. But our skill fails; it is patchy and fluctuant; and, when it fails, misunderstanding of others and of ourselves comes in.

A chief cause of misunderstanding, I shall argue later, is the Proper Mean- ing Superstition. That is, the common belief—encouraged officially by what lingers on in the school manuals as Rhetoric—that a word has a meaning of its own (ideally, only one) independent of and controlling its use and the purpose for which it should be uttered. This superstition is a recognition of a certain kind of stability in the meanings of certain words. It is only a su- perstition when it forgets (as it commonly does) that the stability of the meaning of a word comes from the constancy of the contexts that give it its meaning. Stability in a word's meaning is not something to be assumed, but always something to be explained. And as we try out explanations, we dis- cover, of course, that as there are many sorts of constant contexts—there are many sorts of stabilities. The stability of the meaning of a word like *knife*, say, is different from the stability of a word like *mass* in its technical use, and then again both differ from the stabilities of such words, say, as *event, ingression, endurance, recurrence,* or *object,* in the paragraphs of a very distinguished predecessor in this Lectureship. It will have been noticed perhaps that the way I propose to treat meanings has its analogues with Mr. Whitehead's treatment of things. But indeed no one to whom Berkeley has mattered will be very confident as to which is which.

I have been suggesting—with my talk of macroscopic and microscopic inquiries—that the theory of language may have something to learn, not much but a little, from the ways in which the physicist envisages stabilities. But much closer analogies are possible with some of the patterns of Biology. The theory of interpretation is obviously a branch of biology—a branch that has not grown very far or very healthily yet. To remember this may help us to avoid some traditional mistakes—among them the use of bad analogies which tie us up if we take them too seriously. Some of these are notorious; for example, the opposition between form and content, and the almost equivalent opposition between matter and form. These are wretchedly inconvenient metaphors. So is that other which makes language a dress which thought puts on. We shall do better to think of a meaning as though it were a plant that has grown—not a can that has been filled or a lump of clay that has been moulded. These are obvious inadequacies; but, as the history of criticism shows, they have not been avoided, and the perennial efforts of the reflective to amend or surpass them—Croce is the extreme modern example—hardly help.

More insidious and more devastating are the oversimple mechanical analogies which have been brought in under the heading of Associationism in the hope of explaining how language works. And thought as well. The two problems are close together and similar and neither can be discussed profitably apart from the other. But, unless we drastically remake their definitions, and thereby dodge the main problems, Language and Thought are not—need I say?—one and the same. I suppose I must, since the Behaviorists have so loudly averred that Thought is subvocal talking. That however is a doctrine I prefer, in these lectures, to attack by implication. To discuss it explicitly would take time that can, I think, be spent more fruitfully. I will only say that I hold that any doctrine identifying Thought with *muscular* movement is a self-refutation of the observationalism that prompts it—heroic and fatal. And that an identification of Thought with an activity of the nervous system is to me an acceptable hypothesis, but too large to have interesting applications. It may be left until more is known about both; when possibly it may be developed to a point at which it might become useful. At present it is still Thought which is most accessible to study and accessible largely through Language. We can all detect a difference in our own minds between thinking of a dog and thinking of a cat. But no neurologist can. Even when no cats or dogs are about and we are doing nothing about them except thinking of them, the difference is plainly perceptible. We can also say "dog" and think "cat."

I must, though, discuss the doctrine of associations briefly, because when we ask ourselves about how words mean, some theory about trains of associated ideas or accompanying images is certain to occur to us as an answer. And until we see how little distance these theories take us they are frustrating. We all know the outline of these theories: we learn what the word "cat" means by seeing a cat at the same time that we hear the word "cat" and thus a link is formed between the sight and the sound. Next time we hear the word "cat" an image of a cat (a visual image, let us say) arises in the mind, and that is how the word "cat" means a cat. The obvious objections that come from the differences between cats; from the fact that images of a grey persian asleep and of a tabby stalking are very different, and from some people saying they never have any imagery, must then be taken account of, and the theory grows very complex. Usually, images get relegated to a background and become mere supports to something hard to be precise about—an idea of a cat—which is supposed then to be associated with the word "cat" much as the image originally was supposed to be associated with it.

This classical theory of meaning has been under heavy fire from many sides for more than a century—from positions as different as those of Coleridge, of Bradley, of Pavlov and of the *gestalt* psychologists. In response it has elaborated itself, calling in the aid of the conditioned-reflex and submitting to the influence of Freud. I do not say that it is incapable, when amended, of supplying us with a workable theory of meaning; in saying that simple associationism does not go far enough and is an impediment unless we see this, I am merely reminding you that a clustering of associated images and ideas about a word in the mind does not answer our question: "How does a word mean?" It only hands it on to them, and the question becomes: "How does an idea (or an image) mean what it does?" To answer that we have to go outside the mind and inquire into its connections with what are not mental occurrences. Or (if you prefer, instead, to extend the sense of the word "mind") we have to inquire into connections between events which were left out by the traditional associationism. And in leaving them out they left out the problem.

For our purposes here the important points are two. First, that ordinary, current, undeveloped associationism is ruined by the crude inapposite physical metaphor of impressions stamped on the mind (the image of the cat stamped by the cat), impressions then linked and combined in clusters like atoms in molecules. That metaphor gives us no useful account either of perception or of reflection, and we shall not be able to think into or think out any of the interesting problems of Rhetoric unless we improve it. Secondly the appeal to *imagery* as constituting the meaning of an utterance has, in fact, frustrated a large part of the great efforts that have been made by very able people ever since the 17th Century to put Rhetoric back into the important place it deserves among our studies. . . .

It is no exaggeration to say that the fabrics of all our various worlds are the fabrics of our meanings—the formations and transformations of meanings which we must study with and through words. . . . Whatever we may be studying we do so only through the growth of our meanings. To realize this turns some parts of this attempted direct study of the modes of growth and interaction between meanings, which might otherwise seem a niggling philosophic juggle with distinctions, into a business of great practical importance. For this study is theoretical only that it may become practical.

I have been leading up—or down, if you like—to an extremely simple and obvious but fundamental remark: that no word can be judged as to whether it is good or bad, correct or incorrect, beautiful or ugly, or anything else that matters to a writer, in isolation. That seems so evident that I am almost ashamed to say it, and yet it flies straight in the face of the only doctrine that for two hundred years has been officially inculcated—when any doctrine is inculcated in these matters. I mean the doctrine of Usage. The doctrine that there is a right or a good use for every word and that literary virtue consists in making that good use of it.

"The Interinanimation of Words," from *The Philosophy of Rhetoric* (1936).

8

A Context Theory of Meaning and Types of Context

I have urged that there is room for a persistent, systematic, detailed inquiry into how words work that will take the place of the discredited subject which goes by the name of Rhetoric. This inquiry must be philosophic, or—if you hesitate with that word, I do myself—it must take charge of the criticism of its own assumptions and not accept them, more than it can help, ready-made from other studies. How words mean is not a question to which we can safely accept an answer either as an inheritance from common sense, that curious growth, or as something vouched for by another science, by psychology, say—since other sciences use words themselves and not least delusively when they address themselves to these questions. The result is that a revived Rhetoric, or study of verbal understanding and misunderstanding, must itself undertake its own inquiry into the modes of meaning—not only, as with the old Rhetoric, on a macroscopic scale, discussing the effects of different disposals of large parts of a discourse—but also on a microscopic scale by using theorems about the structure of the fundamental conjectural units of meaning and the conditions through which they, and their interconnections, arise.

In the old Rhetoric, of course, there is much that a new Rhetoric finds useful—and much besides which may be advantageous until man changes his nature, debates and disputes, incites, tricks, bullies and cajoles his fellows less. Aristotle's notes on the forensic treatment of evidence elicited under torture are unhappily not without their utility still in some very up-to-date parts of the world.

From *The Philosophy of Rhetoric* (1936), Lecture II.

Among the general themes of the old Rhetoric there is one which is especially pertinent to our inquiry. The old Rhetoric was an offspring of dispute; it developed as the rationale of pleadings and persuadings; it was the theory of the battle of words and has always been itself dominated by the combative impulse. Perhaps what it has most to teach us is the narrowing and blinding influence of that preoccupation, that debaters' interest.

Persuasion is only one among the aims of discourse. It poaches on the others—especially on that of *exposition,* which is concerned to state a view, not to persuade people to agree or to do anything more than examine it. The review and correspondence columns of the learned and scientific journals are the places in which to watch this poaching at its liveliest. It is no bad preparation for any attempt at exposition . . , to realize how easily the combative impulse can put us in mental blinkers and make us take another man's words in the ways in which we can down him with least trouble. . . . [Richards introduces his "context theorem of meaning" to support the argument that purposes determine discourse. The most important element of the *theorem*—Richards follows Coleridge in using this term instead of *idea*—is the premise that "meanings, from the very beginning, have a primordial generality and abstractness." He covers much of the same ground as that explored in "Realism/Nominalism/Conceptualism" (*Interpretation in Teaching*) (see chapter 14) before turning to meaning as "delegated efficacy," an attempt to avoid simple-minded conceptions of representation.]

I must explain now the rather special and technical sense I am giving to this word "context." This is the pivotal point of the whole theorem. The word has a familiar sense in "a literary context," as the other words before and after a given word which determine how it is to be interpreted. This is easily extended to cover the rest of the book. . . . The familiar sense of "context" can be extended further to include the circumstances under which anything was written or said; wider still to include, for a word in Shakespeare, say, the other known uses of the word about that time, wider still finally to include anything whatever about the period, or about anything else which is relevant to our interpretation of it. The technical use I am going to make of this term "context" is none of these—though it has something in common with them as having to do with the governing conditions of an interpretation. We can get to it best, perhaps, by considering those recurrences in nature which statements of causal laws are about.

Put very simply, a causal law may be taken as saying that, under certain conditions, of two events if one happens the other does. We usually call the first the cause and the second the effect, but the two may happen together, as when I clap my hands and both palms tingle. If we are talking about final causes we reverse them, and the lecture you are going to hear was the cause of your coming hither. There is a good deal of arbitrariness at several points here which comes from the different purposes for which we need causal laws. We decide, to suit these purposes, how we shall divide up events; we make the existence of the earth one event and the tick of a clock another, and so on. And we distribute the titles of "cause" and "effect" as we please. Thus we do not please to say that night causes day or day night. We prefer to say that given the conditions the rotation of the earth is the cause of their succession. We arc especially arbitrary in picking out the cause from among the whole group, or context, of conditions—of prior and subsequent events which hang together. Thus the coroner decides that the cause of a man's death was the act of a murderer and not the man's meeting with the murderer, or the stopping of his heart, or the fact that he was not wearing a bullet-proof waistcoat. That is because the coroner is interested in certain kinds of causal laws but not in others. So here, in sketching this causal theorem of meaning, I am interested only in certain kinds of law and am not necessarily saying anything about others.

Now for the sense of "context." Most generally it is a name for a whole cluster of events that recur together—including the required conditions as well as whatever we may pick out as cause or effect. But the modes of causal recurrence on which meaning depends are peculiar through that delegated efficacy I have been talking about. In these contexts one item—typically a word—takes over the duties of parts which can then be omitted from the recurrence. There is thus an abridgement of the context, shown only in the behavior of living things, and most extensively and drastically shown by man. When this abridgement happens, what the sign or word—the item with these delegated powers—means is the missing parts of the context.

If we ask how this abridgement happens, how a sign comes to stand for an absent cause and conditions, we come up against the limits of knowledge at once. No one knows. Physiological speculation has made very little progress towards explaining *that,* though enormous strides have been made this century in analysing the complexities of the conditioned reflex. The shift, the handing over, is left still as inexplicable. Probably this "learning problem" goes down as deep as the nature of life itself. We can suppose, if we like, that some sorts of residual effects are left behind from former occurrences which later cooperate with the sign in determining the response. To do so is to use a metaphor drawn from the gross behavior, taken macroscopically, of systems that are not living—printed things, gramophone records and such.* We can be fairly ingenious with these metaphors, invent neural archives storing up impressions, or neural telephone exchanges with fantastic properties. But how the archives get consulted or how in the telephone system A gets on to the B it needs, instead of to the whole alphabet at once in a jumble, remain utterly mysterious matters. Fortunately linguistics and the theory of meaning need not wait until this is remedied. They can probably go much further than we have yet imagined without any answer to this question. It is enough for

---

*Another crack at Wittgenstein. Richards considered that Wittgenstein's reliance on the single example of the gramophone was symptomatic of a failure to make the kind of discriminations he thought necessary in discussing signal and message, the channels of communication, and the kinds of code.—ED

our purposes to say that what a word means is the missing parts of the contexts from which it draws its delegated efficacy.

At this point I must remind you of what I said a few minutes ago about the primordial generality and abstractness of meaning and about how, when we mean the simplest-seeming concrete object, its concreteness comes to it from the way in which we are bringing it simultaneously into a number of sorts. The sorts grow together in it to form that meaning. Theory here, as so often, can merely exploit the etymological hint given in the word "concrete." If we forget this and suppose that we start with discrete impressions of particulars ("fixities and definites" as Coleridge called them) and then build these up into congeries, the theorem I am recommending collapses at once into contradictions and absurdities. That was the fault of the old Hartleian Associationism: it did not go back far enough; it took particular impressions as its initial terms. But the initial terms for this theorem are not impressions; they are sortings, recognitions, laws of response, recurrences of like behaviors.

A particular impression is already a product of concrescence. Behind, or in it, there has been a coming together of *sortings*. When we take a number of particular impressions—of a number of different white things, say—and abstract from them an idea of whiteness, we are explicitly reversing a process which has already been implicitly at work in our perception of them as all white. Our risk is to confuse the abstractness we thus arrive at intellectually with the primordial abstractness out of which these impressions have already grown—before ever any conscious explicit reflection took place.

Things, in brief, are instances of laws. As Bradley said, association marries only universals, and out of these laws, these recurrent likenesses of behavior, in our minds and in the world—not out of revived duplicates of individual past impressions—the fabric of our meanings, which is the world, is composed.

So much for the theorem. What are the problems we must use it to construct?

Since the whole business of Rhetoric comes down to comparisons between the meanings of words, the first problem, I think, should be this. How, if the meaning of a word is, in this sense, the missing parts of its contexts, how then should we compare the meanings of two words? There is opportunity for a grand misunderstanding here. It is not proposed that we should try to make these comparisons by a process of discovering, detailing, and then comparing these missing parts. We could not do it and, if we could, it would be a waste of time. The theorem does not pretend to give us quite new ways of distinguishing between meanings. It only bars out certain practices and assumptions which are common and misleading.

The office of the theorem is much more negative than positive; but is not the less useful for that. It will not perhaps tell us how to do much that we cannot do without it already; but it will prevent us from doing stupid things which we are fond of doing. . . .

The context theorem of meaning would prevent our making hundreds of baseless and disabling assumptions that we commonly make about meanings, oversimplifications that create false problems interfering with closer comparisons—and that is its main service. In this, it belongs with a number of other theorems which may be called policeman doctrines—because they are designed on the model of an ideal police-force, not to make any of us do anything but to prevent other people from interfering unduly with our lawful activities. The organization of impulses doctrine of values for literary criticism is in the same position. These policeman doctrines keep assumptions that are out of place from frustrating and misleading sagacity. . . .

Preëminently what the theorem would discourage is our habit of behaving as though, if a passage means one thing it cannot at the same time mean another and an incompatible thing. Freud taught us that a dream may mean a dozen different things; he has persuaded us that some symbols are, as he says, "overdetermined" and mean many different selections from among their causes. This theorem goes further, and regards all discourse—outside the technicalities of science—as overdetermined, as having multiplicity of meaning. It can illustrate this view from almost any of the great controversies. And it offers us—by restraining the One and Only One True Meaning Superstition—a better hope, I believe, of profiting from the controversies. A controversy is normally an exploitation of a systematic set of misunderstandings for warlike purposes. This theorem suggests that the swords of dispute might be turned into plough shares; and a way found by which we may (to revert to Hobbes) "make use of our benefit of effects formerly seen—for the commodity of human life."

The next problem concerns what happens when we put words together in sentences. At least that is a common way of stating it. The theorem recommends us rather to turn the problem round and ask what happens when, out of the integral utterance which is the sentence, we try to isolate the discrete meanings of the words of which it is composed. [It is in] sentences and the interaction between words in the sentence that the most deep-rooted, systematic and persistent misunderstandings arise.

A third set of problems concerns rivalries between different types of context which supply the meaning for a single utterance. These start with the plain equivoque—as when the word "reason" may mean either a cause or an argument. I am simplifying this here to make it a type of a really simple ambiguity. Actually in most occurrences it would be much more complex and not so easily cleared up, as the shifting meanings of "cause" and "argument" themselves show. The context theorem of meaning will make us expect ambiguity to the widest extent and of the subtlest kinds nearly everywhere, and of course we find it. But where the old Rhetoric treated ambiguity as a fault in language, and hoped to confine or eliminate it, the new Rhetoric sees it as an inevitable consequence of the powers of language and as the indispensable means of most of our most important utterances—especially in Poetry and Religion.

Of course ambiguities are a nuisance in exposition as, in spite of my efforts, you have certainly been feeling. But neutral exposition is a very special limited use of language, comparatively a late development to which we have not (outside some parts of the sciences) yet adapted it. This brings me to those large-scale rivalries between contexts which shift the very aims of discourse. When the passions—the combative passion and others—intervene, either in the formation of an utterance or in its interpretation, we have examples of context action just as much as when the word "paper," say, takes its meaning from its contexts. The extra meaning that comes in when a sentence, in addition to making a statement, is meant to be insulting, or flattering, or is interpreted so—we may call it emotive meaning—is not so different from plain statement as we are apt to suppose. As the word means the missing part of its contexts and is a substitute for them, so the insulting intention may be the substitute for a kick,—the missing part of its context. The same general theorem covers all the modes of meaning.

I began by speaking of the poaching of the other language functions on the preserve of pure exposition. Pure exposition has its guardian passions no doubt—though I do not know their names. But they are not often as strong as the poachers and are easily beguiled by them. It has been so necessary to us, especially since the physical basis of civilization became technical, to care at least sometimes for the truth only and keep the poachers sometimes out, that we have exaggerated enormously the extent of pure exposition. It is a relatively rare occurrence outside the routine of train services and the tamer, more settled parts of the sciences. We have exaggerated our success for strategic reasons—some of them good, because encouraging, if we do not too much hoodwink ourselves. (I have aimed at points to be merely expository in [these] remarks, but I know better than to suppose I have succeeded.) We shall find, preëminently in the subject of rhetoric, that interpretations and opinions about interpretations that are not primarily steps of partisan policy are excessively hard to arrive at. And thereby we rediscover that the world—so far from being a solid matter of fact—is rather a fabric of conventions, which for obscure reasons it has suited us in the past to manufacture and support. And that sometimes is a dismaying rediscovery which seems to unsettle our foundations. . . .

———

Facts are no true comforts until we know how to take them; and that is just our problem. They are further items in configurations which we have to learn to understand. This observation long ago gave us our saying about the wood and the trees. There is indeed something reminiscent of the Babes in the Wood in much contemporary scholarship. They wandered up and down and to and fro. They went everywhere but out of the wood and were found in the morning (there was a morning!) under a heap of leaves. The story says that pitying birds buried them so. This seems a pretty fancy. I find it more likely that they collected these leaves themselves and perished through unregulated interest in the variety of foliation.

In less legendary language we do not develop a mind by giving it more facts but by helping it to judge relevance. It is relevance which tells us which meanings belong with which, and in what configurations, for a valid interpretation. The way to strengthen the sense of relevance is by exercising it with simpler problems rather than by adding elaborations.

"Responsibilities in the Teaching of English," from *Speculative Instruments* (1955).

9

The Coalescence of Subject
and Object

In beginning to expound Coleridge's theory of the Imagination, I propose to start where he himself in the *Biographia* (after all his endless preliminaries, warnings and preparations) really started: that is, with a theory of the act of knowledge, or of consciousness, or, as he called it, "the coincidence or coalescence of an OBJECT with a SUBJECT." Upon how we understand these two terms and how we understand this *coalescence* of the two, a large part of our understanding of Coleridge's theory will depend.

And here at once comes up a practical difficulty. Coleridge insists that Philosophy uses what he calls the INNER SENSE and that therefore it cannot "like geometry, appropriate to every construction a correspondent *outward* intuition." For example, a geometer can think of a line. Then if he wishes he can draw one (or image one). The stroke is not the line itself (having length without breadth) but it satisfactorily images the line (as a mathematical line) and it is "an efficient mean to excite every imagination to the intuition of it."

But where operations and acts of the inner sense are concerned matters are not so easy. We are all practised in thinking of lines—we are not all equally practised in using the INNER SENSE:

One man's consciousness extends only to the pleasant or unpleasant sensations caused in him by external impressions; another enlarges his inner sense to a consciousness of forms and quantity; a third in addition to the image is conscious of the conception or notion of the thing; a fourth attains to a notion of his notions—he reflects upon his own reflections; and thus we may say without impropriety that the one

From *Coleridge on Imagination* (1934) chap. 3.

possesses more or less inner sense than the other. This more or less betrays already that philosophy in its first principles must have a practical or moral, as well as a theoretical or speculative side (*B. L.,* I, 172).

As Blake put it, "A fool sees not the same tree that a wise man sees."

Coleridge supposes that these successive levels, as it were of the operation of the INNER SENSE are stages that can be attained—with practice—by the right people; that from notions of our notions we can go on to an INNER SENSE of the act of notioning, of the acts of choosing among our notions and framing them, comparing them and so on, and he begins his philosophy with a certain act of contemplation, a *realizing intuition* which brings into existence what he calls "the first postulate of philosophy" *an instrument to be used in his later descriptions* (as a geometer may postulate a construction of lines as an instrument to be used in geometry).

But this initial act of contemplation is not mere theoretical apprehension such as can be instigated by words in anyone who is acquainted with a language. Nor is it possible for everyone:

To an Esquimau or New Zealander our most popular philosophy would be wholly unintelligible. The sense, the inward organ for it, is not yet born in him. So is there many a one among us, yes, and some who think themselves philosophers too, to whom the philosophic organ is entirely wanting. To such a man philosophy is a mere play of words and notions, like a theory of music to the deaf, or like the geometry of light to the blind. The connection of the parts and their logical dependencies may be seen and remembered; but the whole is groundless and hollow, unsustained by living contact, unaccompanied with any realizing intuition which exists by and in the act that affirms its existence, which is known, because it is, and is, because it is known. The words of Plotinus, in the assumed person of nature, hold true of the philosophic energy. . . , With me the act of contemplation makes the thing contemplated, as the geometricians contemplating describe lines correspondent; but I am not describing lines, but simply contemplating, the representative forms of things rise up into existence (*B. L.,* I, p. 173).

What he is asking us to do is to perform for ourselves an act of contemplation, of *realizing intuition,* at the same time and in the same act becoming aware by the INNER SENSE of what we are doing. Here is the postulate:

The postulate of philosophy and at the same time the test of philosophic capacity, is no other than the heaven-descended KNOW THYSELF (E coelo descendit, Γνῶθι σεαυτόν). And this at once practically and speculatively. For as philosophy is neither a science of the reason or understanding only, or merely a science of morals, but the science of BEING altogether, its primary ground can be neither merely speculative, or merely practical, but both in one. All knowledge rests on the coincidence of an object with a subject.

It will be noticed that Coleridge deliberately makes this postulate seem *arbitrary.* It is an act of the will, a direction of the *inner sense,* a mode of action, or of being, at the same time that it is a mode of knowing. It is that activity of the mind in which knowing and doing and making and being are least to be distinguished.

In order to be able to make this postulate (or to use it) we must have sufficiently developed our inner sense. We must be more than merely aware, we must be aware of our awareness, and of the form and mode of operation of our awareness. The rest of his philosophy is a verbal machine for exhibiting what the exercise of this postulate or this act of contemplation yielded. (As the geometer's drawn diagrams and written theorems are a machine for exhibiting his acts of *realizing intuition*.) We must study it *as a machine*—with a recognition that in the nature of the case it must be a very inefficient machine—useful only so far as it helps us to go through the same *realizing intuitions*.

At this point I had better raise and meet—if I can—an objection. Someone will say, "But this is only *introspection* glorified into a method of research. And introspection is notoriously misleading. The tendency of psychology, as psychology becomes a science, is to depose it and reduce its claims." The right answer to which is, I think, this: that *introspection* (the seemingly direct inspection by the mind of the mind's own processes) is discredited, and rightly, as a means of settling matters *not* within the scope of direct inspection (e.g., whether colour-contrast effects arise in the retina or farther back in the head; how we locate sounds; or whether the eye follows a smooth line more easily than a jagged one) but that there still remains a field in which introspection is not only a possible but an indispensable source of information, and that all modes of systematic inquiry use at some point comparisons whose method is nothing but introspection.

But there is a subtler question than this to be noticed. It may be said that introspection only sees what it expects to see—the framework of assumptions through which it is made. We must reply that this by itself is something, is much, is all we can ask, and all we need. Definitive final results are not to be hoped for in these matters. What we want are possible, useful hypotheses, ways of conceiving the mind that may help us in living.

Self-knowledge is obviously an unusually dangerous phrase—even among philosophical phrases. The mere exercise of introspection, the effort to make out what we are doing as we think, the detection of our assumptions, the tracking down of obscure motives, the observation of components in consciousness that are not ordinarily attended to, and so on, is not to be confused either with the act which supplies Coleridge's initial postulate—the realizing intuition—*or* with the mode of self-creation which Coleridge is going on to use in dividing the Imagination from the Fancy. Introspection is clearly not in itself Imagination: it supplies us as a rule with *notions* only, not with a fresh development of our selves. But we are concerned at present only with Coleridge's initial postulate. His Γνῶθι σεαυτόν is a technique for making certain assumptions—living them in order thereby to discover what it is we are making. As we have seen, Coleridge's theory of knowing treats knowing as a kind of making, i.e., the bringing into being of what is known. By itself, it makes no discoveries except in the sense of discovering what it has made.

One feature of Coleridge's thinking needs to be pointed out early. It is not peculiar to him, though the disorder in his exposition sometimes makes this feature seem specially obtrusive. *After* he has stated some principle (or objection) in a subtle form, with a meaning that no one with a fairly open and curious mind can doubt would be worth exploring, he is apt to repeat something like it, in similar words, but fairly evidently with a meaning by no means the same.

For example, *here* he has taken Γνῶθι σεαυτόν as the first postulate of philosophy—and with an implication that the self that has to be known is a self that is created in the act of endeavouring to know it. "The inner sense," he says, "has its direction determined for the greater part by an act of freedom" (*B. L.,* i, p. 172). This was in 1817.

Fifteen years later he writes as follows:

> Γνῶθι σεαυτόν!—and is this the prime
> And heaven-sprung maxim of the olden time!–
> Say canst thou make thyself? Learn first that trade:—
> Haply thou may'st know what thyself has't made.
> What has't thou, Man, that thou dar'st call thine own?
> What is there in thee, Man, that may be known?
> Dark fluxion, all unfixable by thought,
> A Phantom dim of past and future wrought,
> Vain sister of the worm,—life, death, soul, clod,
> Ignore thyself and seek to know thy God!

A passage, unless I mistake, streaked through, if read dramatically, with the less familiar veins of Coleridge's best poetry. Read it, not dramatically, but for the *prose-sense* and for the feelings towards the doctrines it then presents (scorn, timidity and bafflement) and it is, in almost similar words, directly contrary to the former doctrine. For the earlier Γνῶθι σεαυτόν had promised that in the effort to know ourselves we might in a real sense make ourselves—and these verses seem almost to spit scorn on the endeavour. There is a long and terrible chapter of Coleridge's biography to be read between them.

In the earlier doctrine there is a sense in which to seek to know God may be interpreted as the safest method of knowing oneself. But that was with an altogether different sense for the words "seek to know thy God," a sense which the later verses, unless I misread them, seem to forget or deny. And with this change come other changes in the sense of "self" and "thought."

It may seem that—imitating Coleridge in the respects in which it is most easy to imitate him—I have forgotten that I proposed to begin with *the coalescence of the Subject and the Object*. But the postulate Γνῶθι σεαυτόν is only this coalescence in other words. Coleridge's *Subject* is the Self or the Intelligence, the sentient knowing Mind; his *Object* is Nature, what is known by the mind in the act of knowing. The coalescence of the two is that knowing (making, being) activity we have been considering.

We need here both a free eye and a light hand. We have to make certain distinctions and, while making them, never to forget that we make them for certain purposes only, and that we can unmake them and *must do so* for other purposes. "While I am attempting to explain this intimate coalition, I must suppose it dissolved," said Coleridge. A separated Subject and Object cannot be put together again without the distinction between them lapsing. These distinctions were made only for conveniences of abstract theory and of practical action. The scope of the conveniences is wide, so wide that the distinctions—between the self that knows, its knowing, its knowledge and what it knows—may seem inevitable, established in their own right as part of the order of existence. But for other purposes, as when our knowing *in the act of the realizing intuition* is developing itself, they are not ruling. "There is here no first, and no second; both are coinstantaneous and one." The distinctions are not then being used by the Subject–Object, nor are they useful to us in describing its act (or being)—any more than when a plant is growing we can distinguish what grows, its growing, the growledge and what is grown. Though Coleridge says (*B. L.,* I, p. 180), "To know is in its very essence a verb active," he is often in fact paralleling knowing with growing: "the *rules* of the IMAGINATION are themselves the very powers of growth and production" (*B. L.,* II, p. 65). His clearest statement, in a very important passage in *The Statesman's Manual* (Appendix B) is in these terms:

Further, and with particular reference to that undivided reason, neither merely speculative or merely practical, but both in one . . . I seem to myself to behold in the quiet objects on which I am gazing, more than an arbitrary illustration, more than a mere *simile,* the work of my own fancy. I feel an awe, as if there were before my eyes the same power as that of the reason—the same power in a lower dignity, and therefore a symbol established in the truth of things. I feel it alike, whether I contemplate a single tree or flower, or mediate on vegetation throughout the world, as one of the great organs of the life of nature. Lo!—with the rising sun it commences its outward life and enters into open communion with all the elements, at once assimilating them to itself and to each other. . . . Lo!—how upholding the ceaseless plastic motion of the parts in the profoundest rest of the whole it becomes the visible *organismus* of the entire silent or elementary life of nature.

That in the *products* of knowing we later have occasion to distinguish Subject from Object does not entail their separation in the *process*. The senses of the words change as our discussion moves from the one to the other. We need to take them apart to explain them and to divide off the sphere of natural science (including physiology). We need to take them together to explore the act of knowing by means of the inner sense, and to divide off the sphere of what may be called pure psychology. But since the assumptions introduced for the convenience of these different purposes are different (and thus the terms used in the two spheres have different senses) we cannot bring them together without a mediating method of interpretation. There is thus a gap left between natural science and psychology which thought has not yet succeeded in bridging. Because, we may conjecture, it is a gap introduced only by our mode of formulating the problem.

Coleridge made acute remarks in several places about the pernicious effect of the "despotism of the eye" under which "we are restless because invisible things are not the objects of vision." "Metaphysical systems, for the most part, become popular not for their truth, but in proportion as they attribute to causes a susceptibility of being seen, if only our visual organs were sufficiently powerful." But a diagrammatic presentation of Coleridge's philosophical position, and its difficulties, will, I hope, here economize exposition, and, with this warning, need not mislead. It is no more than a compact *aide mémoire*.

Subject	"Mind"
↓	↑
Aware of (perceiving)	Brain
↓	↑
Object	Receptor (e.g., eye)
(The apparition of a man)	↑
	Light waves
	↑
	Agitations in some physical system

Let us take what has become a "common-sense" view of perception—it is really the view of popular science—and place it on the right-hand side of our diagram, with a gap to divide it from a psychological view of perception on the left in which a Conscious Subject is aware of an Object, say a man.

For Coleridge, of course, there is no right-hand side to the picture; it is absorbed into the Object in the left-hand division which contains all that is known. What I have there labelled the "apparition of a man" is not, for Coleridge, an apparition but the man himself. The Object is not "a something without . . . which occasions the objects of their perceptions" but the man himself. "It is the table itself, which the man of common-sense believes himself to see—not the phantom of a table, from which he may argumentatively deduce the reality of a table which he does not see" (*B. L.*, I, 179). And the Subject for Coleridge is equally not a hypothetical abstraction, a conscious ego about which nothing can be known; but it is an Act of knowing—"a realizing intuition." It is "a subject which becomes a subject by the act of constructing itself objectively to itself; but which never is an object except for itself, and only so far as by the very same act it becomes a subject" (*B. L.*, I, 183).

The coalescence of the Subject and the Object in the act of knowing is a difficult doctrine—partly because it needs practising, partly because other senses of *Subject* and *Object* (and still more of *subjective* and *objective*) are so easily confused with these. For example, we may take *objective* as "outside and independent of my mind or any mind," which would make nonsense of the doctrine. Or we may take *subjective* as "dependent upon wishes, feelings, state of expectation, prior conceptions, and so on," which again is not Coleridge's sense here. And we are likely to be more familiar with these senses—through discussions as to whether Beauty, for example, is subjective or objective.

Another distinction for which *subjective* and *objective* are used is also likely to be confused into the problem. Feelings, desires, pain-pleasure (the affec-tive—volitional aspects of consciousness) may be opposed as subjective, to sensations, images, ideas, conceptions (cognitive aspects of consciousness) presentations which seem to stand *over against* a conscious subject. These appear to be offered to contemplation in a way in which desires, for example, are not. This again is *not* Coleridge's distinction. It turns upon a piece of speculative psychological mythology that he does not use. In his best analyses he transposes feelings, thoughts, ideas, desires, images and passions with a freedom which descriptive psychology has only recently regained. He treats all these elements in the psychological inventory as forms of the activity of the mind—different, of course, and with different functions—but not to be set over against one another in two groups either as products to be opposed to the processes which bring them into being, or as presentations to be set against the reverberations they arouse and which shift them about.

His subject–object machinery introduces no such split between the ingre-dients of the mind. It is for him an instrument for noting, and insisting, that nothing of which we are in any way conscious is *given* to the mind. Into the simplest seeming "datum" a constructing, forming activity from the mind has entered. And the perceiving and the forming are the same. The subject (the self) has gone into what it perceives, and what it perceives is, in this sense, itself. So the object becomes the subject and the subject the object. And as, to understand what Coleridge is saying, we must not take the object as some-thing given to us; so equally we must not take the subject to be a mere empty formless void out of which all things mysteriously and ceaselessly rush to become everything we know. The subject is what it is through the objects it has been. . . .

———

Northrop Frye has written: "The great writer seldom regards himself as a personality with something to say: his mind to him is simply a place where something happens to words." This, as it stands, looks like a generalization from biographies; but that, I think, is largely a *façon de parler*. Language invites us continually to talk about poets under conditions which only entitle us to talk about poems. The substance of this sentence, for me, is that well-organized poems can be studied as places where transactions between words take place.

"How Does a Poem Know When It Is Finished?" from *Poetries and Sciences* (1970).

10

Motivation

We cannot too early consider the part played by the expected satisfaction, the inducement, the motivation which is behind and guides every process of interpretation. No writer supplies the full setting which controls the reader in his reading. He cannot. Always the major part must be left to the reader to bring in. This is perhaps the truism which in practice we most neglect. The writer can at best only use a small selection from the whole setting— taking this as the total situation, all the conditions governing what is going on. What he uses has a nucleus, namely what he explicitly mentions. Round this is a sphere of relatively stable factors, those things which all, on reflection, would agree to be implied, to be necessarily cooperative with what he has actually mentioned. Round these, less and less dependable and stable, are sphere after sphere of more and more doubtful factors which spread out, if we carry our speculative description far enough, to include the whole past experience of the reader. If, and insofar as, communication occurs, vast ranges of these free or unimplied factors must still be somehow ordered so as to secure some correspondence between those active in the reader and in the writer. They are so ordered, if at all, by what Coleridge called "the all in each of all men," the common principles of human life and the routine of normal experience. It seems a shadowy thing on which to depend unless we recognize that it is rooted in our biological continuity one with another.

From this common principle evidently branch all the specialized similarities that training and common studies can induce. It makes them possible, but without them we could go no great distance in understanding one an-

Interpretation in Teaching (1938), chap. 4.

other—as all who have resided, say, in Japan know too well. Hence, since a language is our chief controllable common training, the paramount importance of studies in English for English-speaking peoples. Hence innumerable morals—e.g., the importance of a common body of literature familiar to all—for the teacher and the framers of a curriculum. (That we can no longer refer with any confidence to any episode in the Bible, or to any nursery tale or any piece of mythology is a clear and well-recognized sign of the urgency of taking these things more advisedly in hand.) Hence too the inaccessibility, to all but specially trained readers, of most literature of past ages. We perhaps as a rule can give only enough training to our pupils to hide this inaccessibility from us and from them, without giving enough to build a genuine bridge across the gulf.

The writer, relying upon the common linguistic training, and on whatever other common controlling factors in experience he can, offers at best a skeleton or schema to be filled out by his reader. Looked at from a distance it may seem a miracle that he should succeed, and our wonder must be that understanding is achieved so often and goes so deep, not that it so often fails. But, looking closer, the explanation is perhaps to be found in the extreme interconnectedness of the processes of any single mind. If we thought of experience (as the cruder exponents of associationism used to think of it) as merely a series of impacts on a passive mind, linked together only by frequencies of concomitance and by resultant habit sequences, communication might well seem inexplicable. But such a theory, though it haunts more than a little educational theory—recommending, for example, drill as a mode of improving composition!—is now merely an intellectual curiosity like astrology. It is now agreed, beneath all their differences in phrasing, by all schools of psychology that the mind (or whatever they put in its place) is not a passive substratum, that mental process is from the beginning selective. In other words that experience is not just suffering things to happen to us but a mode of ordering our lives. From this self-ordering, organizing principle comes the sameness upon which communication depends. In addition to the uniformity of experience conceived as offered to us *from without,* there is its uniformity as organized by us *from within;* and here is where the control of inducement over interpretation comes in. We choose, in brief, and the laws of choice are alike in us all, though their outcome, of course, is not.

What we arrive at as our interpretation is what we are satisfied with as the meaning. To write "what gave us satisfaction" might mislead, but, if guardedly taken, it would make the point more vigorously. We may be well content to find an author's remarks "unsatisfactory." There is an inner movement in the process that is easily described as our tendency to find what meaning we please. If sometimes we teachers are included to blame this—as whimsicality, wantonness or obstinacy—when things have gone wrong, we should not forget that we have it equally to thank whenever things go right. For if we ask, Upon what can an author rely to guide his reader to his meaning? the broad answer fundamentally must be this: he must rely upon the right reading being more satisfying than any other reading.

I have left out all sorts of qualifications: "satisfying to whom and in what state of mind and for what purpose?" we must hurry to ask. But that is my point obviously enough here. We must never, if we can help it, forget that nobody ever reads anything for no purpose or in a state of utter indifference as to what he finds it to mean. And we must never pretend that aberrations in interpretation can be considered apart from distortions in the reader's appetitive process. This is why the question of inducement, of motivation, goes to the heart of all the teacher's problems, and all problems of interpretation and expression.

No slight stress has lately been laid upon this doctrine in discussions of the principles of English teaching, but sometimes in an unduly onesided fashion and without recognizing its manifold implications. It is often urged for example that it is no good making backward writers do composition at random, in the blue, merely *as* composition, that unless they are writing about something that interests them, unless they have something they care about to discuss, they will have no genuine impulse to write, no steam behind their wheels, and, with nothing to express, no cause to improve their expression. Well and good so far as it goes—but that, I think it can be shown, is no great distance. Granted that composition-exercises without *any* motive, and interpretation-exercises equally, would be absurdities, this recommendation assumes altogether too simple a view of interests. It has, I suggest, a fatal and obvious defect in that it identifies them with what the psychologizing moralists used to call "involuntary" appetitions and overlooks the immensely important domain of voluntary actions—those namely in which something is done not for its own sake, not for the immediate satisfaction in the action, but for the sake of remoter consequences. The vast majority of the interests on which education depends are plainly of this voluntary type and it is a commonplace of morals and psychology alike that the successful exercise of such voluntary activities, that is the process of attending deliberately for an ulterior purpose to a task which is not intrinsically alluring, generates an *in*voluntary intrinsic interest, if not in the work itself, at least (and it is quite as helpful) in its successful prosecution. In brief, *pride,* reluctance to be beaten, self-esteem are enlisted, no stronger motives than which can be engaged. And with even a slight satisfaction to these—and the least sense of success with the work will yield it—the work itself, becoming identified with an activity of the self, picks up a derivative attraction.

I am here, of course, merely echoing the homilies of innumerable moralists. But there is a more immediate reason for doubting whether the policy of utilizing only or chiefly a pupil's own personal interests is advisable, or for thinking that he will advance best by writing about his hobbies or reading only the literature which has already caught his fancy. It comes from the central place of linguistic ability in man's being as a social creature. Without ability to speak we have no standing, our rank depends upon our capacity to understand and to express ourselves so as to be understood. The incredible intellectual feat that the child achieves in learning to speak had as its chief motive just this enhancement of its self-esteem. If the motive lapses later with the development of a partial command of interpretation and expression, that is because the performer is suffering from a relaxation of the social criticism which originally drove him on. Ideally, his own self-criticism should take its place; failing that or pending this moment of maturity, it is the teacher's business to arrange for the stimulating challenge.

He has to contrive that the pupil becomes clearly aware that he is as yet unable to interpret or to express things that others, whom he regards as no more than his equals, succeed with. A painful process to recommend no doubt. But if it is true that the main reason why any of us can talk or understand speech at all was that we each so hated feeling a fool, this recommendation as regards the motivation of English studies is obvious. It seems that the advertisers who undertake to make us impressive public speakers have been better psychologists than the Drill school of educationists!

Guardedly used, what I may perhaps call the "protocol method" might be employed more widely with advantage. Nothing is more stimulating than to see how others have succeeded with the same task. Nothing more quickly transforms a problem from a mystery to be guessed about into a practical matter that can, and must, be understood. Like other powerful methods it is open to grave abuse; it can bewilder, wound, and frustrate. I should be loath to see it employed without the protection of anonymity. Unless ample leisure for meditation is allowed, specimens of other students' work will not be illuminating. To hear random comments read out soon induces a nervous crisis. But, if these obvious dangers are avoided, I believe that a process of presenting to the class the varied views that any set of comments will supply, might do much to freshen English studies and, by restoring candor and humility, redeem what is too often a dreary and hypocritical ritual.

I assume then, as a general motive which should be dominant both in expression and in interpretation, a desire to esteem oneself as a person capable of saying and of reading things adequately—an unwillingness to be patently silly or inept in these activities. It is this motive which more than any other holds in check the vagaries of the active and passive uses of language. The merit of a literary exercise must, I believe, be judged by the degree to which it invites this motive to overrule adventitious, distracting and more limited interests. No doubt the general motive can be reinforced by special interests, and there is here some weight in the "Let him write about what he dreams about!" doctrine. If he feels that a subject is important, he is more likely perhaps to take care in saying things, or in discovering what is being said, about it. On the other hand this is evidently truer of factual matters than of imaginative. In general, exercises for which revealing tests of adequacy are not able to be applied take up time on which there are better claims.

It is a narrow view of motivation which supposes that an exercise in interpretation or composition merely as such, and taken apart from the special enthusiasms, pursuits or curiosities of the individual, must be devoid of interest or lack incentives. Such a view overlooks the fascination of puzzles and omits to consider how these special interests themselves originally developed.

In most cases perhaps they would be found to have grown at first as modes of self-enhancement; developing, with growth, their peculiar intrinsic attractions. But of course the exercises must be well chosen, they must present themselves as reasonable challenges, as tasks that the learner feels he ought to be able to succeed in. Above all they must call for a kind of effort from him that reassures him as he achieves it; they must not, and here is the fatal objection to most drill, make him feel that he is merely submitting to the compulsion of an unintelligible command. That feeling numbs intelligence at once and deadens just what we are most anxious to awaken. It reverses the right order as between habit formation and insight. Here modern psychology can do the teacher a service. Nothing is more impressive in recent studies of learning than the overthrow of the assumptions on which the drill recommendation rests. We learn by *seeing* how to do things, not by blindly going through the motions. *After* insight, repetition will develop habits that may usefully take its place, but not before. It is strange that these obsolete notions of how learning happens should find such a stronghold in teaching practice, since nowhere should the waste they entail be more apparent.

"When I had once found the delight of knowledge and felt the pleasure of intelligence and the pride of invention," said Imlac, "every hour taught me something new. I lived in a continual course of gratifications." It is these gratifications that are the fundamental incentives to all study. Good teaching offers them incessantly, bad teaching withholds them: and perhaps there is more bad teaching in English than in any other subject. Mathematics used to be notorious too and a comparison might be useful. I understand that methods there have improved, and that more teachers now can transform a dark mystery operated only by mechanical dodges and tricks into an intelligible field for reason.

We must not forget that blind rote and drill kill the teacher as surely as his pupils. Unless we can see a mistake as a problem we cannot make it fruitful for its victim. And only so can we raise the occupation of the teacher of elementary English into a profession that can, without self-sacrifice, attract the talented. The correction and analysis of interpretation and composition can and must be developed into a study worth pursuing for its own sake. But there should be no difficulty in doing this once we realize that it is nothing else than literary criticism descended from its windy heights and restored to contact with its actual facts.

The class-room indeed offers unique opportunities for criticism, including self-criticism. The literary critic who wonders, as he must often do, whether he is of any service to the world, and whether his efforts make any difference to anyone, can find there, if he will modestly descend to minute particulars, an inexhaustible field to cultivate. There, living in the flesh, are all the types of the human spirit; there all the steps which the historian of culture would like to trace are being taken anew; there all the literary discoveries are being made again. There too, and more evidently, the heresies, the confusions, the outworn, exploded, exposed-to-death assumptions that have frustrated so many possible poets and prophets, are being reinvented. Who would be only a paleontologist if the dinosaur still roamed the swamp?

To be more temperate, the varieties of interpretation which a well-chosen passage can elicit do sometimes astonishingly repeat in miniature the characteristics of vanished literary epochs. They are, I suggest, if carefully examined, capable of presenting a fascinating synopsis of intellectual history—not less interesting for being more compassable. As a word or a grammatical form may contain the germ of a whole philosophy, so certain ways of reading carry implicitly with them a characteristic outlook or culture. And apart from these attractions, the detailed study of interpretations has its interest as showing us, again in miniature, many facets of human nature which we ordinarily perceive only as traits of character. On these grounds alone, it would be capable of some justification as a part of general education aside from the help which it may give to the development of linguistic ability. But centrally its value derives from the insight it may give us into how our minds work, into their difficulties, their weaknesses, their temptations and the means of overcoming them. And this insight, which the discerning and skilful teacher can share with and induce in his pupils, is the only source of advance and its chief reward.

One very simple and broad observation—with an obvious accompanying recommendation—can, I think, be made at this stage. It is that a whole literature seems to be missing from the library of pedagogics. The literature namely which would describe plainly and candidly actual procedures followed by teachers in correcting or discussing the compositions of their pupils, and detail the explanations they venture to give of their corrections. The technical journals of the teaching profession compare extremely badly with those of dentistry in this respect. They bulge with repetitive discussions of principles, but where can we find case-histories detailing the treatment recommended for a given confused paragraph? The dentist is ready to tell his *confrères* how he rights a rotting tooth. The teacher seems as yet oddly unwilling to confess in equal detail how he criticizes a bad essay. To do so is of course to invite comment that may be disconcerting, but the man of faith will not flinch from that. The literature that would result if studies of interesting confusions and misunderstandings became as regular features in the professional literature as descriptions of procedures are in the dental journals would soon revolutionize practice. We should begin to profit, as dentists have long been profiting, from one another's mistakes.

It is one thing to insist (as we have all been insisting for years) that the pupil's great need is to attain a mastery of clear and ordered expression. It is quite another *to show, in detail,* how a given paragraph fails or how the pupil can best be helped to see that it fails and to put it right. The first sounds like the end of the matter, which lapses into universal agreement. The second may well be the beginning of a lengthy and valuable dispute. Doubtless for the layman stupidity and bad writing are not things he would willingly linger over. Their study is, he may think, no more his concern than the horrors of pathology—which he leaves to the medical profession. But just who is the analogue to the pathologist here? Who does study misconception with the care it deserves? The teacher at present does not; but who else should? And is the layman's position really as well taken as he thinks? Stupidity is a complaint from which no one can claim immunity, and adults must commonly be their own schoolmasters.

Stupidity is an unduly harsh name for the misinterpretations and frustrations of expression with which we are concerned here. In their less gross and palpable forms they are ceaseless, and we flatter ourselves if we think we escape them ever. Who, asks the moralist, is the just man and perfect? Who, asks the alienist, is not psychopathic? Who, we may ask, interprets, or expresses himself, as well as he might? They are all equally rhetorical questions. The real questions are as to the extent of our loss and the power of the available remedies. That both are much greater than we ordinarily suppose will, I hope, be established in the course of this discussion. That they are strangely neglected is implied. I doubt indeed whether there is another matter as important to mankind which receives as little systematic study, or in which so much might evidently be done if we set to work to do it.

The obvious recommendation which follows from the shortage of detailed case studies of failures is that the professional journals should reserve sections—perhaps under special editorship—for such communications from teachers, and encourage, in correspondence columns, a critical discussion of them. This would provide openings for much thought which at present has no very useful outlet; it would stimulate interest at the very point at which the teacher is apt to feel most need for such stimulation (the correction of papers)—the point at which his work is most apt to seem merely disheartening; it would give him the support of a cooperative venture; he would be able to compare his own troubles with those of his fellows. Instead of a mere ad hoc struggle with a single difficulty, he could feel that he was taking part in a general effort to improve technique and that his thought had a wider usefulness than the ordinary limitations of the school setting present it as having. And there would be a further and obvious use in these communications. They would in time provide an abundant supply, in a prepared and developed form, of just those exercises in interpretation which are a chief need in teaching. They would give us both model problems and a technique of discussion. At present if we offer our pupils a passage to comment upon we are making a somewhat incalculable experiment. Only after watching its strange adventures as it passes through mind after mind are we in a position to see clearly what may best be learnt from it. The experiments which I am reporting in this section of my statement were obviously of very different value from this point of view. They all made, perhaps, too exacting a demand to be of general use. I had to risk this because too easy an exercise would—given the conditions under which my audience submitted itself to me—have cost me more interest than I could afford to lose. But exercises of this type—

through which students must come to see for themselves that what they regard as adequate reading and writing is not adequate—exercises which will prove to them, apart altogether from a teacher's opinion, that they have not nearly mastered the arts of reading and writing, and that without further improvement a large part of their intellectual life is mere folly, such exercises, I am convinced, are a prime need. No one can sit down to invent such exercises. You have to wait until one is revealed to you by what at first seems a happy accident of your own or someone else's stupidity. Then you have to satisfy yourself that it is no mere individual accidental lapse that has occurred but that the troublesome passage is a natural and general matrix of misunderstanding.

To discover the most useful exercises must be a large corporate undertaking. Moreover they must be suited not only to the pupils but to the teachers, and what may sometimes be an arduous process of preparation is required before they are ready for use. The communications and the critical correspondence would both prepare them for the teacher and, which is perhaps even more important, would, whether good or bad, be a valuable exercise *for him* in the considerations which this kind of work entails—exercise which ordinary school work by no means necessarily supplies. Doubtless the editor of such a section would receive plenty of queer letters. The teacher's desk has no virtue to protect him from misinterpreting. But once the point has been granted that the study of almost any misinterpretation may be profitable, the source of the blunder is unimportant. It may even humanize the subject to realize still more often that Fate has us all in its hand here!

In the design of instruction—say, in literacy or in a second language—the actual outcome, the ease or difficulty (better, the discernment or trouble) with which a learner takes a step, is much more instructive to the designer if he has kept himself as little committed as he can be to the *detail* of what he is trying out. Meanwhile, however, constancy and attachment to the *principles* of the design (as opposed to the minutiae of its implementation) are required. For these principles have (or should have) governed the choice of the detail; it is these principles which are really under trial (not some one of a number of possible embodiments), and unless the principles stay constant, fertile interplay between what is looked for (feedforward) and what actually happens (feedback) is precluded. The experimentation will not lead to the strengthening or weakening or emendation of the principles, which should be its main purpose.

"The Secret of Feedforward," from *Complementarities* (1976).

II

The Composing Mind

Much in my account of "The Poetic Experience" [in *Science and Poetry*] is a simplification of doctrines more elaborately expounded in *Principles of Literary Criticism*. Some of these have since seemed to me not so much false as undeveloped and likely to be wrongly taken. In what follows I try to add some of the misleading parts of the picture and with them to redirect the whole design. What should then appear could be, it may be hoped, somewhat more useful to poets than the earlier sketches.

In chief, the connexities *within* any experience that is likely to be called "poetic" in any relevant sense were not brought out enough; nor were the multiplicities and intricacies of its dependencies upon other experience.

Take first what we may rather too easily call ^{di}parts^{di}* of the poem without more than dimly and distantly realizing what a variety of choices we may be offering our interlocutor as to what we are talking of. Its lines are parts; so are its assumptions, its implications, its suggestions, its echoes, its words, its letters, its commas . . . but in what different ways! And often, relations between parts are themselves parts: the length of a line may come to it from other lines (in a sense quite unlike anything to be settled by some measurement), a foot takes its form from other feet, actual or possible; an assonance works by not being a full rhyme. . . . As a shift of mood requires the former mood, so a word may succeed by *not* being the expected word. Or by being surprisingly, just *that*. Such gambits and stratagems are omnipresent and inexhaustibly various in all speech. A wide and often convenient definition

*See pp. 270–73 for an explanation of these superscripts.—ED

Poetries and Sciences (1970), "Reorientation."

of the ᴺᵂpoeticˢʷ use of language makes it simply discourse in which such features heighten the efficiency of the utterance.

To consider how the composing mind, and the recomposing mind of the recipient, manage such devices will be a means of bringing home the connexities I note as understressed in *Science and Poetry*. In the use (and in the recipient's interpretation)—witting, unwitting or betwixt and between—of an alliteration, say, or an assonance a great deal more recognition of structure must enter than we commonly suppose. The structures in question will commonly be cyclic: eddyings, to borrow from Coleridge, eddyings often of eddies of eddies—each subcomponent having the reciprocal, interdependent features of ⁿᵇfeedforwardⁿᵇ and ⁿᵇfeedbackⁿᵇ: i.e., what has happened has set the cycle *for* (fed forward) a consequent. Occurrence, accordant or otherwise at the set point, is reported (fed back) to the larger system sustaining the subcycle so that corrective action, if need be, may be taken.

Perhaps the most pertinent illustration of a feedforward feedback cycle is the drawing of a free-hand circle. First comes the feedforward directive as to the size of the circle. It cannot be begun without that. Then with every inch your chalk travels there is feedback reporting to your nerve-muscle-tendon-joint executives as to violations of the feedforward directives and an issuing of new feedforward as to corrective action if needed. Conceive now that, as serving the free but controlled sweep of your arm, all the contributors—your eye on the alert for aberrations; your nerves as balancing the opposing pulls of the muscles that roll shoulder, elbow, wrist, thumb and finger joints—are all organized in cooperative circuits. Probably we should think of even the smaller subcomponents of these circuits as being also cyclic systems held stable through their dependence upon the wider systems within what they serve.

What is most plainly evident about the overall arrangement is the immense amount of *substitution* it permits. Alternative means are richly available. You can, for example, correct your curve by adjustment at shoulder, elbow or wrist or in varying degrees at all three. If for any reason a step cannot be taken in one way, it can in another. Obviously, this is of the greatest biologic importance. What has, however, to be imagined (as far as may be) is *how* these alternates get selected and alerted and how their precedences, mergers, etc. are ordered. Some sort of communication-system, maybe a variety of them, between subsystems within, across and up and down the multiplicities of hierarchies of control seems to be required.

Among these preternaturals, some of the poetries offer the most reflexive, self-involved examples. Indeed, these are self-editing, sometimes to a degree matched only at the opposite end of the mental spectrum: in mathematics. The modes of self-reference and self-examination are, however, fully as diverse. Mathematics explores itself by mathematical means, poetries by poetic. This self-searching shows itself whenever in composing, or in choice between interpretations, we note how we are guided by the extent to which change in one component entails change in others, whenever we 'see' that if x varies, *p,g* . . . must vary too. The process of composition is indeed a weighing of these entailments, a balancing imposed by the rivalling possibilities of the alternates I suggest that, as with our circle-drawing, we should include alternates of which we do not ordinarily or normally admit we are in the least cognizant.

We are not cognizant of them, but the composing, the growth of the poem, is. Something then in *us* takes account of the innumerable entailments: cooperations and repudiations, in an unhesitating and secure fashion.

What 'we' or 'us' in such sentences can be talking about is no easy matter to decide. It seems perhaps a likely suggestion that "we," in such instances, represents the system of relevant feedforward, which at the moment is being confirmed by feedback. Such a view would accord with the widely agreed fact that our ˢʷweˢʷs keep varying. The ˢʷweˢʷ that is concerned with writing or interpreting a poem seems very closely bound up with what it is doing. By comparison ˢʷweˢʷ which uses its knowledge of the multiplication table seems little involved. Both, however, belong to the big 'WE' that no biographer can ever understand.

Adding, as I suggest we should, influential alternates 'we' do *not cognize* (though the poem does) may restore to the poem the mystery that most poetries seem justly to claim. The poem knows more than we do about itself, and part of its business is to make us feel so. . . . It starts off as a problem: *what to be;* and ends by finding in itself, when successful, what it was seeking. It becomes self-entailed: in Coleridge's formula it "contains in itself the reason why it is so and not otherwise."

So much for the inner connexities which *S & P*, I think, missed. The further connexities, the linkages, selective and corrective, with what has been and is to be, these were—unless I am being unfair—as lightly passed over. The book was perhaps too busy hurrying up the retreat of religion to attend properly to its own business.

These further connexities, through which the poetries can pursue their task of exploring, reassessing, and confirming values, can perhaps be suggested most compendiously by a reminder of what a good enough dictionary could display. Every word, it could show, is connected, directly or circuitously, in every one of its uses with uses of all other words. ˢʷUsesˢʷ here deserves careful reflection. A ˢʷuseˢʷ of the word here is some work it is being asked to do, some task it is required (in cooperation with other words) to help with. We may remind ourselves: (1) that these tasks we ask words to take part in are attempts to cope with situations; and (2) that these situations are complexes within which the utterer and the recipient are necessary and fundamental parts along with, and involved in, the thing to be done.

All this, which is perhaps as a rule 'taken for granted' in thought about what language does for man, if spelled out and then pondered resourcefully, can become, I think, that justification of the poetries—as language well employed on creative tasks—which the author of *S & P* did not quite know where to look for, though he knew that it needs perennially to be sought.

Perhaps he was scared by some silly uses of "creative" and did not feel like venturing upon the others.

> Say can'st thou make thyself?—Learn first that trade;—
> Haply thou mayst know what thyself has made.

Perhaps not even Coleridge knew just how to take that. And probably, few reflective readers will be at all constant in how they take it, though they may agree that among the things that language has to do, to help us in finding improved orders of being may be counted the chief. As Philosophy told Boethius in his prison: "Now do I know the cause of your sickness. You have forgotten what you are."

———

The way of reflection presupposes the responses it considers, compares, and decides between. Any whole presupposes its parts; and all this which it does is their interaction within it. When the responses dry up and the words go blank and we wonder what they can possibly mean, what we do is suspend our suppressing doubts in turn and encourage any response that will come out. The logical contradictions or agreements which then settle whether this response be slaughtered or crowned have the same forms as those which shaped it, but they hold between units of larger scale and the operative universals are of higher order. It seems that the simplest scrap or pulse of learning and the grandest flight of speculation share a common *pattern*, much as the inside of the atom seems to be built on somewhat the same plan as the solar system, and that again to have its analogies with the disposal of the galaxies.

"Warfare of Heart and Head," from *How to Read a Page* (1942).

III

The Meanings of Meaning

Lev Vygotsky, the Russian psychologist, declared that exploration of the relationship of language and thought necessarily begins with "the unit of meaning," arguing his case with the help of the organic metaphor of the living cell. Richards, too, returning to the great theme of meaning, which he and Ogden had so energetically (and inadequately) addressed in *The Meaning of Meaning,* depends on organic metaphors as he continually sets forth the triadic character of the meaning relation. Poetry, he believed, was the best "instrument of research" because the complex interdependencies of words, the activity of metaphor, and other figurative ways of making meaning provide the best opportunity for studying all the meanings of meaning, all the functions of the sign.

In the current critical climate, it is tonic to read Richards forthrightly setting out to discuss ways of thinking about *meanings* and how language *represents* them. He carefully identifies the "defensive isolationism," the "eviscerative abstraction" favored by positivist linguistics, which in its scientism holds that setting aside meaning, purpose, and context allows *language itself* to be discovered. But Richards understood very clearly that what is represented is an interpretation which must itself be represented so that it, too, can be interpreted. The doctrine of the Interpretant does not sanction the absurd notion of an indeterminacy that denies the possibility of reference. The abyss which opens between the signifier and the signified in the dyadic conception of the sign and into which meaning, significance, intention, purpose, authors, and their language are flung, plays no role in a triadic semiotic.

"Meanings Anew," which Richards considered one of his most important pieces, was written nearly forty years after *The Meaning of Meaning* and shows the kind of advance he made, once he was out from under Ogden's controlling influence and had begun drawing out implications of what he had learned about translation. (*Meanings* would not have been called "virtualities" and "dispositional conspiracies" in the 1920s.) He needs to form the concepts of composition and notation and, indeed, of language itself, and watching how he goes about it is instructive. He calls his definitions *propositions,* thereby inviting pragmatic analysis. Richards' style of defining derives from his detestation of disputation: *multiple definition* becomes the principal technique for seeing what difference a science of signs could make in how we read, how we think about language, and how we teach interpretation by showing how everything depends on the way we understand the uses of language and our purposes as we depend on it in thinking and communicating.

Richards' "Theory of Comprehending" offers a full analysis of the model Jakobson had developed of "the communication situation." He shows how this representation, derived from information (or communication) theory, because it muddles signal and message, does not allow us to recognize the interdependence of what we say and what we intend, of text and context, of purpose and discourse. It certainly pleased Richards that Jakobson recognized the importance of situation to any interpretive activity, but the information theory diagram could not properly represent how the situation itself helps to determine our messages. Richards redesigned the diagram to accommodate "comparison fields," but even his comically complicated version cannot represent the process of determination in which feedforward is in dialectic with feedback. Since our messages are meanings, they are means as well as ends: the purposing entailed in making meaning Richards represented in another diagram as the hub of a circle in which he depicts the roles of language. But to give an account of the agentive activity, he turned to metaphor—or myth. Has anyone else writing on linguistics spoken of the soul?

Whenever Richards turns his attention to linguists and their various enterprises, he concludes that they have not *yet* developed the wherewithal to guide them in what they claim to be doing. The *yet* (and it occurs dozens of times) serves two purposes: it is a gentle (sometimes sardonic) warning: "Not so fast! What you're claiming is not yet warranted!" But I think it also expresses a genuine hope Richards had for the electronic media in conjunction with a genuinely modern understanding of language and learning. He thought that linguists, with their mechanistic models, might yet be brought to see that a different perspective, a different direction, was possible, and he wanted to encourage them: he did not want to foreclose the possibility that we are on the threshold of revolutionary change.

As Richards developed his theory of comprehending—at the heart of which was "the comparing activity itself"—he depended on certain instruments of thought, certain "divisions," which he called "oppositions." Though not necessarily antithetical, they are set over against one another so that we can the more readily apprehend the dialectic. One of the chief oppositions is token/type, C. S. Peirce's distinction between instance and law, particular and universal. These oppositions are triadically conceived: there is always the dimension of activity—or *acteevity,* as Richards wanted to spell it, to alert us to its importance.

"Powers and Limits of Signs," written when Richards was over eighty, is quirky and unfocused, but in it he explicitly and eloquently comments on Peirce's semiotic principles. (This excerpt comprises about half of the original text; the other half is a version of his extensive discussion of depiction in "Learning and Looking"; see Chapter 23 in this volume.) The disquisition on translation is actually an explanation of what Peirce means by *semiosis,* the dialectical process of balancing abstract accounts and the experiential record. And of course his perennial insistence on keeping things tentative is an expression of Peirce's principle of fallibilism. His comments on the tenor/vehicle distinction, developed in *The Philosophy of Rhetoric* forty years before, as a token of Peirce's token/TYPE opposition suggests that triadicity is the commanding idea early and late: of Richards' theory of translation as of his theory of comprehending; of his educational designs as of his philosophy of rhetoric. He endeavors always to make the case that we must differentiate without dichotomizing the *what* and the *how,* what we mean and what we say.

Following this essay, I have added a long passage from a notebook in which Richards was working out what he had to say in "Powers and Limits." In both places, he is taking aim at General Semantics, which was virtually defunct by the 1970s, but the cogency of his critique can be tested by substituting "Post-Structuralist Critical Theory" for "General Semantics." Thus, Paul de Man's conception of how words work is a mystical variant of Alfred Korsybski's profound positivism, and his terror of organic conceptions of the symbol resembles the Count's detestation of all metaphors but his own. Another interest of this draft is that Richards remarks, as he fails to do in the essay as published, on "the necessary mutual dependence" of the powers and limits of signs. No modern critic (other than Kenneth Burke) has better understood this dialectic.

12

Thoughts, Words, and Things

Symbols direct and organize, record and communicate. In stating what they direct and organize, record and communicate we have to distinguish as always between Thoughts and Things. It is Thought (or, as we shall usually say, *reference*) which is directed and organized, and it is also Thought which is recorded and communicated. But just as we say that the gardener mows the lawn when we know that it is the lawnmower which actually does the cutting, so, though we know that the direct relation of symbols is with thought, we also say that symbols record events and communicate facts.

By leaving out essential elements in the language situation we easily raise problems and difficulties which vanish when the whole transaction is considered in greater detail. Words, as every one now knows, "mean" nothing by themselves, although the belief that they did, as we shall see in the next chapter, was once equally universal. It is only when a thinker makes use of them that they stand for anything, or in one sense, have "meaning." They are instruments. But besides this referential use which for all reflective, intellectual use of language should be paramount, words have other functions which may be grouped together as emotive. These can best be examined when the framework of the problem of strict statement and intellectual communication has been set up. The importance of the emotive aspects of language is not thereby minimized, and anyone chiefly concerned with popular or primitive speech might well be led to reverse this order of approach. Many difficulties, indeed, arising through the behaviour of words in discussion, even amongst scientists, force us at an early stage to take into account these "nonsymbolic" in-

From *The Meaning of Meaning,* with C. K. Ogden (1923), chap. 1.

fluences. But for the analysis of the senses of "meaning" with which we are here chiefly concerned, it is desirable to begin with the relations of thoughts, words and things as they are found in cases of reflective speech uncomplicated by emotional, diplomatic, or other disturbances; and with regard to these, the indirectness of the relations between words and things is the feature which first deserves attention.

This may be simply illustrated by a diagram, in which the three factors involved whenever any statement is made, or understood, are placed at the corners of the triangle, the relations which hold between them being represented by the sides. The point just made can be restated by saying that in this respect the base of the triangle is quite different in composition from either of the other sides.

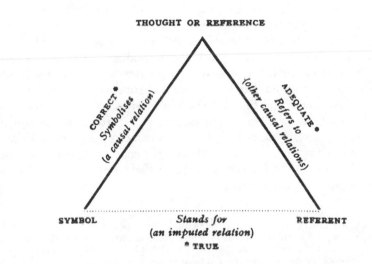

THOUGHT OR REFERENCE

CORRECT *
Symbolises
(a causal relation)

ADEQUATE *
Refers to
(other causal relations)

SYMBOL   *Stands for*   REFERENT
        (*an imputed relation*)
              * TRUE

Between a thought and a symbol causal relations hold. When we speak, the symbolism we employ is caused partly by the reference we are making and partly by social and psychological factors—the purpose for which we are making the reference, the proposed effect of our symbols on other persons, and our own attitude. When we hear what is said, the symbols both cause us to perform an act of reference and to assume an attitude which will, according to circumstances, be more or less similar to the act and the attitude of the speaker.

Between the Thought and the Referent there is also a relation; more or less direct (as when we think about or attend to a coloured surface we see), or indirect (as when we "think of" or "refer to" Napoleon), in which case there may be a very long chain of sign-situations intervening between the act and its referent: word—historian—contemporary record—eyewitness—referent (Napoleon).

Between the symbol and the referent there is no relevant relation other than the indirect one, which consists in its being used by someone to stand for a referent. Symbol and Referent, that is to say, are not connected directly (and when, for grammatical reasons, we imply such a relation, it will merely be an imputed, as opposed to a real, relation) but only indirectly round the two sides of the triangle.*

It may appear unnecessary to insist that there is no direct connection between say "dog," the word, and certain common objects in our streets, and that the only connection which holds is that which consists in our using the word when we refer to the animal. We shall find, however, that the kind of simplification typified by this once universal theory of direct meaning relations between words and things is the source of almost all the difficulties which thought encounters. As will appear at a later stage, the power to confuse and obstruct, which such simplifications possess, is largely due to the conditions of communication. Language if it is to be used must be a *ready* instrument. The handiness and ease of a phrase is always more important in deciding whether it will be extensively used than its accuracy. Thus such shorthand as the word "means" is constantly used so as to imply a direct simple relation between words and things, phrases and situations. If such relations could be admitted then there would of course be no problem as to the nature of Meaning, and the vast majority of those who have been concerned with it would have been right in their refusal to discuss it. But too many interesting developments have been occurring in the sciences, through the rejection of everyday symbolizations and the endeavour to replace them by more accurate accounts, for any naïve theory that "meaning" is just "meaning" to be popular at the moment.

---

*An exceptional case occurs when the symbol used is more or less directly like the referent for which it is used, as for instance, it may be when it is an onomatopœic word, or an image, or a gesture, or a drawing. In this case the triangle is completed; its base is supplied, and a great simplification of the problem involved appears to result. For this reason many attempts have been made to reduce the normal language situation to this possibly more primitive form. Its greater completeness does no doubt account for the immense superiority in efficiency of gesture languages, within their appropriate field, to other languages not supportable by gesture within *their* fields. Hence we know far more perfectly what has occurred if a scene is well reenacted than if it be merely described. But in the normal situation we have to recognize that our triangle is without its base, that between Symbol and Referent no direct relation holds; and, further, that it is through this lack that most of the problems of language arise. Simulative and nonsimulative languages are entirely distinct in principle. Standing for and representing are different relations. It is, however, convenient to speak at times as though there were some direct relation holding between Symbol and Referent. We then say, on the analogy of the lawnmower, that a Symbol refers to a Referent. Provided that the telescopic nature of the phrase is not forgotten, confusion need not arise. In Supplement I, Part V *infra,* Dr Malinowski gives a valuable account of the development of the speech situation in relation to the above diagram. [When Ogden and Richards say that "it is the lawnmower which actually does the cutting," the example is more complex than is suggested and we can imagine how that *actually* would later have been subjected to an inquiry which could have reversed the assertion they make here. Further, it is doubtful that Richards would have stood by the distinction here between "simulative" and "nonsimulative" languages. Any symbol is subject to reflective, dialectical interpretation. The distinction was probably an attempt to differentiate an *index* from a *symbol,* in Peirce's terms. In any case, the example is an attempt to indicate the role of mediation in all symbolization.—ED]

We have, of course, to bear in mind how constantly language leads us to *talk* in ways which do not correspond with our *thought*. I will borrow a convenient label from Roman Jakobson and call it the Sunrise–Sunset, or pre-Copernican, or pre-Einsteinian Style. It may be that many people who use Vulgar Packaging expressions really know better—just as people talking of sunsets have not forgotten, and are not denying, that the earth rotates. I am suggesting, though, that very often people not only use Vulgar Packaging Language but *think with,* and are attached to, Vulgar Packaging THOUGHT. And that these people are finding this scientific lingo: of *message, signal,* and so on an intellectual Godsend.

What's chiefly wrong with it? This. It stands squarely in the way of our practical understanding and command of language. It hides from us both how we may learn to speak (and write) better, and how we may learn to comprehend more comprehensively. Managing the variable connections between words and what they mean: what they might mean, can't mean, and should mean—*that*—not as a theoretical study only or chiefly, but as a matter of actual control—that is the technique of poetry. If anyone is led into a way of thinking—a way of proceeding, rather—as though *composing* were a sort of catching a nonverbal butterfly in a verbal butterfly net, as though comprehending were a releasing of the said butterfly from the net, then he is deprived of the very thing that could help him: exercise in comparing the various equivalences of different words and phrases, their interdependencies in varying situations.

Every word or phrase in a language known to any one person (one utterer-comprehender) is—I have been insisting—potentially linked with all his other words and phrases in an unimaginably multifarious manner. Some words *substitute* for others (in a given situation), some *modify,* some *oppose,* some *exclude* others; some *invite* others, some *repel* . . . it is endless.

"The Future of Poetry," from *So Much Nearer* (1968).

13

Meanings Anew

In thinking about anything so central as our meanings we should encourage ourselves to take a variety of views from different distances and angles and to arrange them so that they supplement and clarify one another. This is hardly our usual practice, thinkers being more in the habit of behaving as though if one view is right any other views which "differ from it" must be wrong. No doubt in some fields that customary practice is useful, but not in considering how we should consider; for that is what we will be trying to do here under the heading "Meanings Anew."

This then will be a view—one of many different views, some others of which may be found in remarks or in assumptions made elsewhere in these essays. These are, I conceive, compatible, but no explicit attempt is made here to compare, to relate, to adjust and reconcile them one to another. That they will appear to conflict may be supposed. We would have to know very little about meanings and about how language represents them to expect otherwise. These other views have arisen in various connections, as serving, they hoped, this or that local endeavor. Any view is shaped by its connections though for convenience we often forget this. What follows is less tied to local service and more responsible to wider claims. It aspires to ask for more detachment, less engagement, and tries to remember as it proceeds that, if so, it has the freedom of a sketch.

Any word as it occurs *livingly* in a sentence that is occurring livingly in a discourse may be questioned in three ways:

From *So Much Nearer* (1968), chap. 5. Notes have been renumbered.

A. As to its interplay as a sound with the sounds of other words.

B. As to its interplay as a syntactic item with other syntactic items.

C. As to its interplay as a semantic agent with other semantic agents.

These three systems of interplay settle the role of the word in serving the sentence as that sentence is serving the situation.[1]

A. This interplay differentiates the word from others and enables it *as sound* to serve B and C. It is an interplay not only with other words co-occurring with it in the sentence and in the discourse but with all other words from which *for its work in the sentence* it needs to be differentiated and to which it needs to be related. It will do no harm here if we conceive a word's work in a discourse on the analogy of an individual's work in an enterprise. The character of the word as sound may be compared to the *appearance* of a worker, its distinguishability from the appearance of other workers. One's appearance *can* have, as not only ambassadors know, more than a little relation with the work he can do.

B. Syntactic interplay too can be approached through an analogy—with such organization of cooperations as is needed on a ship or in a business. Different word classes and phrase, group, clause structures have their duties to and requirements from one another, all ultimately deriving from and sanctioned by the work to be done through their cooperations. Any sentence (*in a discourse*) has its assignment. To fulfil this an internal organization of its components is required. Which of the many possible organizations it adopts for the job in hand is settled by the convergence of a prodigiously, indeed an unimaginably, complex set of determinants offering patterns formerly used in more or less parallel situations in the past. These may be called *Context Pressures* (in the sense of 'context'* defined in Appendix B of *The Meaning of Meaning*.) Another label for these might be *precedents*. Given a sort of work to be done, *how* that sort of work has previously been done naturally comes in, just as it does in any action, such as putting on a shoe. There is therefore much seemingly mechanical compulsion in syntactic interplay. The individual words participating in a sentence may all be changed while the structure of the team (their mutual dependencies) is the same. Syntactical necessities (such as, say, noun–verb accord as to singular and plural: "He eats" but "They eat") are imposed on a *growing* sentence by context pressure[2] from the enormous body of previous situations so handled. This pressure is represented in precedence routines that manage such demands. *His* language (the competence of his ideolect), for any user of it, is the operative system of precedents he has acquired through his traffic in it with other users. The confirmatory and suppressive effects of that traffic vary greatly from user to user and from hour to hour. Hence different degrees of ability in language use. (It is much to be wished that theorists about language would afford

---

*See pp. 270–73 for an explanation of these superscripts.—ED

themselves more opportunity for reflective study of early stages in the acquisition not only of first but of second languages by variously situated individuals.)

Syntactically, for most hearers–speakers, a person's language is a system of choices and entailments which he accepts as his only means of pursuing the verbal tasks (and indulgences) offered to him. Usually, in conversation and in impromptu speaking he only fulfils syntactic requirements to a socially tolerable degree often relatively low—as anyone will agree who has listened to tape recordings of his own performances in what he had hoped were accomplished speeches. When, moreover, he has propitious conditions and something sufficiently unusual to say, he is capable of departing wildly from syntactic routine. We should remember, though, that any grammarian is under severe pressure from his profession to assume (and find) as much autonomous necessity in his subject as he can.

C. The corresponding analogy for semantic interplay would point simply to all the tasks there can be[3] for any enterprise to attempt.

As a semantic agent a word in a sentence is participating in one of those attempts; using its sound, when and as that can help, and its syntax, its powers over and subordination to the other words in the sentence, as these can help. But beyond all that it has its own third world of interplay: with the *situation* within which it is used, with whatsoever perceptions and associations and cognitive schemas are characterizing that situation *and* other situations to which it stands in opposition and in relevant connection; with other words, phrases, clauses, of its own sentence and of other sentences in the discourse; and with words, etc., in other discourses: with all this and much more wheresoever. All these partners in the vast interplay we may conceive as being in various degrees alerted, prepared to have their participation tried out: held in reserve or allowed to step in. What accords or denies them this chance is the failure or success of the momentary phase of the attempt. And often this phase will be little more than a tentative exploration (to see how it might go) of some preliminary to or corrective of an experimental move in what may be only a trial of a tactical device, as helpful or not in a strategem which itself is only a possibility being tested as to its contribution to a larger strategic scheme in the balance with others while the design and choice of the overall campaign yet waits on the local outcomes. In brief, all degrees of complexity of any task may be reflected in the semantic interplay implicit in the weighing of a word. Those with any lively awareness of the intricacy of their own verbal choices tend to grow impatient of oversimple accounts.

This task-reflection and task-handling is both helped and hindered by the syntactic interplay. For the phase in hand the operation tries out sentence forms much as it might try out possible handlings of the task; and the sentence form on trial can have strong influence on—sometimes amounting to control over—more than the mere phase in hand. It can open up, and close down, ranges of possibility of handling. We all know—and the formal routines of administrative communications (officialese) show—how shifting from the active into the passive may enable us to dodge a problem. Compare

> The (?) sabotaged the scheme.
> The scheme was sabotaged.

The passive lets us get on with our account or theory without having to face up to the task of saying who did the sabotaging. Yet it may be important at that point to be explicit and to recognize then and there how much the speaker is or is not able to say.

The interferences and facilitations of both *syntactic* and *sound* patterns are brought out very clearly in the writing of verse, especially verse with an exacting meter and rhyme scheme. Your choice of a rhyme (which you may have to abandon as impracticable) determines, while you keep it, narrow classes of words as alone possible at precisely defined further points. This both limits your search for solutions and suggests possibilities which would never otherwise have come up for consideration. In trying them out syntactic resource is suppled up and extended. It has the metrical demands to meet too. The local phase may thus direct the entire poem, if the poem lets it. The struggle in such composition between overall, intermediate and local design can become very apparent. (This is the most respectable reason for the collecting of first drafts and manuscripts of poems in progress.) What is manifest then is the interplay—semantic, syntactic, phonetic—which is active, if in less evident degree, in all use of language. It is with this in mind that we can now approach the question of efficiency in language.

Traditional assumptions, even though most language users know better, are often distorting—as in the rejection by many "generative grammarians" of all sorts of sentences which an ordinarily resourceful speaker can easily imagine as being highly efficient in the right setting and situation. Specialist training and preoccupation can develop a marked professional disqualification[4] here, due largely to the hangover from the dominion of the grammar master, and also to the hunger the grammarian suffers for some mode of controlling language which will spare him from going into the truly 'generative' question, Who, in what situation, is here talking to whom and trying to say what? Anything, however remote from actualities, rather than ask THAT. It is this shrinking which develops artificially abstractive concepts of grammar. It combines with the traditional training of grammarians.

Historically, syntax developed first; phonologic and semantic studies (under those names) are latecomers. Even very up-to-date treatments of linguistic theory as a whole still commonly take syntax as the prime problem, leaving the sounds and the meanings of sentences to be somehow, as subordinate matters, adjusted, tucked into grammatical formulations. But, in the normal case, we speak to say something; and what we have in mind to say shapes what we say, within, normally, an accepted grammatical structuring. *In written prose,* especially in what we are likely to call formal prose, the structures that grammarians have long ago described (and canonized) still rule ("as a rule"). We fit what we have to say into them. But in verse, in poetic utterance, as in its contrary—random, informal improvisation—other structures very frequently are chosen as being more suitable and efficient, as managing the appropriate requirements and exclusions as to meaning better than a more explicit handling. In much speech that is under high pressure, practical conditions, urgencies, needs . . . disallow conventional prose structures ("talking like an *old* book") and prefer structures better adapted to the actual aims and situation. They can also, of course, be worse adapted and fail, as with incomprehensible ejaculations. In air-ground communications the need for precision, succinctness, clarity and absence of ambiguity has led to the development of a highly formalized and artificial exchange of locutions. Such forms are misrepresented if we blanket them as agrammatical, or as exceptions, breakdowns, relaxations, licenses, departures from grammar. When they work well they are merely other grammatical arrangements better suited, in the situation, to the service of the dictating meaning than the conventional written prose arrangements would be. The point is that if we can conceive the situation fully and accurately enough we will find the justification for the grammatical structure to derive almost always from its service to the semantic aims of the utterance.[5] Some semantic aims are, for safety, convenience and economy in operation, conventionalized. For *them* it is safe, convenient and economical to use conventional routines of expression. Other semantic aims, being different, are better served by other, nonroutine grammatical arrangements. In brief, both sound relations and grammatical relations between words are ancillary; they serve utterances in their task of coping as best they can with meanings.

In the normal case, the unit of utterance will be a sentence. The one or more words in it will participate in its work in ways which usually entail the subordination or sacrifice of their other possibilities to its purposes. They are doing their duty to the sentence whose business it is to exact this duty from them. Only so can it profit from them and do its duty thereby, to previous or following sentences, all endeavoring to contribute to a discourse which is aiming somewhere. And the aim is the utterance of a meaning. The subordinate parts are utterances of contributions to that meaning, in the sense that they modify, redirect, amplify, limit, qualify in manifold ways, that meaning, including how we hope the recipients will take it.

In all this, each part—from the sound elements which cooperate to form the words on up—has a double task: to *combine* with the rest in the overall undertaking and to *exclude* whatever is not contributory to it. Each part has both to help with the sailing of the ship and to repel boarders. It has composition and opposition in hand.

Composition is the supplying at the right time and place of whatever the developing meaning then and there requires. It is the cooperation with the rest in preparing for what is to come and completing what has preceded. It is more than this, though; it is the exploration of what is to come and of how it should be prepared for, and it is the further examination of what has preceded and of how it may be amended and completed.

Opposition is a necessary complementary to composition: the two entail one another. Bishop Butler safely enough remarked that "Everything is what it is and not another thing." (An utterance G. E. Moore took for his motto.) The remark becomes more illuminating if we remake it into: "Everything is what it is *through* not being any other thing." (To ask whether, and, if so, how and *how far* these two are different in meaning here is a pertinent exercise in reflection.) Any meaning, at least, is what it is through selection. It has the features it has as opposed to others it might have. It is *this* meaning NOT *that;* and any subordinate contributory meaning within it has to be *this* NOT *that* as its service to the more inclusive meaning. Of the most inclusive meanings, those that would seem to presume to profess to tell us in a measure what it all is and what we are (so it has been held in Vedantic, Taoist, and other traditions), all that can be said is, "Neti, neti," *not that, not that;* the positive utterance being beyond our means.

For utterances that are within our means, however, each contributor does what it can to help by keeping out other things which would make the meaning other than that which it is becoming and is to become. In many ways this work of opposition, of excluding possible alternatives, is more open to analytic study than the work of composition, for it is reflected in, and indeed generates, systematic classification by division from more fundamental contrasts: is ↔ isn't, this ↔ that, here ↔ there, now ↔ then . . . on up. If we compare these last three contrarieties we find little or no priority to accord to any one of them. *This ↔ that* are the purest pointers with the least content to them, the least characterizing committed. *Here ↔ there* spatializes, *now ↔ then* temporalizes; and we note a new opposition in *then: then in the future ↔ then in the past.* By the space–time, time–space analogy we find the analogue in *there: there ahead ↔ there behind.* Compare now *ahead, in front, before.* We notice that, as between *ahead ↔ in front, ahead* carries a suggestion of forward motion (full speed ahead) which *in front* can be quite free from. In *there before us,* whether or not it lets in this component of traveling: [sw]"the past is behind us, the future before[sw]", will depend upon the more inclusive overall meaning and on what in the circumambient wording, in the setting, or in the situation, is present to *encourage* or *discourage* it.

I have been trying with these elemental examples to illustrate (1) how opposition works and how complex and delicate its tasks are; (2) how much analogy enters both into the threats to the required meaning and into the defenses; and (3), with [w]"encourage[w]" and [w]"discourage[w]", how what has been roughly called exclusion above can be a matter of degree and to be considered rather by psychological than by such physical metaphors as *in* or *out.* With positional and directional components this is especially so. With nouns and adjectives concerned in routine communications, a binary, *on ↔ off* opposition is more frequent. Visual items, for example, may be *colored ↔ not colored;* if colored, *uniform ↔ not uniform;* if uniform, *saturated ↔ not saturated;* if saturated, *primary ↔ not primary;* if primary a limited number of alternates— each in opposition to the others—compete: red–orange–yellow–green–blue–indigo–violet.

I have chosen an example here into which ingredients of color-theory have entered. Here we have another type of threat to a required meaning. Most speakers of English have, most of the time, no particular color-theory in mind, but a required meaning may very well need a specific structuring of the opposition field of its key-terms which only a particular theory can secure. Most discussions of such topics as concern us in these pages are in this situation, and most misunderstandings in such fields arise through interventions of theories which make the opposition field for the utterer unlike the opposition field for the recipient. Wider, clearer recognition of the probability of this, more diligent search for the sources of misunderstandings are the only remedies experience suggests. It may be hoped that these will increasingly take the place of the contentions, debates, refutations, rejoinders, the legal-logical collieshangies . . . that are more customary. . . .

Language is an instrument for the pursuit and control of meanings. Meanings are hard to talk of in part because to talk of them at all we have to find some selection from them which will serve to describe themselves; we are having to fashion sentences, paragraphs, discourse, which may serve as a vehicle for beings which though they are not verbal and can reject any offered verbal vehicles on occasion can for the most part in many fields only find themselves and come to completion through the use of vehicles of one order or another. Any sentence such as the last, which is attempting to describe meanings and consciously exemplifying the insecurities and uncertainties of its task, can hardly help recognizing how at every turn offstage murmurs of "Neti, neti" are a shaping influence in its composition. It was this, perhaps, which put the word "pursuit" into our fundamental proposition: a reference to hunting which may remind us that what we mean is something we can always be mistaken about. The peevish "I wish you would say what you mean" and the proud "I say what I mean and mean what I say!" are ignoring an essential fact of the matter. Another important recognition is that the danger of speaking misleadingly of meanings increases with each new or old technical term we employ, if the technical term is, as it usually is in this subject, a condensation from a theory: as with ʳsaturationʳ and ʳprimaryʳ in the example on page 149. (An ˢʷexampleˢʷ in the sense which is exemplified in ˢʷmake an example ofˢʷ someone—make him into a warning to others.)

What these excuses and alarums are doing here is preparing for a gloss on ʳan instrument for the pursuit and control of meaningsʳ as used in the opening sentence of the paragraph above. ʾInstrumentʾ, ʾpursuitʾ, and ʾcontrolʾ perhaps need little more treatment than may be taken from a dictionary. But ʾmeaningʾ is not so manageable. About all that a dictionary offers is "what is meant."

What seems to be shown is that while useful, acceptable and relevant senses for ʷinstrumentʷ, ʷpursuitʷ, and ʷcontrolʷ are available, ʷmeaningʷ (perhaps because it is our handle to itself) is still in need of a resourceful clarificatory entry. Such an entry would not, of course, *tell* us how we ⁿᵇshouldⁿᵇ use the word here. It couldn't do that, but it could help us to make out how it can best serve with ^sw^instrument^sw^, ^sw^pursuit^sw^ and ^sw^control^sw^ the purposes governing our proposed formulation: *Language is an instrument for the pursuit and control of meanings.* The hope is that our practical knowledge of (our ^sw^know-how with^sw^) the other words in this formulation can become enough to show us what we should be talking about *here* with ^w^meanings^w^, on which ^sw^know-how^sw^ is caught more often than not off balance. It should be that which will satisfy the requirements and exclusions set up by the rest of the proposition. Our question thus can be: "What should ^w^meanings^w^ here be doing if this formulation is to be (as it seems to be) evident and true?" And our directives can be: "Find a task for ^w^meanings^w^ which should make the formulation so" and, "Give an account of ^w^meanings^w^ able to explain why the word should be a source of so much trouble."

It will be noticed that ^w^should^w^ is here taking over major responsibilities. ^sw^Should^sw^ is too important a component of all meanings to be left out of any inquiry into 'meanings'. As it enters here, it is a variable amalgam of prudence, probability and ethics: Compare: "You *should* say 'He does' not 'He do.'" "The murderer *should* be taking up his gun about now." "You *should* admit your doubts if you feel them." In general the participation of *should* in this discussion should be salutary: modest, tentative, doubt-provoking and allaying.

It may be admitted that this way of approaching the problem deliberately brings together to the crucial point all the hardest ingredients in it: what 'requirement' here should be and what 'satisfaction'; what the criteria should be for 'evident' and 'true'; and what 'should' should be saying for us on each of its appearances. This approach, in fact, runs directly counter to strong preferences for dealing, where we can, with difficulties piecemeal, for finding formulations which isolate points for separate treatment whenever possible. Its excuse is that, in this matter of a *wise choice*[6] of a ^sw^meaning^sw^ for ^sw^meaning^sw^ here in this formulation, the ways in which we take 'requirement', 'satisfy', 'evident', 'true' and 'should' as well as the words in the formulation are jointly and cooperatively relevant. Their meanings here should be an explicative display of this relevance.

Is it not strange and interesting that a proposition, "Language is an instrument for the pursuit and control of meanings" which, if we read it and reflect upon it with a view to checking it against all we know of language, instruments, pursuit, control and meanings, will seem to be obviously in accord with that knowledge, can yet turn, if we start asking certain sorts of questions, into what easily seems an empty quest? And that ^w^meaning^w^, a word which we use so often and in so many ways with such unperturbed security, can so readily be made to seem an intelligential will-o'-the-wisp?

Let us now ask what it is that the meanings employed in and referred to by our formulation have to do.

1. They have to mediate for the individual in his thinking, feeling, willing, desiring, loving, fearing, suffering, enjoying . . . between all his cognitive,

affective and volitional activities and that actuality with which these activities are concerned. They are what we [sw]think of[sw] and what we [sw]*think with*[sw] when we think—whether we think of our own right-hand thumbnail, an honest man or a centaur; they are what we feel when we admire a dancer or dread an interview; what we want when we covet a yacht or a moment or two of peace and quiet for undisturbed reflection. In each case we find when we think more carefully and self-critically that—though we talk otherwise—it is not actuality that we [nb]directly[nb] think of, feel or want, but no more than a representative of actuality, something which may or may not faithfully correspond with actuality, as we learn in the outcome through our disappointment or surprise: further meanings which emerge to teach us better. 'Actuality' itself, which we can only think, talk of or feel or seek by way of meanings, is further off. We deal with it through meanings. Our meanings, it is true, are themselves part of actuality, as we are, but our traffic with the rest of it is only through meanings. Actuality is that with which we so deal and probably we should not try to say much more than this about it.

2. Meanings have also to mediate between individuals, be their common world[7] to them, their common representatives of actuality. They are *not,* as we are thinking of them here, private events, concoctions of an individual, conceivings produced in independence by his central nervous system or his mind. His nervous system and his mind are dependencies along with other meanings. Meanings are public, in any way that any beings can be public. All our most acceptable examples of public objects: a President, the Post Office, a bus line or a stove are meanings, forms through which individuals, however separate in other ways, may act and react upon one another, inherit, build, maintain, and develop their common world.

3. Meanings have further to be capable of truth and falsity; be true if actuality supports them, false if it does not. If actuality supports them too continuously and completely, we are apt just to mistake them for it, taking a thumbnail to be neither more nor less than what we may think it is. The biologist, the chemist beyond him, the physicist farther beyond and the philosopher farther still have other accounts to offer. But even the truest, the most endlessly verified meanings are not actuality. Meanings are falsifiable; actuality is not. Meanings are what we think *of,* feel, will and the rest, as well as what we think with. They are that portion of actuality through which we deal with the rest, and as actual themselves they share in actuality's incomprehensibility. And yet, to repeat, all our thinking, feeling, willing . . . is a traffic with actuality via meanings, via meanings resulting from our joint and several labors of opposition and composition. Those apt to mistake meanings for the actualities they represent should consider the different views we develop[8] of one another, e.g., a lover's view of his lass and hers of him, as compared with others' opinions of either; a nation's image of itself, as compared with other nations' views. Other people, most of all those we think we know best, are for most of us the most fateful fabrics of meanings we enjoy— solider than our own selves, which are also, as we think *of* them, fabrics of

meaning, central, highly determinative and doubtful. But not even our own selves, as thought *of,* can be identified with any further actuality. No vision is that *of* which it is. No meanings are that which they would represent.

4. Meanings have to serve not only as instruments with which we attempt to explore, invite, accept, defend ourselves from and adjust ourselves to actuality, but even more as instruments by which we attempt to order meanings themselves. They are, in fact, usually so busy reorganizing one another under the impulsion of events that they have little energy left over for concern with either language or themselves. Thought and feeling and will are radically, biologically, evolutionary-wise *revisional.* Theory of them, theory of meanings is so too. As it finds itself so, it comes to take its arrangements, even those which most satisfy its requirements, as essentially tentative: a thought that comes home comfortingly at the end of four such paragraphs as these.

The next question to ask of meanings, the tissues of which all our worlds are formed, is as to their relationship to the notations—here principally linguistic—through which we attempt to distinguish, to order and to control them.

The familiar instance of a notation is writing. But it is worthwhile reflecting that notation relationships occur within many different partner systems and that the writing–speech relationship is not wholly representative of them. In a more general sense, whenever one course of events leaves a record in another course of events by which it can be by some means in some degree represented, we may call this a notation relationship. The configurations of the groove in a gramophone disc, a barograph tracing, tracks of a fox and a hare . . . the unknown continuant conditions in the brain which enable an episode to be recalled, the dispositions which allow acquired skill and knowledge to be available anew, are instances. Obviously each of these is different in important respects from the others. From the groove we can get back the music; from the tracing, data toward a description; from the tracks, a hypothesis; from the continuants, a memory; from the disposition, the return of a power. From writing what we hope for is the reconstruction of a meaning. In each case the record gives us ways of reconsidering the originative course of events.

In this sense, what we hear of our own voices as we talk may be called a notation of our speech, so may whatever we feel of our motions of articulation. These three commonly serve one another. Try silently reciting a favorite passage before and after taking your tongue firmly between your teeth. You can learn to overcome the effect but at first you will notice a difference. If for any reason, we have difficulty in speech, trying to speak, listening to the sounds we make, and attending to what our mouth movements feel like, all these contribute jointly to our performance. Add to them our trains of imagery of what the sounds *should* sound like, of what the motions (as felt) *should* feel like . . . and we see that in picking up merely the pronunciation of a few new phrases of an unfamiliar tongue, we are exercising a highly complex cooperative activity in which a number of concurrent streams of endeavor, running in different but intercommunicating channels, are in *feedforward* [see chapter 20 in this volume] and feedback circuits together, reciprocally prompting and critically controlling one another's performance.

It is permissible to conjecture that no learning occurs without some such arrangement as this: whereby, to use the simplest model, two streams in different channels (ear and eye, or perception and image, for example) are jointly concerned to interpret a sequence of events. Each, in competition with the other, feeds forward whatever its information affords to help the other, and then, in turn, puts itself into the best posture to receive and evaluate the feedback. Each thus becomes not only the competitive inciter to the other but the controller and reviser. Such collaboration requires, of course, that there be adequate means of translation available somehow. The eye is handling color and shape; the ear, tone and duration. Yet they cooperate, superlatively, in conversation. Somehow or other they understand one another excellently, or we could not live. After all, we locate sounds through reflex eye swivelings controlled by differences of phase in the two ears. It may help us in trying to imagine how we handle meanings to remind ourselves of the resourcefulness of the cooperative senses through which we come to have any sensory meanings at all to handle.[9]

Meanings and language are essentially in a notational relationship. It has been suggested above that the partnerships of multiple diverse channels in merely echoic behavior (as in just learning how to pronounce a new word in a foreign tongue) are intricate enough to stretch the imagination. We must not expect that the partnerships developed in the notational relationships between language and meanings will be any simpler. Recall the sketch of linguistic workings offered above. At innumerable points in its three rings (phonologic, grammatic, semantic), opportunities arise both for support to and interference from participants within the growing language-meanings structure. (Language over meaning, i.e., language/meaning it is, for the most part, in the speaker; meaning/language, for the most part, in the recipient.) Seeking its own development, the fabric of meanings may attempt to charge what comes to it as language with grammatic and semantic duties the words refuse to carry. Meanwhile the words' own affiliations and oppositions may be trying to provoke, perhaps, drastic changes among the meanings. This unruly contention between the steeds as to where the chariot is to go is as characteristic of these language–meanings, meanings–language relationships as it was of Plato's original pair.[10] Meanings and verbal schemas are both incessantly launching feedforward explorations, both as to what load the verbal vehicle can carry and as to what developments the meanings can accept. And the feedback from these, to the writer who is reconciling *How to say it?* with *What should I be saying?* is what shows him how indispensable these notational relationships have been to the development of mind. In brief, meanings serve as notation for phrasing as much as phrasing (on the deadly usual view) serves to record meanings.

Any self-attentive person can witness to all this. What has seemed to have been said earlier can come almost continuously under revision from what the rest of the sentence and the sequent sentences are saying. Feedforward–feedback circuits confirm or amend what the discourse ahead is again to amend or confirm. Add in imagery, *not* as some sort of decoration or epiphenomenon, but as a critical and often subversive commentary, checking, through its own notational relationship, the validity of the meanings being developed and of the verbal expression they are receiving. Add in, further, the openings that etymological and metaphorical resources so assiduously supply for divergent developments or for obstructive resistance. At times (as every author, together with his readers, should agree) it seems a continual miracle that sentences attempting to say anything at all *new* can go on making sense.

The inhibiting character of these speculations has been put first; the encouraging note should follow. Perhaps some comparisons between walking and talking can supply it. Normally we no more ask how we talk than we ask how we walk. Both walking and talking are, in a considerable though as yet unassignable measure, *learned activities,* in which most of what has been learned has become, normally, automated. We have *learned how.* In our brilliant early years we learn to adjust our steps to the ground we are traversing much as we learn how to fit our utterances to the situations with which they have to deal. Only rarely do we become consciously cognizant of distinct features of the continuous field of intake from which our equilibrium as walkers depends. But if we are carrying a full glass, supporting somebody, descending a steep-enough declivity, or have strained a back muscle, the discriminative and selective character of the activity becomes highly apparent. And in our most casual, automated walking, the same though unnoticed mutual dependence of each part of our movement upon other parts is keeping us from a fall.

In more than a few ways walking can be taken as a type-specimen of what notational relationships may do for us. In every moment when we are walking, our balance, as our weight goes onto one foot, is being computed by the nervous system, notation-wise, in terms not only of whatever the transference of our weight to the other foot will require (and must exclude), but of whatever unevennesses in footing we may be meeting, whatever we may be reaching for, whatever we may be swinging in our hands as we carry it, whatever may be the tilt of our head and whatever changes in tempo and/or direction our distance-receptor signals may be warning us to prepare for. And all this is being done in terms of notations from feedforward–feedback cycles requiring fine accuracy of timing and coordination, in parallel serial loops, and using labyrinth reports together with muscle–joint–tendon outcomes signaled from all over the body. All this, and Heaven knows how much else— as the cragsman, the river logger or the boxer is in the best position to realize—our walking takes without worry in its stride.

This comparison of talking with walking is not "an analogy only." The two are instances of a general principle. All true activity has this organic character, this mutual though hierarchical dependence of part upon part and of outcome upon whole. Only through this can the activity meet the needs it has to serve. And no activity—least of all speech—can be usefully described without regard for its use to the organism, what it does to help it to continue living. For this inescapable reason, the recurrently fashionable efforts of linguistic theorists to treat language as "a self-sufficient universe" in isolation from "the world that language attempts to talk about" are self-destructive. These dream-motivated efforts are abortive attempts to make matters simpler than they can be. Language, like bodily movement, is a way of dealing with that same world. All reflective attempts to describe how language works are inseparably dependent upon recognition of the varieties of the work language undertakes, fails in or achieves.

In walking there is nothing quite like the gross difference between the production of a stream of speech sounds and the conduct of a course of meanings, unless it be the rhythmic swing over from bearing the immediate responsibility for the support of the body to supplying what is needed, on release, as check. Each leg system alternates between these. In talking, a somewhat analogous alternation sometimes appears. In one phase the sentence has the stage, uttering what has just been and is being thought while meanings wait around to see how well they are being treated and stand by to make any needed corrections; in the next, meanings are being generated and arranged, getting ready to let words record them. But often the connections are closer, more finely intermeshed: the arrival of a word and of a meaning may be indistinguishably welcome, or a proffered word because of an accompanying meaning is instantaneously dismissed.

Reasons in plenty lead us to expect the greatest variability in all this, both between individuals and within the same individual in one hour of one morning. Some of these reasons are on the frontiers of 'inspiration'; others border on fatigue; the topic, its familiarity, its own coherence, the depth of treatment being attempted . . . the audience, the noise level . . . there is no end to factors that may come in. What, however, is essential to the notational relationship is the way in which the two or more streams of activity can alternately and all but simultaneously pivot upon one another. A sentence can hold meanings steady while other meanings work to revise or support them: alternately, meanings are held firm (but by what who knows?) while sentence after sentence tries itself out against and by them. In imagining these encounters we are reminded again that linguistic form is three-ringed (sound, syntax, sense) and that it may be carried by full speech, subvocal talking, imagery of various sorts and by writing. And writing itself may be either visual words or the motions of penciling and typing. (There is good reason for expecting that many who fail to learn to read via a pencil could learn via the typewriter, if the invitations to them to experiment were rightly sequenced.) There is ground for supposing that many differences in compositional competence may not be unconnected with the fullness or sketchiness, the permanence or fleetingness (pen, pencil or voice) of the utterance with which meanings have to "come to terms" to use a tough concept in a grim matter. We all know people who speak well enough but are helpless pen in hand—and others who are ready-enough writers, but quite unable to talk consecutively, except perhaps on the telephone. In this last case, it could be that past fear of feedback from the interlocutor's facial expression is sometimes the source of the inhibition.

The complexity of linguistic form has been stressed above. Much speculative neurology has been concerned with ways in which perceptual motor activity can simplify itself, can develop stable-state routines which can represent (act for, serve as immediately available models for) recurrent *types* of situations requiring appropriate action. No doubt the activity in talking is vastly more intricate than that in walking, but it is a reasonable conjecture that the same possibilities for self-simplification are used in both. We seem indeed to know a good deal via introspection about good *and bad* ways of making recurrent problems of meaning as easy for us as we can. How intricate they still will be is obvious enough to imagination whenever it *is intent to apprehend* what linguistic workings must be if they are to do what they must: each item being a node in a spreading multifold network, a member of almost endless overlapping sets of alternates and in yet other ways exigently selective. Only through all this can it serve. And we should not suppose that the fields of meanings it serves can be simpler. But in fact we do very obstinately so suppose. When *we are not intent to apprehend what must be* we behave as though managing meanings was as simple as billiards and had much the same beguiling obviousness about it. Most minds feel a strong reluctance to face up to the intricacies of their meanings any more than seems strictly necessary. We pretend, for example, that billiards is simple. The physicist (or the expert in a different way, feeling the effects of the weather on the cloth) can tell another story.

In general we make whatever we can as simple as we can. "What we want," cries a character in H. G. Wells' *The New Machiavelli*, "is thick thinking: thinking that will stand up by itself!"* This was in opposition to the hero's slogan, "Love and fine thinking." We most of us use thick thinking, as thick thinking as we can, whenever there seems a chance that it will do. Unhappily most of the time it won't do, though it may take us a while to find out that it is betraying us. Bacon's experienced pen well records that "As in the courts and services of princes and states it is a much easier matter to give satisfaction than to do the business."[11] Our meanings are ever most insinuating courtiers. We discover through the outcome that plausibility really is these instrumentalities' second name.

Among the tasks in which we should not use any thicker thinking than need be are attempts to say what they are. The most tantalizing and baffling

*The opposition here between *thick* and *fine*, which Richards borrows from H. G. Wells, marks a different range of meaning from that which Clifford Geertz borrows from Gilbert Ryle—between *thick* and *thin*. Only the second suggests that substantiation is not just by "detail" and "specifics" but by what we take them to mean. Interpretation is the thickening agent.—ED

part of a theory of meanings has always been the discussion of their status. Certainly, they cannot be identified with the realities—the things, events, facts, possibilities—they would represent to us. They cannot because they can be falsified; they often, and can be shown to, misrepresent. And, as certainly, they are not identical with any *particular* conceivings, fancies, images, depictions, notions . . . that people thinking *with* and *of* meanings have as they think with and of them. These *particular* conceivings, etc., just *won't do* what meanings have to do. These conceivings, etc., are events in individual minds. The [sw]meanings[sw] we are here concerned with are no such thinkings; they are what such thinkings are [nb]of[bb] and/or work [nb]with[nb]. The thinkings are particular and private; the meanings are general and public.

This 'of' and this 'with' here carry, of course, very dubious and puzzling meanings—matched if not outdone by the 'representing' duty which meanings aspire to fulfil—for the things, events, facts, possibilities on which their verification or falsification depends.

Thus we have:

1	2	3	4	5
conceivings, etc.	'of' 'with'	''MEANINGS''	'representing'	things, etc.

To make this thicket the more tangled and obscure (it can be compared with Dante's at the opening of the *Inferno* and with Plato's in *Republic*, 432D, when something like a track of Justice is found) we have to add that the first and last columns are quite usually described as [sw]meanings[sw] and that 'of', 'with' and 'representing' are often made [sw]the relation of meanings[sw]. Moreover, swarms of theories, hypotheses, explanations, etc., frequent the thicket, offering accounts of how images, etc., depict (are pictures of) fact immediately, and of how knowings are, in a manner, becomings of what they know. The impulse *to simplify somehow* is here at its strongest. Though only an audacious person would profess to be as happy here as Br'er Rabbit, it is perfectly true to say that, whether we know it or not, in this briar patch we are "born and bred." The separation of [sw]meanings[sw] from [sw]psychological happenings[sw] on the left and from [sw]states of affairs[sw] on the right will doubtless seem unnecessary and repellent. Its ground has been indicated above; meanings have to mediate in two ways: (1) between action and the situations action is attempting to meet; and (2) between participants in communication. For both duties meanings must have the status of *generals* (or universals) not that of *particulars*.

(1) Action can be accorded to situation only through recurrences of general characters (see *The Meaning of Meaning*, Appendix B).

(2) Two or more communicators (or the same thinker at different times) must have sufficiently the *same* meaning present to them.

This is, of course, recognized to be the most resistant as it is the most central and recurrent problem in philosophy. Whatever may be said here will inevitably occasion every sort of misinterpretation, although the chief aim of any account of meanings may well be to lower the probability of these. The last paragraph, for example, might seem to risk a reader's confusing sameness in what is cognized with sameness in the cognizings.[12] That confusion would destroy the tenuous, precarious understanding here hoped for. An account of meanings must somehow explain how understandings as well as misunderstandings are possible.

To do so it has to recognize that meanings must be *general*. This recognition, if taken as seriously as it deserves, frees us from some unfruitful doubts—from exaggerations of our isolation among them. It is an enheartening doctrine.

But it is well to remind ourselves that this "way of ideas," Plato's solution of the problem of sameness, has traditionally its dangers: temptations to elevate to overweening status what are but conjectures. Socrates (*Republic*, 506E) declined further flight as "an undertaking higher than the impulse that keeps me up today" and this essay on meanings must refrain too. The meanings we aspire to are servants of purposes that clearly transcend ours. Chief among their services may be to explore, illuminate, clarify and even amend these purposes, an exceedingly exalted role.

Such a view of meanings naturally invites us to conceive of them as being analogous to a language, a universal language through which we communicate with reality. It is an invitation which not a few—Herbert, Jonathan Edwards, Wordsworth among them—have accepted. This too, as oracles and prophesyings in all ages have shown us, has its dangers. A theory of meanings can best guard us from them by reminding us of the force of the conditions through which it is prone to err.

NOTES AND GLOSSES

1. *situation* The prominence given to this word in this paragraph reflects not only the considerations behind the stress on ʾsign situationsʾ in *The Meaning of Meaning* but prolonged concern with both the teaching of the beginnings of second languages and learning to read. The design of instruction in both these ⁿᵇsituationsⁿᵇ peculiarly requires and permits close study of the structure of the tasks being presented. These tasks can only be conceived and compared in terms of the situations in which they arise and from which they are derived.

   For maximal effectiveness the series of sentence-situation (SEN/SIT) parallels offered to the learner must be kept as simple and as evident as possible. The designer must therefore examine the structural relations between the situations he uses as carefully as he does those between his sentences. It is in the course of doing so that he becomes most fully aware of the linkage between actuality and language. As he opposes one SEN/SIT with another, he has to see to it that the respect in which they are opposed is minimally confusable, for the learner, with other respects which might come into the question. The designer's main instrument for exploring this is language. And language (as he knows or should know) is capable of confusing such investigations in a high degree. So he will do well to use whatever further instruments for exploration he can. Two of these are *action* and *depiction:* the use of enactments and of iconic representations or images. If he can check and support his *verbal* (symbolic) discernment of the situation with these two other modes of representation, he can work far more safely. And he soon comes to see that what he needs for himself—a cooperative, mutually corroborative cross-checking by the three channels—is just what his pupil needs for secure learning that will build self-critical self-reliance. As Jerome S. Bruner has lately and rightly been insisting, these three, the enactment or performance, the iconic, or picturing, and the symbolic or verbal, are "three parallel systems for processing information and for representing it—one through manipulation and action, one through perceptual organization and imagery and one through symbolic apparatus." (See *Toward a Theory of Instruction,* Cambridge, Harvard University Press, 1966.) These three are not "stages": they may be "emphases in development"; through all our lives they should be cooperative resources helping toward comprehension. It is such considerations which show how idle and artificial are attempts "to describe the structure of a sentence *in isolation from its possible settings in linguistic discourse (written or verbal) or in non-linguistic contexts (social or physical)*." For a typical series of SEN/SIT sequences illustrating the recommendations to which analysis and experimentation lead, the reader may consult *English through Pictures,* Books 1 and 2, and *First Steps in Reading English,* I. A. Richards and Christine Gibson (New York, Washington Square Press, 1961).

2. *context pressure* The distinction between 'contexts', as here used, and 'settings' is useful. May I use again a passage from the Preface of my *Interpretation in Teaching*. "(1) A word, like any other sign, gets whatever meaning it has through belonging to a recurrent group of events, which may be called its *context*. Thus a word's context, *in this sense*, is a certain recurrent pattern of *past* groups of events, and to say that a word's meaning depends upon its context would be to point to the process by which it has acquired its meaning. (2) In another, though a connected sense, a word's context is *the words which surround it in the utterance* and the other *contemporaneous* signs which govern its interpretation.

"Both senses of context need to be kept in mind if we are to consider carefully how interpretations succeed or fail. For clarity we may distinguish the second sort of context by calling it the *setting*. It is evident that a change in the setting may change the context (in the first sense) in which a word is taken. We never, in fact, interpret single signs in isolation. (The etymological hint given by *inter* is very relevant here.) We always take a sign as being *in some setting,* actual or implied, as part of an interconnected sign-field (normally, with verbal signs, a sentence and an occasion). Thus, insufficient attention to the accompanying sign-field . . . which controls the context . . . is a frequent cause of mistaken understanding. But equally, no care, however great, in observing the setting will secure good interpretation if past experience has not provided the required originative context." As Bruner has recently put it, "Unless certain basic skills are mastered, later, more elaborated ones become increasingly out of reach." This unhappily is true of all mental endeavor at all levels. To continue from my Preface: "The interactions of what I am calling the contexts and settings are as intricate and incessant as life itself. . . . Sign-fields by recurring, generate contexts . . . and which contexts are operative (how the signs are read) is determined later by the new settings." (1937)

3. *all the tasks there can be* The selection of these tasks by the speaker, the sorts of attempts he makes upon them, his perceptions of their success or failure . . . all this is as much a matter of *context pressure* as his selection of a pronunciation, an intonation (A), for example, or of a grammatical pattern (B). But the context pressures in semantic choice and strategy (C) are (or should be) far more various, subtle and mutually accommodating than with (A) and (B). There is always a danger in linguistics—it is an occupational hazard—that we will try to conceive the 'unimaginably complex set of determinants' which may be operant in (C) on the model of those relatively simpler sets appropriate to (A) and (B).

4. *professional disqualification* Thus, typically, **John demands Harry* and **John believes love* are ruled out on transformational grounds (Paul M. Postal, "Underlying and Superficial Linguistic Structure," *Harvard Educational Review*, Spring 1964, p. 256). Yet any competent dramatist could write a dialogue in which these sentences would effectively say exactly what the developing situation requires. These * (starred) unacceptables cheer up the ordinary reader's perusal of this literature. They often seem to derive from the linguist's not having taken enough to heart his own declaration: "Most important, however, is the fact that a full linguistic description must contain a *semantic component* whose task is to assign each sentence a *meaning*" (ibid., p. 259). No doubt this "most important" truth is not saying here quite what we may think it should. Most of these utterances are private code messages exchanged by the devout. But at least it contrasts pleasantly with the denunciations of meaning as linguistically irrelevant that used to enliven analogous pages.

5. *service to the semantic aims of the utterance* In practice a description of these aims and a full and close enough description of the situation calling it forth often turn into two sides of the same coin. It is this that makes the current self-denying ordinances of generative grammar so frustrating. "Just as linguistic theory as such does not specify the relation of semantic markers to the nonlinguistic world, so also it cannot deal with the relations between a speaker's experiences, verbal or otherwise, and the utterances he produces" (Postal, op. cit., p. 264). A queer nemesis appears here: the Behaviorists denied themselves introspection; Chomsky attacked Skinner's attempt to describe verbal behavior on that basis as "hopelessly premature" (*Language*, Jan.–March, 1959). Now, echoing that famous review, his followers are fashionably denying themselves almost as much as ever Skinner did. Meanwhile to those ready to use every helpful source of information all these preclusions already seem ill-grounded and comically out of date.

6. *wise choice* These complexities, and the choice of such a phrase as "wise choice" here, in place of remarks about 'fact-finding', reflect the status, in the hierarchies of consequence, of what we are inquiring into. Meanings—whatever else we may find to say about them—are man's means of conserving and extending his unique powers as the most resourceful species known. His powers derive from his complexity in sensory–effector resource and its attendant flexibility. If we investigate his highest instruments ('meanings' for which language serves as an instrument) with apparatus comparable to those he developed to study arithmetic, macroscopic physics, descriptive botany, logic . . . we wreck our subject matter, destroy our preparation. Such misapplications of inappropriate techniques (though at

present barely avoidable) disqualify the inquiries in which we attempt to use them.

7. *their common world* A further discussion of the positions here indicated may be found in my *Coleridge on Imagination,* Chapter Seven, "The Wind Harp."
8. *views we develop* Compare "Complementary Complementarities" in *The Screens and Other Poems* (Harcourt, Brace & World, 1960).
9. *any sensory meanings at all to handle*

> One eye sees—what to one point is shown,
> A figure almost flat, depthless, and dull.
> Our two eyes join their fields, the sieves unite,
> Their lines of sight converge: a rounded, full,
> And living image on the Screen is thrown.
>
> Our two ears do the same: what one could hear
> By the other's limits finds itself unbound,
> The two together in their differing phase
> Locate our sound; but not alone through sound:
> Reflex eye-searchings orient the ear.
>
> Thus do the senses—no more led to strive,
> Named for an omen—make the World of Sense
> The model for the Mind; nor less for State.
> Its fateful summary of experience:
> Consentaneity alone will thrive.
>
> From "The Screens"

10. *Plato's original pair:* Phaedrus, 68.
11. *do the business: Valerius Terminus.*
12. *sameness in the cognizings* There are important questions as to when and how far (if at all) differences in cognizings in different minds need prevent them from cognizing *sufficiently* the same meanings. Comparisons between cultures—African, American, British, Canadian, Chinese—necessarily raise these questions; the answers may very likely be decisive for hopes of a unitary human advance.

We seem, in fact, to be in much the same ridiculous position in which Socrates found himself in the middle of Book IV of the *Republic* (432). What we have been seeking has been under our feet (or back of our eyes) all the time. To distinguish, relate, and mediate between the modes of language, or the species of meaning, we need no more than, and no less than, Philosophy. It is a dismaying conclusion to an age much more aware of the perils than of the powers of the study and radically in disagreement as to what Philosophy should be or how it should proceed. But perhaps this way of redefining Philosophy, as the study whose business it is to mediate between the modes of language, may encourage others than myself. It is, at least, my way of whistling in the dark. And with the help of another hint from Plato I can even see something not unlike a dawn.

The Guardian was to be a product of an education designed with the needed care to fit him for his office. What studies will best prepare the instrument *we* have in mind? I have argued that neither theory separately, nor suasion will do it—nor yet a mere mixture of the two. What remains then? A method of inquiry and a technique for judging which is familiar in many fields and indeed characteristic of the learned professions. Somewhat oddly, it seems to be without a recognized general name or even a distinguishing prescription. Perhaps, though, there may be a reason for the absence of this prescription. For when I set myself to write one, as a mere putting down of what I see, I am brought back again to Socrates' embarrassment at having to come out with the definition of Justice. This remedy so painfully sought turns out to have been in full sight all along, familiar to oblivion point, obvious to nonexistence, and veritable to incredibility. Keeping things in their proper places is indeed all we have to do.

Before training for this supreme task can be effective certain conditions have obviously to be fulfilled, certain aptitudes must be active in the student. Vigilant field observation; responsive immersion in the actual, in its full concreteness, before, during, and after the passage of the abstractive processes which yield perception; endlessly returning, self-correcting care for the *how* as well as for the *what* and the *why* and the *whither* of the concern, the wondering itself; an unwinking lookout for analogues in all respects however remote, and avid curiosity about all modes of analogy and parallelism; unfailing symbolic lubrication, keeping the formulation and the form, the name and what it names, the cry and the pang, the command and the desire . . . the utterance and what it utters . . . from jamming together; and, above all perhaps, an itch to see how things look from other angles; these—with enough drive behind them—are among the necessary foundation virtues on which the training works. I have phrased them as ideals here, but all training presupposes them as actuals in some measure, however imperfect. Though they can be developed, we may doubt, with Plato, whether they can be induced. Description of them, however, feels otiose, as any description of reflection does, since those who understand know already.

The training which requires these virtues advances them by recognizing them—that is their chief reinforcement—and by affording them opportunity for exercise. Their nature settles what will do them most good. Their first need is an abundant provision of examples of skilled and less skilled interpretations, specimens of minds at work in the interactions of words undergoing, experiencing, enjoying, checking, comparing, and recording them. There are various ways of collecting this material.

"Emotive Meaning Again," from *Speculative Instruments* (1955).

14

Realism, Nominalism, Conceptualism/Logic, Metaphysics, Psychology

A prologue, like a Spirit Calming Ceremony preceding a Noh play, may itself take a dramatic form. I offer this, then, as a sort of curtain-raiser, a short scene in which three of the most powerful intellectual forces of our tradition are brought face to face with one another. This short play tries to appraise both the situation from which they derive and what, severally and jointly, they can do about it. The title of this prelude might be "Sameness." Or "Recurrence"; or "Again" would do as well.

How can things be the same, or recur or come again? It looks a reasonable question. If we ask flatly: Can they? we get two vigorously opposed answers. One is brisk: "Why, yes of course!" The other is the sad "Never again!" It has sometimes seemed that Western philosophy originated in and has hardly been able to go beyond the contrast of these two answers and that Plato and Heraclitus must be refining them still—some would say in Elysium; others, in Limbo.

It will be noted that I have dressed these answers up with my "brisk" and "sad." I have made them much more emotional than they need be. In certain moods people will make them switch places: "yes" will voice resentment; "no," approval. It depends on the things and the answerers. But all these endless emotional and evaluative possibilities—likings and dislikings, hopes and fears, disappointments and deliveries—are, for this prologue, but incidentals: they supply background and off-stage music. Its action is between three strong and confident, and historically most contentious, rivals, offering each his own theory of sameness, each his account of how samenesses come

Beyond (1973), Prologue.

about and of what saying that things are the same really means. These three bear old and familiar names honored by adherents, though sometimes somewhat abusively used by opponents. They are Realism, Nominalism, Conceptualism.

For Realists things are the same through participating in, sharing in, imitating, being occurrences of, manifestations of, instances of a Universal. Familiar but more ambiguous names that have been more used in place of *Universal* are *Idea* and *Form*. Often these are qualified by *Platonic,* since Plato, or the Socrates he presents to us, is supposed to have invented or discovered this account of sameness. It might be fairer to say that they found it in their language; that they developed into a philosophic instrument what had for ages been a handy device for asking questions about and exploring meanings. Commonly, the illustrations used are drawn from august or at least dignified topics. Socrates in the *Phaedo* takes the Beautiful, the Good, the Great, the Equal as his instances and holds that the safest answer to a question like What makes beautiful things be beautiful? is the occurrence in them of Beauty—in some high sense, the same in them all. As to other sorts of answers, his advice is that we should "distrust our experience and, as the saying is, 'be afraid of our shadow.'"

This was Socrates at seventy on the last afternoon of his life. But Plato is at great pains to show us also, in the *Parmenides,* a "very young" Socrates, seemingly fresh from happening on the Forms. He excites the admiration of Parmenides and Zeno by his eagerness. Parmenides sets out to demolish the doctrine and begins by asking Socrates whether "hair, mud, dirt or any other trivial and undignified objects" have Forms distinct from things we can handle. Socrates confesses that this thought has troubled him and, at times, forced him to retreat, for fear of falling into abysmal nonsense. That, says Parmenides, is because Socrates is still young. He will get over such fears when philosophy has taken firmer hold of him. What Parmenides does bring out are the difficulties, recognized ever since, in explaining the relation between an instance and that of which it is an instance: between the many *the*'s on this page and the one word THE. Typical problems for Realists to consider here are whether the many *the*'s on the page (configurations of ink) represent the printer's *the,* the linguistic *the* (which may appear in handwriting and in speech, actual and imagined), the mental *the,* which may be used in thinking though in no way uttered . . . in brief, all the troubles attending the word *word.* Happily, as we shall see, Nominalists and Conceptualists have equally all these troubles to attend to.

Just *how* particular things partake of, or belong under, the Forms which make them what they are is not something explicable in terms of other relationships—relationships, that is, which are not themselves instances of it. The moral is that we have to accept this question as unanswerable. We have nothing deeper or clearer through which to answer it. All we can do is linger with it awhile until our feeling of the queerness of the situation we are in becomes familiar.

Dismayed at or repelled by the situation, Nominalists prefer to explain sameness through the names or labels that are applicable: all *the*'s may rightly be so called. It is the label which unites them and makes them *the*'s. Here, too, we may note as equally queer this dislike of the Unanswerable, this suspicion of it as "bordering unduly on the ineffable," this eagerness to rid the world of all but 'fully comprehensible'* items, this supposal that it can be so rid. All this timorousness is hard to make out. What conception of 'fully comprehensible' and of 'fully comprehended', we should ask, do these thinkers enjoy?

What C. S. Peirce, stepping aside from older philosophic language, called the "type–token ambiguity" is well exemplified by the printed page, the instance from which Peirce took his label. On this page you are now reading there occurs the letter *t*. There is only one letter *t*. And yet there are two of them in the word *letter,* three on the average in each line, and towards a hundred on the page. The one and only letter *t* is the *type;* the hundred or so occurrences are tokens of it. The same opposition between what occurs and its occurrences can be noted, of course, wherever it is looked for. It is invaluable and indispensable. Language could not work without it. Nor could life go on. The human make-up is a type—actualized with differences in the writer and in whoever may read him. A cup of tea: that is one thing, the type; its tokens are drunk by the million. In most cases no inconvenience and no risk of confusion arise. Good, bad, indifferent: Lapsang Souchong at its most fragrant or stewed tannin, tea is tea; we can praise or condemn any token of it we taste. But in our praise or our condemnation itself the same opposition will be at work. We will be assigning tokens to types and recognizing types from tokens—just as in this paragraph we have been offering tokens of the type *type* and of the type *token*. In brief, meanings must be in some respect general if they are to be useful. Strict and utter uniqueness is merely a limiting notion: self-destroying, inapprehensible, and ineffable. An occurrence which was in no way *like* any other could not be an occurrence; nothing would be occurring. Uniqueness, in other words, is a matter of degrees of likeness in relevant respects. A unique occurrence is no more, we must conclude, than different in certain respects from any other.

By and large, few troubles develop from our use of the same word for the type and for the tokens. We see at once whether the letter *t* or an actual, individual *t* is being spoken of. Our concern is with what the tokens can convey, the meaning we take as type. I have suggested that the type–token relationship is of such consequence for theory of interpretation and theory of action that it might well be symbolized in printed discussion by the use of capitals for types and of lower case for tokens.

Among the topics for which confusion between token and type can readily arise and be, moreover, especially unfortunate, theory of meanings and its quasi translation or paraphrase, theory of situations, endure a bad eminence.

See pp. 270–73 for an explanation of these superscripts.—ED

In both we have, as addressers and as addressees, to watch our steps as warily as we can. Thus a 'meaning' may be:

1. An occurrence: a design, at one specific instant, in an addresser to communicate a specific message to an equally specific addressee. It is an event (dated and placed) hoping to induce, through a signal, the coming about of an exactly similar, reciprocal event in the addressee. (Such is often our presumption: we can probably agree that communicators would do well to replace the 'exactly' aim by something less demanding. Perhaps by "more or less" or by "very.") That is a token-use of "meaning"—a single specific occurrence.

2. In the type use it should be recognized that thought about the type–token relationship remains mysterious to itself. Attempts to describe or to explain it, from Plato or Sankara on, are never satisfying—no doubt because we have, in these attempts themselves, to use this very distinction itself. We are concerned here with something so central to and so inseparable from thought that intelligence can hardly turn round in upon it, either to give some account of it or, more ambitiously, to account *for* it. "We cannot know the knower of knowledge" (*Brihadaranyaka Upanishad*).

There has always been a suasive temptation to overlook or to refuse to accept the consequences of this continuing, indeed inalienable, control by types. The history of Nominalism is full of rich evidence. Most minds, perhaps all, however much or little they may be consciously aware of it, balance between the instance, *the labeled*, the easily identifiable *thing*, recordable, able to be attested in court at need, and the quite other sort of entity, the TYPE. Theory of semantics, with its "period-piece" predilections as to what the ways of science should, professedly, be, has for more than a generation been heavily nominalistic. It has preferred (at any cost) to deal with easily identifiable items that could be entered in an inventory, presented in an account (bankruptcy proceedings, maybe, in the background?) rather than with unaccountable matters—to call them that—such as *invite* questioning and the kind of exploration which knows in advance that depth after depth will endlessly open to it. The virtue which Nominalism has really aspired to is tidyness, everything in its place. We can all respect this aspiration; it tries to defend us from our countless aberrations, and we can understand why, for innumerable Nominalists, this aim has been adventurous and challenging. But there are other intellectual invitations and some of them are (in the currencies here in question) more rewarding.

A fine recent prominent instance of nominalistic care and of concern for methodological decorum will be found in Nelson Goodman's bold and well-sustained *Languages of Art*. For him, talk about properties, characters, universals, classes, types is "informal parlance admissible only because it can readily be translated into more acceptable language." "I prefer," he says, "to dismiss the type altogether and treat the so-called tokens of a type as replicas of one another." The continuing and indispensable help of the type in "readily be translated," and in "more acceptable language," and in any fuller account of "replicahood"—and, in fact and indeed, in any attempt to give some account of how every word and every letter (or every phoneme) in every utterance is *re*cognized is here typically overlooked. The necessities behind *sameness* are by no means so docile, so ready to vanish at the word "dismiss." . . . As apology Goodman proffers:

In all this, the aptness of an emphasis upon labels, of a nominalistic but not necessarily verbalistic orientation, becomes acutely apparent once more. Whatever reverence may be felt for classes or attributes, such classes are not moved from realm to realm, nor are attributes somehow extracted from some objects and injected into others. Rather a set of terms, of alternative labels, is transported; and the organization they effect in the alien realm is guided by their habitual use in the home realm. (p. 74)

Such fancy metaphoric comment on metaphor tells its own story. Those labels are no more 'transported' (poor convicts) than classes are moved or attributes pumped out or in. All this is poetry bobbing up in the wrong place, in the midst, in fact, of an overly conscientious logic forgetful of what it serves. What we should not be forgetting, however, is that while such nominalistic scruples deter even the best-qualified inquirers, we are suffering heavy losses, on every cultural front, from our failure to look more deeply into what we are doing and into how we should be doing it.

As remedy we should start by recognizing that this mystery is at the heart of all comparings. We can and do use discernible samenesses and differences both in the token-fields and in the type domain. We perceive that a letter t is imperfect, and also we know—though in another way—that t is a different letter from i. These are all t's:

$$TTTtttTTTtttTTTtttTTTttt$$

and these all i's:

$$IIIiiiIIIiiiIIIiiiIIIiii$$

With such things as letters, type–token ambiguities give us little trouble. We have in fact learned how to handle them in learning *how to read*. But there is another and a higher sense for *how to read*. We are concerned there, not with configurations of inkstains, but with meanings and situations. With these we are incessantly liable to mistake token-field matters for type-domain problems. As in trying to read some handwritings we keep taking defective instances for different letters, so in most of our communications our chief practical difficulties (as opposed to theoretical deficiencies: insufficiently refined concepts) come from confusions of these two orders. The miscreations thus induced cross with misapprehensions as to the jobs the sign elements in the sign complexes are undertaking. It is not surprising that misunderstandings play so large a part in our lives. The wonder is rather that they are not more frequent.

With this type–token opposition in mind it is tempting to speculate a little further. The printing illustration we have been using is one of the simplest, most easily analyzed cases that can be found. For convenience in computer use, less and less confusable code elements will no doubt be devised while, at the same time, briefings for computers are developed, enabling them to handle more and more complex code systems. Some sort of compromise between these two trends will be arrived at. This illustration can serve us here as a type specimen.

Every token, we can assume, will—given powerful enough microscopy— be found to be, in some respect and in some degree, different from any other. No two handwritings, no two voices, no two pairs of ears or eyes deal with words in quite the same way. Make the mesh fine enough and differences will appear. Nonetheless, each member of a token set, through differing from its fellow members, represents a type, and it is the type so represented which matters to meaning. Somehow we allow for these differences (within limits) and through the token apprehend the type. Thus, on the telephone, despite the noise in the channel and the peculiarities of the instruments through which the signal (the *token* stream) comes to us, we get the bonding *type,* and thence, maybe, the message. The message is what we are concerned about. In a similar way, when we rephrase 'what we have to say' we can regard the meanings of the rephrasings as tokens of that single coercive though questionable 'what we have to say'—and pass thence to a meaning as type. As we tolerate imperfections in a handwriting, in our interlocutor's pronunciation, in the telephone signal, in our hearing and vision, so, too, we tolerate obscurity, vacuity, and pleonasm—acceptable defects in what we receive as token phrasings. Our concern is with what the tokens can convey, the meaning we take as type. Going yet a step further, the situations dated and placed, within which and under the control of which communications are attempted, must equally be regarded as tokens. Every instance of a SITUATION that gives meaning to something that is said is—as an event, an occurrence, an occasion—a token. Here again we are only derivatively concerned with the actual and more or less unique complexes of dated and placed circumstances (the tokens). It is the SITUATION they exemplify and represent (their type) which is the guide we question as to what is being said and what it is we may have to do.

All this is true enough. Yet we ourselves, as tokens, have ever to deal, immediately, only with tokens, and be to others only tokens: tokens fearing or hoping as much even as Job, himself, that they are radically unable ever to be confronted with their type.

In between Realists and Nominalists stand Conceptualists. Sameness for them arises, they might say, not from the shared Universal or the appropriate replicahood of the label, but from correspondence with concepts, representational mediators, mental or neurological.

And yet, with every word through which they may say so, both the pervasion of the type and the replication of the token-label are equally inevitable. For indeed the central original question, What is sameness? remains unsolved in all three positions. Jointly, perhaps they illuminate it somewhat. Severally, each quite patently begs it. What is it to *share,* to be *appropriate,* to *correspond?* These are questions that have to be recognized as reappearances in various disguises of the old unanswerable sameness-with-difference problem.

With sameness, of course, as these hyphens indicate, belongs difference. Neither can work without the other. As we phrase our sentences, however, there are subtleties of appeal to our audience (without and within) which often distinguish ˢʷnot different fromˢʷ and ˢʷthe same asˢʷ, ˢʷnot the sameˢʷ and ˢʷdifferentˢʷ. But strictly or 'logically', as we say, or for a simple computer, the two are a binary pair. They are, it seems likely, the most indispensable of all the tools of rational treatment, the tools without which none of our other tools can be contrived. Why, then, should it be so hard to say anything useful about them? Why does it seem maladroit and unmannerly to drag up any such question? There may be sound reasons—though not reasons which are easy to set forth and convey.

It will be noted that our play is beginning to take on a queer appearance: that of an attempt at the answering of an Unanswerable, the apprehension of an Inapprehensible, the explication of an Inexplicable. Traditionally, of course, recognition that X is incomprehensible has not deterred people from attempting to comprehend it. Rather the contrary, indeed. Such recognitions serve as the stringing of the bow. In the outcome, what is shifted may well be what goes under the name of comprehension. So here. After formulations such as *That wherewith we inquire will not serve inquiry into inquiry* or *The work it can do is the explication of the hypothesis,* we take to looking for analogies, parallels, parables, metaphors, similes—to find, then, always sameness–difference back again in, and on, our hands. We have not overcome the problem, but we may have come to be on better terms with it.

These similes, high (how encompass the All?) and low—indeed down to the ground, as with bootstrap lifting—recondite or familiar, farfetched or homely, all set us searching for the principle: the common source whereby they seem to help us to understand our situation. Their very diversity pushes the communality further up into the abstract in a way to make us revere the more than superb daring of Shelley's "Pinnacled dim in the intense inane." (To be trusted to understand *that* is truly restorative and Promethean.) Among these parables some look like etymonic puns—the endless paronomastic play of the Dictionary. For example, consider the word *term.* Any discourse is *limited* (given its bounds) by the terms (meanings, expressions) it employs. The units of which it is composed settle (determine) how much it can cover—as choice of center and radius fix circumference. What we begin with—our choices of samenesses and differences, our operative meanings— decides (cuts thoroughly, cuts down) where we will extend to, how far and in which directions. And it is from these limits that we may learn what those originative, creative choices were. In our beginnings will be found our end and from our end we may discover our beginnings—and in all the senses of *end* from terminus to purpose.

With this last word we step into theology. Realism, Conceptualism, Nominalism become no longer merely logical positions, claiming as such to be neutral as regards man's true being, the possibility of his immortality, and his relationships to other beings; they show themselves as, in fact, decidedly partisan. It is true that devices can be excogitated which disguise these trends. While discarding "the strange doctrine of abstract ideas"—whether as a Realist or as a Conceptualist might frame it—Bishop Berkeley, for example, can make his Nominalism seem pious doctrine by having ideas "imprinted on the Senses by the Author of nature." In general, special cases apart, Nominalists have been the "No Nonsense!" party, impatient of what they have deemed metaphysical lumber, Realists (better called, perhaps, Platonists) the party of those readiest to welcome strangeness, and Conceptualists the middle-minded travelers unwilling to commit themselves to any extreme position.

To describe them so, in terms of their fears—Nominalists not wanting to be taken in, Realists not wanting to be left out, and Conceptualists hoping to avoid both dangers—is to make this great controversy largely an affair of diverse temperaments. That it has so often been marked by merciless intolerance fits with this. So does the inconclusiveness of the outcomes. Historically, the debate flares up and dies down rather as though the participants at first had high hopes and then came to despair of being persuasive. Such situations develop fierce repugnancies, strong enough to make the antagonists unable to conceive one another's positions. Socrates put this vividly. After warning Crito to be careful and not say anything he doesn't really believe, he goes on: "I know there are never many who think like this, and that those who do and those who don't can't help despising [feeling contempt for] one another." Despise, feel contempt for—not too strong a description of how Realists and Nominalists have often regarded one another's views on universals. More than a mere wish to defend one's own position appears; an active need to disparage the opponent's motives and habits of mind takes part. Indications, these, of the moral–volitional components in these choices. It is interesting that such attitudes do not infect the earliest phases of thought about universals; they are absent in Plato's discussions—notably in the *Parmenides*—and in Aristotle. Later disputants have too often shown no such good manners.

Another characteristic of this oldest and most central of philosophic controversies is the queer remoteness from other issues in which it has been conducted. . . . A partial explanation is that the Logicians who took over did not like to admit failure. This and the previous characteristics may be connected. Psychology has had something to say about the flight from actuality that may accompany defeat. And Logicians, it is observable, from Aristotle on, have been signally unable, for one another and for the laity, to say what Logic is. As Bertrand Russell delightedly pointed out—to Tarski, Carnap, Willard Van Quine, Gödel, and a few others who had met to decide just this—they deserve to be sacked for not knowing what they are doing.

In more than one respect, Nominalism pairs off with Logic, Realism with

Metaphysics, Conceptualism with Psychology. The Logician, preoccupied with technique of proof and more abstracted, professionally, than any others from the accidentals of actuality, can willingly labor at his own mystery within an extremely low cognitive vacuum, his being a 'formal' study. The Metaphysician, on the contrary, his polar opposite, ideally takes all knowledge as his concern. In the Western tradition, an insatiable thirst for every sort of instruction has, from Plato and Aristotle onwards, been traditionally a sign of the philosophic mind. Not the mere acquisition of the knowledge, but the finding of an intelligible order in or for it has been the Metaphysician's aim. Inevitably, this makes him early acquainted with, indeed, overfamiliar with, unintelligibility. He learns to tolerate it more easily than others. He grows accustomed to high pressures from incomprehensibles. . . .

To such a one universals (which make the Logicians so "cough in ink and wear the carpet with their shoes") are his life breath. In between, the psychologist (of the William James variety) accepts his own mind, and by analogy the minds of others, as his more than sufficient field. Noting his own fluctuations, he can hope to understand both Nominalist and Realist better than they can one another. In a measure he has been both. In another sense than that of Aquinas, for him, knowing something is a way of becoming it; or, rather, to have been is a way of having known.

With such experience and the inclination to experimentation it gives him, he is ready to play imaginative games with possibilities. And he need have no more than temporary attachment to his conjectures. William James is our exemplar in that unwearying play. And it is he who will best remind us of what thinking, and the selection of likenesses with differences through which it proceeds, is for.

I confess that I do not see why the very existence of an invisible world may not in part depend on the personal response which any one of us may make to the religious appeal. God himself, in short, may draw vital strength and increase of very being from our fidelity. For my own part, I do not know what the sweat and blood and tragedy of this life mean, if they mean anything short of this. If this life be not a real fight, in which something is eternally gained for the universe by success, it is no better than a game of private theatricals from which one may withdraw at will. But it *feels* like a real fight,—as if there were something really wild in the universe which we, with all our idealities and faithfulnesses, are needed to redeem; and first of all to redeem our own hearts from atheisms and fears. For such a half-wild half-saved universe our nature is adapted. The deepest thing in our nature is this dumb region of the heart in which we dwell alone with our willingnesses and our unwillingnesses, our faiths and our fears. As through the cracks and crannies of caverns those waters exude from the earth's bosom which then form the fountain-heads of springs, so in these crepuscular depths of personality the sources of all our outer deeds and decisions take their rise. Here is our deepest organ of communication with the nature of things; and compared with these concrete movements of our soul all abstract statements and scientific arguments—the veto, for example, which the strict positivist pronounces upon our faith—sound to us like mere chatterings of the teeth.

Indeed, we may marvel at the confidence, as of folk terribly at ease in Zion, with which philosophers can in their argumentative preoccupations forget what they are about. Why should anyone be attempting rebuttals of others? What is their thinking in the end for?

The continuing theme, the labyrinth's clue, is this Why: this pursuit of the Unanswerable. What it should be if found may be intimated, hinted at, in countless ways. None of them do more than offer the mystery to us again. In them all, whether as discourse or as poem, with more or less self-recognition, Knowledge turns upon itself to admit itself to be ignorance. . . .

Two major, shaping positions, for me, interact here: the interdiction figured by the forbidden fruit and the Socratic tenet that Knowledge—could we attain it—would be Virtue. The two, when truly coactive, are more capable of collaborating than either may seem apart. Contemplation of Eve's trespass, though in some it leads to "spitting from the mouth/The withered apple seed," can set its hand to the same task Socrates recommends to Phaedrus: "I am not yet able, as the Delphic inscription has it, to know myself; so it seems to be absurd, when I do not as yet know that, to inquire into extraneous matters." What he is setting aside here as postponable is rationalistic explanation of myths—such as that of the Tree. He is advising Phaedrus that to find out how not to be mistaken as to the kinds of knowledge most needful is the overruling task. And if the philosophy prayed for at the close of the dialogue is the offspring of wonder, and though, when young, it is cognitively omnivorous, its end is to learn how to choose.

Choice thus brings us back to the two principles, the two processes of putting together and setting apart, of which Socrates is a lover (*Phaedrus* 266B). To those skilled in such decisions about sameness and difference, he has hitherto given the name *dialecticians*. "Whether the name is right or wrong, God knows." But any so skilled he "follows after and will 'walk in his footsteps as if he were a god.'" And his aim is "to know whether I am a monster more complicated and furious than Typhon or a gentler and simpler creature to whom a divine and quiet lot is given by nature."

What seems certain about this inquiry is that theories of sameness and difference can further it only by helping us to see more distinctly what we are doing. They are not candidates among which we have to choose; they are variously useful ways of approaching our choices as to how we combine and divide. Sameness–difference as an ultimate opposition must use more than one approach. To compare them is to examine, in a perspicuous type specimen or exemplar, other sets of necessary oppositions: those between what we see and how we see it (the Homeric and the Platonic views of living), between what is said and how it is said (Book II of the *Republic* and the poem of Job), between any utterance and what it would utter.

As all know, 'the same thing' (so to call it) may be represented in different ways; and those ways themselves may mean different things as the fields, the settings, differ within which they are taken.

This situation, this necessary conjunction and opposition of an utterance and what it would utter, we cannot escape from; it is instanced again in every attempt we make to account for it. We deal with realities only through representations of them, and we need all the aids we can be given in remembering this.

Among such aids a pair of terms introduced for the discussion of metaphor may be generalized (though with some change of sense) and be useful. Let ˢʷwhat is to be saidˢʷ be the Tenor, and ˢʷthe way of saying itˢʷ be the Vehicle; and their relation be represented as $\dfrac{\text{Tenor}}{\text{Vehicle}}\left(\dfrac{\text{T}}{\text{V}}\right)$, as though the Tenor were a passenger riding in some sort of car. The image may usefully remind us that the events, the situations, we are dealing with have vector character: the utterance is trying to go somewhere. Setting it out so, we may the more conveniently bear in mind that we apprehend any V (and thereby, we would hope, *its* T) through comparing with other V's.

In my parenthesis I wrote "*its* T" to bring out a question. In practice we take for granted that one and the same T may have a variety of V's—indeed, a considerable number of them more or less fitting, appropriate, *serviceable* (our choice of words here is, of course, itself an instance of what it is discussing). Looking closer, thinking through a better lens, we will be likely to conclude that any change from V_1 to V_2 will in some respect and to some extent (important or not) result in, entail, *convey* a different T. As he changes from one car to another, the passenger becomes in some respect and degree different.

Nothing could possibly be more familiar to us all than all this. It is instanced, illustrated, in all our perceptions or recognitions of everything. What we do not sufficiently consider, however, are (1) the degree to which any V takes its character from the *settings* in which it occurs and (2) the degree to which it is shaped by other V's which (in that setting) are or are not *substitutable* for it—able or not to replace it in this or that respect. The process of prehending a V, of selecting, deciding between ways to take it, is almost entirely (1) a noting of what comes with it (before and after) in the unit to which it belongs and (2) a recognizing of its compatibilities and *in*compatibilities with other V's which might be offered. This noting and recognizing may be explicit or tacit: supported by conscious examination and experimental trial or merely assumed, with a latent readiness to observe and to accept or reject if called upon. Change what comes with it (1), and its relations to other possible and impossible V's (2) are changed.

I have put this as though with the hearer, the reader, in mind; but it holds, too, of the speaker, the writer. He, too, is guided (1) by what comes (and can and/or must come) with it in the unit and (2) by the substitution field. In any more or less successful instance of communication, addresser and addressee are guided alike.

These cardinal truths, these hinges of all thought, haunt our every reflective remark. We are prone to regard them as offering chiefly threats to communication, and neglect to notice the immense services of the flexibilities they afford. Did these fundamental conditions of utterance not hold, how miserably limited would be our powers; how little we could think of, and how little would be what we can receive and somehow, with luck, convey.

So ends my curtain-raiser.

––––––––

No one will deny that there are meanings (or call them that: virtualities, dispositional conspiracies) which are active before they embody themselves. The process of writing a poem—in many instances—consists in cajoling an unembodied something into its incarnation. The formal aspects of poetry—rhyme, meter, etc.—are largely dodges which have been propitious in slowing down selection and widening the scan. Before it has found itself in its words by finding the words for itself, that *something else* has as little overt character, is as indescribable, as a name that we are failing to recall.

"The Future of Poetry," from *So Much Nearer* (1968).

15

Toward a Theory of Comprehending

Looking back, across more than a score of years, on the considerations with which *Mencius on the Mind* was concerned, it seems to me now that the togethernesses, the mutualities, of those considerations were omitted. There were distinctions made and differences stressed between sorts of meaning, but why they should be so made and so stressed hardly became apparent. The last chapter, "Towards a Technique for Comparative Studies" [see Chapter 2 in this volume], was suitably tentative in title and in treatment. It stammered away persistently, but what it was trying to say never, *as a whole*, got said. I have some doubts whether any whole was in any steady way in the mind of the sayer. The book was written hurriedly, in a whirl of lecturing on *Ulysses* and on *The Possessed*, during a first teaching visit to Harvard. It was worked up from notes made between Tsing Hua and Yenching, under the guidance of divers advisers, and written out with much of the feeling one has in trying to scribble down a dream before it fades away. The intellectual currencies of the Harvard scene, not to mention Leopold Bloom and Stavrogin, were driving out those Chinese *aperçus* all the while. Then the only manuscript was lost, stolen by Li An-che's cook by mistake. It lay on a house roof for some months, tossed there by the thief the instant he perceived how worthless it was. Then odd pages began blowing up and down the *hutung;* rumour spread and a search was made; it was found and returned to me—just in time to be compared with the proofs of a second version I had been recollecting back home again in Cambridge, where yet another local logical game had been offering yet other guidelines to be avoided. All useful experience, no

Speculative Instruments (1955), chap. 2. Notes have been renumbered.

doubt, in guessing about *what* makes *what* seem to mean *what*—*when, where,* and to *whom*—but not then and there conducive to a single comprehensive view of comprehending.

This, I now suppose, is what one should attempt to form. I suppose too that a first condition of the endeavor is a recognition of its inherent wilfulness. It is purposive; it seeks. If asked *what* it seeks, its only just answer should be: "Itself." It seeks to comprehend what comprehending may be. What is sought is the search.

Yet it advances. When it looks back upon its earlier phases, what it most notes are the things it took for granted *without* having put its requests into any but most indefinite form. It can bring the request and the grant nearer to terms for ever without any fear of arriving. The process of refining its assumptions must be just as endless as the endeavor itself.

Through these assumptions it divides and combines—dividing in order to combine, combining in order to divide—and simultaneously. Whatever it compares is compared in a respect or in respects. These respects are the instruments of the exploration. And it is with them as with the instruments of investigation in physics but more so: the properties of the instruments enter into the account of the investigation. There is thus at the heart of any theory of meanings a principle of the instrument. The exploration of comprehension is the task of devising a system of instruments for comparing meanings. But these systems, these instruments, are themselves comparable. They belong with what they compare and are subject in the end to one another. Indeed, this mutual subjection or control seems to be the ἀρχή[1] for a doctrine of comprehension—that upon which all else depends.

There is a seeming opposition to be reconciled here. We may suppose there to be a hierarchy of instruments, each caring for those below and cared for by those above. Or we may suppose the system to be circular. I have leaned here toward a position somewhat like that of the constitutional monarchist who supports an authority which is itself under control (see Aspect 6 below). The same question seems to me to appear again as: "How should we structure the most embracing purpose?" and this I take to be an invitation to an inquiry into Justice on Platonic lines.

This mutual control shows itself in any segment of activity (any stretch of discourse, for example) as accordance and discordance of means with ends. Ends endeavour to choose means which will choose them. The entirety of activity, if, obeying Aristotle, we may venture to attempt to conceive it, seems to consist of *choices*. Initial choices would be free; but, when choice has been made, the subsequent choices are bound thereby while the choice is held. An interpretation knows only a part, often a very small part, of the entailments of its choices. These entailments may later seem to it to be "brute fact"— something in no way and in no measure due to its choices, something upon which their success or failure depends. This is the defectiveness of the choices—made too soon or not made when choice was needed.

Enough of these preliminaries. They seemed necessary to the introduction here of the word LET as the first and all-important move in this undertaking. Let *let* rule every meaning for every word in every sentence which follows. These sentences will seem for the most part to be in the indicative, but that is for brevity and for custom's sake. Everything which seems to be said in the indicative floats on a raft of optative invitations to mean in such wise. Any theory of meanings which can serve as authority, as more embracing purpose, to a theory of translation is concerned with the mutual tension of whatever can be put together to serve as that raft.

Such are among the reflections which translation between diverse cultures can occasion. How may we compare what a sentence in English may mean with what a sentence in Chinese may mean? The only sound traditional answer is in terms of two scholarships—one in English, the other in Chinese. But a scepticism which can be liberating rather than paralysing may make us doubtful of the sufficiency of our techniques for comparing meanings even within one tradition. How can one compare a sentence in English poetry with one (however like it) in English prose? Or indeed any two sentences, or the same sentence, in different settings? What is synonymy?[2] A proliferous literature of critical and interpretative theory witnesses to the difficulty. It seems to have been felt more and more in recent decades. Is there any reason to doubt that analogous difficulties await analogous efforts for Chinese? They may well have been attending the conduct of that language all along.

These troubles come, perhaps, in part from insufficient attention to the comparing activity itself. How do we compare other things? Let us see whether what we do in comparing boxes or rooms can be helpful in suggesting what we might do in comparing meanings. What would a sort of geometry of comprehendings be like? With rooms, we need, in the simplest cases, three dimensions. With length, breadth, and height ascertained, we have gone some way toward discovering how far one room is like another. Would it be useful to ask in how many "dimensions" meanings may agree or differ? It might be wise to drop the geometric word and generalize at once. Let us say, then, "in how many respects"—remembering that meanings may, if we so wish, be compared in an indefinitely great number of respects or in as few as will serve some purpose. The purpose decides which respects are relevant. This is true of rooms, too. So our problem is one of choice. What is the simplest system of respects which would enable us to compare meanings in a way serviceable to the translator's purposes? (As three dimensions serve us in comparing sizes and shapes.)

I have just called this a *problem*. If a problem is something which has a solution, I should not have done so. In my opening sentence I called such things *considerations,* hoping thereby to suggest that they are fields of unlimited speculation—held within only the most unlimited framework that even sidereal space could symbolize—and not, as problems in a branch of mathematics may be, formed and given their solutions by the assumptions which set them up. What this theory of meaning should be or do is not in this narrow sense a problem.

It is, on the other hand, the most searching of all considerations, for it is concerned with arranging our techniques for arranging. Since the system of respects is set up to serve our comparings, the respects in it must not be too many or too few, and they will probably vary with the comparing. But this cannot itself be described except by means of the respects which serve it, being the comparing which these respects implement and enable. (Similarly, the comparing of sizes and shapes cannot be described except by reference to the spatial dimensions.) In brief, we make an instrument and try it out. Only by trying it out can we discover what it can do for us. Likewise, only such trial can develop our comprehending of what it is with which we seek to explore comprehending. Thus what ensues will be a depiction of the whereby and the wherefore as well as the what.

We may begin by adapting the conventional diagram of the communication engineer to our wider purposes [see Chapter 23]. In translation we have two such diagrams to consider as a minimum. There will be (say) a Chinese communication for which we find ourselves in the role of Destination; and we assume thereupon the role of Sources for a communication in English. But since other communications in Chinese and other communications in

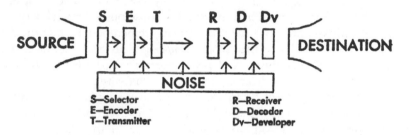

S—Selector   R—Receiver
E—Encoder   D—Decoder
T—Transmitter   Dv—Developer

English, having *something in common* with the present communication, come in to guide the encodings and decodings, the process becomes very complex. We have here indeed what may very probably be the most complex type of event yet produced in the evolution of the cosmos.

Between two utterances[3] the operative *something in common* whereby the one influences the other may be any feature or character or respect whatever and can be itself highly complex. It may be some conjunction of respects. The comprehending of any utterance is guided by any number of partially similar situations in which partially similar utterances have occurred. More exactly, the comprehending is a function of the comparison fields from which it derives. Let the units of which these comparison fields consist be *utterances-within-situations*—the utterance and its situation being partners in the network of transactions with other utterances in other situations which lends significance to the utterance. Partially similar utterances made within very different situations are likely to require different comprehendings, though language is, of course, our collective attempt to minimize these divergences of meaning.

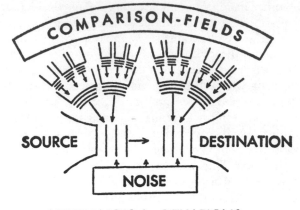

UTTERANCES-in-SITUATIONS

A comprehending, accordingly, is an instance of a nexus established through past occurrences of partially similar utterances in partially similar situations—utterances and situations partially covarying. The past utterances-within-situations need not have been consciously remarked or wittingly analysed; still less need they be explicitly remembered when the comprehending occurs. Thus the word *comparison* in the technical term "comparison-field" may mislead. It is not necessary that the members of a comparison-field—widely diverse utterances-within-situations as they may be—should ever have been taken together in explicit analytic scrutiny and examined as to their likenesses and differences. The discriminations and connections (dividings and combinings) which arise in the development of meaning are, in some respects, *as though* this had been done. Sometimes they are so produced; but, for the most part, they need no such elaborate reflective procedure. Let me generalize "comparison" here to make it cover whatever putting together and setting apart (however unremarked) has been operative in the formation of the nexus. The routine of concept formation and of discriminative behaviour even down to what we might call merely perceptual levels has an interesting resemblance to the highest activities of systematic conceptual classification. It is as though the nervous system had been taught Mill's Joint Method of Agreement and Difference.

What I have been sketching applies, for the translator, in the first place to the Decoding and Developing of the Chinese utterance. In the second place it applies to the Selecting and Encoding which (it is hoped) will produce an utterance in English acceptable as a translation from the Chinese. But, plainly enough, the covaryings of utterances-within-situations for English are other than they are for Chinese. Any translator has acquired his Chinese and his English through "comparison-fields" which are different and systematically different in structure: different not only with respect to the ways in which utterances change with situations, but also with respect to those changes that are significant in utterances (e.g., phonemics) and with respect to those changes that are significant in situations (e.g., status recognition). The comparative linguist could, if he wished, illustrate this for the rest of his natural days. And it is one of the pedagogue's reasons for preferring a "direct" method to a "translation" method in beginning language learning. He finds that by keeping to one language only he can provide comparison-fields (through sequences of sentence-in-situations) which are more effective, that is, more propitious to full and deep comprehending later on. This structuring of experience will of course differ with our aim. The linguist—for his purposes—will set up one schema of respects in which comparisons will be made; the pedagogue—for his purposes—will set up another. What schema will a translator set up to serve as a theory of the sorts and interrelations of meanings to guide him in his own tasks?

Limitless in their variety, these tasks present themselves, the words, phrases, sentence forms and the situations, and the meanings, to be compared being as varied as the ways in which they may be compared. How are we to choose the respects (or dimensions) which will serve us best as headings under which to arrange those similarities and those differences of meanings which the translator must try to discern in one language and to achieve in another? In the concrete, in the minute particulars of practice, these comparison-fields are familiar enough; though we tend to forget, as scholars, what we must often, as pedagogues, recall: that these comparison-fields go back into infancy. All we have to do is to arrange, in a schema as parsimonious as adequacy will allow, a body of experience so common that if the purposing of our arrangement could be agreed on, there might be little we would then differ about.

Let us turn our communications diagram through 90 degrees now and look down it. Here is a cross-section of the activities to be found there, made at the points where what is prepared for transmission and what has been decoded and developed may be supposed—in a successful communication—to resemble one another most nearly. I have marked and numbered for labelling the seven divisions in my proposed schema.

1. Points to, selects. . . .
2. Says something about, sorts. . . .
3. Comes alive to, wakes up to, presents. . . .
4. Cares about. . . .
5. Would change or keep as it is. . . .
6. Manages, directs, runs, administers itself. . . .
7. Seeks, pursues, tries, endeavours to be or to do. . . .

1. Indicating
2. Characterizing
3. Realizing
4. Valuing
5. Influencing
6. Controlling
7. Purposing

Let us label these *sorts of work* which an utterance may be doing with two or more sets of names, academic and colloquial—on the assumption that communication will be made more probable if we use here a multiplicity of largely equivalent indications. I am numbering them for convenience of reference; but I do not want to suggest that there is any fixed temporal order, that first we Select, then we Characterize, then Realize, then Value, then would Influence, then Organize and then Purpose. Nor is there any constant logical order. Let us keep these jobs as independent one of another as we can. In individual cases we will find many sorts of detailed dependence, but let us put none in by definition.

In applying this schema to translating, we can ask of two utterances in two languages:

1. How far do they pick out the same (or at least analogous) things to talk about?
2. How far do they say the same (or at least analogous) things about them?
3. How far do they present with equal vividness and/or actuality, weak or strong?
4. How far do they value in the same ways?
5. How far would they keep or change in the same ways?
6. How far are the dependencies and interplay between 1, 2, 3, 4, 5 and 6 itself, the same in them both?
7. How widely would they serve the same purposes, playing the same parts, within the varying activities they might occur in?[4]

Let me label this sevenfold event which my diagram depicts COMPREHENDING, as comprehensive a name as I can find. Any full utterance does all these things at once, and invites all of them in the comprehender. In some instances, however, one or more of these dimensions, aspects, powers, functions, jobs, variables, parameters, components, ingredients, tasks, duties (all these words are in need of the comparative study my diagram should be an instrument for) will shrink toward the null, the vanishing point. There is swearing and there is mathematics. In swearing there *may* be nothing but 4, 5, and 7; in mathematics only 1, 6, and 7 may matter. It would appear that 7 never lapses; without purposing, without the feedforward which structures all activity, no utterance and no comprehending. A full comparison between two utterances (between an original and a translation of it, for example) would require us to discern what all their dimensions, aspects, functions may be and compare them as to each and as to their relations within the entire comprehending. In comparing boxes or rooms, we need three dimensions; in comparing comprehendings, we need, I suggest, at least these seven.

Even of a single comprehending we can ask our seven sorts of questions: Under 1, we ask WHICH things are being talked (thought) of? Under 2, WHAT is being said of them? Under 3, EVEN so? Under 4, SHOULD this be so? Under 5, WON'T YOU (WON'T I)? Under 6, HOW? Under 7, WHEREIN, WHEREBY, and WHEREFORE, TO WHAT END?

Of these, 1 and 2 may be felt to be more narrowly, more clearly, *questions* than the others; and 3 especially may seem to be rather a wondering than a questioning. Under 3, what is in question is the nearness and fulness with which something is to be present to us. *Doubting* ("is this so or not, possibly, probably, certainly?") belongs (in this schema) rather to 5 or 6 ("to be accepted or not, and how?").

Let us consider these functions in turn.

Indicating and *Characterizing* will need less comment than the others. They have been more discussed, for they correspond to the distinction logicians make under the labels "Extension–Intension" and "Denotation–Connotation." In the logicians' use, the denotation of a term is whatever may be covered by the term and the connotation is the set of properties (characters) anything must have if it is to be so covered. But there is also a well-established literary use of "connotation" in which the connotation is 3, 4, and 5 in my diagram rather than 2 (which is likely then to be called the "bare, or mere meaning"). These two uses of "connotation" parallel what may be the chief difference between scientific and poetic use of language. There is some parallel, too, with what I have discussed (*Interpretation in Teaching*, p. 311) as the rigid and the fluid uses of language. If we make Characterizing be "*saying something about* what is being pointed to," we have obviously to narrow down the meaning of "saying." It can open out to take in anything that an utterance can do, anything in any way said, suggested, evoked, hinted, required, and implied (the literary connotation), or it can be kept down to the logician's connotation—the "definition" (as it is sometimes put) of a term.

The last paragraph illustrates—as must any attempt to write about the language we use or should use about language—the heavy duties we have to put on quotation marks. I have suggested that we should develop sets of specialized quotes, as a technical notation by which we could better keep track of the uses we are making of our words, and I have tried out the use of a few such quotations marks in that book and elsewhere.* . . . Once we recognize to what an extent thinking is a taking care of and a keeping account of the conduct of our words, the need for a notation with which to study and control their resourcefulness becomes obvious.

sⁿIndicatingˢʷ or ˢʷSelectingˢʷ—especially if we picture it to ourselves with the image of a pointer (an arrow as of a wind vane)—may seem unstable. It can be so; but some of our selectings are the most constant things we do. Angus Sinclair puts a further point well: "What is thus loosely describable as the selecting and grouping which each of us carries out is not an act done once and thereby completed, but is a continuing process which must be sustained if our experience is to continue as it is. If for any reason it is not sustained, i.e., if for any reason a man follows a different way of grouping in his attention, then the experience he has will be different also. Further, this requires some effort. . . . Knowing is not a passive contemplation, but a continuously effort-consuming activity."[5]

*See pp. 270–73 for an explanation of these superscripts.—ED

Sinclair's ˢʷgroupingˢʷ seems to be my ˢʷCharacterizing, Sortingˢʷ. We have, in English, what may seem an excess of analytic machineries to help us in distinguishing ˡitsˡ from ˡwhatsˡ, that is, Indicating, 1, from Characterizing, 2. Such are (in most uses): for 1, ʷsubject, substance, entity, particular, thing, being, group, classʷ; for 2, ʷpredicate, attribute, property, quality, relation, character, essence, universalʷ. A large methodological question which can seem to fall near the very heart of any endeavour to translate philosophy is this: does use of different ˀanalytic machineriesˀ entail difference of ˀviewˀ? I put my ?'s in here to remind us that both ˢʷanalytic machineriesˢʷ and ˢʷviewˢʷ have to do with little-explored territories though they are surrounded by the most debatable land in ˀthe Western philosophic traditionˀ. Current use of most of this machinery is erratic: at a popular level it cares little which of the above words are employed; more sophisticated use varies from one philosophic school to the next. There is little likelihood of increased clarity unless some new factor enters. The exercise of choice required when thinking which is remote from ᑫthe Western philosophic traditionᑫ—thinking which uses, perhaps, no such machinery—has to be thoroughly explored in English, might be just such a new factor. The distinction between Indicating and Characterizing, and their queer interplay, might, through translation studies, become again the central growing point for thought.

Realizing, 3, needs more discussion here, though what the discussion should bring out is something familiar to everyone. The two meanings we separate most easily in this cluster are exemplified by: (*a*) "She realized how he would take it" and (*b*) "He thus realized his ambition." It is with (*a*) that we are concerned, though the background influence of (*b*), ˢʷrealizingˢʷ as ˢʷthe becoming actual of the possibleˢʷ, is frequently apparent. This duality may be as relevant to Chinese modes of ˀknowledgeˀ as it is to some Aristotelian doctrines of becoming.

Within (*a*), two lines of interpretation offer themselves: (i) it may be taken as equivalent to ˢʷShe imagined vividly and livingly how he would feelˢʷ; or (ii) ˢʷShe foresaw how he would actˢʷ. (The vagueness of ᵒᶜtake itᵒᶜ reinforces the ambiguity of ᵒᶜrealizedᵒᶜ.) This exemplifies a frequent shift in ˢʷrealizeˢʷ: the shift between a lively, concrete, actualized presence and a cognizance of implications and consequences which may be (and commonly is) highly schematic. A statesman may realize what the outcome will be all the better for not realizing too vividly how X may feel. It thus appears that while the use of ʷrealizeʷ in (i) does entail a high degree of Realizing, 3, in my schema, ʷrealizeʷ in (ii) does not. The entirety of apprehension which is ascribed by remarks such as "He fully realized," and the contrast with "He didn't at all realize," can be handled in terms of 1, 2, 5, and 6.

What is highly realized may be distinct, explicitly structured, detailed, ˀdefiniteˀ in most of the senses of this strategic word. But it may equally well be very indefinite. That unlocatable, indescribable, almost unidentifiable qualm which is the first emergence of nausea is something which can be Realized to the full without as yet being Characterized in any but the sketchiest fashion. Conversely, Characterizing may be most complete and minute without much Realizing having developed. In fact, fullness and detail in Characterizing frequently prevent our Realizing, though the details may be offered expressly to increase it. On the other hand, many devices—from headlines to the routines of the dispatch editor and the commentator—reduce the reality of what is presented. Much that is called 'sensationalism' has this effect. We may suspect that this is sometimes its justification. We need to be protected from the wear and tear of actuality. It would not be surprising if this wrapping-up professed to be unwrapping.

> Human kind
> Cannot bear very much reality.

Nonetheless, increase in Realizing is in general accompanied by increased particularity in Characterizing, and by increased choosiness and discrimination in the Selecting of what shall be Characterized.

Realizing is very frequently brought about through metaphor, as may be illustrated by the following vivid account of a moment of Realization from Virginia Woolf:

Suddenly, as if the movement of his hand had released it, the *load* of her accumulated impressions of him *tilted up,* and *down poured in a ponderous avalanche* all she felt about him. That was one sensation. Then *up rose in a fume* the essence of his being. That was another. She felt herself *transfixed* by the intensity of her perception; it was his severity: it was his goodness. [*To the Lighthouse,* Modern Library Edition, Part I, Sect. IV, p 39, IAR's italics.]

Metaphor, however, can serve under all my headings. It is worth remarking with regard to Chinese–English translation that the great traditional metaphors of Western thought play so large a part in shaping our conceptions that a study of any metaphors which have played a comparable part in Chinese thought suggests itself as possibly a key move. Examples in the Western tradition would be: the metaphor of conception used in the previous sentence (see *Phaedrus,* 276E); the analogy of the Self and the State from the *Republic,* and the tripartite structure of both; that other Platonic metaphor of intellectual vision, the eye of the mind; the comparison of the idea of the good with the sun; the metaphor of light as truth generally; the metaphor of inspiration; and, from Hosea, the metaphor of a marriage contract between the Lord and Israel, and indeed the use of the ideas of love (not sex) and fidelity in theology. These great originative structurings have acted in the West in innumerable minds which have had no notion of how important such metaphors can be. It would be hard to say, indeed, of the Self–State analogy whether thought about personality or about government has been the more influenced by it, for the traffic has been two-way. Where such a metaphor is absent in Chinese or where Chinese has a traditional metaphor which English lacks, the loss in translation is likely to be grave. The remedy is, perhaps, through a deeper, more systematic study of metaphor. Assistance in such studies is, of course, one of the aims of the schema of comparisons offered in my diagram.

Valuing, 4, is a modern philosophic battleground, the dispute being in part whether the language of valuation, obligation, and justification is to be comprehended in some peculiar fashion or fashions (as ‼emotive‼) or in the ordinary way of description. For the purposes of comparative study of meanings, this warfare, on which so much time and talent is being spent, may not be important. It is not clear that any decision would help us to compare meanings better. It may be wise to hold that: ʳEvaluationsʳ are a form of ʾempirical knowledgeʾ, which might put considerable strain on our concepts of ʾempirical knowledgeʾ; or it may be wiser still to hold that will and desire may enter into valuations in more ways than those in which they enter our type specimens of empirical knowledge. To decide which view would be wiser, we would have to be able to make comparisons between meanings beyond our present scope. What does seem certain is that, *as an instrument for the comparison of meanings,* our diagram should avoid prejudging this issue. It should be able to represent the opposed positions more justly; they look as if they were almost equally in need of restatement. But notice here how ᵒᶜshouldᵒᶜ and ᵒᶜjustlyᵒᶜ and ᵒᶜin need ofᵒᶜ appear in this very remark. Any formulation of these considerations is itself valuative as well as factual; the conflict it hopes to adjudicate is alive in the bosom of the judge. The difficulties ensuing from this I shall discuss under Aspect 6, the Management, Control, or Administration of Comprehending. Meanwhile, my diagram assumes that ˢʷValuingˢʷ is different from Realizing, Characterizing, and Indicating; and that it ʾshouldʾ be defined in such a way as to avoid implying any fixed relations to them—though, of course, the interplay between all three will be varied, incessant, and all-important. All study of language and thought *in action* is both an exemplification and enjoyment of this kind of interplay.

As another precaution, we may leave the full variety of Valuing unconfined. We are concerned here not only with all the attitudes which may be uttered by the aid of ʷgoodʷ and ʷbadʷ, ʷrightʷ and ʷwrongʷ, ʷbeautifulʷ and ʷuglyʷ, ʷpleasantʷ and ʷunpleasantʷ, ʷimportantʷ and ʷtrivialʷ, but with the ranges of love and hate, desire and fear, hope and despair, belief and disbelief. These fields are all polar, and there is a middle zone where it may be doubtful whether any valuing is going on and whether it is positive or negative. So Valuing may often seem to lapse.

Similarly, and perhaps as a consequence, Influencing, 5—that part of a Comprehending which endeavours either to change or to preserve unchanged, to be changed or to remain unchanged—may be too slight to be remarked. If we ask what it is here which would change or be preserved, it may be best to reply ˢʷthe onflowing situationˢʷ and to remind ourselves that this ˢʷonflowing situationˢʷ is at least twofold. It is (*a*) that motion of affairs within which the Comprehending is proceeding; it is also (*b*) the Selecting, Characterizing, Realizing, and Valuing, and the rest, through which the

Comprehending is taking account of and dealing with (*a*). It is what is happening *and* what we take to be happening. We are lucky when these sufficiently accord. Influencing—the keeping of the stream of events so or the changing of it—concerns (*u*) as offered to us in (*b*) and, within (*a*), it includes our adjustment to the not-us as well as the adjustment of the not-us to ourselves. In general, a Comprehending is concerned to change part of the onflowing situation and keep the rest unchanged. Something has to remain unchanged; there has to be some continuant, if change is to be possible: so at least we may be wise to suppose.

Controlling or Administering, 6, has to do with these decisions as to what it will be wise to suppose, and with what arises through these supposals. Wisdom, we may remember, "lies in the masterful administration of the unforeseen."[6] We may be highly surprised to discover what we are supposing. The supposals may be conscious, and arrived at through explicit reflection and deliberation and choices wittingly made, or they may be unwitting, picked up from the tradition or from the accidents of habit formation. And they may concern every aspect of meaning—from Selecting round to Controlling, this would-be executive, itself. Many of our most important supposals concern the nature of meaning and the connections of the sorts of meaning with one another, in brief, the very topic our diagram should help us to explore.

It is here, in this aspect of the mind as a self-ordering endeavour, as a government hoping to maintain itself, that compromise appears most clearly as the practical art of the translator. To ask: Where in general will compromise be most needed? is to try to divide the fields of possible discourse. There are areas of settled routine—much of trade, for example—where the fixed and comparatively simple structuring of the things and events to be dealt with allows of a fine practical equivalence between the languages used. Wherever there is a clear operational check upon Comprehendings this happy condition is likely to prevail. Mathematics, physics, the strict sciences can be translated without loss—by the introduction of the technical term and the use of the type-specimen, the model and the operational definition. Here functions 1, 2, and 6 are serving a Purposing so general that it can hide behind the ordering, 6, of what is said, 2, about what, 1. But as discourse grows less abstract and hypothetical, more entire and actual, the probability of loss and therefore the need for choice and compromise become greater. With narrative and philosophy and poetry insofar as the growth and history of the language and of other social and cultural institutions enter in, a self-denying statute is required. If we take Ethics to be "the bringing to bear of self-control for the purpose of realizing our desires"[7] we have to decide which of our desires must give way to which. The translator has first to reconcile himself to conceiving his art in terms of minimal loss and then to balance and adjudicate, as best he can, the claims of the rival functions. His question is: Which sorts of loss will we take in order not to lose what? And answering that is in practice a series of decisions, 6, on behalf of a policy, 7, which may very well have to declare itself openly, in a preface or in footnotes. The mind–state analogy is at work all through, it will be perceived. The translator is called upon to become a statesman and serve a limitless oncoming state. His chief advantage over his analogue is that he can, sometimes, go back and undo his mistakes. He can cancel and choose again. But for the rest his practical sagacity must accept the hard commonplace truths: if we try for too much, we will get less than we might, and what we can go on to do will depend on what we have done and are doing now.

Translation theory—over and above the aid it may afford the translator—has thus a peculiar duty toward man's self-completion, to use a concept which seems to be suggestively common to the Chinese and the Western traditions. We are not weather vanes, 1; we are not filing systems, 2; we are not even agonies or delights only, 3; we are not litmus paper, 4, or servomechanisms, 5. We are guardians, 6, and subject therefore to the paradox of government: that we must derive our powers, in one way or another, from the very forces which we have to do our best to control. Translation theory has not only to work for better mutual comprehension between users of diverse tongues; more central still in its purposing is a more complete viewing of itself and of the Comprehending which it should serve.

NOTES

1. *Arche* foundational or guiding principle. Richards preferred the concept of dependence in describing the architectonics of ideas.—ED
2. See, e.g., Willard V. O. Quine, "Two Dogmas of Empiricism," *Philosophical Review,* Vol. LX (1951).
3. I need a highly general term here, not limited to any mode of utterance, such as *overt* speech or writing. An act of comprehending may itself be regarded as an utterance, being a rebirth, after passage through the lifeless signal, of something more or less the same as the original which was transmitted.
4. A possible eighth division might be Venting (that one of the multifarious meanings of the word *expression* which seems least well covered by my seven). Utterances from a simple "Ouch!" or "Ooh!" up to *The Divine Comedy* can be regarded as drive-reducing—in terms, that is, of the psychology of the utterer. But, since the purposes of a psychological investigator are not those of a translator, I would expect different schemas to be suitable. And to me, at present, this respect seems well enough taken care of—for the translator's purposes—through my seven which may *all* in their varying ways be drive-reducing. I am indebted to Dr. Irving Singer for making me see the need for this note, and to Charles Morris' *Signs, Language, and Behavior* (New York: Prentice-Hall, Inc., 1946) for suggestions contributing to my schema.
5. Angus Sinclair, *The Conditions of Knowing* (London: Routledge & Kegan Paul, 1951), p. 35.
6. Robert Bridges, *The Testament of Beauty* (Oxford, 1939).
7. Collected Papers of Charles Sanders Peirce, I, 334.

Messages are generated by Contexts; they are conveyed by signals. Messages are living. They are animated instances of meaning, determinations from the context field; the signals which convey them are dead. My thinking, doubting, wondering at this moment is living activity; so is the nerve–muscle–joint process guiding my pen as I compose my Message. But the motions of the pen itself are inanimate, as are the configurations its point is tracing on the paper, the signals. The typist, the printer, the library, etc. all put the page before you. As you read the inanimate lines of print, a living activity of thinking, doubting, wondering—despairing perhaps—arises in you. That is the Message coming into being again. It was not in the pen or on the page. So too with a speaker: his postures, gestures, facial expressions, actions and the rest, together with what his voice does in the soundwave channel—anything that videotape can take down: all that is signal, merely. Not until it is interpreted by some living recipient does anything that should be called the Message appear. It is essential to a Message that what forms in the Addressee (or other recipient) should be of the same order of being with what has formed in the Addresser. He may get it all wrong (and often does) but there is an IT. The two apparitions are both meanings. But a sound track and a system of meanings are not things of a sort, able to agree or disagree. The distinction between Message and signal (Context and physical channel) is indeed a *pons asinorum* in linguistics.

"Factors in and Functions of Language," from *Poetries: Their Media and Ends* (1974).

16

Meanings as Instruments

[A sample of Every Man's English* at work in semantic description]

At the heart of language control is the use of words (or, better, their senses) as instruments in looking closely at or into the senses of other words. They help us to separate the parts which make up these senses and to see more clearly how one sense may be, in this way or that, the same as or different from another. They are our apparatus for comparing and connecting senses, for taking them to bits and putting them together again.

At first, we may think that, to be useful, an instrument word should itself be very clear, straightforward and simple, have no more than one fixed sense, and keep to it without changing in any way from one use to another. But if we keep a sharp eye on some of these words we soon learn that this is not so at all. These important words in fact ask for careful watching, and if we watch them enough we come to see that they could not serve us so well if they were not free to take on different powers to meet the different sorts of work they have in hand. The thing to do is not to be surprised by these changes but to learn how and why they take place and be ready to profit from them.

Among the most interesting of these words is *simple* itself—a word that certainly looks as though it should be simple. Far from it.[1]

---

*Richards' label for his variant of Basic English. He probably echoed Coleridge, who, in commenting on Wordsworth's phrase "the real language of men," wrote as follows: "I object . . . to an equivocation in the use of the word "real." Every man's language varies, according to the extent of his knowledge, the activity of his faculties, and the depth or quickness of his feelings. Every man's language has, first, its *individualities;* secondly, the common properties of the *class* to which he belongs; and thirdly, words and phrases of *universal* use" (*Biographia Literaria*, II, chapter 17).—ED

From *Techniques in Language Control* (1974), chap. 8.

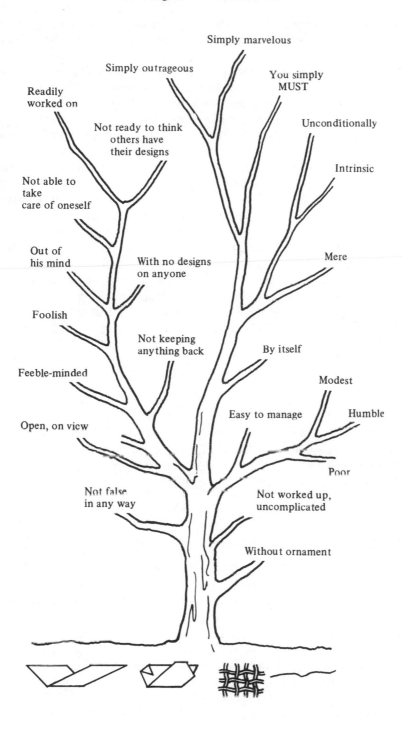

Simply marvelous

Simply outrageous

You simply
MUST

Readily
worked on

Not ready to think
others have
their designs

Unconditionally

Intrinsic

Not able to
take
care of oneself

Out of
his mind

With no designs
on anyone

Mere

Foolish

Not keeping
anything back

By itself

Feeble-minded

Modest

Humble

Open, on view

Easy to manage

Poor

Not false
in any way

Not worked up,
uncomplicated

Without ornament

Let us make a picture of its senses in the form of a tree with a stem springing up from a root sense and branches stretching out in a number of directions.

At the root of this tree we may put a picture of a sheet of paper with only one fold in it. And let this one-fold sheet be compared with and taken in opposition (as opposite) to a sheet with many folds in it.

This opposition between *simple* (L. *simplex: sem*-as in *semel* "once" + -*plex* "fold") and *complex* (L. *complexus* "embrace, connection, network" = more-than-one-fold, i.e., *manifold*) starts the development off and, as we will see, controls it throughout. It may help if we add another pair of pictures of another opposition here at the root: a picture of one thread by itself to be compared with a picture of threads going over and under one another as in a cloth or twisted together, over and under to form a braid.

The root area then of *simple* is of something being *by itself,* as opposed to being together with other things in more or less complex relations to them. The next step on from being by itself, open like an unfolded sheet, is being two-fold, being double. Thence we have *duplicity,* a word with very bad suggestions: of seeming to be of one sort and being of another.

By opposition with this we have a branch of senses stretching out from: "not false in any way, true" through

"open, all on view"

"not keeping anything back or secret from other people"

"saying no more or less than what one has in mind"

"with no designs on anyone"

"not ready to think that others may have designs on anyone"

therefore, "readily worked upon by others, easily taken in by them and made to believe what is not true to serve their purposes"

"not able to take care of oneself"

"foolish, feeble-minded"

"out of his mind"

"not responsible for his acts or thoughts."

As the picture attempts to suggest, up to a certain point to say of someone that he is "simple" can voice high approval. It may well be that there is nothing better than to be completely sincere—clear and direct with oneself: in C. S. Lewis's words "seeing what he sees and playing no tricks with his own knowledge of purpose" (p. 171). Then suddenly this branch takes a down turn: the simple one is no longer able to take care of himself. He may not play any tricks on himself but other people can and do. He ends up as "just too simple" with no power to see what is going on about him, or to look after his own interests and purposes, wise or foolish.

We have put this in as a left-hand branch. On the right let us start another branch with the idea that what is simple is without ornament, with nothing done to it to make it specially pleasing, not worked up to have any added attractions. Things, ways of living, dress, food and the rest are simple in this sense when they are uncomplicated (not made complex). At this point, the branch divides. What is not complex is not hard to take in or to work. So one part of the branch takes us to "easily managed" with a side suggestion that such things are natural as opposed to things made complex by art. The other part of the branch turns away to the idea that poor people have to live simply, they haven't enough money for anything more. And with this comes the thought that simple people living simply will do well not to try to seem to be more important than they are or to seem to have more than in fact they have. The branch which has been down to "poor" then takes an up-turn to "humble" (makes oneself seem, to others, unimportant) and "modest" (not putting too high a value on oneself).

Such suggestions are frequently more powerful than true. We all know that things like telephones and airplanes are made more complex than they need to be so that they may be easier (simpler) to operate. And that life can be much simpler with a refrigerator, a washing machine, and a vacuum cleaner than without them. And we know too how not having enough money can make it more necessary to seem to have it, not less.

Let us look now at the middle stem of the tree which has put out these branches. The root, the chief opposition, is the same. What is as it is, *in and by itself,* is opposed to what has other things added to and mixed up with it, as conditions or outcomes. So, taken *in, by and for itself,* it is taken "simply"; all the rest on which it may be dependent or which may be dependent on it is kept out of the account. This use of "simply" is a way of saying that this is how we are taking it.

There is a very deep idea here, harder to get at than it may seem. Possibly, we cannot, in fact, take anything so.[2] But we can certainly think that we are taking a thing so, *by itself.* Then, as C. S. Lewis points out, if we say of it, simply so taken, that it is good or bad we seem to be saying something with much *more* weight than if we said, "under these conditions, or because of these effects I am for it or against it." And this may be why, as he suggests, we so frequently use "simply" as simply a way of making *more* noise about what we are saying and forcing it more strongly upon those we are talking to.

It may be added that to discuss such a word as *simple* as we have been doing in this sample of Every Man's English—without a full and representative selection of examples—is to be less than just to the powers of the word. All who can should turn to Lewis' own pages, and we all should go on thinking of the ever-changing views of what is simple in certain senses which developments in the sciences give us.

Let us turn now to the word "*sense.*" In most discussions of words and their senses, of whether something that is said makes sense, of whether when we put it in other words it has the same or a different sense and so on, we behave as though no question need come up as to how we should be taking this word *sense* itself. And most of the time, no doubt, we are quite right in going on so. We would never get anywhere or get anything said or done if we stopped to ask such questions about every word we use. On the other hand this word *sense* is so very important, does so much work for us and such different sorts of work, that we can probably help ourselves not a little and help this word and the other words we talk about with it to do their work better, if we do take a few pages here and put down some of the chief things known about it.

SENSE

Let us see then what a tree picture of the senses of the word *sense* may look like.

We may put as roots the Latin verb *sentire,* with its parts, *sensus* and *sentiens* and nouns from them: *sensus* and *sententia.* A wide, general stem or trunk sense can be pointed to from different sides by "feel, know, take in, experience, learn, get, have in mind, go through, undergo." There are also connections with Latin *sentis* "a path" (footway) on which the feet feel their way in the night, and maybe with Old High German *sinnan* "to go, to journey, to think." Probably we should take all these possibilities as *not* in early times opposed to one another. For example, "feeling" can often today be taken as separated from and opposed to "thinking." In early use of Latin it may be doubted if a question: "Are you thinking or feeling?" could have been asked or could have meant anything. And the same would probably be true, in most cases, of the young child today.

Our tree's stem, however, soon divides so markedly as to make it almost two trees with common roots. The division comes from an opposition as deep and important as that between "outside" and "inside." This is the division between what we see, hear, touch, taste and smell—the outer world, in short—and what we somehow find going on in our minds when we note how we are thinking, feeling, hoping, fearing, willing and desiring—the inner world of our experiences. The things we learn of through our senses as against the conditions of mind we are conscious of within ourselves: these two are the first and the chief branches or stems through which later branchings are organized.

It is interesting to note how independent the two can be. No one is ever in much doubt as to when the word "sense" is talking about seeing, hearing, etc. or about ways of thinking, feeling, etc. This is surprising in view of the fact that seeing, hearing, etc. are all ways of knowing and our uses of "experience" readily cover both the outer and the inner worlds. C. S. Lewis gives us (p. 152) two lines from Pope which are both equally about these two sorts of sense but use opposite words for them. They show very clearly how well we can separate them:

What thin partitions sense from thought divide.[3]
While pure description held the place of sense.[4]

quot homines, tot sententiae

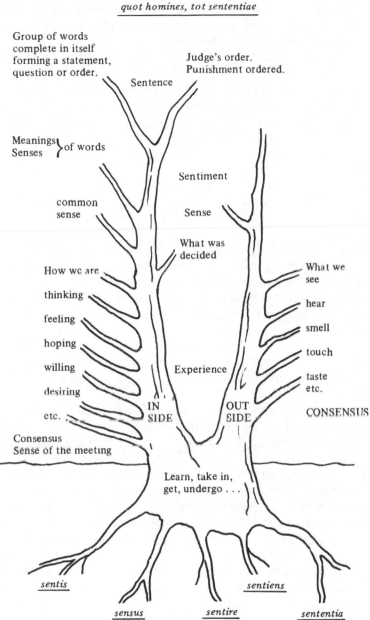

Group of words
complete in itself
forming a statement,
question or order.

Judge's order.
Punishment ordered.

Sentence

Meanings
Senses } of words

Sentiment

common
sense

Sense

What was
decided

How we are

What we
see

thinking

hear

feeling

smell

hoping

touch

willing

Experience

taste
etc.

desiring

etc.

IN
SIDE

OUT
SIDE

CONSENSUS

Consensus
Sense of the meeting

Learn, take in,
get, undergo . . .

sentis

sentiens

sensus

sentire

sententia

The first is saying "Between what the eye etc. can see etc. and our thoughts about it, the walls are very thin." The second is saying "Here no more than an account of what could be seen etc. was given in place of what was needed, namely, serious and interesting thought."

Taking up now the outer-world branch, we may note first that physiology and psychology have added to the old list of the five senses. We have an uncertain number of ways of knowing the positions, motions, and condition of our bodies and of their parts. If you are out of breath, if your heart starts "thumping," if your foot "goes to sleep" and so on . . . , incoming news of what is taking place tells you about it much as incoming news tells you that someone is waving to you. So too with heat and cold and with pressures and tired muscles and with pains. It may seem strange to put some of these sense-events in the *outer* world. They may seem so much inside us. They come from inside our bodies, it is true. But that is not the same thing as being in *us*. We will therefore add these "other senses" to the old five of our outer-world branch.

What we have chiefly to note about all these incomings of news is how smoothly they work together. What one sense has to tell us, as a rule, agrees very well with what the others are saying. There is a very highly developed *consensus* (in the physiological sense, agreement of different organs, parts of us with special work to do, in effecting a purpose). In all this helpful cooperation we have something very unlike the angry fighting between different views that is so frequent in the inner world. In turning to that branch now, let us hope that this promising order among the inputs can serve us as an example in our attempts to discover better ways of ordering thought and its outputs.

From *sentire* "to think" came *sententia* and in English "sentence" has had and has a number of special senses. In Middle English it could be used where we would now use "opinion" and sometimes for "deep and well-based opinion." We have come to use "sentence" chiefly for the words as opposed to what they are saying, for a group of words complete in itself forming a statement, question, or command. An important sort of sentence is the statement-order in which a judge gives out his decision: "What was the sentence?" "The sentence was six years." "He is serving out his sentence." Here we see the sense of "sentence" moving from the words the judge said to what was ordered and so on to the punishment itself.

"Sense," like Middle English "sentence," can be used to show approval: "That's talking sense!"; or disapproval: "There wasn't much sense in what he said." Approval and agreement commonly go hand in hand; we naturally approve of that with which we agree. The danger is that when we do not agree we are so ready to twist what has been said. There are other dangers too: we twist other people's words in order to make them seem to agree with us as well as to be able to attack them. Or again, we may take others to be thinking as we would think when in fact they have quite another view. What is known as "the sense of the meeting," the *consensus* in the political sense, is sometimes far from being what most of the people represented had in mind. We would do well to write up over our doorways and weigh daily the old saying from Terence, *quot homines, tot sententiae.* "There are as many opinions as there are men." It might help us to take more pains about the senses we give to words. Hard though it is to see clearly enough into our own thinking, it is far harder to make out the thought of others. No trouble would be too much that truly could help us in this and increase our powers here. To turn two lines from Milton's *L'Allegro* to another purpose than his—in so doing we would be

> Untwisting all the chains that ty
> The hidden soul of harmony.

Clearly this sort of work on the senses of words and their connections can be taken very far. Commonly the force of a word in a situation (used under certain conditions) comes to it from and depends on the fact that in other situations it will have other senses. Here, we have attempted no more than to present—in a specimen of Every Man's, controlled language kept very near to Basic—two pictured accounts of the branchings of the senses of two of the chief words through which we attempt both to control and to make clear what we take to be said. Though all words are instruments, these two with a few more, of which "instrument" itself is one, do the greater part of the work. Inside "instrument" (that through which something is done), *stru-* represents *struct-* as in "instruct" and "structure," with a root idea of building. We may learn again from these great words how much of what we can do depends on our instruments, on what we find to work with.

This is not an altogether comforting thought. As the physicist discovers that any account he can give of subatomic events depends upon the instruments he is using in his experiments (Niels Bohr's Complementarity Principle) so here—at the other end of the simple to complex scale—here, in our attempts to control our meanings (the most complex undertaking we know of), what we can do depends equally upon the instruments we are using. And these instruments themselves are meanings. No train of thought could better make us see—as with the "humble" and "modest" senses of "simple"—why we do well to ask ourselves, again and again and carefully, what we are doing in our thinking. And to ask this again about our answers. . . .

NOTES

1. We are deeply in debt here to C. S. Lewis's very clear and well-ordered account of the words *simple* and *sense* in his most helpful *Studies in Words*, Cambridge University Press, 1960 and 1967, where the needed examples will be found.
2. This, which may seem a strange sort of doubt, is Plato's. In his *Sophist,* The Stranger from Elia offers this account of what truly is or has being: "I suggest that anything truly is that has any sort of power to control any other thing or be con-

trolled, in however small a degree, by it . . . . I am putting forward, as a mark of things that truly are, that they are nothing but power." (In Every Man's English.) For Francis Cornford's way of saying this and his observations on the Greek word here translated as *power,* see his *Plato's Theory of Knowledge,* London, Routledge, 1935, p. vii and pp. 234–39. On the connection with present-day physics, see *So Much Nearer,* pp. 107–08.

3. *Essay on Man,* 1, 226.
4. *To Arbuthnot,* 147.

In writing something down according to an explicit convention (or in Morsing it), the rules are fully worked out; they are familiar and available to give rulings. In the other cases, in any instance of enterprising and adroit use of language, the rules are conjectural merely and as yet, in fact, barely conjecturable. Meanwhile, however, in more than a little of the talk about coding and decoding that goes on there is present, I fear, a suggestion that Morsing and composing are closely alike. I have listened to "communication theory" being offered to teachers-to-be in such a way that you would suppose that to speak or write well is no more than to emit—in parallel with strings of received notions—the clichés that have the highest probabilities. What is odd is that some who are ready to call themselves ˢʷeducatorsˢʷ have a difficulty in seeing why such a degradation of crude usage theory should be debilitating. An account well suited to the purposes of the communication engineer may be highly misleading as an instrument in teaching writing and reading. I am not doubting that the engineers' formulation has been convenient in phonology, but only whether its extension into higher levels of linguistics may not need the especial attention of critics. I hazard the guess that higher levels can help out lower levels more frequently than lower higher.

"Variant Readings and Misreading," from *So Much Nearer* (1968).

There is an important use of words—very frequent, I suggest, in poetry—which does not freeze its meanings but leaves them fluid, which does not fix an assertorial clip upon them in the way that scientific prose and factual discussion must. It leaves them free to move about and relate themselves in various ways to one another. Probably this freedom should be thought of as a matter of degree, but as degree suggests measurement and we are not in sight of measurement here—do not know what we should seek to measure—we can do no more at present than recognize a necessity of vagueness. That is not to say, however, that the meanings in these fluid sentences are vague.

They may or may not be—as meanings in rigid prose may or may not be. *Vagueness–precision* and *rigidity–fluidity* . . . are different dimensions. In fluid language a great many very precise meanings may be free to dispose themselves in a multiplicity of diverse ways.

"Poetry as an Instrument of Research," from *Speculative Instruments* (1955).

17

Some Glances at Current Linguistics

... A generative theory of language (of those languages at the least in which Western Man's view of himself is incarnate) cannot do without a knower. It cannot handle any of the words which can replace *know* in "I___that my soul liveth" or indeed any but sentences about neutral "its" and "theys." It cannot even say what grammarians should be doing. To be truly generative an account of language must find a supreme place for a knower down in the ultimate profundities of its deep structure.

This is not, of course, a proof of, or even an argument for, the necessity of a soul. These considerations may invite but do not require any such belief. They are a part, however, of the explanation of the resentment shown against common speech (and of some of the toadying to its less respectable manifestations) which has been so marked among positivist–behaviorist theorists of languages. The unfair advantages of a theological inside track are indeed provoking. Moreover, and this was more often the major consideration, this 'knower* so snugly ensconced in the very heart of the subject is so pathetically fallible, so groundlessly confident, so often and so evidently mistaken. The privileges and pretensions of introspection are so immense, its punditry so arrogant, its fraudulence sometimes so patent, its equivocations often so bare that Behaviorism was perhaps inevitable.

In all this the interweavings of other factors, other ambitions than the academic should be noted. As the possibilities of the computer, of automation and of data-processing were increasingly recognized, their techniques

See pp. 270–73 for an explanation of these superscripts.—ED

From *So Much Nearer* (1968), chap. 4.

developed, and their military significance appreciated, wishes for a comparable linguistic engineering became pressing. And not only in the hope of soon attaining practicable machine translation but for other communication problems as well. The amount of recent work in linguistics—especially on theories of grammar and, of late, semantics—which has been supported by the Signal Corps, the Army, the Air Force, the Navy and the National Science Foundation tells its own story. This question of the source of the wherewithal can be important. Those who supply the necessary funds may reasonably expect to receive in return something which really looks like value for their money. Those who endeavor to produce this not unnaturally assume the appropriate professional manner. Much of their most intent reading has, for many of them, been in a literature composed for these patrons. The importance of the ⁿᵇright ⁿᵇ stance, the right lingo, the right resource is well understood by experts "expert beyond experience" in every field.

Among these resources one in particular is noticeable enough in modern linguistics to deserve comment. As most examiners well know, when a question has been asked and the examinee hasn't an answer, an account (the lengthier and the more elaborate the better) of some conditions any answer must manage to meet can often earn a good mark. It looks at least like a step in the right direction and toward something. Hence, if I mistake not, some of the recent prominence in linguistics of theorizing on theory-construction—theory cubed, at least, and to higher powers sometimes—given as much mathematical style as may be. Math is the Queen now to the patrons as Theology was in monastic days. We may note, however, the obscuration, the doubts below the dazzle of the panache, the occultation of assumptions, the palming of the point . . . with which premature mathematical treatment has often, ever since Plato, troubled thought about language.

Another source of unreality in much contemporary linguistics is timidity in facing up to the problem of 'the linguistic community'. This phrase, if we took it literally, would ask us to assume that all the hearers–speakers we are considering as belonging to it are alike in their linguistic behavior in all relevant ways. Any close and alert examination of perhaps any linguistic community can show, from indisputable factual record, so much variation in regard to almost any linguistically interesting feature of this behavior that the phrase 'linguistic community' takes on a sardonic air. This is an actuality we have many strong motives for minimizing; to keep up our *morale* we have to pretend a good deal of our time that mutual understanding is occurring when we really know very well that it isn't; really close and deep accord in interpretation is unusual and astonishing; communication so far as it succeeds deceives us as to its failures; meditation upon the matter can induce a melancholy and a sense of loneliness; and if we speak or write about it we will incur charges of morbidity and exaggeration. Nonetheless, a critical study will show that degrees of efficiency in any but trivial communications are as stated.

It is notable that the sentences grammarians use as specimens in their expositions are usually such as are little likely to be misinterpreted. And where they do touch upon ambiguity there is commonly an eccentricity and artificiality in the examples which may be symptomatic. The real hazards of language are conspicuously *not* represented. Samples taken from political, moral, religious, methodological *and linguistic* discussion would give a very different impression. Studies of language which avoid dealing with those features of language which have been most frustrating to our efforts to inquire into our deepest needs may justly be described as superficial. And this in the face of innumerable and ever-increasing practical needs to clarify and try to remedy our multiplying misunderstandings, at a time when there are clear risks of our cultures falling apart. The most indispensable efforts of education are in fact addressed to lowering these probabilities of misapprehension. We should not forget how much of the justification of linguistic studies is to be found in the improved communication to which—it has been hoped—they may lead.

Let us look then at how linguistics has been handling its task of selecting the hearers–speakers whose verbal conduct it aims to study. Two opposed tendencies may be remarked. On the one hand there are those who have become interested in differences and have inquired into the variants of spoken and written utterance and (to a lesser degree) of comprehension or interpretation in the recipients. These variants, as we all know, arise through many circumstances. There are as many dialects—regional, occupational, social, cultural—as you have the patience to distinguish and the energy to order through your type-specimens and descriptions. Many individuals operate in a number of such dialects: classroom, at home, with the gang and so on. These circumstantial variations, which commonly go along with switches in gesture and port, are often called *registers*. Expressions and responses suited to one occasion are unsuited to another.

Look closer, consider as minutely as you can how individuals differ one from another and not least in how they distinguish between occasions. It is a slogan in contemporary linguistics, endlessly re-echoed, that language is 'creative', that people are incessantly saying things that no one has said before, instead of merely repeating phrases they have heard. Go over some of your acquaintances in imagination and listen to a selection of TV ads (or try a Pinter play), and wonder to what extent that is true of which of them. Here is another respect in which *ideolects* (as linguists name the tacit competences of individual hearers–speakers) differ. Anyone who has been a teacher or a clinician or an administrator knows how deeply hearers–speakers differ not only from one another but day by day and hour by hour from themselves. We need, in fact, to extrapolate the series: *Language, Dialect, Register, Ideolect,* and to supply some name for the momentary competence of an individual within a specific ambiance of circumstances. (Would *Compos* conceivably meet this need? X's *compos* then would theoretically range from that of Shakespeare penning *The Phoenix and the Turtle* down to that of the autistic child achieving his first uses of language.)

Against this background of diversity of competences what do the systematic theorists, exponents of the converse tendency, do? They invent a remarkable construct, highly abstract and only after some reflection identifiable, which they refer to as "a fluent speaker." I do not know who invented this remarkable figure or why he is called "fluent" rather than "preternatural." On page 481 of *Structure of Language,* by J. A. Fodor and J. J. Katz, he is thus described. Note that he is introduced as though he were a real person and not a figment. But clearly he is a concoction on the lines of a frictionless inclined plane or a perfect gas—not to say a perfect gas-bag.

"A fluent speaker's mastery of his language exhibits itself in his ability to produce and understand the sentences of his language, *including indefinitely many that are wholly novel to him* (i.e., his ability to produce and understand *any* sentence of his language)." The italics are theirs. They add in a footnote, "There are exceptions, such as technical words that the speaker does not know, sentences too long for the speaker to scan in his lifetime and so on," which lets us see with what concern for actuality the writers are conceiving their subject. Probably "wholly" in "*wholly novel*" is due just to carelessness, to inattention to the essentials. Anyone faced with a sentence wholly novel to him is in the position of the beginner in a new language who has met none of its words before nor any of the constructions in which they are being used. It is fun to imagine this fluent speaker producing and understanding such sentences so freely. The weasel word here may be "his" in "his language." That could contract the segment of the language he is so skilled in to just those sentences, few or many, that he *can* produce and understand. Notice further the assumption in "produce and understand" that of course this gifted chap can compose anything that he can comprehend. If he can understand Shakespeare he can write like him, can he? A semantic theory that ignores the differences between passive and active competence as well as the problems of degrees of understanding is a revealing exhibit.

I have lingered over this crazy* construct, the *fluent speaker,* because it illustrates the abstract unreality of much modern theorizing, and may remind us of the ease with which an artificial set of problems can be substituted for those that are professedly under study. This fluent one, as he is described, corresponds to nothing. In practice, however, his description would probably come down to something like this: "A speaker who can produce and understand (more or less) any sentence which we, the authors, are going to use *as specimens* in our pages."

But this, it will be felt, is hardly adequate as a key construct with reference to which a theory undertakes "to determine what mechanisms a semantic

---

*For all his long years in the United States, Richards remained uninfluenced (so far as I can see) by American habits of speech. Thus *crazy* here probably does not mean "nutty" or "wild" but "distorted," "irrational," and "unstable." On the other hand it is not improbable that Richards enjoyed the overtones of this word in this situation. Which of his superscripts would be appropriate I will not venture to say.—ED

theory employs in reconstructing the speaker's ability to interpret sentences in isolation."[1]. . .

The more closely we consider any sentence that is saying anything dependent on what has come before it and/or of any consequence for what may be to come, the more intimately interwoven[2] are grammatical form and semantic import. It is only by using exorbitant and inapplicable definitions for 'grammar', 'grammarian', 'describe', and 'setting'—on the lines of that offered for 'fluent speaker'—that such claims as the following can be made: "Grammars seek to describe the structure of a sentence *in isolation from its possible settings in linguistic discourse (written or verbal) or in nonlinguistic contexts (social or physical)*."[3] Ask how the necessary comparisons can arise or can be carried through without consideration of possible settings or how anyone acquires or employs a language, and the heroic degree of this eviscerative abstraction becomes evident. The mummies that result have no communication. Only that fluent speaker, I fear, could have converse with them. The authors explain: "The justification . . . is simply that the fluent speaker is able to construct and recognize syntactically well-formed sentences without recourse . . ." etc. A theory of the construction of semantic theories which displays as a banner heading:

LINGUISTIC DESCRIPTION MINUS GRAMMAR EQUALS SEMANTICS

is not reassuring. It hardly leads us to expect penetration. What we find are other fancy constructs, e.g., persons who do not speak English but are equipped with a completely adequate grammar of English. This again may make us wonder how theories with such slight relation to actuality can be helpful. . . .

NOTES

1. *in isolation: Structure of Language, Readings in the Philosophy of Language,* eds. Jerry A. Fodor and Jerrold J. Katz (New York: Prentice-Hall, 1964), p. 491. The phrase 'in isolation' as here used needs expansion. It may mean ˢʷwithout any apparently helpful actual settingˢʷ. The authors have been discussing an anonymous letter containing only a single sentence. With this construct they seem to suppose that they have eliminated influence of setting. But have they? In practice (in a way which is most relevant to theory) an anonymous letter is a powerful setting in itself. It puts the reader to work imagining possible composers, etc., and trying to select from among them. A scrap of paper blown off a dump will do the same to a lesser degree. There are, as most people well know, systematic resources, available to utterers and receivers alike, which supply conjectural settings when needed and supplement normally sufficient settings as required. And, though these authors argue to the contrary, a communicator's "ability to interpret sentences" is very largely his ability to make judicious choices from among such alternative possible settings. All this reliable common knowledge, which could supply solid ground for an account of how people do in fact come to understand, more or less, what others say to them (and of how they in turn manage to say things to others) is here summarily brushed off for the sake of that fluent speaker.

2. *intimately interwoven* Compare Chomsky. "In general, as syntactic description becomes deeper, what appear to be semantic questions fall increasingly within its
scope." See "Current Issues," p. 51, in *Structure of Language,* p. 77. Compare with
this: LINGUISTIC DESCRIPTION MINUS GRAMMAR EQUALS SEMANTICS, p. 483.
What has happened here to phonology as well as to grammar and to semantics?
3. Fodor and Katz, op. cit., p. 484.

Grammatical theory cannot possibly be a closed system. The facts it attempts
to order are a selection of the acts of men. So too, it may be said, are the
facts of mathematics. But mathematical thought restricts itself to certain
clearly defined aspects of things, their numerable and quantitative aspects, or
in the case of geometry, to properties which can be defined ab initio. It proceeds only in virtue of these definitions. But grammar has no such definitions
to support it. If it had, it would no longer be an inquiry into the uses of
language; it would cease to be an empirical comparative inquiry and become
a deductive symbol system.

"What Is Grammar?," from *Interpretation in Teaching* (1938).

18

Powers and Limits of Signs

Our starting point can be Roman Jakobson's admirably forthright formulation:

For us, both as linguists and as ordinary word-users, the meaning of any linguistic sign is its translation into some further alternative Sign, especially a sign "in which it is more fully developed" as Peirce, the deepest inquirer into the essence of signs, insistently stated.[1]

Jakobson's opening qualification here is highly significant: both as distinguishing linguists from ordinary word-users, and as indicating that there are also other-than-ordinary, or special, USES of Language. . . . [Richards describes certain special uses—of teachers, learners, playwrights, advertisers, pornographers, poets, political sloganeers—all "determined by the character of the situation governing the communication." He then returns to the passage quoted from Jakobson, closing in on "is its translation."] . . . The word *is* here marks, I take it, an ellipsis, itself calling for expansion, calling for a sign in which its own meaning is more fully developed. What should our expansion be? When we have settled that, we will be readier to answer questions about "its translation." The most helpful "further, alternative sign" among those that occur to me is, I think, "can be clarified by." I find myself loth—through a resistance which hardens as I experiment—to accept a reading that takes *is* more literally: e.g., "is nothing other than," "is, in fact, actually" and such. Perhaps this resistance reflects possibilities in the reading of "its translation"—to which we may now turn.

From *Poetries: Their Media and Ends* (1974), chap. 2.

In common with very many other words ending in *-tion*, TRANSLATION may represent either a process of translating or the product that is the outcome of the process. I take it to be the process which is being talked of here, not the product. This probably is the cause of my difficulty in taking *is* more literally. With TRANSLATION as product, I seem to see less clearly how any one such outcome could be said to be the "meaning of a linguistic sign." But with TRANSLATION as a process of weighing, comparing, amending, adjusting possibilities of interpretation, selecting, testing etc., etc., I seem to find myself much nearer to a viable view. As process, TRANSLATION allows for the flexibility, the adaptability, the manifold resource of most of the meanings I have had dealings with. Figuratively, the process view offers us cells cooperating; the product view, merely bricks in a wall.

A related set (system, rather) of ambiguities with TRANSLATION seems worth exploring here. Jakobson neatly presents three kinds of translation:

1. Intralingual translation or REWORDING . . .

2. Interlingual translation or TRANSLATION proper . . .

3. Intersemiotic translation or TRANSMUTATION . . . an interpretation of verbal signs by means of signs of non-verbal sign systems. (p. 233)

His essay in *On Translation* is largely devoted to bringing his extraordinary range of knowledge to bear on (2). I confine myself to (1) and (3).

Relatively little explicit analytic discussion of the organization of nonverbal sign systems has, until recent times, been available. (1) and (2), being more accessible, have preempted attention. It is easier to talk about our words than about the other-than-verbal signs which may very likely be our necessary means of comparing and controlling what our words are doing.

We must recognize that Peirce's doctrine, along with its encouraging positive aspects, has a negative interpretation which can be grimly forbidding. Many have taken it as denying that we can do more in exploring our meanings than switch from one phrasing to another and on again to yet others. Positivists, Behaviorists and their Nominalist allies, who make it a point of conscience to enact and obey self-denying ordinances in matters such as the occurrence and use of concepts and of images—visual, mobile, tactile, kinaesthetic, gustatory, olfactory and the rest—have seemed to wish to empty the mind of all but verbal equivalences and to substitute word-play for thinking. But SUBSTITUTABLE and EQUIVALENCE, along with COMPARE and CONTROL, are terms whose meanings are as explorable as they are important. Human education indeed might well be described as learning how to explore them.

The key question is: "How do we decide whether an expression is or is not equivalent to, substitutable for, able to replace . . . another?" If we answer: "By comparing," we have then to try to say what we are comparing with what and how we do it. And, as we do so, we have again to decide whether or not our account is 'satisfactory',* 'sufficient', 'able to explain the facts', 'intelligible' . . . and so on. These expressions again we have to compare (bearing in mind our account of comparing). We see why Peirce held that interpretation is a conversation without an ending.

What are we comparing? Not the expressions alone—apart from their meanings. But these meanings they have: what is our mode of access to them? Must we not have other means than just our phrasings through which to focus our attention on them and, as we say, make them out? Here is where our nonverbal sign systems come in, supplying us with (theoretically illimitable) cultivatable resources for noting within ourselves, to ourselves, how the meanings we are comparing are alike or unlike, require, preclude, supplement, in general are related to, one another. The meanings compared are relations within the overall fabric of sign systems.

The nonverbal sign systems are of two orders: public and private. If we ask ourselves what corresponds to a nod or shake of the head or a face we would like to pull, on occasions when we must give no sign of what we think, we will have these two orders conveniently present for comparison. There are batteries of such questions we may ask ourselves (without necessarily "putting them into words") that similarly can destroy any contention that thinking is nothing but internal speech. What is a forgotten name which you know is none of those suggested? How do you know what you have to say before you know how you will say it? What is a plan before it is begun to be worked out? Or any movement before it is made? When we recall, moreover, modern accounts of the signaling systems which control cell-growth and co-operation in the body, to try to substitute subvocal speech for thinking looks absurd. The point is that we are beginning to have better ideas about how we think, about what thinking must be like.

Nonetheless, if we are ready to let parapsychology go on crying in the wilderness, we only communicate with others through public signs, verbal and nonverbal. With ourselves we have only too many modes of communing. We do talk to ourselves and more than a little; but guiding and controlling these internal colloquies too is THOUGHT: a capacity to compare meanings.

Along with a re-conception of thought should go a more developed idea of meanings. It is not surprising that meanings—through the last fifty years—have been variously out of favor in psychology and in linguistics. Doctrinaire dogmatisms apart, much of the recurrent head-shaking and shoulder-shrugging over 'meaning' has sprung from a fair recognition of its enigmatic status. The forbidding side of Peirce's view represents a wish to replace meanings by more examinable fabrics—unduly limiting them, to "further alternative verbal signs" and overlooking the indispensable cooperations and constant support of the nonverbal sign-system components. His fundamental insight, however,—that the meaning of any sign consists in its relationship to other signs—retains all its value.

*See pp. 270–73 for an explanation of these superscripts.—ED

This relationship may extend very far. As any word may be conceived as related, via the words most immediately connected with it, to all the other words in the language, so some at least, of the nonverbal sign-systems have, span by span, an analogous though less extensive and inclusive connexity. Consider what the composer is doing in the auditory field and what relationships his phrases may have to other possible phrases. For each phrase, its relationships, at that point within the setting of the composition, are its musical meaning. Compare too what the tennis-player is doing in the optical–motor–kinaesthetic–tactual field. His strokes too can be thought of as having meanings—their relationship, rich and subtle or poor and crude, to his other possible strokes.

These relationships are highly complex. If we think of them as associations we risk making them seem too mechanical, and must remember that all activity is purposive. Throughout there is selection and control of means by ends. Jakobson performed a fine service to theory of meanings when he reminded linguists[2] that there are traditionally two kinds of association: (1) by SIMILARITY–OPPOSITION and (2) by CONTIGUITY. These operate in collaborative rivalry. A meaning is what it is through (1) what it is like and unlike and (2) where it is in its setting. A term with no opposite or a term by itself alone would be meaningless. X is HERE through not being THERE. And it is THERE through not being HERE. But without an X to be here or there, no meaning arises. (It may be worth adding that a number of what look like very important but unhappily insoluble problems seem to arise through forgetting this. But that does not make them less painful or important. The theological troubles of omniscience and omnipotence are the prime examples, linked as they are with the nature of defect. Evil seems a very high price to pay for the possibility of good.)

Our most variously powerful nonverbal sign-system is depiction: our iconic use of visual signs. Many of its aspects naturally parallel those of other signs. Thus a depiction, e.g. a visual image, may occur in degrees of vividness and presence varying from hallucinatory strength to the faintest, minimal, rudimentary sketch or indication—*without,* in some respects at least, loss of efficacy. So a sentence, heard in the mind's ear, can be reduced to a mere fragment, barely of a syllable, without losing meaning adequate to the occasion. Depiction too has, very evidently, its private and its public sectors. Consider how we decide whether a portrait is or is not "a good likeness," or whether any drawing is or is not "right." We evidently have our internal means (not necessarily confined to more or less veridical visual images) by which to check (control: etymon, CONTRA, 'over against' what is on a ROLL) the meanings that public signs may offer us. Depiction has not as yet received anything like the attention and study it deserves—either in semiotic or in theory and practice of education. In semiotic, to consider how depictions work can serve as valuable CONTROL over accounts of how verbal language works. The metaphor by which we call depiction a "visual language" is deeply instructive. In education, what depictions can do and how they do it are, both of them, among the largest relatively untapped resources the educator might command.

It is fitting that the semiotic of depiction should itself use depictions: with which to distinguish and hold clear for study the cooperative factors in depictive communication. Let us begin with a

$$\frac{\text{SITUATION(SIT)}}{\text{SITUATION (SIT)}} \text{ and a } \frac{\text{PICTURING(PIC)}}{\text{PICTURING (PIC)}}$$

Here the CAPITALS v SMALL CAPITALS contrast represents C. S. Peirce's TYPE v TOKEN distinction. In the last two sentences (SENTENCES, SENs) the graphic contrast between Caps and small caps (between C and c) represents the semiotic distinction (between an instance, c, and that of which it is an instance, C). In these SENs both verbal and nonverbal signs are cooperating in a way which deserves fuller exploration than can be attempted here.

What I have called a GRAPHIC contrast is not DEPICTIVE, for it will not do to describe C and c, as picturings of C and c (otherwise the indispensable distinction between a picture and that of which it is a picture would lapse). On the other hand, in $\frac{\text{SEN}}{\text{SEN}}, \frac{\text{PIC}}{\text{PIC}}, \frac{\text{SIT}}{\text{SIT}}$, the line under SEN and over SEN can properly be regarded as a depictive sign of the relationship between TYPE and TOKEN, between what is instanced and instances of it. As with all signs it can be read in various ways (varying with the setting and purpose: the "sit"). Thus it may be indicating just this token status, or it may be going further and telling us that our dealings with Ts are mediated only through TS (TYPES being known to us and dealt with by us only through TOKENS; no TYPE being seen or smelled or touched or even thought of except through TOKENS of it). In other words, TYPES have to be carried by TOKENS; what occurs, being timeless and placeless, must be represented by datable, locatable occurrings. And this division line may be read (in yet another sense: VERBALIZED, WORDED) as "over," or as "is conveyed by" and so on.

Inevitably, in using such a line we are inviting an immensely powerful system of meanings: those deriving from the $\frac{\text{numerator}}{\text{denominator}}$ relationship to intervene, if and when they can. I mention this to illustrate the point made above that any meaning has to defend itself from interpretations not relevant. Indeed its resistances to these usually define what it is. There are exceptions to this. One is exemplified by the fact that a depiction, say, of the relation of a point to a line, if taken strictly as concerned only with their positions on a plane, is definite in ways in which no verbal transmutation of it normally can be. All we can do, in words, is to indicate and approximate. That is why architectural depictions are so useful. No verbal description can take their place. And any builder's performances based on them will depart, less or more, from what they depict. But this definiteness attends only while they are being regarded as visual statements of relations between items on a plane. Let them be taken as PICTORIAL representations of objects in space and they become as open to misinterpretation as any verbal description could be.

Such a notational device and the semiotic reflections it prompts can help to protect us (1) from confusions between TYPES and TOKENS and (2) from confusions between "what is said" and "our ways of saying it." Both must—as far as possible—be avoided, if we are to trace successfully the powers and limits of depiction and of its cooperations with verbal signs. . . . [There follows an explanation of "modes of exploring situations," which is a version of what is set forth in "Learning and Looking" (see Chap. 23). In conclusion, Richards returns to the Jakobson statement with which he began.]

The linguist knows, in the sense of being able to state, discuss, support or refute them, innumerable things about languages which the ordinary word-user does not, in that sense, know. The ordinary user may be an admirable word-user (even a Shakespeare) without any of that knowledge. He has another sort of knowledge of the language, a know-how with it, which serves him in its place. Furthermore, there is little or no evidence that the linguist's knowledge would necessarily help the ordinary word-user, if he had it. People can have a great deal of linguistic knowledge and yet be inferior word-users.

There is, however, one branch of special linguistic knowledge which can help everyone, though it is not enough just to have it; we must learn to use it. This branch has no safe and handy name, but it can be readily described. It is the art of conscious comparings of meanings and of the explicit description of them through linguistic signs.

The lack of a safe name for this art is not hard to explain. In part it is due to the enigmatic status of meanings; they were felt to be such dubious entities that few could be sure what was being done when they were discussed. In part it is due to people giving the art names much used for other things: RHETORIC, for example, EXEGESIS and, worst of all SEMANTICS, including Korzybsky's General Semantics. Two good names exist covering parts of this study. LEXICOLOGY: the knowledge and skill and judgment required for good work in preparing articles in a Dictionary. But the art of comparing meanings requires ability to see what the setting of a meaning is as well as discernment as to which parts of a Dictionary article may be relevant. Study of SYNONYMY suffers from similar drawbacks.

Indication of a few principles of this fundamental art, strangely neglected in schools eminently useful though it is, will help to show what it should try to do.

1. Cooperation and Interference. One has just been mentioned: the dependence of meanings on the meanings of other words surrounding them in the setting as well as upon other factors in the ambience. What should be brought out is how what a word does is changed by a change made elsewhere

in a passage. In this, words behave very like people engaged in what should be a cooperative undertaking.

This principle emerges from comparisons between alternative phrases. To risk overstating it: any change in the phrasing entails some change in the meaning of a sentence. Sometimes it is a change that matters, sometimes not. To question WHY is continually a penetrating thrust of inquiry.

2. Tenor and Vehicle. A long while, some forty or more years ago, I tried to further inquire into metaphor by introducing two new terms (to be technicalized, if possible) to replace the appalling welter of highly ambiguous phrasings that labored to distinguish (1) what was being said (offered, presented) from (2) the way in which it was being said (offered, presented). They were: (1) TENOR, (2) VEHICLE, to stand respectively for the what (the Tenor) and the way (the Vehicle). I did not then, I think, so generalize, being too close to the problems of metaphor. Nor did I write the distinction down depictively as $\frac{T}{V}$, making V into SIGNANS and T into SIGNATUM. I did however realize, then as much earlier, that what T, the Tenor, would represent could not normally be unaffected by changes in V.

Notations have strange powers (as has been frequently shown in the history of mathematics). They can simplify and make routine what otherwise might call for an effort of thought, a recalling of principles. Korzybsky (the Apostle of General Semantics, mentioned above; he was not averse to being introduced to gatherings as Count Korzybsky, the Time Binder) tried, in his *Science and Sanity,* in its day a gospel for a cult, to introduce various useful notations to serve as reminders of what we all know but frequently forget. Typical was the sign *etc.*—to remind us of the rest that should be in our awareness more often than it is. He proposed to abbreviate it to ., or .. as it was placed in the midst or at the end of a sentence. This doubtless, would be a salutary procedure, though so inconspicuous a sign would be likely to be overlooked or treated as a misprint. I have tried out, myself, a set of specialized inverted commas with various intents. One of these is concerned with the Tenor–Vehicle terminological innovation mentioned above. It is the affixing, as superscripts, of ᴽʷ_____ᴽʷ in place of ᴽʷquotation marksᴽʷ, to distinguish words and phrases which the writer knows may very possibly be taken by the addressee in senses seriously different from that in which he hopes to have them understood. sw_____sw is short for SAID WITH, which is again an abbreviation of ᴽʷsomething that may be said withᴽʷ. The implication is that language at that point, as it can be used for the particular purpose being pursued is deficient (at least, as the writer can use it). And that, failing a perfectly fit term, something known to be less than fully efficient is being used. The indulgence of the reader is being begged for and his guessing capacity being alerted by the little alphabetic fleas perched so round the word or phrase.

This notational device, neither complex nor exacting, can serve, I believe, several compatible purposes. It can warn the reader to ^{sw}step warily^{sw} and to ^{sw}select wisely^{sw}. It can, furthermore, help to defend us from an error into which we far too frequently fall: the mistake of supposing that our statements are doing more than they possibly can, that they are indeed putting the very truth down on the paper. One of Korzybsky's most famous metaphoric slogans is useful here: "The map is not the territory." In a cool moment we may perhaps suppose we couldn't think it is. And a moment later we find ourselves so doing, and realize once more how great is the power of signs and at the same time how strict their limits.

3. Object and Meta-Languages. A third principle of this art of comparing meanings will seem from one point of view to be the same thing said in another way. It can be put as an injunction: Don't confuse statements about things with statements about the language used in the statements. In other words: Distinguish between object-language and meta-language. Object-language is talk about "the context referred to"; meta-language is about the code being used in the communication. But, here again, we must distinguish without separating and remember that a sentence can very well be both referential: tell us about something, and metalingual: tell us about the code. If I say: "That is quail," I may be telling someone something about a bird. How much I tell him will obviously depend upon how much he knows about quails already. Or I may be telling him something about the word *quail*: That it is the name for a certain sort of bird. What is referential for one addressee may be metalingual for another. Into all comparisons of meanings, all attempts to assess and describe the powers and limits of signs in their actual operation, the inevitable differences enter. Occasions differ, speakers differ, recipients differ. In spite of which human communication can somehow be maintained.

NOTES

1. "On Linguistic Aspects of Translation," in *On Translation,* ed. Reuben A. Brower (Cambridge: Harvard University Press), pp. 232–33.
2. R. Jakobson and M. Halle, *Fundamentals of Language* ('s-Gravenhage: Mouton & Co., 1956), pp. 60, 80, 81.

If we take seriously and try intellectually to live up to Peirce's doctrine of the Interpretant (^r_____^r) we get the broad overall indication both of these powers and limitations and of their necessary mutual dependence. Efforts of thought can run primarily and equally in an endless struggle against them and a forced acknowledgement of them. This view can have more drastic consequences than are commonly remarked.

A naive enough view we might conjecture would be that we have some ability, apart from signs, to think of: to apprehend: entertain in our minds,

what a sign is *of* and to compare this with what the sign professedly represents—so controlling and if needed correcting it. For example, when I say
"I'm alive" my meaning does not seem to me to be confusing to the other
sentences partially or wholly substitutable for it. Peirce's doctrine for all its
encouraging positive aspects has a negative aspect which denies this and tells
us that all we can do is to compare a sign with other signs which we may
take to be more or less substitutable for is. If we ask about 'substitutable':
about how we tell whether our other signs (farther or less far developed) can
be substituted, the answer comes in a reapplication of the doctrine: we receive yet other signs (ᵂequivalentᵂ . . . ᵂreplaceable byᵂ . . . able to do the
work of ᵂsubstitutableᵂ). If indeed by this, we allege in protest that comparing all these (unless it go deeper than counting and listing their letters, giving
some phonologic, syntactic, etymologic account of their sign particularities);
if it is to be any *semantic* account requires some other sort of access to their
meanings by which how much they agree and differ may be judged, the reply
comes that if we are to communicate to others (or to ourselves) any of such
alleged observations or perceivings we have to do so again through signs.

In all that, it will be recognized, we are on familiar ground. Old arguings
on imageless thought, direct as opposed to mediate awareness and so on
come to mind. Not that this should disturb us unduly. In so central a matter
(and in accord with the Peirce doctrine) should we expect no more [i.e.,
anything more] than substitutable signs?

We must communicate with others through signs: granted. But must we
with ourselves? We often do talk with ourselves, indulge in very elaborate
and explicit internal colloquies, but have we not a power—sometimes at
least—to dispense with any sign vehicle whatsoever: or to reduce it to or
beyond the vanishing point? Different people/thinkers (and perhaps the same
thinker at different times, being under different influences) will answer dif-
feringly. It seems, though, that we can have immediate awareness of our own
meanings.

One of the sources of the Peirce doctrine itself has been a wish to substitute
for meanings some fabric of the other sign particularities mentioned above.
Some aver that their immediate dealings with their meanings are with fabrics
at least as much affective–volitional–conative and purposive as cognitive and
that we are concerned with them as representing what we would seek, fear,
hope for, cling to, avoid through undetectable ranges of situations we may
find ourselves in. So conceived of, meanings, it can be thought, are a more
necessary part of the furniture of cohesive existence than have often been
made out as being.

Yet, granting that, the vast powers signs as vehicles of meanings so conceived could possess and exercise, the consequent severity of their limitations
must be granted too. Whatever may happen between a mind and itself, traffic
between minds (parapsychology still crying in the wilderness) is conducted
wholly through signs and moreover, it ensues, is concerned only with signs
and with the mutual control by signs of signs. Signs, we must admit, are

composed of the above particularities—but it is a far cry from these to what we commonly suppose (and show ourselves as supposing in our behavior) we talk about and deal with together. A rigidly accepted doctrine of the interpretant gets rid of things and people except insofar as we are content to let them be merely ˢʷas it wereˢʷ be no more than relatively continuing complexes of probable possibilities of further sign-patternings. It is not the least of the powers of signs that they can make some thinkers sometimes (at their philosophic desks) suppose themselves to be thus content.

An important but neglected reflection should attend all such discussions. Whatever view is adopted, it applies also/equally to every term and more in the discussion itself. Metalinguical discourse can and should, of course, be distinguished from discourse at the ˢʷ"I'm alive"ˢʷ level. We can and do go up higher. The sentences so far in this paragraph are meta-metalingual. This last was meta-meta-meta. We can imagine an endless hierarchy of discourse about discourse . . . and construct model samples of it, though much care is needed in identifying any utterance as being of any one level. For example, "That was a quail" might be a remark identifying a fleetingly viewed bird. Or it might be a piece of instruction in the use of the word "quail." Or, very commonly, both at once. And with upper metalingual utterances we may find that they are working at several levels simultaneously. Any rulings (on the analogy of logical Theory of Types) would be hazardous and would probably apply not to language in use but only to artificially contrived models. It seems safe therefore to hold that remarks about how language works are themselves instances of language at work and therefore subject to their own import. (More than a little methodology seems to be in this case.)

Turning now from these broad overall considerations let us examine some specific instances of sign-operations noting there too how power and limit, are ordinarily co-implicatant: the power entails/requires the limit; the limit enables the power. . . .

From *Notebook* 37.

IV

Design for Escape

In his comments on translating from the Chinese, Richards spoke of "Comparative Studies"; when he helped devise Harvard's postwar curriculum, what he meant by "General Education" had something in common with this idea of an earlier time. Language was, of course, central: "There is no study which is not a language study, concerned with the speculative instruments it employs." This is yet another way of declaring that interpretation is central to all criticism.

The analogy which meant most to Richards was that between discourse and the state, as when he models Universal Studies on the United Nations. He believed deeply that the "implementarities" he was inventing and demonstrating were worthwhile, not because they offered bright new evidence for his theories, but because they addressed illiteracy, which he saw as the most urgent political and moral problem the world faces. Richards believed that today's illiterates stand at the threshold of a new world, just as the populations of the Homeric era had stood between oral and written discourse. He did, indeed, believe that literacy made a crucial difference, *not* because people lacked "cognitive" ability without it, but because reading and writing—representation in graphic form—improved the mind's capacities by opening another "channel." He never tired of punning on *media* and *medium* and *means*—noting their dialectical relationship, with one another and to ends. Feedforward, purposing, noting sames and differents—all that was made easier by literacy.

The two most important principles of Richards' pedagogy are that the *how* comes out of the *what* and that language is "the supreme organ of the mind's self-ordering growth and development." By looking and looking again at what he is doing, the learner learns: Why? Because looking again is interpretation, and interpreting engages the mind in an activity of forming and transforming. The powers of mind and of language can each be described in terms of the other: what they share is the power of seeing–knowing, of apprehending, of composing *oppositions*. Oppositional structure is common to perception and to predication, to metaphor and memory-and-envisagement. As Richards explored how one "channel" can help another—how writing improves listening, how seeing aids thinking, etc.—he continually referred to "the all-in-each" of human nature, a phrase from Coleridge, and the expression of a principle of Romanticism that importantly balances "individualism." Only in the perspective of a triadic semiotics does this idea have heuristic value; otherwise, it is a Utopian fantasy.

19

General Education in the Humanities

Once upon a time, somewhere, perhaps, when our forefathers lived in simple tribal societies, a man could get a good general education through docile acceptance of the current ideas. It is not so now. Any man, today, has to fight for his moral life to get one. And the hardest part of the fight is the effort to go on asking what a general education is, what is the good of it and what it is for.

No one can tell us what it is—in so many words. The words mean little or nothing unless somehow we know already what they would say. The answers have to be about what man is, what he may be and what he should be. We do not learn these things from short statements, however well they are phrased, or from long treatises, however persuasive. How can we learn them then? This is exactly our first question, "What is a general education?" over again.

One way of learning them might be through familiarity with the best that has been thought and felt by the greatest minds of the past. And it seems sensible to start with the earliest of these. If Poetry, Religion, and Philosophy are the main confluents of the traditional Western human being, if they are the chief tributaries of the river in which we, as individuals, are little whirls or eddies, then a knowledge of their headwaters should help. Homer, the Old Testament, and Plato are these headwaters. These ancient authors in a sometimes distressing fashion are authors of more than books. They made and make *us* up—whether we know it or like it or not. They are the founding fathers of our tradition, and guide even our attempts to be rid of it.

Speculative Instruments (1955), chap. 11.

So put, this can be an alarming thought. Freud has taught us to be uneasy about paternal influences. We may well wonder how long—on through the millions of years which (until nuclear physics dawned) lay before Western civilized man—how long are these Big B.C. Three to rule him? "Origins are inescapable" is a formula which will bear a great deal of interpretation. Our questioning of it in particular instances makes up most of general education: the inquiry into the hierarchy of the questions, *or* which questions should come before which?

The first great questioners seem to us, too often, to be *answerers*. That is our fault. We misread them, forgetting that no man says anything new and important unless under the urge, or after the tension, of questions. Homer may at first sight seem an exception; but what is Achilles but a question? Do not ask me what it is. The only way to know it is to know the *Iliad*.

When one knows it, one comes to doubt that easy opening sentence I began with. Homer is tribal education at its height. Perhaps all education is questioning and good education is simply ordered questioning leading to what we—with planet-dwellers' indifference—are equally willing to call the highest or the deepest questions?

Knowing and questioning, of course, require one another. We understand nothing except insofar as we understand the questions behind it—and that is never very far. Near the close of Canto IV of *Paradise*:

. . . Our intellect is never satisfied unless the Truth illume it, beyond which nothing true extends. In that it reposes, as a wild beast in his lair, so soon as it has reached it: and it can reach it; otherwise every desire would be in vain. Because of this, doubt springs up like a shoot, at the foot of the truth; and it is nature which urges us to the summit from height to height.

Short of the summit, truth from which no doubts spring up is dead.

The Old Testament—as soon as we begin to see what comes before what among its writings of a thousand years—is an unparalleled exhibition of titanic questionings followed by wooden-minded formalism and miscomprehension. It enacts before us, on the grandest scale, the perpetual human tragedy—the transformation of originative inspiration into the neat note and devout observance of the make-the-grade examinee.

Thus the Old Testament can present to us—against an appropriate background of fears and thunders—what general education is *not,* together with much to suggest what it might be. Plato too—without the fears and in what feels like perfect spring weather, though historians know better—shows us two sides. Some will tell us that the source there of general education is Socrates—shining through an increasing haze of Plato's "dear gorgeous nonsense," as Coleridge called it. It seems more likely that both must share the praise, as well as the blame, of inventing the art which is still man's best hope and worst bane—the art of conscious controlled interrogation which turns so fatally into a technique of purblind disputation. Here again something which is not general education displaces how much which suggests what it might be.

To the end—wherever the pursuit leads us—we gain general education only by asking what it is. But we cannot ask such a question in the void. It does no good to interrogate merely the words *General Education*. We must have materials—samples to examine—while remembering that it is our business to be examiners, not examinees. We must not let the routines and mechanics of the learning–teaching trade get in the way. We must not forget that it is *samples* we are examining. Samples of what quality? Samples of what?

The question is general education at work again.

———

This is not a political, it is a cultural crisis. The political crisis is a by-product. Its source is not economic, not geographic (geopolitic), not even governmental or administrative; it is philosophic, it is in the strain between unreconciled views of man and of how to seek and secure his good. But one side has learnt how to put its views into effect, while the other has not.

On the one side are those who see men as particles pushed about by external forces, and their desires, opinions, and beliefs as mechanisms which may be manipulated—in their interests or in the interests of the manipulators, it little matters which. On the other side are those who see a man, not as a thing but as a sovereign person—however poorly prepared to rule himself. And while the manipulators find in every development of mass psychology, every study of public opinion, every extension of communications, new power to their hands, the humanists are still busy wringing theirs. And yet, if they cannot rise to the responsibility the juncture puts upon them, who can?

Perhaps those in the sciences and in the humanities who are open to reciprocal influences can. It is only in and through education—at once more scientifically and more humanly conceived—that our remedy will be found. Religion, poetry, science, politics, in separation, do not have it. Only a recreated organon, the United Studies, can give it. The world needs that as much as it needs a world government. The parallels will bear pressing: how can a United Studies admit Science without the liquidation of the traditional human being?

The answer, it seems, is: only by a cross-over, by learning from science how to make the humanities accumulative too. Thereby they would acquire a future as well as a past, a growth pattern as well as a tradition. The smiles or shudders with which many a modern humanist will greet such a remark show how far unscientific misapplications of mock-scientific procedures have clouded the picture. It need not be so. The teacher of English . . . should remember his *Republic* (531D) and recall what the task of dialectic (its prelude ended) was for Plato, and how constantly metaphors from genetics led his thought on the teacher's art (*Phaedrus,* 277; *Republic,* 495). But references to

Plato . . . will only depress those educators who would ban the *Republic* lest its use in schools breed another Sparta. A teacher who would truly follow the tradition which stems therefrom will see that education has as yet barely begun. . . . He will ask himself, not supinely but actively, whether the failure of nonaccumulative studies to advance is not due to the hugger–mugger, promiscuous, leave-it-to-nature style in which the seeds of all things are being strewn over the would-be student's mind.

From "Responsibilities in the Teaching of English," *Speculative Instruments* (1955).

20

Toward a More Synoptic View

Language I take to be pre-eminently *the learnt activity* of man, and *learning* itself to be the chief current mode of evolution, of world advance. I am struck, accordingly, by the vigorous attempts which Language Theory (Scientific Linguistics) and Learning Theory (Scientific Behaviour Study) have recently been making to achieve something like AUTARCHY or independence or isolationism, and by their revolt against or withdrawal from most other studies (their breaking off of diplomatic relations). I take Philosophy to be most usefully the overall name nowadays of the diplomatic services between the studies. I think this attempt to break away, to secede, on the part of these new sciences, Linguistics and Behavior, is dangerous *for them* and *for others*. Both dream at times of intellectual world-conquest. Linguistic Science and the study of Behavior alike have a certain young ruthlessness and regardlessness.

I am using this grand analogy (which is Plato's) between the not-at-all Universal Studies and the not-at-all United Nations to explain why in what follows I am concerned with diplomatic–philosophic STRATEGY for the further study of language rather than with any specific investigations of any part or any attempted overall picture. Perhaps the only other grand analogy which has had any comparable role is that to which this group here has recently given such impressive development: the organism–machine analogy.

Let me begin with a doubt, a pervasive and penetrating doubt—truly a bosom doubt. It concerns the language to use in these or any other remarks about language.

Speculative Instruments (1955), chap. 10.

The very instruments we use if we try to say anything which is not trivial about language embody in themselves the very problems we hope to use them to explore. The doubt comes up, therefore: how far can we hope to be understood—or even to understand ourselves—as we use such words? And in the lucidity of this doubt the literature of this subject can take on a queer appearance. Must confidence be in inverse ratio to the security of its grounds?

This situation is not, of course, peculiar to the study of language. All studies suffer from and thrive through this. The properties of the instruments or apparatus employed enter into, contribute to, belong with and confine the scope of the investigation.

I can perhaps best put this more or less uncomfortable though familiar point and show its relevance to the strategic problem: How may the study of language be advanced? by using a quotation from J. R. Oppenheimer (*Scientific American,* September 1950, p. 22), his formulation of Bohr's *principle of complementarity*:

The basic finding was that in the atomic world it is not possible to describe the atomic system under investigation in abstraction from the apparatus used for the investigation by a single, unique objective model. Rather, a variety of models, each corresponding to a possible experimental arrangement and all required for a complete description of possible physical experience, stand in a complementary relation to one another, in that the actual realization of any one model excludes the realization of others, yet each is a necessary part of the complete description of experience in the atomic world.

It is . . . not yet fully clear how characteristically or how frequently we shall meet instances . . . in other fields, above all in the study of biological, psychological and cultural problems.

It may be worth speculating for a few moments on the sequence in which recognition of some such principle of *Instrumental Dependence* as this has struck the various studies as necessary. Mathematics, I conjecture, . . . may have been the earliest study forced to ask itself about its intellectual instruments. The simpler the properties of the instruments the easier it may be to take account of them. If so, we might get some such sequence as this: Mathematics, Physics, Chemistry, Biology, Sociology, Psychology, Anthropology, Poetics, Dialectic. The parallelism of this sequence to the scale of increasing complexity of subject and to cosmic history or evolution would be not accidental. Furthermore, it might be held, the higher up you go on the scale of complexity, the MORE of the mind you bring in as apparatus or instrument of the inquiry. A mathematician, as mathematician, uses one branch only (though a prodigious branch) of human ability; the anthropologist has to be more many-sided, the student of poetics (I venture to say) more complete still.

Corresponding to all these studies are characteristic uses of language. Poetics, I suggest, is faced by the most complex of them. Above Poetics I would put only Dialectic as being concerned with the relations of Poetics with all the other studies and with their relations to one another. Dialectics would thus be the supreme study, with Philosophy as its Diplomatic Agent. All of them are *both* subject matter and language studies. That is the chief point here: there is no study which is not a language study, concerned with the speculative instruments* it employs.

Let me linger a moment with Anthropology because of the close ties and great influence it has recently been having with Linguistics. Its chief methodological problem . . . I can put compactly with a quotation from A. L. Kroeber, "Anthropology," *Scientific American,* September 1950, pp. 87–94:

> Anthropologists now agree that each culture must be explained in terms of its own structure and values, instead of being rated by the standards of some other civilization exalted as absolute—which in practice of course is always our own civilization. This principle leads, it is true, to a relativistic or pluralistic philosophy—to a belief in many values rather than a simple value system. But why not, if the facts so demand?

This "basic principle of the relativistic approach" is fairly plainly a half-way house not permanently tenable. It would be better to say: an early *staging place* not nearly half-way—perhaps only a millionth part of the way, if you can imagine this metaphoric distance being metaphorically measured. It is a negative defensive step, an anti-imperialist move, necessary and desirable, of course, but not at all a sufficient principle for an overall *comparative* study. It is parallel to the linguistic principle that the structure of a language is not to be described in terms of the structure of some other language (English grammar in terms of Latin, or Hopi in terms of English).

What the linguistic scientists have been doing is fashioning a growing sys-

---

*I have commented on this phrase as follows: (1) IAR noted that he had originally taken the phrase "speculative instruments" from Coleridge but that he hadn't been able to find it again. This mystic motif of the lost source is charming to contemplate, but my guess is that he couldn't find it because it isn't there. In the *Cratylus,* Socrates says: "Then a name is an instrument of teaching and of distinguishing natures, as the shuttle is of distinguishing the threads of the web. . . . And the shuttle is the instrument of the weaver?" (388) What the weaver makes provides the radical metaphor of *text*: our instruments are the names by which we differentiate; with those differentiations, those sortings, we weave the fabric of discourse. On the other hand, a shuttle is not speculative; IAR needed some way to supplement the metaphor of weaving, which suggests the constraints of lexical meaning and syntactical structures, however tentative they might be, with the idea of knowing as vision; *speculation,* which combines seeing and knowing, gave him his metaphor. *Speculative instruments* is, I think, IAR's amalgam of Plato and Coleridge. (*Rhetoric Society Quarterly,* X [Fall 1980], 205.) (2) Richards might have remembered a phrase of Othello's as he is explaining that Desdemona's presence will not interfere with his following orders:

> . . . when light-winged toys
> Of feather'd Cupid seel with wanton dullness
> My speculative and officed instruments
> That my disports corrupt and taint my business,
> Let housewives make a skillet of my helm. . . . (I. 3. 268–72).

(*New Literary History,* XIV [Autumn 1982], 77—ED.

tem of *instruments for comparing*: instruments able to put diverse language into a common frame. They are not, of course, attempting to examine and describe Hopi in Hopi or Kwakiutle in Kwakiutle. They are working out overall apparatus which can be, they hope, used for the examination and description of all languages. It may well be that any one such apparatus will for ever be unable to describe every feature of language. A ʳcomplementarityʳ situation may very well arise.* But the apparatus hitherto devised keeps within narrow limits as to *which* of the features and functions of languages it is as yet ready to give an account of. . . .

Most natural behavior (as distinguished from some artificially isolated behavior—in some learning-theory experiments, for example) shows feedforward. All activity (ACT-EEV-ITY, I'd like to say, putting a vocal tag on the word to show that it's here being used technically with a certain definition behind it. Scots have a reputation—which may be excessive—of knowing what they mean. And it is G. F. Stout's account of activity that I am using)— all acteevity depends on, and is made into acteevity by, feedforward.

Take looking for something, hunting, searching, for example. We do not *find* anything unless we *know* in some sense what we are looking for. Nor do our humblest cousins among the animals. (I'd like, here again, to put vocal tags on *find* and *know*. They are correlative terms here. We may happen on something but we don't *find* it unless we are looking for it. *Finding* is the end-phase—in both main senses of ʷendʷ—to the acteevity of searching. Something is fed forward by coincidence with which that acteevity reaches its terminus and goal.) . . .

In my pocket are some pennies and a dime. I am going to find the dime by touch and partly by hearing: by the feel and sound of my finger-nail scraping on the milled edge of the dime. Something is being fed into my search (and into your observation of my search) which will, when the search reaches its END, tell the acteevity that it is successful.

Very probably some of you will have been saying to yourselves that talk about ʼfeedforwardʼ is just falsifying metaphor and that there is nothing here but TAPING (as with the instructions given on tape to a computation engine before it is set to work)—for a special run of manipulative–perceptual mechanism, plus resort to a memory store, plus *feedback*. And that the same holds good for all cases of so-called acteevity at all levels. If so, that transforms the question into one about *taping,* about the source of ad hoc tapings in organisms and their dependence on more general tapings. Tapings seem to be hierarchic, or to form an enclosure series—the widest, most inclusive or overall tapings being least determinate. These feed forward, for their own maintenance and performance—guide and protect themselves by feeding forward— subordinate, narrower, more specific instrumental tapings and these do the same again and so on.

Feedforward, for me, names the peculiar character of tapings which arise in the service of more generic, more inclusive, tapings. And, as such, the adequacy of any description or *valuation* of any acteevity depends upon recognition of the source of its feedforward. . . . I am by profession (1) a critic, (2) a pedagogue, especially concerned with teaching beginning Reading and with the early stages of teaching a second language. Criticism and pedagogy thus for me constitute two fairly high-level feedforward systems tending and guiding two extensive worlds of relatively specific acteevity. And in both, though in different ways, *design*—a flexible fitting of means to ends—is nearly everything.

In Criticism, radically a valuative acteevity, the difference between better and worse utterances is in design. Poor speech and writing is poor either because it is not attempting anything worth trying or because it is inefficient. (The design, mind you, may be, and most commonly is, unwitting.)

This Principle of Efficiency is, I think, little more than a recognition of the enclosure series I have just mentioned, the hierarchical service: the ad hoc tapering serving the wider aim which serves the wider, wider still, and the widest aim. . . . And since language is inescapably a social acteevity which only comes into existence with, and owes its whole character to, mutualities among men and within communities, the study of language, even in the most elementary stages, has to be a dependent of that highest generic taping which may be called ethics. It is concerned—endlessly—with standards and validity. It must be as *normative* through and through as, for example, the study of *medicine*.

How many other studies also must be? Must all? Medicine must be. But how about Biology as a whole? Is not that *Normative* in the sense that of each organism studied the student asks: "How far is this a good, typical (i.e. normal) specimen?" Even of a disease we have "a beautiful case"—one which is serviceable for feedforward.

We call, for we see and feel, the swan and the dove both beautiful. . . . Absurd would it be to make a comparison between their separate claims to beauty from any abstract rule common to both, without reference to the life and being of the animals themselves . . . or on any ground indeed save that of their own inappropriateness to their own end and being, their want of significance as symbol and physiognomy. (Raysor: *Coleridge's Sh. Crit. I*, p. 196.)

Here we have the anthropologist's "relativistic approach" back again—in the service, this time, of aesthetics. But I am inclined to suggest that all studies whatsoever are normative in this sense by the very fact that their statements only work through agreements among users—ad hoc mutual and self-tapings—to use them so and not otherwise. Insofar as someone does not so use them the overall taping—the purpose of the discussion—is not (normally) served.

There are, of course, any number of inquiries—in linguistics as in every other study—which look, and will be strenuously maintained to be, *non-normative*. But still there are overall questions for every such inquiry which are normative: (1) What is this for? (2) What is its bearing on other inquiries? (3) Are the conditions which generate and control the inquiry being observed? These put them within wider acteevities wherein they are judged—factually, yes, but more than factually too.

Naive scientism with its autarchic policies can be a threat to us all here. There are vast areas of so-called purely descriptive linguistics which are a grim danger at present to the conduct of language to education, to standards of intelligence, to the reserves in theory and in sensibility of the mental tester: the danger is the worse for the keys to opportunity being so often in incompetent hands. The appeal to mere *usage*: "If it's widely in use, it's O.K.," is a case in point. Every useful feature of language was *not in use* once upon a time. Every degradation of language too starts somewhere. Behind usage is the question of efficiency. Inefficient language features are not O.K., however widespread their use. Of course, to the linguistic botanist it is important to preserve all varieties until they have been collected and described. But that is not the point of view of the overall study of language, its services and its powers. That overall view is, I am insisting, inescapably NORMATIVE. It is concerned (as every speaker and every listener is always concerned) with the maintenance and improvement of the use of language. And for this reason, the "scientific objectivity" of which many a linguistic scientist is so charmingly vain (like the boy with his first bicycle) is out of place when it tries (as it does) to interfere with education or criticism.

No doubt the job of "collecting and arranging the facts of speech" has been much interfered with by silly normative prejudices in the past. Linguistics and medicine may be expected to develop analogous fads and quackeries. But that does not excuse retaliatory aggression. Here then is a place where philosophy, the diplomatic agency of dialectic, must intervene. It has to *protect* studies from the interferences of other studies, yes. But it has more to do. It has also to help studies out of *self*-frustrations due to their ignorance of what other studies can and should do for them.

A Synoptic View therefore—truly Universal Study—would have more than police functions; it should be advisor-general and therapist as well. And yet what exquisite discretion it would have to employ if it were not to impair the due freedom for growth in the autonomous studies! On the other hand, an extended Complementarity Principle would amount to no slight Charter of Tolerance. Indeed some may fear it as a beginning of anarchy. Such high organization is a long way off, however; and it will be better to consider what steps might be taken toward it.

Let us remind ourselves once more that it is not a 'theory' or 'doctrine' we are in search of but a development of comprehending. I am shutting ^{sw}doctrine^{sw} in too narrowly in this remark: making it too merely a chain of statements (all 1, 2, 6, and 7: see p. 181) and neglecting the *wholeness*, the mutuality of control among the dimensions or respects which has been characteristic of so much teaching. I did so deliberately because this very question: "Do the structures of the typical utterances of different studies differ?" is perhaps a good one to set out from. By 'structures' we should mean here ˢʷconnections between the various respects from in the comprehending ˢʷ. Mere difference in subject matter would be, in most cases, far less important: a difference in 1 chiefly and derivatively in 2. But differences in Selecting can speak for much more, all the way round to deep divergence of Purposing. They need not, of course; but it is when they do that the real difficulties of approaching a Synoptic View confront us. It is then, for example, that the religious and the scientific, the poetic and the ethical consciences can divide the mind.

Once again, it is not an *account* only of these difficulties which we need but a way of meeting and accepting them. And the chief use of an account might be as an aid to our honesty in judging whether we were or were not facing them. The cultures of the world offer us a wonderful display of man's capacities for self-deception:

> The gigantic anthropological circus riotously
> Holds open all its booths

but a few hours of any self-observant person's life can provide almost as rich and a nearer demonstration. How to be? How to reconcile the possible modes of being? That is no theoretical question but the choice of choices.

It may seem odd to equate *this* with the reconciliation of the warring studies and to take the faculties of the mind and the Faculties of a University into a serious pun together. It may seem odder, perhaps, some day not to do so. For the knowledges, though the gaps between them have been widening, interfere with people's modes of living ever more deeply. . . . We take what a College can give us as serviceable guidance today in far more than professional affairs. This is part of the transition from culture to education—a perilous transition, no doubt, but hardly new or, on our ordinary time-scale, sudden. If Mr. Eric Havelock is right, Socrates was put to death for trying to replace apprenticeship—association with and imitation of the knowledgeable—by instruction, and it looks as though the founding of the Academy itself was an early and decisive step in an interminable and necessary process.

It is easy to talk eloquently about freedom in the pursuit of truth and the democratic method. But what we need is to induce the struggle between the rival forces repeatedly on a small controllable scale so that the different outcomes of the choices shall become apparent. The world crisis, "Shall we accept others' views (good or bad) to learn to see?" is reproduced inside every genuine experiment in interpretation. Appeals to principles are very well— *after* the principle has grown into something to appeal to. And so are right answers, theoretical analyses and demonstrations—*after* the learner has shaped in himself the terms in which they must be read. There is no short cut, and none is recommended; but to say so is not to leave things to nature. In other subjects we do not. To teach English is no doubt more difficult than to teach Mathematics or Chemistry; English is so very much more complicated. But that is no reason to despair or to think that the learners may therefore be left to master their language unaided. . . .

The gap between theoretical analysis (of the mechanics of metaphor, say, or of the variations of "definite") and the practical handling of language in the conduct of thought . . . is only serious if we overlook it, or think that further analysis *by itself* will fill it. It becomes easier to cross as we examine it, for study of the gap is itelf the bridge. This study must be made from both sides. To build the bridge and introduce his students to build it with him is the teacher's business.

"Rhetoric," from *Interpretation in Teaching* (1938).

21

Literature, Oral–Aural and Optical

My title is itself a miniature example of the problem I would discuss: "Literature, Oral–Aural and Optical."

I think man must love confusion. Otherwise he wouldn't pronounce "oral" and "aural" alike, as if there were no difference between speaking and hearing and no point in separating the doings of the mouth and the ear. Writing, of course, distinguishes them. Any reader can see the difference between "oral" and "aural." But as most people, I believe, most often say them, they sound the same. Speech takes them and their meaning together, in a large loose sort of unity. Writing, in this instance, tries to use their etymons to clear things up.

I want to speculate a little in this talk on some of the differences between speech and writing when used for their most ambitious purposes: for poetry and philosophy. I am talking still in a writing-conscious era when in spite of radio, tape, and the soundtrack, the WORD is still, first and foremost, the written word, and more specifically the printed word, not the utterance of a voice. And the sentence is still something that offers itself to the eye in static precision—there before us to be examined—frozen stiff, as it were, to be sliced up and dissected by the leisurely, piecemeal, analytic mind served by the corresponsive eye, whenever we chose to linger and explore. The written sentence and its meaning stand over against the eye—to be looked into. But to the ear a spoken sentence is more like a fluctuant, resonant pulse of our inner history, gone by almost before it is completed. That is the great contrast

Complementarities (1976), chap. 26; originally a radio talk, broadcast in 1947.

I want to play with. It may be rather important now that speech and the ear are getting their chance to stage a comeback.

This contrast has had more than a little to do with the history of literature. Isn't it remarkable . . . that we haven't any word for "literature before writing"? Isn't it monstrous that one should have to talk about aural literature or preliterate literature, meaning by that something that isn't necessarily ever written or read, needn't be any concern of the man of letters, isn't made up out of letters but out of sounds, isn't literature at all, but direct vocal utterance: This shows, doesn't it, how thoroughly *writing* has stolen the show? The very mother-art from which literature sprang hasn't even a name among us.

Literature is born and reborn on the summit of Everest. It is a very odd thing, but in literature the best in each kind comes first, comes suddenly, and never comes again. This is a disturbing, uncomfortable, unacceptable idea to people who take their doctrines of evolution and of progress oversimply. But I think it must be admitted to be true. Of the very greatest things in each sort of literature, the masterpiece is unprecedented, unique, never thenceforth challenged or approached. The rule seems to be that stated in the refrain of "Green grow the rashes, O": "One is one and all alone and evermore shall be so."

Think of the *Iliad*, of the Book of Job, or in prose of the earliest "J" narratives in Genesis or of the "Court History of David" in 2 Samuel 9–20. That court history is the first historical narrative there is, written about 1000 B.C.— 500 years before Herodotus, the "Father of History." The scholar's judgment on it seems to be that as narrative prose it is utterly unmatched in its kind by anything later in the Old Testament. The same thing seems to hold of later masterpieces, each in its own kind. There is no rival to Plato or to Vergil or to Dante, or to Cervantes, and no second Shakespeare or Milton. I don't know any satisfying explanation of this strange general rule. It feels as if it were somehow deeply significant and seems to herd with myths of the Fall of Man and the Golden Age. But it is not a myth, I believe, but a historical generalization.

We pen-conscious and print-minded people have to make no slight effort if we are to imagine what happened in the minds of speakers and listeners before writing came in. Our habits and attitudes are shaped by our experience as readers and by our optical training in analysis. We are ready to compare and connect and distinguish and abstract in a thousand ways which were hardly, if at all, possible to the preliteracy listener.

All this has its advantages and disadvantages for us, both as speakers and listeners. It helps us, sometimes, to avoid some sorts of nonsense, though it may well expose us to other sorts. It lets us interfere consciously with our minds in their work of grasping the meaning. It makes the whole job of understanding—or misunderstanding—more complicated than it need be. These habits of comparing and abstracting, which come from the way in which words (and their meanings too, as we think) stand before us separately in print, enable us to ask pertinent questions, but they invite us also to raise points which have nothing to do with what is going forward.

In contrast, for the preliterate's *ear*, words in discourse are not separate items, open to time-free contemplation, they are crests or troughs in a stream, parts of a wave pattern. It is arguable that the preliterate could swim, as it were, in the sea of meaning while we only paddle and splash along its edges. However this may be, my point is that the reading mind and the speech-centered preliteracy mind tackle apprehension in different fashions.

Homer illustrates the difference well. Readers coming to Homer under their own steam are often puzzled by a lot of things which this difference may help to explain. Homer's similes, for example, adorn the events they are attached to; they do not as a rule present or elucidate the action. They don't make us see *that* more clearly; they ask us to imagine some other event which may be remarkably unlike and unconnected with what is being described. There is usually no scope for the cunning discoveries of deeper correspondencies in which metaphor-curious *readers* of poetry so much delight. Homer's audiences were not looking for such things. They were attending to something else.   '

Some of the troubles which Plato had with Homer's morality may have had the same explanation. There we have the first and greatest *writing* philosopher turning with what seems a malicious but anguished unfairness against the universal provider, the educator of Greece. Eric Havelock has suggested that we may see in Plato's rejections of Homer the revolt of the writing mind's mode of apprehension against the *preliterate* mind's other, less abstract and intellectual, ways of ordering itself. The contrast is not simply between poetry and philosophy. Poetry is often, in technique, philosophical; and the aims of philosophy may be poetic. Moreover, the origin of philosophy, like that of poetry, is in aural not in optical composition.

Socrates—as against what Plato wrote—didn't write anything. He conversed instead. What he said is something we have more or less to guess at. Whatever it was, and whether Plato reported of it accurately or not (first-class opinions have been poles apart on that) Socrates' conversation does really seem to have done more for philosophy than all the writings of all the philosophers ever since. For it settled what sort of thing philosophy, or the discourse of reason—as it has been practiced in the West—was to be.

Socrates, in a word, invented philosophy. If John Burnet was right, he also invented something else—which goes with philosophy and has been even more influential. He invented the soul. Before Socrates, so Burnet thought, nobody ever anywhere had had any conception of what, ever since Socrates, has been in mind when the word "soul," in his meaning for it, is considered. When, at his trial, Socrates says that the only thing that matters is to care for one's soul, the best that his judges could have made of that, Burnet suggests, is something like "Be good to your ghost!"—without any of the implications that one's soul really is oneself and is what knows and chooses.

Now whether we like reason and the soul—and believe in them—or not, there is no doubt that they are among the most decisive inventions ever made. They are not obvious or natural discoveries by any means. They are not chairs or shoes; they are more like the electron. And they seem to belong to the Western tradition and are unparalleled in other traditions. Without them, *we,* of the tradition, would not, any of us, be what we are. The questions we ask and the sorts of ways in which we try to answer them . . . the very *we's* we take ourselves to be and the sort of thing we take *thinking* to be . . . all these are outcomes of these inventions. So it is interesting that the man who made them didn't write anything.

Socrates may have had a prejudice against writing. Plato gives him—in the *Phaedrus* (274c–277a)—a very curious little story about the invention of the letters:

"I heard, then," says Socrates, "that at Naucratis, in Egypt, was one of the ancient gods of that country, the one whose sacred bird is called the ibis, and the name of the god himself was Theuth. He it was who invented numbers and arithmetic and astronomy, also draughts and dice, and, most important of all, letters. Now the king of all Egypt at that time was the god Thamus . . . To him came Theuth to show his inventions, saying that they ought to be imparted to the other Egyptians. But Thamus asked what use there was in each . . . when they came to the letters, 'This invention, O King,' said Theuth, 'will make the Egyptians wiser and will improve their memories; for it is an elixir of memory and wisdom that I have discovered.' But Thamus replied, 'Most ingenious Theuth, one man has the ability to beget arts, but the ability to judge of their usefulness or harmfulness to their users belongs to another; and now you, who are the father of letters, have been led by your affection to ascribe to them a power the opposite of that which they really possess . . . you offer your pupils the appearance of wisdom, not true wisdom . . . for they will read many things without instruction and will therefore seem to know many things, when they are for the most part ignorant and hard to get along with . . .'."

"Socrates," says Phaedrus, "you easily make up stories about Egypt or any country you please." But Socrates goes on:

"He who thinks, then, that he has left behind him any art in writing, and he who receives it in the belief that anything in writing will be clear and certain, would be an utterly simple person . . . every word, when once it is written, is bandied about, alike among those who understand and those who have no interest in it . . . for it has no power to protect or help itself."

Instead of such words, the true teacher will use "the legitimate brother of this bastard [sort of speech] . . . [and sow,] in a fitting soul intelligent words which are able to help themselves and him who planted them, which are not fruitless, but yield seed from which there spring up in other minds other words capable of continuing the process for ever, and which make their possessor happy, to the farthest possible limit of human happiness." Socrates is notably serious here.

There are more modern inventions—aren't there?—of which we can echo

Thamus' remark. "One man has the ability to beget arts, but the ability to judge of their usefulness or harmfulness to their users belongs to another."

Radio (and videotape) are technology's long-delayed reply to writing. It might (if the god Thamus were its guide) give us back some of the things we lost by the invention of letters. Not that we can or should give up reading and writing or the useful habits of reflection and analysis and private judgment they have developed and encouraged. These are part of the human equipment now—to be denied to no man. But—if the speakers can resist its temptations and control its vagaries, and if the other conditions which worry the critic of radio are righted—listening might (it is permissible to dream)— listening might give both philosophy and poetry a new communality and with it a new roundness and wholeness, freeing them from the pharisaical regard for the recondite.

Reading, silent reading, is manifestly antisocial activity. When Augustine first saw a man reading to himself silently (it was Saint Ambrose) he was deeply shocked. He knew Ambrose was a good man, what he did couldn't be wicked . . . but still!

Listening, in contrast, tends to communality. What is listened to, by choice, in common, speaks to "the all in each of all men." This may be low and trivial. But it may, as the *Iliad* and Job can remind us, deal with man's highest and most momentous concerns.

The *Iliad* and the prewriting narratives of the Old Testament were products of public competition. They were the winners, the things which best pleased and continued to please, their audiences through a series of elimination trials. I do not think it is being sentimental or romantic or nostalgic to stand in some awe of the judgment of those early audiences—who listened and judged Homer and the "J" narratives of Genesis. They had this advantage over us. They were expert audiences, experienced in what they judged. They knew the stories. The form and style they were to be told in had been settled. The audiences knew in general what to look for, as farmers do at a sheepdog trial. So they could concentrate on how well it was done. They didn't have to wonder what sort of a game this was, or what the rules, if any, were, or what the player was trying to do. They knew all that, and could devote themselves to judging his play.

The result was a sort of economical functional efficiency, if you like that way of putting the point. Furthermore, the *Iliad* is a collective product—in shaping which the discernible preferences of the audience, shown then and there, had an immediate effect on the poets. Kipling puts it beautifully: "Unless they please they are not heard at all." The poets could not rely on posterity to recognize their unappreciated merits. To address posterity you need a pen. The result was that posterity has been kinder to these aural composers, whose work was breath on the wind, than it has been to any *writers*.

Then, into this mode of composition came the new influence of writing. As to how it came in—that is all speculation. Early inventions often spread slowly and unevenly. Perhaps writing was used in commerce for centuries before poets took it up. When they did the effect was to freeze the traditional stream, making it viscous first, then solid and fixed. We may guess, perhaps, that there was a final stimulative effect before the scribes and the editors took over and speech, the living voice, gave place to the text and the *book* came to the throne.

The early books inherited the powers and organization of the oral tradition. That is a large part of the explanation of their immense influence ever since and of their miraculous massive preeminence. I am thinking not only of Homer and the Bible but of the founding books of most of the great cultures. The Vedas, Analects, and Mencius are good examples. They are the spoken word attributed suitably to Confucius or Mencius, written down later. I am not sure that the preeminence of Plato's earlier dialogues doesn't have the same explanation. Perhaps Socrates knew what he was doing in not writing. But the point is that the new techniques of composition through writing, when superimposed on the old techniques of speech, produced extraordinary results.

Well now. The book, at last, so it is said, is being deposed. Its successor is this microphone before me which looks so inattentive and unresponsive. The question is: whether the new or restored opportunities now offered to speech, when superimposed on the established techniques of reading and writing, can work the miracle again. My own feeling is that they can and may.

With speech, skill with these expressive resources seems often quite independent of the lexical repertory. Those who use the fewest and least selected words can sometimes use tonal implications most effectively.

Writtens in contrast to *spokens* have no such resources. A very few simple devices: capitals, italics, underlinings, exclamation points—these can mark emphases and, less reliably, some tones of dispute. The services of all the rest of the vocal means have to be supplied, for *writtens,* otherwise—by special choices in vocabulary and phrasing. This contrast—which makes writing seem for some purposes so inadequate—is highly useful in the earlier phases of learning to read. Not only does it greatly simplify the choice of the sorts of sentences reading should begin with but it helps us to bring the question: "how would you say it?" sharply to the learner's attention. It makes him realize that he and not the printed form of the sentence has that point to settle. Thereby it fights against that meaningless word-by-word rendering of sentences which is so deadly an enemy of intelligent learning. It also highlights the peculiar authority of the sentence as the unit of meaning within the wider context. It is the sentence which says something, the words being only its servants in so doing. Any early reading program can be tested by the degree to which it succeeds in making the learners show that they understand this. The very poverty of the *writtens* in means of expression can be used to direct their attention to these two major points: What is the sentence saying and how would you speak it?

"Instructional Engineering," from *The Written Word* (1971).

Two arts—the art of reading poetry and the reciprocal art of listening with discrimination to such reading—can now be developed as never before. They depend upon recognition of the *reading voice* as our prime and indispensable instrument for exploring and comparing meanings. And we have to recognize, too, the equally indispensable cooperative work of the written notation, of print, in the study of meanings. Those who have proposed the dropping of reading-writing from education know too little both about how meanings have developed and how men have become more human. These thinkers are—it should be said forcibly—inadequately prepared for the role they have assumed.

The Uses of Literature. Harvard English Studies, 4. Ed. Monroe Engel (Cambridge: Harvard University Press, 1973), pp. 207–24.

22

The Reign of Writing

The statistical nature of *messages* is entirely determined by the character of the source. But the statistical character of the *signal* is actually transmitted by a channel . . . is determined both by what one attempts to feed into the channel and by the capabilities of the channel to handle different signal situations. . . . Error and confusion arise and fidelity decreases, when, no matter how good the coding, one tries to crowd too much over a channel.

Warren Weaver, *Recent Contributions to the*
Mathematical Theory of Communication

The style of this version has been shaped by many aims. I hope and believe that they have settled their worst differences behind the scenes. But no one who has ever thought about the translation of remote texts can suppose that there is an ideal version for any *general* purpose. My compromise has at least tried to be conscious, to know what it is giving up for what, and to accept consistently its own limitations. A brief account of these "behind the scenes" deliberations will be the best way to explain how this version differs from others and why it should have been made.

Let me say first, if I can, what I take to be the chief *general* interest of the *Iliad* for present-day readers. I stress the word "general" not only because the *Iliad* has a place in so many programs of General Education, and because work in one such program first made me feel a need for some version of this kind, but because specialized scholarship today rarely has any direct concern with the general reader. Its own business has become too exacting. And the scholar today tends to forget what the unprepared reader most needs and is apt to offer some introductory steps to scholarship in its place. The general reader's first need is to see for himself why and how the *Iliad* should matter at all to him in these days. Contemporary opinions about the highly conjectural facts of its origin and circumstances do not, I think, help us to see this. Nor need we expect that better opinions still would be more helpful. After all, until only the other day most readers have been without any reputable views whatsoever on such points.

From *The Wrath of Achilles: The 'Iliad' of Homer, Shortened and in a New Translation* (1950), Introduction.

The chief general interest of the *Iliad* is that we can find in it the ancestors to very important things which are still characteristic of European or "Western" culture. Among these are tragedy; the problem character; domestic comedy; an ironic skepticism as to divine concern with or control of human endeavor; certain admirations for the individual will in its pride, and for the heroic conflict that elicits this pride; and, over all, a poetic enjoyment of the foreknowledge of death. "Whence cometh wisdom? and where is the place of understanding?" asks the Book of Job: "Destruction and Death says, 'We have heard a rumor thereof with our ears'" (28:22). The *Iliad* is the place where that rumor sounds most insistently and with least competition from messages purporting to be more certain. It is a rumor to which modern ears are certainly being tuned.

An anthropology we can as yet only dream of would be needed to say whether these things are really as peculiar to and distinctive of European culture as they seem (or where the limits of this construct, "European culture," should be set). But certainly in our tradition, the *Iliad* is the primal appearance of them—an appearance so clear and so heightened by the strangeness of the setting that it is actually easier to discern and meditate upon these traits in the *Iliad* than in the more complex and cross-bred lineaments of its cultural descendants. The great figures of the *Iliad* are very obviously more than life size. They resemble the glass flowers of the celebrated Harvard collection in being easier to comprehend than any field specimens we may pick for ourselves. And it is not only their physical aspects that are exaggerated: the power to lift a stone, "one that two men could not lift as men are." Their scale in every aspect is magnified as much as Ares and Athene are on Achilles' shield—"the people at their feet are smaller"—among whom we may count ourselves along with all other actual persons. Most evidently, certain of their passions are enlarged. Achilles' wrath and his sorrow strike us as exorbitant; our own tracks are not as his. And the momentum of these passions is as remarkable; nothing can halt or divert his anger against Agamemnon except a still greater anger against Hector (and himself) which channels it off. This second rage is so extreme that in the end it offends even the gods, and illustrates once for all the etymologic sense of *wroth* as "crooked, bad." Behind both the anger and the sorrow (in its early phases, at least) is an exclusive self-regard and an oblivion of others which socialized consciences find hard to conceive. A modern nationalist is apt to think that such nonparticipation in the war effort deserves a court-martial and a death penalty. It may help us to compare Achilles not with an individual but with a nation; we may then find that the behavior of most great powers is still only too Achillean. This vanity, this tenderness for our honor, which we no longer dare nurse for ourselves, we can still indulge when we have transferred it to our cause or to our country.

For good or for evil these traits have been essential parts of the spiritual physiognomy of the West. We must consider each for himself whether they are components of an elixir or of a poison. It is idle to ask how far Homer, directly and indirectly, has been responsible for their continuance. We do not know enough about spiritual genetics to say. The point rather is that in the *Iliad* we can study these things in a peculiar purity. The very fact that the setting is strange and remote to us, that the concomitants are often unintelligible or conjectural only, throws what we share with Hector or Helen or even with Hera into relief. When all else differs, what is in common stands out most clearly. And no one can say that what he recognizes in the *Iliad* is not his own deep concern. . . .

A version that will let us consider these things as undistractedly as we may must give up some other aims. Among them will be the attempt to reflect the *language* of the *Iliad*: its archaism; its decorative stylized figuredness; its artificiality, and most of its characeristics as a medium for oral extempore composition. A very large proportion of the *Iliad* consists of line-beginnings, lines, and line-endings which the poet could use very freely over and over again, knowing them to be metrically satisfying and sufficiently neutral as regards the context of what he was saying to raise no difficulties for him or for his audience. Most of the stock epithets annexed to the characters, the formal openings and transitions, and many of the similes and descriptive fillings are essentially ready-made *rests,* for the poet and his hearers, by which the strain of composition, and of comprehension for the listeners, can be lessened. They are, of course, by no means inert matter or mere scaffolding; but they have, as it were, a general not a specific duty. They are cells of the poetry that have been found, through generations of experience in public recitation, to serve best as connective tissue, supporting without hindering the more important cells in which the main work of the poem is being forwarded. In a prose version, addressed primarily to a reader's eye, not to a listener's ear, most, though not all, of the necessities of oral epic are best omitted. In print they do not have effects at all like their effects in a flow of metrical utterance.

On the other hand the reign of writing looks like it is drawing soon to a close. The radio may be restoring to the ear some of its original priority in "literature." The very fact that the highest achievements of verbal communication have to be named with a word which implies letters is evidence of the deep change that the invention of writing made. Between the age of Homer, whenever that was, and Plato's time, were born the concept and the abstraction, as the literate have known them since. And it is this shift from concrete, image-borne, continuous presentations to the products of analysis, comparison, and definition which chiefly comes between a present-day reader and the preintellectual world of Homer. It is impossible to doubt that writing was a prime agent in this change. The eye can linger over individual words and phrases. It can isolate them for reflection. Writing indeed can separate them as they can hardly be separated in preliterate speech. It can give them a distinct and questionable standing, and expose them to a discussion which purely oral–aural communication barely permits. When we stop to consider what is being said, we are probably using powers of controlled,

selective attention which we owe to experience with writing. A chief difficulty in rendering the *Iliad* is to remember that it is not concerned with ideas
as we have come to understand ideas. Its meanings are more rounded, self-
supporting, and whole. Without being any less selective in their own way
they are not discriminated and prepared for logical manipulation. Thus the
attempt to say with modern English what the *Iliad* says in preliterate speech
must reckon with a radical change in *saying* itself. It is not only that different
things are said, and said in different ways, but what is done in and by the
saying is different.

One resource in this predicament is to return to the condition of the listener, and one motive behind this version has been to make something which
can be read aloud without discomfort and grasped by a listener without ov-
erfrequent lapses of attention. Its germ, in fact, was a presentation of "The
Anger of Achilles" in eight fifteen-minute readings for the Lowell Institute
Co-operative Broadcasting Council. From classroom efforts, I knew that
available prose versions would not do. No reader, without feeling unbearably
stuffy, can mouth any long sequence of such sentences as: "Strange goddess,
why art thou minded to beguile me thus? Verily thou wilt lead me yet further
on to one of the well-peopled cities of Phygia or lovely Maeonia, if there,
too, there be some one of mortal men who is dear to thee, seeing that now
Menelaus hath conquered goodly Alexander, and is minded to lead hateful
me to his home. It is for this cause that thou art now come hither with
guileful thought." Helen vanishes completely behind such a veil of disused
forms. The listener might gather she talked some sort of antique and never
actual lingo, but not that he would miss anything by switching to another
station. A much simpler and more natural language was clearly needed. . . .
The steps that slope down from this toward a version in truly contemporary
English are slippery and I have not been tempted. To change the image, I
have felt that such a version, though it would be more "readable" in a sense,
would be too open to what communication theory calls *noise:* "additions to
the signal not intended by the information source."

All through, in fact, I have been haunted by the engineer's diagram of a
communication system.

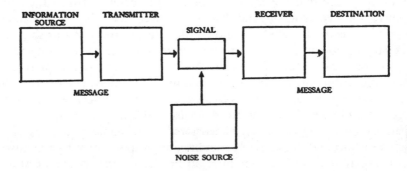

From *The Mathematical Theory of Communication* by Claude E. Shannon and Warren
Weaver, University of Illinois Press, Urbana, 1949, pp. 5 and 98.

Here Homer (whatever that may be) is the *information source*. I (certain subsystems, rather, in me) am the *transmitter*. I encode certain things my information source seems to give me in a *signal* which keeps up through the printed pages that follow. You (certain subsystems, rather, in you) are the *receiver*. You take in the marks on the paper which you recode again as sentences and hand on to the *destination*. This destination is the part of the diagram that has most of the appropriate poetic indefiniteness. It balances the mystery of the source which was "Homer." Whither, indeed, is all this directed? We have no better answer to give than Homer had. And as we wonder about that, the importance of the *noise source* needs no stressing—here, in the context of the first of all the poems which

> have power to make
> Our noisy years seem moments in the being
> Of the eternal Silence.

Further reflection on this diagram makes us aware that its great central gap is repeated; that between the information source and the transmitter, between the receiver and the destination, as between the transmitter and the receiver, come the noises—with an iteration most incident to hollow men. It has been my hope that by a certain simplification imposed on what I took from Homer and by a certain generality imposed upon my signal, I might diminish these noises. But I realize that the real enemy I contend with is a taste for noise.

Wisdom or folly? Some among computer aficionados can almost persuade themselves that their monster servants can be taught to tell them which is which. Computers can, no doubt of it, tell us any amount which may be helpful: what many of the circumstances are, what decisions have been taken in similar circumstances and with what outcomes. They can be made to show us—with more exactitude than our imaginations can compass—what someone or other has told them will be relevant to our problem. But of the WHAT ELSE that may be relevant they are uninformed. It is up to us to be somehow cognizant of, susceptible to and judicious with that illimitable WHAT ELSE. That is the testing point. Here comes in the difference between living by the book of rules (and the computer is but a book with a built-in selective reader) and living by the judgment–instinct, that ultimate responsibility which is seen in all true action and most clearly in the creative arts. Another way, this appeal to the relevant WHAT ELSE, of reaffirming the concluding declaration of Shelley's *Defence of Poetry:* "Poetry is the unacknowledged legislation of the world."

But, someone may reply, will not computers, by taking immense intellectual burdens off our shoulders, free us for precisely these tasks of ultimate choice, these legislative acts? While fearing that they will not, we may hope so. It is obvious that the great slave-based communities and others rich in service have owed much of their accomplishment to their servitors. A man or woman alone, doing his-her everything for his-her self, commonly does little or nothing else, noble or nefarious. We are almost all of us products of the assistance we can accept. Equally, we are potential victims of those who, for whatever motives, high or low, would like to run things for us. These are reflections to be borne in mind now that we are so soon to come into competition with those who will have intellectual instruments of a million or a billion mind-power at their disposal. Like all power sources, the computer is not going to lessen responsibilities but increase them.

These may seem gloomy prognostications. They can equally, with a small shift of policy, become a summons to the highest of imaginable endeavors—the reconstitution of man in the new image we can now conceive for him.

"Computer-Conveyed Instruction," from *So Much Nearer* (1968).

23

Learning and Looking

Learning . . . and looking. Why not the more usual order: "Looking and learning"? Well, for one thing, to suggest that there may be a real problem here and perhaps a big one. Why do I so often look and look and yet totally fail to learn? Isn't it perhaps that I haven't learned *how* to look? May not looking—in many sorts of situations—be a skill, an activity which has to be more or less laboriously acquired? Isn't there an art of looking? Or, rather, are there not many special *arts of looking,* into the cultivation of which much more could go than merely a lot of experience and a modicum of interest? Are there not, in many special fields, propitious procedures, techniques of training, already developed, which can help people coming newly into any of them to learn how to look, to profit *more* and profit *sooner* from their successes *and* their failures? And are there not even, perhaps, general principles to be formulated and tried out and perfected? Is it not possible that we are letting a good deal of potential ability remain unelicitated by leaving *instruction in looking* to the chance mercies of undirected Nature?

You will, of course—at least I hope you will—have been saying "Quite so!" to all this. After all, are there not for bird watchers, airplane spotters, license plate spotters, etc.—and in botany, in chemistry, and in many fields of clinical diagnosis—highly developed techniques for systematic elimination and precise identification? The birder on the lookout for warblers knows just what to go by in his observations; so does the pathologist squinting down his microscope. And in most of these activities the selection of what to look for has been worked out by elaborate, deliberate analysis and made over

From *Design for Escape* (1968), chap. 4.

thereby into a resource available to *anyone* who will take a relatively very small amount of trouble.

All most encouraging—especially if we ask ourselves why such techniques should have developed so successfully in some fields but not in others. We conclude that in these developed fields people have come to know what they are doing, but that in others (some of greater moment) they as yet don't.

What I shall be trying to explore with you are some simple, familiar questions about the use of depictions in helping people to learn how to look and how thereby to learn. . . .

Opposition and *comparison*: these are the chief intellectual tools in the study of PICTORIAL language—as they are in the study of VERBAL language. Parallel to the VERBAL literacy problem there is the more neglected problem of PICTORIAL literacy, the task of learning to handle depictions. It is variously reported that many cultures in Africa and elsewhere have traditionally made little or no use of two-dimensional depiction even for decoration or amusement. And peoples of these cultures are said to find special difficulty in understanding pictures which in the Western tradition are clear to everyone from childhood up. They do not, apparently, see the depiction as *representing* anything. Critically assessed evidence on these points is scanty.

Further experimentation on the development of two-dimensional representation in children growing up within pictorial traditions such as ours is much needed. So is a wider study of play, use of toys, etc., in the cultures compared. There are cultures which don't seem to have invented the toy. Relevant too would be structural analysis of the depictive or iconic aspect, separated, so far as may be, from the symbolic use, of Chinese and Egyptian writing.

Let us begin with the initial contrasts of position in space and in time as they may be represented in speech, in action, and in depiction.

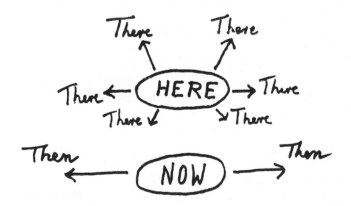

Here and *there* are intelligible only in contrast one to the other. So too with *now* and *then*. Pedagogically they have a peculiar claim to priority. *I am here now* is always, unequivocally and indisputably, true. A speaker may be wrong or misleading in almost everything else he says, but not in this. Furthermore, these initial oppositions enable *I am here, You are there, He is there (here), She is there (here)*, and so on, to be very clearly enacted and demonstrated to and by beginning students. Sentences and performances can here be verifiably, unmistakably, and memorably accordant. So too with

> *I was there.   I am here.   I will be there.*
> *He was there.   He is here.   He will be there.*

and so on.

The prepositions—those that are in their central senses handlers of spatio-temporal relationships (*of* and *for* are the exceptions)—share this demonstrability, provided we keep at first strictly to their physical work carried out through the clear physical oppositions in position and direction they mark. This set of spatiotemporal position and direction words can be represented in their central senses in one diagram (see p. 246). And with suitable sentences they can all be represented both in speech and enaction.

It is important for a learner to begin with these physical senses, because only from these do many of their metaphoric uses become intelligible. For example, *at, on, in*.

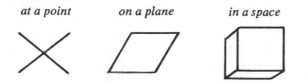

at a point   *on a plane*   *in a space*

From these oppositions uses such as *at* 10:15 *on* the first Monday *in* January *in* 1968 can be understood. And more remote metaphoric uses too. Thus something may be *in* or *on* one's mind:

To have something *in* one's mind is commonly to have a convenient and perhaps comforting resource available; but something *on* one's mind is as a weight pressing down, a burden.

This last example naturally takes us on to the role of opposition and comparison in physiognomy.

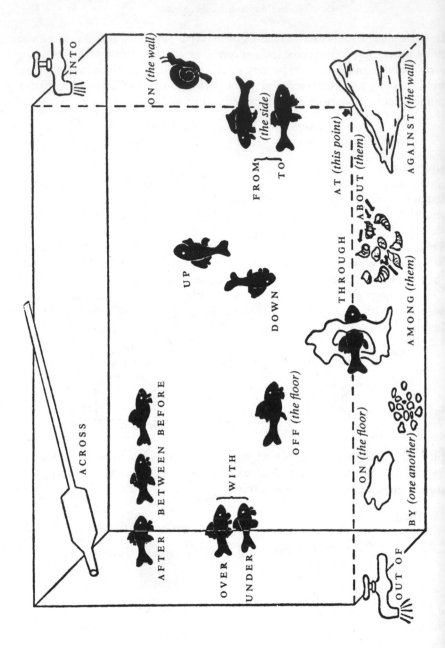

INTO

ON (the wall)

FROM
(the side)
TO

AGAINST (the wall)

AT (this point)

ABOUT (them)

THROUGH

UP

DOWN

AMONG (them)

ACROSS

OFF (the floor)

AFTER BETWEEN BEFORE

ON (the floor)

WITH

BY (one another)

OVER
UNDER

OUT OF

It is fitting, is it not, that the man who has most aptly characterized the role of COMPARISON in the study of depiction should have been the original deviser and pioneer of the comic strip: Rodolphe Töppfer (1799–1846). I take my quotation and examples from page 11 of Dr. Wiese's brilliant translation of Töppfer's "Essay on Physiognomy" in her delightful *Enter: The Comics* (Lincoln: University of Nebraska Press, 1965, p. 11):

First, one must never forget that any human face, however poorly and childishly drawn, possesses necessarily, by the mere fact of existing, some perfectly definite expression. Since this is true—quite apart from the question of knowledge, skill, or study, it follows that anyone observant or curious can discover what gives a particular face its special expression. If he tries to determine the deciding features by conjecture only, he may spend a lot of time for results that are inconclusive and problematic. But in fact one does not normally take such a course. You don't meditate: you make a new face. Right away the points of likeness remain constant, the differences stand out, and you are on your way to seeing with high accuracy which modulations of the line make the first face look stupid and the second harsh. Here's an example, and to make it more convincing I shall adopt the style of schoolboys.

Now this is surely the most elementary form of the human head—the crudest, most puerile you can imagine. What strikes you about it? Just this: since it cannot exist without wearing an expression, it has one indeed: the look of a stupid, stammering fellow, not even too sad about his lot. To tell straightway what produces this expression is not too easy, but anyone who cares to do so can find out quickly through comparisons. I draw another face: and I see it is less stupid, less stammering, and if it is not blessed with wits, at least it has a certain capacity for concentration. With no trouble at all, I note that this is mainly because I have brought forward the lower lip, reduced the space between the eyelids, and brought the eye closer to the nose. Now multiply the faces to make more comparisons, and you have already begun to acquire some understanding

of physiognomy, independent of any studies from nature, casts, noses, eyes, or ears. For with each face I can go through the process we used in comparing the second with the first.

In Töppfer's spirit then we have an experimental inquiry to pursue. But we will work at the other end of the scale from his. Physiognomies ("phyogs," we used to call them at school) are the most complex and subtle signfields there are. We will choose—for our study of learning via looking—the simplest examples we can find: cases where the three components, the *situation*, the *depiction* (or enaction) and the equivalent *sentence* are as unambiguous and as clear as they can be.

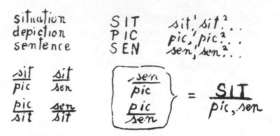

I have two things to explain about this.

1. I am using the Capital Letters SIT, PIC, SEN and the lower case sit[1], sit[2], and so on, to mark a fundamental contrast for any theory of communication (and indeed for any theory of anything whatsoever): the truly ultimate opposition between occurrences and whatever they are occurrences OF. I have put this TYPE v. token opposition into my Capital v. lower case symbolism. So, we will be reminded of it automatically. A main virtue (power) of Notations is to keep useful things in mind for us.

2. The other thing to explain is this line over pic and under sit $\frac{\text{sit}^1}{\text{pic}^1}$ which may be read verbally in various ways, as "is conveyed by" or "from" ("*via*") or "tells."

$$\text{Thus } \frac{\text{sit}^1}{\text{pic}^1} : \text{you see what the situation is from (via) the picture}$$

$$\frac{\text{pic}^1}{\text{sit}^1} : \text{you see what the picture is } of \text{ from the situation}$$

$$\frac{\text{sit}^1}{\text{sen}^1} : \text{the sentence tells you what the situation is}$$

$$\frac{\text{sen}^1}{\text{sit}^1} : \text{the situation tells you what the sentence is.}$$
$$\text{(If you are deaf enough that's so all the time.)}$$

The last pair are more complex and more instructive.

If what we are concerned with is communication between intelligential systems—and not merely echoic repercussions among robots—we have to recognize that $\frac{\text{sen}^1}{\text{pic}^1}$ and $\frac{\text{pic}^1}{\text{sen}^1}$ are abbreviations. There is a SIT, which is not represented in the above, highly active in both of them. More fully, when picture tells us what a sentence says and when a sentence tells us what picture is *of* there is a SIT which is common to them and mediating between them. Picture and sentence "mean the same thing," we say; they are two different means of representing the same situation. We can depict this with

SIT

en¹, en²...
pic¹, pic²...
sen¹, sen²...

With this as background—and having in mind also populations failing to learn to read verbally and unable as yet to use pictures—let us now look at a few very simple depictions of oppositions.

My first group will raise some problems of two-dimensional representation of two-dimensional situations.

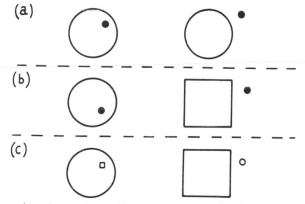

(a)

(b)

(c)

These DEPICT situations we can DESCRIBE verbally. With (*a*), *It is inside* and *It is outside* will do the trick. But (*b*) and (*c*) for more reflective handling. These situations can furthermore be ENACTED in many fashions. They are enacted by the point of the pencil in the process of drawing the circle and placing the dot. Or in Africa, say, we can lay down a loop of cord (or scratch a ring in the dust) and station something or someone inside it or outside, and so on. . . .

These three: *enaction, depiction, description* are the three fundamental notations with which we may represent oppositions of situations. . . .

Compare:

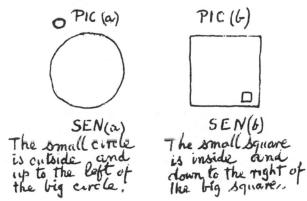

PIC (a)

PIC (b)

SEN(a)
The small circle
is outside and
up to the left of
the big circle.

SEN(b)
The small square
is inside and
down to the right of
the big square.

As *visual* statements PIC(*a*) *and* PIC(*b*) say much more than the verbal statements can. SEN(*a*) and SEN(*b*) could equally well cover a wide range of different cases. But PIC(*a*) and PIC(*b*) precisely *fix or create just one*.

As merely visual statements this is so. Taken, however, not as *visual statements* but as *depictive*, as *pictorial statements* about the relations of objects not *on* a plane but *in* a space, this visual definiteness vanishes. A pictorial statement can no more say just where the objects are, or what their space relations are to one another, than any verbal translation can. The circle "up to the left" might be a sphere as far away as the setting sun behind a tennis ball in the foreground. Or the circles might be two billiard balls. Similarly the small square might be a box of any size at any distance seen through a window.

To explore another source of indefiniteness and ambiguity. What happens here?

How do we translate this? As a *visual* statement of configurations on a plane we have no trouble. How convenient it is that we know the appropriate geometric and punctuation terms! We can say: "The question mark is up to the left of the ellipse and the exclamation mark is down the right of the parallelogram." But suppose that we were not sophisticated in these ways. Suppose that we had to describe what we see without any such terms, or, worse still, with quite other culturally determinant conventions. Suppose our culture made us see the question mark as a hook upside down and the exclamation point as a man without arms or legs upside down! What then? We would have a situation more like those which arise in much reading and those that new inquiries and genuine learning are faced with.

It was said above that scientific inquiry into learning has to take the principle of opposition by which any notation works very seriously. Not surprisingly, since this principle is so fundamental to science itself: as the systematic inquiry into *what varies with what while the rest is treated as remaining constant*. What *varies with what* while what else can be supposed to remain the same? Is not that the question which systematic investigation (and not only into learning) seeks to answer through its practice of making situations (and notations for them) as safely *comparable* as possible?

We have been comparing visual and depictive statements with sentences: two systems of notation. We also considered enactions—a third system (or system of systems) of notation. There may be much to be learnt about learning through study of the interplay of notations belonging to different media. To take the chief example: What the eye can see and the ear can hear endlessly supply complementary notations for one another. They can offer one another competitive statements by which each can check its own. Each can serve as an instrument by which the other can control and adjust its own oppositions, compositions, and comparisons. The service is reciprocal and cooperative. As you speak I watch your expression to help me toward what you mean and what I hear you say governs how I take your frown. With these advanced developments we are familiar. What have not been sufficiently studied in minute particularity and with a view to general theory and controlled application are the elementary cooperations of ear and eye in learning. And, specifically, the ways in which very simple verbal and visual statements, *duly sequenced together,* can be used to prompt, to control, to correct one another. The visual and the verbal channels can help one another in elementary learning of languages AND in the handling of situations through *language* and *depiction.* They can help far more systematically and effectually than designers have in general as yet realized. And it is through improved design of instruction using planning mutual control of doing, seeing, and saying, of enactions, depictions, and sentences, that the increases in effective capacity we so badly need can chiefly be brought about.

Seeing as well as saying is an activity that can be developed through cultivation. No one knows how much further it might be developed if we really took it in hand and studied how to help people with it. It might be like pole-jumping, say, or modern rock-climbing or modern business management. Suddenly almost anyone can be helped to do what almost nobody could do before. We much too readily suppose that talent in seeing, and in other sorts of discernment, is just natural or native—you have it or not. It can be exercised, why, of course. But can it be taught? We troop children through galleries and museums—somewhat to the affliction of those who go there to look. But very rarely and, as a rule, only in the service of some *specific* field of study, do we use reasonable means to help a child to explore for himself what he does when he sees and to help him check himself and others and find out how to look and observe better . . .

What is needed—and not only in this period of world crisis—is NOT so much some improved philosophic or psychological doctrine, though no one should despise that—as sets of sequenced exercises through which millions of people could explore, *for themselves,* their own abilities and grow in capacity, practical and intelligential, as a result. In most cases perhaps, this amounts to offering them *assisted* invitations to attempt to find out just what they are trying to do and thereby how to do it. . . .

Programming, of course, is just *curriculum on the cellular or molecular scale.* What should be taken before what and taken along with what? What earlier steps will best prepare the learner to take the next step?—and so on all the way back to the earliest controllable, arrangeable steps and all the way on to the point where the learner is ready to see for himself what he should go on to try to do.

Let me contrast two opposed or polar components in programming,* which nonetheless, for all their opposition, must necessarily and inevitably cooperate.

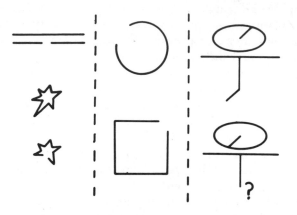

On the left we see "fill in the missing bit" tasks, completion exercises under the guidance of *Association by Contiguity*. On the right we have a completion exercise under the guidance of *Association by Similarity*—by analogy, sameness in difference. In the middle we have completion exercises which are analysable cooperations of the two, in part Contiguity, in part Similarity. Actually Contiguity and Similarity are always present and active together, but sometimes the one, sometimes the other is *dominant*. This cooperative yet contrastive relation between Contiguity and Similarity can be illustrated with two finger games:

What's missing?
Contiguity.

What's the analogue?
Similarity *in difference*.

*See "The Metaphoric and Metonymic Poles" in *Fundamentals of Language* by Roman Jakobson and Maurice Halle (The Hague: Mouton & Co., 1956). "This bipartition is indeed illuminating. Nonetheless, for the most part, the question of the two poles is still neglected, despite its wide scope and importance for any symbolic behavior, especially verbal, and of its impairments."

It can be illustrated with the alphabet. Compare: abc?ef with a:c:d:? In the programming of language learning, and probably of most instruction, it is analogy, similarity in difference—identity of structure ordering diversities of material—which should be dominant almost throughout. Contiguity should become dominant only to take care of anomalies and accidents—exceptions in spelling, for example.

All modes of programming of course require that what has been previously noted remains able to influence what follows: programming being the designed shaping of that influence and its direction on the imminent future.

Even in a series of noting operations, which is as nearly pure contiguity actions and as nearly mere redintegration as possible, the filling-in of the missing bit requires retention of the pattern.

a) *Contiguity:*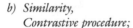

As the contrastive procedure invited becomes more elaborate these retained controlling patterns have to become more faithful and yet adaptable.

b) *Similarity,*
   Contrastive procedure;

In the above diagrams: (*a*) offers us

1. the guiding pattern in which we have to compare and note the relations of the parts and their alternation;
2. the problem in which we have to see what has to be supplied and
3. in which, guided by (2) as well as (1), we see and draw the answer;

(*b*) offers us something more complex:

1. a pair of forms to be compared;
2. a modified version of one of these forms, from which we have to supply
3. the other form similarly modified.

In (*b*), it is evident, we are doing much more than in (*a*). We are, as in (*a*), completing a two-dimensional configuration retaining for the ellipses the relation of the pattern quadrilaterals—but further, we are studying how a thing looks from another angle, another point of view. If, as is likely, we see in (b_1) "on the left, an envelope with a stamp in it" and, thence, "on the right, a circular mat (or plate) with a coin on it," ($b_{,2,3}$) this *pictorial* statement will be verbally translatable by: "If a stamped envelope (which, seen vertically from above, is two rectangles) has from a certain angle the appearance of the parallelograms in (2), a plate with a coin on it will have from that angle the appearance of the ellipses in (3)."

We are, we all know, wonderfully skilled in recognizing forms from varying angles—though the appearances they present may be extremely different. We have to be so skilled if we are to survive. Experiments show, however, that this skill is highest and most widely shared when the forms are those of familiar and standardized types: *recognized* (or common) forms, we call them. In my terminology, these are standard SIT s. . . .

[Perceptual exercises] prove suggestive of analogous problems and processes in other fields—not least as to the ways in which readers interpret sentences. Even the most sophisticated professional critics indulge—to an extent that few can bear to realize—in randomly erratic readings without any suspicion of what they are doing or any sense that there may be other interpretations more just than theirs. The only remedy for these high-grade extravagances (as for the helpless semiliterate), it seems more than likely, is a method of teaching beginning Reading which leaves less scope to guessing and develops reasonable techniques for self-controlling study. What this should do is to offer the beginner sequences of opportunities to discern—optically and intelligentially, pictorially and verbally—how the cooperating words in the sentences we put before him *require* and *exclude* as they build up together what the sentence says. For far further than has, until recently, been imagined, the development from zero of an apprehension of the structure of English can be paralleled by a pictorial sequence. Thus an iconographic means becomes available of showing how language works, a hieroglyphic notation helpful (in context and sequence) equally to language learning and to the development of pictorial literacy. This should not be surprising. Verbal and pictorial languages are, both of them, after all, *notations* for representing situations. The structures of each are reflections, under different limitations, of the structures of possible situations.

Moreover, it is very doubtful whether situations—and our lives are our copings with them—can be identified, distinguished, and compared at all without use of some notation. To enter a new language through such a joint use of verbal and pictorial notations is to be given an introduction to systematic exploration at the simplest and most practical and corrigible level. In other words it is an initiation in SCIENTIFIC METHOD: in learning how to look—to see, in case after calculated case, how what is different fits in with what is the same. . . .

———

The patient toil of scores of teachers is going every day, in courses about the appreciation of poetry, into the effort to make children (and adults) visualize where visualization is a mere distraction and of no service. And little books appear every few months encouraging just this gross misconception of language. For words cannot, and should not attempt to "hand over sensations bodily"; they have very much more important work to do. So far from verbal language being a "compromise for a language of intuition"—a thin, but better-than-nothing, substitute for real experience—language, well-used, is a *completion* and does what the intuitions of sensation by themselves cannot do. Words are the meeting points at which regions of experience which can never combine in sensation or intuition, come together. They are the occasion and the means of that growth which is the mind's endless endeavor to order itself. That is why we have language. It is no mere signalling system. It is the instrument of all our distinctively human development, of everything in which we go beyond the other animals.

"The Command of Metaphor," from *The Philosophy of Rhetoric* (1936). (References are to a book by T. E. Hulme.)

24

Paraphrasing in Basic

[In the concluding essay of *So Much Nearer*, "Toward a World English," Richards provides a short account of Basic English and an explanation of what he saw as its chief role, a way of auditing the meanings of our "key *general* ideas." He then turns to a consideration of how translation into Basic could improve the way we read. He begins by quoting F. L. Lucas writing in 1937 about *Interpretation in Teaching*.]

"I used to think it the object of English to make people well read. I have come to see that its aim must be to teach them how to read. They have the rest of their lives to read in." Alack! Thirty years have shown us that, unless they become teachers or publishers or editors or reviewers, students of English don't read more than they can help. Yet the aim of *teaching them how to read* remains what it was. What are the possible lines on which this aim may proceed? All, I believe, who are aware of the extent to which both prose and verse are currently misread even by seemingly well-qualified readers are agreed that training in some form of paraphrase or gloss is the best remedy for it. But the use of paraphrasing in schools is often so unsatisfactory that we may well feel that the remedy brings in as many evils as the disease.

Paraphrases in general divide into two types. There is the paraphrase that merely replaces the words in the original with rough synonyms, leaving all the doubtful parts of the meaning unillumined. This exercise of shuffling synonyms about is merely deadening to whatever germs of interpretative capacity may exist in the student. It may be agreed that the less he is subjected to it the better.

From *So Much Nearer*, (1968), chap. 10.

But the alternative is almost as bad. Here to write a paraphrase is to compose another passage made as nearly as possible a rival to the first. Rarely tried with a prose original, with poetry it is an invitation to write another poem—in prose—on a partially similar theme. As such, it is an exercise whose effects are often very far indeed from an improved comprehension of the original. This is the kind of paraphrase the more promising kind of pupil usually produces and he deserves our sympathy. For the terms of the task set him are something of an outrage on his sensibility. He is given an original which presumably he respects; he is asked—under the unfair condition that he may use none of the best words because these have been used already by the original poet—to build up a cluster of words, which will, so far as he can contrive, be an equivalent. The better reader he is, the more closely will he realize that what he is being asked to do is something not only presumptuous but impossible and absurd.

The exercise of writing a Basic paraphrase escapes all this. We are there playing a game: giving under strictly binding rules and conditions as accurate a representation as we can of the meanings of the original. But no one will expect our version to achieve a perfect translation. It is *not* claimed that a passage of Ruskin or Shakespeare can be reproduced without loss in Basic, or with that (rather remote) fidelity with which a good French version will render it. Sometimes, indeed, and with a frequency which is to many people at first surprising, passages of great English writing will be found to be already almost in Basic. A comparison of the Basic version and the Authorized Version of the Book of Ruth provides a striking example. But in general our poetry and our more ornate and elaborate emotive prose are not reproducible in Basic. Shakespeare has single lines in Basic:

> Making the Greene one Red

for example, but the line above that

> The multitudinous Seas incarnadine

defeats a Basic version, if from that version we expect anything like the integral effect of the line. But, and this is another point at which a misunderstanding of the purpose and use of a Basic version is extremely likely to occur, no such expectation is invited. Its use is quite other. Though it cannot reproduce the total effect, it can, item by item, display as many of the ingredients of sense which go into producing that total effect as any other analytic medium, and as clearly. The space, the notion, the expansion, the coming on of the waves without number and without end; the shock when the idea of blood is joined with that of water, "water, water, everywhere," and the way the Seas seem not only to be colored with the blood but themselves to become Seas of blood; all this with the suggestion in *incarnadine,* so full of fear and so deep-rooted in the part of the mind which is not conscious, of a living existence that is suddenly given to the waste of blood; all this may be put (I have been writing in Basic since the word *medium*) as completely, if not as delicately, as in any other language.

What are difficult to describe in Basic are not the *ideas* which may be divined in and extracted from the original but the nuances of feeling which result from them and from such other factors as the rhythm. But in any exposition these are difficult to display; and there is, I believe, a very strong case to be made for saying that the exercise of attempting to describe them is not a valuable one. It too easily becomes a debauch, an outflow of unregulatable sensibility. The valuable exercise is the analysis, the tracing out of the sense items, the ideas and their articulations—for these are a main part of the springs of the effect. To study them is to penetrate to the body of poetry; to describe effects is to play with shadows.

The typical instruction for a Basic exercise, I may accordingly suggest, should be this: "Make a Basic version; then, in normal English, point out where and how your Basic version fails (if it fails) to do justice to the original, and if it distorts it, say how." By such an instruction we should avoid the danger of the Basic version being supposed by the more weak-minded or ill-advised pupils to be "just as good" or "really what the poet ought to have written, or meant to say, if he had not been wanting to make it look pretty."

We may now consider what changes in the design of Basic English are likely to be proposed as a result of the varied and extensive use it has received. The chief of these concerns Ogden's treatment of verbs. Basic English is not the only instance of a design for which it is the very feature that most appealed to the designer, as his best contribution, the later seems most to need changing. His policy with verbs was to Ogden his master stroke, the step which made Basic English possible. On many copies of the Basic English Word List he even managed to squeeze in his NO "VERBS" claim with the following model statement: "It is possible to get all these words on the back of a bit of notepaper because there are no 'verbs' in Basic English." Naturally enough, it was this claim which most of all drew attention to Basic and this feature which more than any other aroused opposition.

What Ogden did was this: Guided by some suggestions from Jeremy Bentham, he selected a minimal set of verbs, *come, get, give, go, keep, let, make, put, seem, take; be, do, have; say, see, send; may, will,* which could—in conjunction with other words in Basic—*substitute for* (take the place of) all the other verbs in the language. As the punctuation suggests, these verbs fall into four groups. The first ten (*come* to *take*) are names of irreducibly simple acts. *Seem* somewhat resists this classification or indeed any description. It is easiest to think of it as complementary to *be.* (We *seem* wise and good perhaps; we *are* perhaps foolish and bad.) But the others name what we do, or what things do, and between them they cover our doings, and the doings of things, in a peculiarly comprehensive fashion. Into the meanings of other verbs comes some component able to be carried by one or more of these operators (as *enter,* for example, has a meaning of *come in,* and *meditate* has a meaning which may be carried by *give thought* or *take thought*). And this is what has been meant by the claim that Basic has "no verbs." Its use of these superverbs or operators allows it to dispense with the rest.

Next come *be, do* and *have,* which get such a lion's share of the work in English either as full verbs or as auxiliaries. Then come *say, see, send.* These are luxury conveniences in Basic and not strictly indispensable. We could cover their uses with other Basic words. When we *say* something, we *put* it into words; when we *see* something it *is* in view or we *have* it before our eyes; when we *send* someone we *make* him *go,* and so on. But these periphrases would be awkward, and these three words are of such general utility that it is better to have them on the list. Lastly come *may* and *will,* auxiliaries of possibility and permission, and of futurity.

An immensely strong case can be made for this extremely drastic restriction of verbs *as a design for early stages in learning English as a second language.* These are the verbs which can do most work in the language. They are verbs which must be mastered in any case if the learner is to attain any real competence. This plan gives them early an extraordinary amount of exercise: at first in situations which make their meanings enactively, visibly and pictorially clear and unambiguous. Later come extensions. It is here that the argument for revision arises. Why not, both for paraphrasing purposes and—after a certain stage—for the foreign learner, use *as verbs* all the general words on the Basic List that admit of such use? There are some two hundred that may be so used though in strict Basic they are nouns only: *account, act, air, answer, attack, attempt.* . . . And there are useful verbs contained in Basic nouns: *addition, adjustment, advertisement, agreement, amusement.* . . . There are others still, such as *argue* (argument), *attend* (attention), *behave* (behavior), *believe* (belief), which are no trouble to the English speaker—though they give a learner something further to note and remember.

What results from this redesign is of course a language much nearer than Basic to standard English, a language easier to speak in and to write (for the native), but harder, to an undetermined degree, for the learner. It is commonly proposed further that *can* and *must* (not Basic words) be added, along with varying numbers of others: *ask, bring, buy, find, think,* and so on . . . to yield a language which would still be restricted but would seem until analyzed to have almost the full powers of normal English.

[It is easy to see that in terms of aims discussed earlier] this suppled-up Basic would differ little in coverage (1). It would be far more acceptable (2). As to ease of acquisition (3), it might well cost more than double the toil for equal coverage. This last point could without great trouble be determined by experiment. Appraisal as to (4): Insight into meaning, on the other hand, is a far more tricky matter, not in the least so readily settled. Those who have done most work upon this question and had most opportunity to compare pure Basic and verbed-up Basic as media for paraphrase are far from certain about the balance of advantages. Judgment in the matter turns on a very great number of minute analyses made with varying success by students of varying ability. What seems to emerge is that while it is undoubtedly easier to write paraphrases in verbed-up Basic, the degree of *insight into the original* which results often seems to be markedly less. The higher cost in time and toil of the more restricted Basic version seems for many to be repaid in superior understanding.

A policy that on the whole seems recommendable may be stated as follows:

A. For the learner entering English, when a secure command of the Basic eighteen verbs has been *attained in their physically enactable, depictable uses,* go out from Basic into verb uses of other words through already acquired Basic phrases: start saying "He changed it" for "He made a change in it" or "He got it changed." A habit of explaining the new through paraphrase in the old can thus be built into the expansion of the learner's English.

B. For the English speaker, joint use both of verbed-up Basic and of pure Basic with as much comparison between the versions as can be undertaken.

C. Another step of redesign for Basic seems desirable. It goes along with much-needed cultivation of pictorial literacy. There seems no reason to attempt to limit the intake of words for which a simple picture, or sequence of them, can unambiguously present the meaning. Ogden's category of pictured things, his 200, would thus lapse. Many of them would, of course, come in early for a beginner as means of expanding and exercising his sentence-situation command. But there would be no attempt to make him learn them ahead of his need for them in his *use* of the language.

As a medium for paraphrase, the vocabulary resulting from this last enlargement would seem to have great advantages over pure Basic. In place of the question, "Is this word on the List or not?" we have "Is this thing depictable?" The gearing of language into actuality is thereby increased. And the responsibility of deciding whether or not the paraphraser sufficiently *understands* is put where it belongs, *on him.* Attention is directed to where it is most needed in controlling the structure of the meaning in place of being dissipated over points of no consequence, which nonetheless can waste much time and trouble.

Paraphrase—though I have given it here such prominence—is only one of a wide range of exercises which the use of a selection from English on the model of Basic suggests. The detail of the study of the advantages and disadvantages of one type or another of limitation; the arguments for the inclusion of this or that word or family of words, of this or that construction; sorting games with the Word Lists; the collection and classification, for example, of nouns that work as adjectives too; hundreds of investigations into what words can and cannot do; how they support and control one another; the varieties of opposition; the limits of analogy . . . there is no end to the invitations to exploration set on foot by this representation of a whole language through a part. Nothing more naturally prepares the mind to cultivate its powers of systematic reflection than these wordgames which are in fact nothing less than inquiries into how meanings serve one another and how they serve and are constrained by reality.

The dissatisfactions with customary "English" studies touched on above are *bitterly* felt the world over. They are reflected in the fluctuations of pedagogic views of 'grammar'* as well as in much energetic searching for new curricula for "English" to match those, from which so much has been hoped, for Science and Mathematics. It may be that what has been sought, as Socrates discovered of justice (*Republic,* 432D), "has been rolling under our feet from the start" and that we have been "like people hunting for what they hold in their hands."

But the new curricula to be designed have duties more ambitious and more exacting than those they must replace. It is not only 'English' that is failing us; the roots of an elementary school ˢʷMental and Moral Philosophyˢʷ have been left unwatered and the real sources of our cultures starved. Our thought and our means of thinking, though distinguishable, are interdependent. The way to recover a truly *elementary* education (one which provides, nourishes and liberates the elements) is through the same experimental curiosities as to how language works which give the child speech. But when he comes to writing let us give him sequenced explorables—to sustain and encourage in him the concept of an intelligible world. . . .

Normally a word works only through the cooperations of other words. These restrictive–permissive, controlling–enabling interrelations, which tie the utterances possible within a language into a system, give us our means of distinguishing between variant readings and misreading. Once again, we must never forget that the system in living languages is nowhere fixed or rigid, though it will, no doubt, be more rigid in certain regions of use than in others. The interrelations correspond to the needs the language has met and is meeting, to the tasks it has attempted and is attempting to perform. As need and task change, the interrelations undergo strain which may be met by adjustment and by growth. Here is where novelty, in phrasing and in interpretation, enters, the opportunity for variant reading and original utterance.

We are not far here from valuative considerations. The analogies I have mentioned with a society and an organism suggest that we may properly be concerned with linguistic *health,* whose connections with "whole" we should keep in mind as well as its forward-looking implication: we would not say anyone was in good health if he were unable to continue so for some while. It may be very deeply doubted whether any great language has ever really been left to its own devices unsubject to effective criticism from those who were, by privilege or by profession or by poetic or social endowment, unusually well able to use it and to judge how it should be used. The language arts, after all, are arts. Perhaps we should not take too seriously those who seem to claim authority from linguistics as a 'science' to tell a rather helpless gen-

See pp. 270–73 for an explanation of these superscripts.—ED

eration that what is said by enough people thereby becomes what *should* be said. (Are we to think that what is thought by enough people thereby becomes what should be thought?) And yet in this age of the advertiser ('Everybody's buying it') there is occasion for concern. It is not quite enough to leave the matter to the experience of anyone speaking or writing with care, reflection, and intent. In selecting our phrases are we seeking (1) what most people in our situation would most probably say, or (2) what will best do the work in hand? Only in a very exalted linguistic community indeed would 2 be in general the same as 1; it would be a diseased community in which there was widespread doubt which to prefer. Similarly with interpretation. What we should seek is not the sense that is, or would be, most widely accepted, but that which most fully takes into account the situation the utterance is meeting and the integrity of the language. It was with this in view that I inserted in my diagram DV (development) after D (decoding). There should be—although it may slow reading down—a cyclic mutual dependence between R, D and DV, as with S, E and T. [See p. 179.] In spite of Plato's jokes in the *Phaedrus* the chief service that writing and reading can do us is to help us to reflect: to reflect, *Deo volente,* to some purpose. Counting hands in interpretation cannot do that. Misreadings may, as scholarship frequently discovers, be universal through long periods.

Most speech and writing, and most interpretation, is not, I have urged above, as conscious as the word 'seek' above may suggest. Commonly a series of possible phrases or interpretations offer themselves (more or less schematically), and our choice is not ordinarily guided by highly explicit considerations. It is this that makes a crude usage doctrine dangerous; it can present *the thing to say* in a fashion which blurs the vital distinction between *what I should say here* and *what is said.* And this is not only for the form but for the content of the utterance, as admen and opinion promoters have noted.

To sum up, a sound account of interpretation must build into itself a duty to be critical. A linguistics that is properly aware of the processes through which language grows in the individual and of the effects that his attitudes to language can have upon its health in him must be concerned with pedagogy and with what sorts of assumptions are spread in the school. Poor pedagogy in the thinking of linguistic authorities is in its own way quite as alarming as bad linguistic doctrine in the classroom.

After all this my definition of 'misreading' will still have to lean on much more than has been said if it is not itself to be most variously misread. In this it corresponds to the statesman whose responsibilities as guardian expose him to misrepresentation. He does well not to formulate his policies in ways that give handle to his opponents. My definition too will be well advised not to do more, seemingly, than advance a modest request: "For the purposes outlined above and on the appropriate occasions, may *misreading* mean the *taking of a sentence in such a way that the equivalence relations of one or more of its parts to the rest of the language lapse* and thereby, if such taking were to continue, harm would be done to the language—due regard being given, in applying this criterion, to the necessity for change in language activity with change in the situations to be met, and, in general, to the health of the language."

"Variant Readings and Misreading," from *So Much Nearer* (1968).

25

Sens/Sits

Far too often we find language, along with alleged visual aids, serving not as a means of exploration but as a screen protecting actuality from inquiry and as a substitute for thought and action just where thought and action are most urgently required.

For this meshing of language into actuality there is needed a watchful application of meaning-theory. Sentences, which should be the units in language learning, take their meanings from the situations within which they are used. At first a sentence may be carried by, may ride on, the situation in which it occurs. The situation is its *vehicle*. That is the *passive* use of language. Later, in *active* use, the sentence can carry the situation.

Since sentences and situations *vary* together, sentences are best understood through the learner becoming able to see—as concretely and immediately as possible, through actual *use*—how and why sentences have to change with situations and situations with sentences. The important link is not between an individual utterance and the individual occasion in which it takes part; the important links are between types of sentences (SEN s) and types of situations (SIT s). Individual utterances and situations do not recur. What can recur and be the basis for learning are *types,* not *tokens*—in the sense in which there is only one word THE, the type, but three tokens of it in this sentence.

Ideally, the structuring of language in a learner's mind and the structuring of his world grow together. It is through this covariance in structure that language learning, rightly sequenced, can become the supreme instrument in developing effective capability. Only by suitable sequencing can the learner

From *Design for Escape* (1968), chap. 1.

be led to compare the structure of the language as he uses it with the structure of the situations it is representing. . . .

All language works through opposition. Any utterance does what it does by excluding other utterances which would do other things. To arrange sequences of SEN–SIT s so that through the parallelism of opposing situations and opposing sentences this operative structure of the language enters in and possesses the learner: that is the task of the designer.

Insofar as that happens, *the structure of the new language* and the structure of actuality and action in the learner *grow together.* Grow together: mesh into one another and become one source of power. Teaching a new language can and *should* be the *building* of a new world. As a rule, of course, it is nothing of the sort. . . .

Our two distance receptors—the eye and the ear—are incredibly skilled in their collaboration and complementation. It is hard to understand why they have not been used for millennia far more, and more intelligently, *together* in helping the language learner and in helping him, through his new language, to learn, from the start, much more than just another language. . . .

In a reasonably well-controlled design the radically contrastive structure of language can be linked with the correspondingly contrastive structure of the world through sequences of depictions made as systematically contrastive. . . .

If there are ways—*and there are*—of making the earliest steps in controllable, designed education: e.g., learning the beginnings of English and Reading, from the start, an understanding use of notations (graphic and pictorial), an implantation of reasonable, enquiring, and responsible and self-critical *thought,* truly we should not be neglecting them. Neither learning to read, nor learning a second language has been that sort of thing heretofore. . . . And let us not forget that most of the world's population have still to learn to read and that to fail in *that* (as some very highly favored areas are showing us) can be destructive. It can be as destructive as real success can be restorative and releasing. Real success, in this as in how much else, is *seeing what you have to do and thereby how to do it.* Those who learn so are being turned into effective teachers themselves—a point of importance in view of the shortage of even moderately competent or trainable classroom operators. With what can be done in mind, to watch—in China, in India, in Africa, and nearer home—the ordinary mangling of the necessary distinctions, the bored and distracted rote repetitions of locutions reduced thereby to meaningless parrotings, the inevitable antics, the distraught teacher's interventions; all this can be no slight lesson in the balancings of hope and of despair. . . .

The sovereign incentive for all learning is the learner's awareness of his own learning power. Coleridge stated a profound perception very simply when he said: "I call that alone genuine knowledge which returns as power." It is fundamental too that a learner can know that knowledge is returning thus in him *as power.* As he knows this, he enjoys—to divert some phrases of Hobbes's *The Elements of Philosophy* to other ends than Hobbes's—"The inward glory and triumph of mind that a man may have for the mastery of some difficult and doubtful matter, or for the discovery of some hidden truth" and this enjoyment, this *inward glory and triumph* is the reward, the reinforcement, the motive builder, that designers of instruction can rely on. To quote Coleridge again, the learners should be "carried forward, not merely or chiefly by the mechanical impulse of curiosity, or by a restless desire to arrive at the final solution; but by the pleasurable activity of mind excited by the attractions of the journey itself." The attractions of the journey itself— not any adventitious jolly-ing up, or sugar-coating, not any persuasiveness or spell-binding from a teacher or appetite in the learner for enhanced self-esteem. No. The intrinsic excitement of the student's own exploration of the intelligible order is what should be at work. . . .

When we consider the dehumanizing and even brutalizing conditions amid which so many children have to grow up—the narrow channels, mere peep-holes, open to them on other people, people so often disturbed to the point of incommunicability—their need for reasonable commerce, for sympathetic and comprehensible exchange, for reciprocal give and take of thought and feeling needs no stressing. Far too often the chances of mutual understanding that a teacher in a crowded classroom can offer them shrink to nil. All that comes is another series of bafflements added to

> the heavy and the weary weight
> Of all this unintelligible world

which is already making alienation their probable fate. Real contact with an instructing mind, real participation in a joint exploration can often be the one thing that can lighten—relieve *and* illumine—minds so endangered. But to design instruction so that such contact, such participation occurs is not something a teacher faced with some forty pupils, many of them in revolt, can be honestly supposed to do. It can be designed however by a team of two or three who can use computer-collected and analysed data from what has happened with partially similar pupils before.

Design indeed is engaged not only with the structure of the presentation. It is concerned with the structuring of the activities of the investigating mind of the learner. It can order these by arranging the oppositions displayed in its sequences so that *they* show the learner what he has to take in. When these indications are confirmed and rewarded by success, a peculiar thing happens. The learner has divined three things, how the game goes, what he has to do, and how the teaching mind is playing it. This triple concern puts the learner into a cooperative and creative contact with what is being studied, with his own endeavors, and with the would-be helpful presentation offered to him. While trying to form his own ideas, he is also attempting to penetrate the veil and to participate in the thinking of others. . . .

[Richards concludes by quoting "the most prophetic passage of *Prometheus Bound*," in which Shelley salutes the apparitions that will visit us, concluding

"The wandering voices and the shadows these/Of all that man becomes."]
When we raise the question of standards, it is to this standard that we must
repair. Is it strange to affirm that the ultimate aim of all the arts, including
these, is to present to man his guiding image? Strange perhaps to minds
subjected to the views of recent decades, not strange to the main tradition
which did not think of the arts as alienated. But this guiding image is nothing
less or other than the shaping mode of that knowledge which returns as
power. This is the fundamental theorem, I take it, for any view of Vision.

———

"Notes on Principles of Beginning Language Instruction" were prepared by
I. A. Richards for a UNESCO conference in Paris held on June 19, 1947.

1. We learn a new sentence or sentence element by seeing how it applies in a situation.

2. We teach by so presenting the sentence and the situation together that this is seen.

3. In what follows, the abbreviation SEN–SIT will be used for this unit made up of
a sentence in the situation which gives it meaning.

4. Teaching a language effectively consists of inventing, arranging, presenting, and
testing SEN–SIT s.

5. For each language there is an *ideal order* in which its SEN–SIT s should be arranged.

6. In this ideal order:
   a) The ambiguity of each SEN–SIT, in its place in the order, is minimal.
   b) Each SEN–SIT prepares for those to come.
   c) Each SEN–SIT is confirmed by those which follow.
   d) Disturbance by new SEN–SIT s of SEN–SIT s taught earlier is minimal.

7. An organic sequence in which each step supports and is supported by the others
may be achieved by GRADING. Grading, thus understood, is a qualitative matter
of the relations between parts in the sequence—not a quantitative matter of the
number of words, etc., taught in successive lessons.

8. When the structure of the sentence corresponds to a structure easily perceived in
the situation the SEN–SIT is said to be clear.

9. Good grading begins by using SEN–SIT s which have as few elements as possible
and are as clear as possible.

10. The structure of a sentence appears to a learner through his perceiving how its
elements vary with the corresponding element in the situation. Structure is the
form which persists though the values of the variables change.

It is here.
It is *there*.
He is there.

11. The words we choose in teaching structure through changes in the variables should be widely useful words.

12. Useful words are:
    a) Those through which the learner can USE his knowledge as quickly and widely as possible.
    b) Those which best prepare for the instruction which follows.
    c) Those with the help of which other useful words can be explained.

13. In English the most useful words (and as a rule the most frequent) are:
    a) The structural words in the first column of the Basic English Word List.
    b) The names of the most demonstrable (picturable) common things and their qualities.

14. Among them we should use first those which yield the clearest SEN–SIT s.

15. It seems wise to postpone interrogatives until the affirmative word order has been established.

16. As the learner advances through such a series of SEN–SIT s, he must be exercised in their elements and structures—not through mere repetition but through experience of new SEN–SIT s *using* the learnt elements in varying structures and *using* the same structures with changed elements.

17. Such grading makes any recourse to the mother tongue unnecessary. It should be avoided because it revives:
    a) *Constructions* used in the mother tongue, the chief source of broken language learning.
    b) *Phonemes* of the mother tongue, the source of mispronunciation.
    c) Bilingual associations in place of SEN–SIT s. These prevent "thinking in the new language," which is possible from the first.

18. Translation, a desirable exercise at later stages in the learning of a language, is a cause of much confusion and wasted effort for the beginner. A graded presentation—through rightly ordered SEN–SIT sequences—can entirely replace "equivalents" and explanations in the mother tongue.

Appendix, from *Design for Escape* (1968).

What shall we do with the powers, which we are so rapidly developing, and what will happen to us if we cannot learn to guide them in time?

Preface to the 1928 edition, from *Principles of Literary Criticism*.

[Bringing subjects] "into connections, in a comprehensive *synoptic* view of their relations with one another and with what truly is" which Plato considered a University to be for: what good would all this do? Suppose the subjects, the faculties (in the individual and in the University), the studies: History, Poetry, Theology, Logic, Government, Biology—rearrange them and subdivide them as you will—suppose that these studies came to understand one another so well that they could give up their war?

"The Idea of a University," from *Speculative Instruments* (1955).

———

There is an analogy between the conception of the world order and the design of a language which may serve man best. The choice of words for that language and the assignment of priorities among their duties can parallel the statesman's true tasks. And it is through what language can offer him that every man has to consider what should concern him most. If rightly ordered, and developed through a due sequence, the study of English can become truly a humane education.

"Towards a World English," from *So Much Nearer* (1968).

———

After all, what is any helpful discourse ever doing, whatever the topic, but showing an audience just this: how to practice what is preached.

"Introductory," from *Techniques for Language Control* (1974).

Richards' Specialized
Quotation Marks and Key

Richards considered ambiguities "the very hinges of all thought," but they obviously cannot function as hinges unless they are recognized. Many of his techniques for close reading—or "close thinking," as he claimed—were intended to guide a recognition of ambiguity. His suspicion of the misuse of definition led him to invent alternatives, chiefly "multiple definition" and interpretive paraphrase or "vertical translation." His own favorite device for alerting the reader to the work of a particular word or phrase was what he called "Specialized Quotation Marks," first introduced in *How to Read a Page* (1942) and printed in subsequent books—key and explanation. They started out as a parody of a then new rhetorical gesture. The General Semanticists had persuaded many academics (and public figures too) that the only reality was what could be measured empirically (they had no notion of the pervasive role of interpretation) and that language which was "abstract" should be signaled by a gesture of making quotation marks in the air. To lecture on, say, *moral man* in *immoral society*, was to risk developing arthritis, since each term would require gestural quotation marks. Richards meant his marks, his "alphabetic fleas," to suggest how complex a matter it is to establish *context* and *tone*, to differentiate *type* and *token*, *referents* and *reference*, *signal* and *message*, different kinds of *code*, and so on. With the subsequent appearance of psycholinguistics, Richards slyly renamed them "Meta-Semantic Markers."

I have retained them wherever they occur, but without the conviction that they actually function as he had hoped.

SPECIALIZED QUOTATION MARKS

We all recognise—more or less unsystematically—that quotation marks serve varied purposes:

1. Sometimes they show merely that we are quoting and where our quotation begins and ends.

2. Sometimes they imply that the word or words within them are in some way open to question and are only to be taken in some special sense with reference to some special definition.

3. Sometimes they suggest further that what is quoted is nonsense or that there is really no such thing as the thing they profess to name.

4. Sometimes they suggest that the words are improperly used. The quotation marks are equivalent to "the so-called."

5. Sometimes they indicate only that we are talking of the words as distinguished from their meanings. "Is" and "at" are shorter than "above." "Chien" means what "dog" means, and so on.

There are many other uses. This short list will suffice to show how heavily we overwork this too-serviceable writing device. Some of these uses accordingly are taken over by italics, but there again ambiguity easily arises. We italicize for emphasis (of several kinds) as well as to show that we are talking about words themselves or about some special use made of them. In speech, of course, many of these subtleties can be handled by intonation and pausing, though not with high uniformity or equally well by all speakers.

In most discussions of meanings, quotation marks will necessarily be given an inordinately heavy task to perform. This there is no avoiding. In all interpretation work we have to be able to hold up words and phrases for separate and special attention, and we have to do our best to indicate what our attitudes to them and to their meanings are. It is somewhat absurd, indeed, that writers have not long ago developed a notation system for this purpose which would distinguish the various duties these little commas hanging about our words are charged with.

I continue here with an experiment first tried in my *How to Read a Page* in using a range of special symbols that take the place of the usual quotation marks. They will be small letters placed, as quotation marks are, about the words, the phrases and the sentences they single out. A key to this notation follows. It will be found in practice, I believe, that two glances at the key prepare the reader to recognize, without consulting it anew, what I suppose myself to be doing when I use the notation. It gives us a compact means of commenting on the handling of language—more comprehensible, less ambiguous and less distracting than the usual devices of parenthesis, qualification and discussion. I believe it will abridge both the optical and the intellectual labor of the reader.

KEY

^w. . . . . .^w   indicates that the word—merely as that word in general—is being talked about. The marks are equivalent to "the word." E.g., "ᵂtableᵂ may mean an article of furniture or a list."

^r. . . . .^r   indicates that some special use of the word or phrase is being referred to. The marks are equivalent to "Please refer to the place in the passage we should have in mind here." E.g., "ʳNatureʳ for Whitehead is not Wordsworth's ʳNature.ʳ"

[?]. . . . .[?]   indicates that our problem is What does this word say here? Not whether anything it seems to say is acceptable or not. The marks are equivalent to "Query: what meaning?" There is no derogatory implication. Most ?important? words are, or should be, in this situation.

[!]. . . . .[!]   indicates surprise or derision, a "Good Heavens! What-a-way-to-talk!" attitude. It may be read !shriek! if we have occasion to read it aloud.

^{nb}. . . . .^{nb}   indicates that how the word is understood is a turning point in the discussion, and usually that it may easily be read in more than one way or with an inadequate perception of its importance. The sign is short for *nota bene*.

^{sw}. . . . .^{sw}   indicates that the reader is invited to consider "Something that may be said *With* ˢʷ——.ˢʷ" The marks are short for "Something said With." They are useful when we need to remind ourselves of the very different things that may be meant by the words we are using, and may well be read "Said warily."

ⁱ. . . . .ⁱ   indicates that other senses that the word may have in other occurrences may intervene. The marks are equivalent to "Intervention likely."
By extension

^{di}. . . . .^{di}   would mean "Danger! Watch out!" and

^{hi}. . . . .^{hi}   would mean "Helpful intervention."
In contrast, a word or phrase to be read as having no relevant relations to any other senses in other places, actual or possible, could be written

^t. . . . .^t   to mean "technical term" defined and fixed in this employment.

ⁿ. . . . .ⁿ   indicates that the word is the name that is being used and that we know what it names, though we may not think it a good name. The sign is equivalent to "the so-called ——."

[oc]. . . . . .[oc] to show that occurrences of a word—Peirce's [r]token[r]—are being talked of.

[q]. . . . . .[q] query: what meaning?

Lastly why should we not use the mark =, equivalent to, to indicate that the words or phrases it links are to be taken as having the same [?]meaning[?] for the purposes in hand? This escapes the unfortunate suggestion: that whatever the first is talking about [!]really is[!] the second. The usual device is to write "(i.e., ——)," which too often carries the suggestion that somehow we have no need to ask ourselves what the second explanatory word or phrase is itself standing for here. An equally troublesome device is to add "(or ——)," which commonly offers us a dangerous, usually a crude, ambiguity. [w]Or[w] then may be presenting an alternative thing or just another *name* for the same thing.

Primary Sources

The Meaning of Meaning (London: Kegan Paul, 1923).
Principles of Literary Criticism (London: Kegan Paul, 1924).
Practical Criticism (London: Kegan Paul, 1929).
Mencius on the Mind: Experiments in Multiple Definition (London: Kegan Paul, 1932).
Coleridge on Imagination (London: Kegan Paul, 1934).
The Philosophy of Rhetoric (New York: Oxford University Press, 1936).
Interpretation in Teaching (New York: Harcourt, Brace, 1938).
How to Read a Page: A Course in Effective Reading, with an Introduction to a Hundred
    Great Words (New York: W. W. Norton Company, Inc., 1942).
The Wrath of Achilles: The Iliad of Homer Shortened and in a New Translation
    (New York: W. W. Norton Company, Inc., 1950).
Speculative Instruments (Chicago: University of Chicago Press, 1955).
So Much Nearer (New York: Harcourt, Brace and World, 1968).
Design for Escape: World Education Through Modern Media (New York:
    Harcourt, Brace and World, 1968).
Poetries and Sciences: A Reissue of Science and Poetry (1926; 1935) with Commentary
    (New York: W. W. Norton Company, Inc., 1970).
The Written Word (with Sheridan Baker and Jacques Barzun) (Rowley, Mass.:
    Newbury House Publishers, 1971).
I. A. Richards: Essays in His Honor, ed. Reuben Brower, Helen Vendler, and John
    Hollander (New York: Oxford University Press, 1973).
Beyond (New York: Harcourt, Brace, 1973).
Poetries: Their Media and Ends, ed. Trevor Eaton (The Hague: Mouton, 1974).
Techniques in Language Control (Rowley, Mass.: Newbury House Publishers, 1974).
Complementarities (Cambridge: Harvard University Press, 1976).

Index of Richards'
Speculative Instruments

There is no study which is not a language study,
concerned with the speculative instruments it employs.
—I. A. Richards, "Toward a More Synoptic View"

Speculative instruments is the name Richards gave the ideas we think *with,* the meanings that provide the means of making further meaning in any field of inquiry. I intend this index to serve the same sort of purpose for which Kenneth Burke devised his *Lexicon Rhetoricae* (in *Counterstatement*)—that is, to explain the ideas (and the terms which name them) central to the exploration of certain concerns. For Richards, they were practical criticism, the logical task of interpretation in the making of meaning, the organic character of method, and the pedagogical and political implications of the study of misunderstanding and its remedies. His philosophy of rhetoric is at once a semiotic and a hermeneutic: it depends *from* (as he liked to say) principles of signification and interpretation. The terms, that is, the names of the ideas necessary for the articulation of these principles, and the practice they generate, constitute this index.

The various terms can be represented as oppositions, clusters, and ratios but not, I think, as hierarchies. Begin with any one term and you will find that in relating it to others, new relationships emerge—causalities, effects, resonances. For instance, following out the relationships *comparing* has to *choice* and *control,* and to *opposition* and *dependence,* will prepare a reader for Richards' argument that *purposing* is central to all language use. Considering the relationships among these terms and the ideas they name can illuminate the thought of this critic, who has been characterized as a highly unsystematic thinker, idiosyncratic if not downright cranky. Richards is indeed not systematic, in some senses, but if his philosophy of rhetoric is not architectonic, it is nonetheless coherent.

Activity IAR suggests pronouncing *activity* with a Scots accent—*acteevity*—to alert us to its importance. Activity is essential to Coleridge's conception of Imagination, the forming power which stands opposed to "Fancy." The active mind is antithetical to the passive use of conventions, of the unquestioning acceptance of doctrine. *Activity* supplants behavior as both term and concept, once IAR's psychology develops a philosophical footing. "Language I take to be preeminently the learnt activity of man, and learning itself to be the chief current mode of evaluation, of world advance" (*SI*, 113).

Those who, like Raymond Williams, have found fault with Richards because of his focus on individual competence have not noted the contexts of individual activity, as he conceived it. The all-in-each is "rooted in our biological continuity one with another" and is realized (made manifest) in communication situations. It is certainly true that as we first come to consider a text, attempting to see how the words work, introspection is essential, but as readers we are never *isolatoes,* and reading is never merely personal. As a variant of his favorite analogy of discourse and the state, Richards observed that "like the words in a sentence we are meaningless unless we take our senses from one another. The individual alone is nothing; though the whole takes its values from the individuals within it."

All-in-each IAR deploys this phrase of Coleridge's as another name for the soul. It counterbalances the idea of Romantic "individualism." The all-in-each of human nature is an interpretation of what it means to say that Man is *Homo sapiens sapiens* or that the power of symbolization is species-specific. Without this presupposition of a universal capacity, a theory of interpretation is mechanistic, with meaning set aside as an illusion and interpretation itself reduced to a matter of decoding. The all-in-each is the inborn capacity to see likeness and difference, to sort and gather, to *see as.* The signals the brain receives and transforms are coded, but they are not what is meant by *perception* and *reflection.* The all-in-each is a triadic concept.

All we can ever prove by factual evidence is *an act*—that the author wrote such and such words. But what he meant by them is another matter. Our conclusions there must rest, as best they may, upon another sort of consideration. Fundamentally they rest upon analogies—certain very broad similarities in structure between minds: "The all-in-each of every mind," as Coleridge called it. (*CI*, 14)

Ambiguity We cannot know for sure: ambiguity is entailed by mediation. Consequently, all representation must be subject to review; all interpretation to reinterpretation. Ambiguities are "the very hinges of all thought" because as we reflect on them, we will be relating what is said to what is probably meant. For that reason, Richards suggested that it might be preferable to speak of the *resourcefulness* of words.

In contemporary critical theory, *ambiguity* has been set aside in favor of *indeterminacy,* which appeals to poststructuralists as a bolder concept. But indeterminacy belongs to what Peirce calls Firstness: because it is unrepresented, it cannot be an object of inquiry.

William Empson, IAR's most illustrious pupil, tried to identify "seven types of ambiguity," but the taxonomic aspect of his study is far less important than his subtle sense of how syntax and semantics work together, of how contexts and subterranean currents determine how we read and re-read. Empson's later book, *The Structure of Complex Words*, is dedicated to "I. A. Richards who is the Source of all ideas in this book, even the minor ones arrived at by disagreeing with him."

Choice For IAR, the theory of choice supplants the ancient metaphysics of freedom and necessity and the psychology which isolated "will" from other "faculties." *Choice* means acting purposefully, and the purposeful choice of words serves as a pattern for all choices. As IAR deals with such practical problems as how to sequence the oppositions by which a learner can learn to learn, he never forgets the larger purposes of literacy. Peirce considered that all philosophical inquiry, including all critical inquiry into method, had as its question of questions, "What is Man to become?" Whether consciously echoing Peirce or not, Richards held the same opinion: the "arch-inquiry" implicit in such questions as "How can we teach?" "What do we seek to learn?" "What can we know?" is "What are we to become?" and for IAR, that question had a political urgency. He saw survival—of values, of the planet—as the arch-purpose of all choice. "A discussion of the reasons for the choice of words—which too often seems a trivial exchange of whimsies—can become an introduction to the theory of all choices" (*PR*, 86).

Comparison IAR introduces his theory of comprehending by remarking that at the heart of all interpretation, knowing, and meaning making is "the comparing activity." He notes that Coleridge called it "the sunshine power," the means to illuminate and clarify. IAR never reduces comparison to a rhetorical device typical of one or another of "the modes of discourse." Whether he is discussing the role of comparison in perception, word study, vertical translation (interpretive paraphrase), or metaphoric structure, the emphasis is on the sorting and gathering, the identifying and abstracting that constitute the process by which we discover, create, and establish meanings. "We develop our abilities to discern meanings through comparison" (*Complementarities*, 107).

Complementarity IAR understood that the chief consequence of triadicity is that *all knowledge is partial*. A theory of knowledge must therefore acknowledge the role of perspective (and purpose). Since the angle from which we regard that which we would understand determines how and what we see, we need different perspectives. The act of interpretation requires keeping ourselves alert to contexts and purposes, making interpretations multiple and keeping them tentative. "The two main criteria for a complementarity situation are (1): that the experimental setups should be mutually exclusive and (2): that the separate outcomes should support, complement one another." To demonstrate the principle, IAR suggests the following experiment:

Crumple up a handkerchief, hold it about a foot away, identify a peak among its crumples, and then compare fully how its ridges look as you alternately shut one eye or the other. Try drawing the two landscapes. Notice, further, that not only the two forms differ, but the colors of their slopes are different—if one eye is exposed to a light, to the sun, or to a lesser illuminant and the other eye is in the shade. (*Complementarities*, 114)

Complementarity is not an option but a necessity; it is IAR's insight that we can make a virtue of that necessity. "We only come by our own view of our position through our attempts to imagine the views of others" (*Beyond*, 27).

Richards had the idea long before he had the term; in *Coleridge on Imagination*, he wrote: "Since any account of these shifts [in meanings of *Nature, Mind, see*] must itself use positions, the gap [between two doctrines of projecting and finding] will reappear as between various accounts of these. To suppose otherwise is like hoping to see all their sides from one view point. The gap we cannot escape but we can recognize it" (pp. 161–62).

Context   A supplement to *The Meaning of Meaning*—printed in the final third of that astonishing book, next to the astonishing appendices, which include excerpts from Peirce's correspondence with Lady Welby—is entitled "The Problem of Meaning in Primitive Languages." This paper by Bronislaw Malinowski, which was to become a classic in the field of ethnography, explains the difference between analyzing "dead, inscribed languages" and "a primitive living tongue, existing only in actual utterance," offering a version of Ogden and Richards' "sign-situation," which he calls "the context of situation." The concept is mangled in modern sociolinguistics when *context* is taken to refer to the circumstances of oral "discourse," whereas literacy is said to occur when "speech" is *decontextualized!* This theft of the term is consonant with the positivist hermeneutics which deprives texts of their contexts, leaving them with only *intertextuality*.

In the preface to *Interpretation in Teaching*, IAR explains two meanings of *context*:

1. A word, like any other sign, gets whatever meaning it has through belonging to a recurrent group of events which may be called its context—a certain recurrent pattern of past groups of events. To say that a word's meaning depends upon its context would be to point to the process by which it has acquired its meaning.
2. A word's context of the words which surround it in the utterance, and the other contemporaneous signs which govern its interpretation.

IAR's contextual theorem of meaning as set forth in *The Philosophy of Rhetoric* owes something to Bertrand Russell's correspondence theories and is too close to the idea of *substitution* to serve the purposes Richards was defining. Ironically, it was as he developed his critique of the use made by positivist linguistics of information theory that IAR came to reconceive context. The inadequacies of Jakobson's "communication situation" led him to invent the idea of "comparison fields," which allowed him to suggest the interdependencies of experience and purpose, of feedback and feedforward, and to develop the idea of analogous representation in depictive and enactive modes.

Control IAR named his last book *Techniques in Language Control,* intent as always on avoiding guessing, on assuring that the activity of interpretation be directed by purpose. Exercising control is the function of choice, the exercise of freedom. And just as the chief function of education is the cultivation and protection of freedom, so assisting in the development of control is the central function of pedagogy. "The art of learning is the growth and control of ideas" (*HTRAP,* 25).

For IAR, the body was the primordial speculative instrument and the control of physical capacities and powers he saw as analogous to "language control." He often called on his experience as a mountaineer to point up the similarities between climbing and the use of language. He would surely have delighted in the pedagogy of Tim Noble, a teacher and mountain climber in Wiltshire, who, understanding the equivalency relationship of tenor and vehicle, has reversed the figure: teaching his students the art of rock climbing in the local quarry, he calls on their lessons in reading poetry, so that knowing something about how words work becomes a guide for learning how hands and feet work in getting up the quarry face.

Dependence IAR, who calls on a wide range of English literature from Chaucer to Robert Lowell, borrows from John Donne the important word *interinanimation:* the idea that intention inspirits language is transformed by that interior *in,* in a way that reminds us of the heuristic power of language. Mutual dependence of words in discourse and thought is modeled by the state and, in turn, this interinanimation of words models the relationship of theory and practice.

There is an analogy between the conception of a world order and the design of a language which may serve man best. The choice of words for that language and the assignment of priorities among their duties can parallel the stateman's true tasks. And it is through what language can offer him that every man has to consider what should concern him most. (*SMN,* 266)

Dependence rather than foundation is IAR's master metaphor for the dynamic process whereby practice takes its direction from theory, and theory is revealed for what it is by how we use it:

We are seeking *stabilities,* it is true, but in Plato's image these stabilities are not gained . . . by building them up from foundations of defined assumptions but through their *dependence* from a first principle or master rule of all being. (As gravitation—that sketchy image of dialectic Reason—keeps the universe stable in its freedom; rather than the Elephant standing on the Great Turtle's back which supports the world in the old fable. But how to keep our philosophy from becoming a Great Turtle is always our problem.) (*HTRAP*, 239)

Dialectic From his earliest days at Cambridge University, IAR expressed a hearty dislike of "disputation." In debate, "the disputant is commonly too busy making his points to see what they are." IAR's emphasis is, rather, on what we do with our minds, but this is not a private or merely "psychological" matter. Mental activity takes place in situations—and these are, of course, interpersonal. Dialectic entails dialogue and, although IAR did not himself develop techniques of dialogic action in the classroom, his philosophy of rhetoric is supportive of attempts to do so. "What should guide the reader's mind? Our awareness of interdependence, of how things hang together, which makes us able to give and audit an account of what may be meant in a discussion—that highest activity of REASON which Plato named 'Dialectic'" (*HTRAP*, 240).

Experiment From the time he and Ogden first assembled their assertions about the meaning of meaning as a contribution to a *science* of signs, to his final book, *Techniques in Language Control*, IAR's commitment was to demonstration, not disputation; to exploration, not dogma; to design and control through purposeful choice, not guesswork in combination with authoritarian doctrines. He declared that the classroom should be a "philosophic laboratory" (*SI*, 104) for the study of how words work, and to that end he thought of his "techniques" as heuristic and pragmatic experiments. Reading and writing are both experimental in the sense that what is being sorted and gathered is to be formulated in tentative terms and brought to the pragmatic test.

When he lectured, IAR often (always?) threw texts on a screen, exactly as if they were biological specimens or art objects on slides. Poetry he called "an instrument of research" because it offered occasions for "the study of how words work." In all his techniques, the central principle was that any formulation should be tentative: "IF we put it this way, what difference would it make to our practice?" "IF we worked with this assumption about contexts, how would it change the way we proceed?"

Feedforward IAR's purpose in problematizing the language of cybernetics was to demonstrate the impossibility of accounting for meaning and purposes if we rely on information theory. *Feedback* must therefore be matched by *feedforward*. IAR enjoyed deploying such terms, but the semiotic principle here is precisely the same as that which Coleridge identified as "the forethoughtful query." Feedforward and feedback; intention and context; purpose and situation: IAR never attends to one without the other.

IAR illustrates the dialectic of feedback and feedforward by the example of drawing a freehand circle, an enactive analogy. And in his definition of composition, we can see how the principle works in linguistic terms:

Composition is the supplying at the right time and place of whatever the developing meaning then and there requires. It is the cooperation with the rest in preparing for what is to come and completing what has preceded. It is more than this though; it is the exploration of what is to come and of how it should be prepared for, and it is the further examination of what has preceded and of how it may be amended and completed. (*SMN*, 119–20)

Instruction Richards' intense awareness of social contexts strengthened a conviction that education had a therapeutic, if not a redemptive, role. "When nature and tradition, or rather our contemporary social and economic conditions, betray us, it is reasonable to reflect whether we cannot deliberately contrive artificial means of correction" (*PC*, 301). *Education*, as theory, is always matched for Richards by *instruction*, as practice. His educational designs were always conceived of as classroom procedures and generally referred to as *experiments:* he believed that interpretation is an art, but the actual demonstrations were described in terms of laboratory procedures.

Pedagogy for English teachers (for humanists generally) is frequently a matter of modeling: "Watch me think." (Those who still lecture will frequently defend the practice by some such claim.) IAR wanted the student to watch *himself* think, but that did not mean that there would be no need for instruction. Teaching was never seen as an "intervention" but as offering "assisted invitations" to students to look carefully at what they are doing, *thereby* learning how to do it. Given the "all-in-each of every human mind," the main challenge of instruction was to order a sequence of such assisted invitations so that "the lure of the task itself" would provide the motivation, without "adventitious jollying up." Instruction was a matter of offering guidance, assistance for gaining control, thus freeing students from the habit of guessing. Instruction must seek to develop sequences which can lead the student to exercise "the sovereign power of comparing" as he recognizes "the partially parallel task." To assure that the sequence is apprehendable, it is essential to eliminate all *distraction*.

Instrumentality Early on, IAR had defined a book as "a machine to think with," taking Le Corbusier's definition of a chair as his model. A machine for IAR is always a means. Coleridge wrote that words are not passive tools but instruments; when he called language "the blessed machine," he clearly was not thinking of it mechanistically. Nor is IAR when he speaks of "logical machinery" and so on. The instrumentality of language—its heuristic power—is central to IAR's philosophy of rhetoric. "All meanings are means, are instruments, and inside *Instrument* it is somewhat more than a pun if we find *instruction*, since it is through instruments that we form problems. If so, the super-problem is to find means of making the greatest possible variety of means available: the widest and freest choice of instruments" (*SI*, 151).

Metaphor IAR's contribution to the study of how words work in metaphor is the pair of terms, *tenor* and *vehicle*. Understood in dyadic terms, this is no advance: tenor/vehicle then is only an updated version of language as the garment of thought. But taken in triadic terms, with a recognition of Thirdness, the element of transformation being symbolized by transport and conveyance, tenor/vehicle can be a powerful speculative instrument for studying the structure of all linguistic functions.

IAR called poetry "an instrument of research" because he thought it provided the best means of studying how words work: poetic discourse represents dramatically, as it were, the interinanimation of words. As we attend to the interdependence of tenor and vehicle, we are learning to attend to the same kind of relationship that holds between language and thought; learning, that is, what Vygotsky meant by declaring that the study of that relationship must begin with "the unit of meaning."

A word may be *simultaneously* both literal and metaphoric just as it may simultaneously support many different metaphors, may serve to focus into one meaning many different meanings. This point is of some importance, since so much misinterpretation comes from supposing that if a word works one way it cannot simultaneously work in another and have simultaneously another meaning. (*PR*, 18–19)

Method "There is no way of arriving at any Sciential end but by finding it at every step." That precept of Coleridge guides IAR as he continually sets about finding ways of finding. We discover what our theory means only when we put it to the test and for IAR that meant teaching: the pedagogical imperative is at the heart of his philosophy of rhetoric, as it is central to Coleridge's theory of imagination. The aim of method—the nexus of theory and practice—is to make accessible to the all-in-each of every mind *what* is being attempted and thereby *how* to make the attempt. That the *how* comes from the *what* (in practice), as the *what* comes from the *how* (in the case of theory), is a fundamentally pragmatic principle, and indeed IAR's conception of method owes as much to C.S. Peirce as it does to Coleridge. All that we know is known in some form; the aim of method, therefore, is to aid the recognition and representation of such forms. IAR understood as well as any modern critic that meanings are our means of making meaning and that to realize this heuristic power of meaning requires that we attend to our representations of meaning—not confusing token and type (example and concept); not neglecting context and purpose; not muddling signal and message or conflating the two senses of *code*.

Richards' techniques for the control of meaning have neither explanatory power nor pedagogical point unless they are seen in the triadic perspective. Thus *paraphrase*, if it means we substitute a statement of the message for the text, is "heretical," as some New Critics held. But paraphrase in the service of an interpretive activity becomes the only way to represent an understanding of how what is said is related to what was (probably) meant. The "seemingly revolutionary doctrine of the Interpretant" requires that we see critical activity as a reflective process. Just as discourse is enabled by the "virtuous necessity" of limits, so method is empowered by following the experimental procedures of multiple definition and vertical translation.

Opposition IAR took the concept of opposition from Ogden who had seen its uses as he developed Basic English. *Opposition* is "the name for the need to choose between alternates which must be changed as circumstances require." The Saussurian principle that language is a system of differences is comparable; the syntagmatic and paradigmatic axes and the metonymic/ metaphoric difference are both analogous to opposition by cut and by scale. (The banks of a river exemplify the former; the ends of a thermometer, the latter.) The two kinds of opposition represent the distinction of continuous and discrete degrees, which is central to both "poetries and sciences"—to colloidal chemistry and to Swedenborg's doctrine of correspondences alike. In short, opposition is a very powerful concept and IAR found it indispensable in all his techniques of comparative studies. "All living use of language (as opposed to psittacism: one of Ogden's favorite words) depends upon the user's discernment of how what is being said differs, *significantly,* from other things that might be said instead." [Richards' Introduction to C. K. Ogden, *Opposition* (Bloomington: Indiana University Press, 1967), pp. 12–13].

Organic For IAR, the body is the primary speculative instrument: he continually notes the role it plays in physiognomic perception, enactive representation, and the primary abstractions provided by our sense organs. He considered interpretation "a branch of biology" and suggested that we think of meaning "as though it were a plant that has grown—not a can that has been filled or a lump of clay that has been moulded" (*PR,* 12). He defined language as "the supreme organ of the mind's self-ordering growth and development" (*SI,* 9). These organic metaphors of language and thought are not "figurative," if by that is meant clothing ideas in memorable dress; rather, they represent conceptions otherwise virtually inexpressible.

Like Coleridge, IAR held that "the rules of Imagination are themselves the very powers of growth and production." All factors and functions of language are described in organic terms because they are organic in nature: meanings are alive; interpretation is a process of growth. As we follow IAR's argument, it becomes clear that it is the nature of the organic to be not a directionless or undirectable process but a dialectical determination which it should be our aim to learn to control through reflecting to some purpose.

Purpose When he designed his yantra to represent the seven functions of language, it was *purpose* that held the center, the hub of the wheel. (See p. 181.)

In a Preface to *How to Read a Page,* IAR wrote that "its ultimate theme is Purpose; its own purpose being to offer, through a clearer eye for what we do as we think, a juster position for living."

Reflection Reflection is intrinsic to meaning-making; indeed, there is, properly speaking, no meaning until and unless it emerges in the process of interpretation, which of course includes the interpretation of interpretation. Our capacity not merely to recognize or to interpret but to continually audit emergent recognitions and interpretations—this consciousness of consciousness is what Coleridge called "the sovereign power." Reflection, like recognition, is dependent on process. The circularity of this process—familiar from the metaphor of the hermeneutic circle—explains how it is that *recognition* is entailed in cognition: it not only results from cognition but is itself the precondition of cognition.

The Imagination—"the prime agent of all human perception"—is best represented by acts of perceiving which are, simultaneously and correlatively, acts of apprehension and comprehension. IAR supplies the following from Coleridge as a gloss for his use of the phrase "instrument of reflection" in characterizing Basic English (*SMN*, 267):

"And man became a living soul."
He did not merely *possess* it, he became it. It was his proper being, his truest self, the man *in* the man. . . . Nothing is wanted but the eye, which is the light of this house, the light which is the eye of this soul. This *seeing* light, this *enlightening* eye, is Reflection. It is more, indeed, than is usually meant by that word; but it is what a *Christian* ought to mean by it, and to know too, whence it first came, and still continues to come—of what light even this light is *but* a reflection. (*Aids to Reflection*, Aphorism IX)

Looking—which always entails looking *again*—is IAR's chief emblem for reflection or consideration, which he liked to analyze as a *sidereal* enterprise. We cannot merely *see*; we must always *see as*. This fact becomes a symbol for another, that "meanings arise only through recurrence and what is unique would be ineffable" (*IT*, vii).

Representation For IAR, representation means symbolization—the representation of a representation; that is to say, it entails intention, purpose, choice, and ambiguity. But "representation" is not "indeterminate"; it is emergent in the semiotic process of interpreting our interpretations. In Peirce's semiotics, each sign requires another for its interpretation, the Interpretant (reference) of one sign thus becoming the Representamen (symbol) of the next. There is an "object," but our task as critical readers is to conceive this object as a referent with a context, in a situation which is crucial to its meaning: "Meanings are generated by contexts."

Because IAR's theory of comprehending is a triadic semiotic, it can help us identify certain dangers which are largely ignored in contemporary critical theory: *signal* and *message* must not be muddled; *tokens* (instances, cases) must not be confused with *types* (universals); the *initial terms* in any account of meaning are themselves meanings and are thus subject to interpretation. For IAR, as for C. S. Peirce, there are no data; nothing is simply given.

Representation in IAR's pedagogy is entailed by "practice": theory must be re-presented in actual demonstrations; method must be realized in actual techniques; ideas must be depicted, enacted, set forth in multiple definitions and in different "channels." IAR's enthusiasm for "audiovisual" aids was boundless because two "channels" are better than one: seeing what you hear, writing what you see, hearing what you read are all central to his ideas of language learning. An English professor who in his youth had been a T. A. for Dr. Richards once told me of the job he was assigned when he accompanied IAR to local high schools. The mission was to persuade teachers of the uses of Basic English versions of the classics, especially *The Wrath of Achilles,* IAR's translation of the *Iliad.* He wanted them to hear how the original sounded and to create a context for that sound. The T. A. would attach one end of a jump rope to the radiator and then, as IAR intoned the Homeric hexameters, he would turn the rope so that it struck the floor rhythmically: that was the Aegean Sea breaking on the shore. In *Practical Criticism,* IAR had noted T. S. Eliot's observation that the internal combustion engine had "altered our perception of rhythms."

From the first, IAR depended on diagrams and sketches to represent his representations; they engage the mind because they must be deliberately interpreted. Representation in IAR's demonstrations and techniques is guided by two principles: opposition and sequence. Opposition frames the choices necessary to representing and interpreting purposes; sequence lays bare the structural form of sentences and discursive representations so that we can see what comes next, what varies with what, how the *how* can be drawn from the *what.* Sequence is the way to assist the learner in discerning "the partially parallel task." Cognition depends on re-cognition.

System   Any semiotic system is necessarily dynamic and recursive and is therefore unstable; the purpose of method is to assure that systems are not rigidified. Of course, we seek stabilities, but they can never be final and should never be taken as absolute.

IAR speaks of the systematic character of ambiguity in explaining that ambiguities are not random, personal, or pointless—not mere puzzles with a key. The system of which they are characteristic is *discourse;* they are inevitable because language represents, mediates, and must be interpreted. Ambiguities are "the very hinges of all thought" because it is in translating, transforming, and interpreting them that we can focus on the relationship of what seems to be said to what seems, in the developing discourse, to be meant.

In his microrhetoric, IAR attends to how words work by understanding discourse as a system in which "the opening words have to wait for those that follow to settle what they shall mean—if indeed that ever gets settled" (*PR,* 50).

IAR's argument that we should consider poetry as an "instrument of research" is warranted by the conception of language as systematic:

Consider what we know in knowing some part of a language. We know to some extent which words will *work how* with which, in the varying vicissitudes in which we meet them and in which we may try to use them. Every word, through this potential work, this network of possible cooperations, is connected *via* other words with all the rest in a *living*: a growing, changing, decaying lexical structural would-be system. That system has its claims—as we know—to be *you*, in your case, or *me*, in mine. I don't myself support these claims, but this much seems certain: the quality of our living—not only of our thinking, but of our feeling, desiring, willing, and the rest—is most intimately mixed up with the state of order–disorder within our lexical–structural would-be system. And Poetry, as I have been saying, is our exemplar of that would-be system at its most entire—being most itself. (*SMN*, 176)

Translation IAR's experience first with Basic English and then with the translation of Chinese texts strengthened his conviction that the study of how words work requires techniques which can assure that mediation is seen not as a barrier but as a heuristic. Translation is not a matter of substituting one word from one language for another from another language, nor does language represent reality by substitution. Interpretive paraphrase, which he called "vertical translation," and multiple definitions were techniques intended to alert us to the role of context and to the control words exert on one another. Translation demands attention to exactly those factors and functions which modern linguistics, by an "eviscerative abstraction," has removed from consideration. Translation was for IAR the chief type-specimen of that activity by which we relate what we think is said to what we think is meant.